PLURAL BUT EQUAL

HAROLD CRUSE

PLURAL BUT EQUAL

A Critical Study of Blacks and Minorities and America's Plural Society

QUILL

WILLIAM MORROW
New York

Library of Congress Cataloging-in-Publication Data
Cruse, Harold.

Plural but equal.

Includes index.
1. Afro-Americans—Civil rights.   2. Afro-Americans—Politics and government.   3. United States—Race relations.   I. Title.
E185.615.C78   1987   305.8'96073   86-28519
0-688-08331-5 (pbk.)

Printed in the United States of America

First Quill Edition

1   2   3   4   5   6   7   8   9   10

BOOK DESIGN BY OKSANA KUSHNIR

. . . As the agitation which culminated in the abolition of African slavery in this country covered a period of fifty years, so may we expect that before the rights conferred upon us by the war amendments are fully conceded, a full century will have passed away. We have undertaken no child's play. We have undertaken a serious work which will tax and exhaust the best intelligence of the race for the next century. . . .

From the opening address at the founding convention of the National Afro-American League in Chicago, January 1890, by T. Thomas Fortune, the league's principal founder.

PART ONE
Introduction

What happened to the black civil rights movement after the high point of its 1960s thrust and accomplishments? Did that historic movement for social change achieve all of its implied goals of "racial equality," "equal rights," "freedom," "black liberation," etc.? Such a question in the 1980s, of course, raises the important question, What *were* the social, political, economic, and other implications of those implied goals?

Today, during the *post*-civil rights era of the Eighties, most blacks feel that the goals of the Sixties have not been fully achieved. Here, hindsight suggests that the end of the Sixties represented the waning of the *cycle,* a civil rights cycle. A "cycle" is described as a "course or series of events or operations that recurs regularly and usually leads back to the starting point." Nineteen eighty-six, ironically, represented the first opportunity fully to celebrate the Martin Luther King official holiday, and the main theme of this King celebration called upon all Americans to "rededicate themselves to work toward the kind of society" that King envisioned. Martin Luther King's vision was first adumbrated during the late 1950s and the 1960s, which suggests that blacks and whites in the Eighties ought to recall the first proclamation of King's vision, i.e., the starting point of the civil rights cycle that began and ended with his demise in 1968. But in this regard it is easy to forget the beginning and the end of the first civil rights cycle, roughly 1868 to 1896, the period

in which civil rights issues related to the constitutional ratification of the
Thirteenth, Fourteenth, and Fifteenth Amendments were bitterly contended in a struggle in which black civil rights advocates were beaten
down in abysmal defeat. It would be almost sixty years before the American racial climate would sanction the enactment of another civil rights
cycle.

However, even before the 1980s, many American whites, probably
the majority, believed that blacks had received just about everything in
the way of "special treatment" that the civil rights movement had demanded; in fact, they believed blacks had gotten "too much." Thus, the
resurgence of the white conservative establishment in the Eighties was
actually triggered, in part, by a reaction against what were called civil
rights "excesses." As one result, the white liberal establishment ran out
of the political means and public policy influence further to implement
civil rights increments. As early as 1970, a leading white liberal journalist-
advocate called the demise of the turbulent black Sixties "The Lost
Priority."*

Inasmuch as black Americans represent the largest nonwhite minority
in the United States, and also the one most publicized in the evolution
of minority issues, a better understanding of the consequences of the
Sixties can be achieved only through a historical examination of the
origins of the movement itself. How and why did the modern civil rights
movement begin?

A critical reason why such an examination of the real origins of the
twentieth-century civil rights movement is not simplistic is because the
NAACP was *not*, as is commonly believed, the first effort on the part of
historic black leadership to establish a civil rights organization. Why the
NAACP was not the first became a major determinant in what it became
as the major twentieth-century civil rights organization. During the last
decade of the nineteenth century, both blacks and whites had attempted
a number of short-lived conferences to deal with the "problems peculiar
to the Negro."[1] The most significant attempt, and the one that gained a
degree of national attention and critical response, was the National Afro-
American League (1887–1908).

It was not generally understood during the heyday of the Sixties that
the modern civil rights movement had an important history that had

---

* See John Herbers, *The Lost Priority: What Happened to the Civil Rights Movement in America?*
(New York: Funk & Wagnalls, 1970).

interacted with practically every major American reform, radical, labor, or progressive movement of the twentieth century; that it was not a fortuitous aberration inspired or plotted by "subversive" elements bent on promoting anti-American domestic unrest. But the ahistorical character of our mind-set affects even historians when dealing with the racial factor in American developments. Truths are evaded and consequences ignored. Thus, it was not accidental that in the first comprehensive black history, *From Slavery to Freedom* (1947), written seven years before the historic *Brown* decision, the National Afro-American League was not even mentioned.

The National Afro-American League was founded on the initiative of T. Thomas Fortune, a well-known journalist and newspaper editor who in 1887 called for the creation of an organization led by blacks "to fight for the rights denied them."[2] After three years of intense effort and lively debate on the pros and cons of such a venture, the National Afro-American League was formally organized at its first convention in Chicago in 1890. The convention agreed on a six-point program: (1) the securing of voting rights; (2) the combating of lynch law; (3) the abolition of inequities in state funding of public school education for blacks and whites; (4) reforming the southern penitentiary system—its chain gang and convict lease practices; (5) combating discrimination in railroad and public travel conveyances; and (6) discrimination in public places, hotels, and theaters.

With the exception of the last item, all the racial issues in the league's platform were either peculiar to the southern states or else more stringently enforced in that region than in the North. This was especially true because the league was established just ten years after the demise of Reconstruction, when practically all the advances blacks had won as a consequence of the Fourteenth and Fifteenth Amendments and the Civil Rights Acts of 1866 and 1875 were rapidly being eroded in the South. The launching of the National Afro-American League coincided with the South's concerted move to disfranchise and completely remove southern blacks from participation in the political life of the region. Beginning with Mississippi in 1890, every southern state had by 1910 rewritten its state constitution to establish white supremacy and to impose legal segregation based on race and color in all areas of social and institutional life. Hence, the 1890s offered an unfavorable social climate for a civil rights organization as bold and pioneering as the National Afro-American League. Thus, it was not surprising that not a single issue in the league's six-point platform ever received public or federal support on a local, regional, or national basis except for item number three: racial inequities in funding public school education for blacks and whites. And even here, federal and regional interest was not prompted by the platform of the National Afro-American League, but by the Blair Education Bill, which had been introduced in the national legislature in 1881, nine years before the league was established. Yet the Blair Bill was the one public issue around which the newly formed league could meaningfully agitate until the bill was killed in the Senate in 1890.

From 1890 to 1908, the National Afro-American League struggled to establish itself as a legitimate civil rights protest organization organized by and for, and supported by, blacks themselves. In 1898 the league changed its name to the Afro-American Council. This change was one of the consequences of the extended controversy that plagued the organization from its inception. The league became the battleground for conflicting black leadership philosophies that emerged in the 1890s. The question of leadership ideals centered mainly around the personality of Booker T. Washington, who emerged in 1895 as the most prominent black leader acceptable to whites, both liberal and conservative, in the North and South. Thus, in the historical arena of black civil rights, the league provided a debating platform for the seminal leadership ideals of not only T. Thomas Fortune himself, but of W.E.B. Du Bois, William Monroe Trotter, Booker T. Washington, Bishop Alexander Walters, Ida B. Wells, and several others not so well remembered today.[3] The programmatic approaches to civil rights argued out among black leadership factions within the league were carried over into the NAACP in 1909, and never ceased to be fundamental conflicts from 1909 to the 1980s. The only factors that changed were the emphases and the circumstances.

For the brief period 1890 to 1891, the league argued the pros and cons of the Blair Education Bill, which "proposed to meet the dilemma of Southern Educational backwardness by spending large sums of federal money for public schools" in the southern region. After the Blair bill was defeated, the league struggled to establish its legitimacy in the face of predominantly hostile white opinion generally, and with only limited white liberal support in the North. Typical of southern attitudes was the opinion expressed in a Charleston, South Carolina, newspaper: "The colored people, it is certain, have nothing whatever to gain by organization in the race or color line. This merely strengthens racial divisions . . . and strengthens the very groups who are strongest in their opposition to the very rights which Negroes are demanding."[4] A Georgia newspaper declared: "There is no conceivable direction in which an organization can do the Negro race any good, it might do great harm."[5] However, northern liberalism of a certain variety "gave qualified approval to the League idea, but pointed out that lawsuits, which would have to be the chief weapon of the organization, would require money. Failure to raise the necessary funds would do further harm to the reputation of Negroes by furnishing evidence of their alleged lack of practical ability."[6]

The twenty-year history of the Afro-American League (and/or Council) proved that the inability to fund its program was not the only major problem. The real internal difficulty was the league's inability to argue out a functional consensus among the deeply divided intraracial ideals related to the fulfillment of black citizenship in American democracy. How to secure and maintain progressive black public school education was only one of a number of conflictual programmatic issues the league had to contend with. How to advance and defend black citizenship aspirations in politics, economics, and education confronted the league with options and alternatives, none of which were very promising at the turn of the twentieth century. Thus, in the long run, the National Afro-American League failed in its mission, though its failures led to the founding of the NAACP, which was destined to become the major civil rights organization in the United States in the twentieth century. During its waning years, certain members of the original Afro-American League, among them W.E.B. Du Bois, as a last gasp effort, attempted to have the defeated Blair Education Bill revived. But by then the chance of such a revival in Congress was nil. By the last decade of the nineteenth century it was clear that on questions of racial democracy the northern white liberal community had elected to abandon southern blacks to the *fait accompli* of complete disfranchisement, stripped of all semblance of political status and participation. The post-Reconstruction sentiments that dominated southern affairs in the 1880s and 1890s determined that the Blair Education Bill, the most progressive piece of legislation to be considered during that time, was doomed. Considering the impact that black public school education would have on civil rights legislation sixty-four years later due to the *Brown* Supreme Court decision of 1954, it is instructive, by way of introduction, to review briefly the social and political implications of the Blair Education Bill when it was on the legislative agenda almost a hundred years ago.

The Blair Education Bill was named for Senator Henry W. Blair, Republican from New Hampshire, who, as chairman of the Senate Education and Labor Committee, introduced the measure in 1880. The bill proposed to spend large sums of federal money on public school education as follows:

> Seven million the first year, $10 million the second year, $15 million the third year, and then by decreasing stages to $5 million the eighth year, for a total of $77 million. The annual appropriations were to be divided among the states in proportion to illiteracy. This formula would have directed approximately 75 percent of all federal education aid to southern states, since illiteracy rates were far higher in the South than anywhere else in the country. An appropriation of $15 million, for example, would have provided close to or more than $1 million for each of eight southern states (Virginia, North Carolina, Tennessee, South Carolina, Georgia, Alabama, Mississippi, and Louisiana). None of these states spent anywhere near that amount for public education in 1880. The Blair Bill, however, did not provide outright gifts. It required that recipient states match all federal assistance with at least an equal amount from its own or local resources. . . .[7]

After the Blair bill first passed the Senate in April 1884, for six years it was the subject of lively debate, especially in the South, and seemed to have a fair chance for success. In support of his bill, Senator Blair noted that "millions of southernors, black and white, were growing up in absolute ignorance of the English alphabet," a sentiment that was broadly shared both North and South. By 1880 the idea of federal aid to education was increasingly popular in southern thought and had wide support. In fact, of all the Reconstruction programs, only federal aid to education commanded enough public support, North and South, to stand the least chance of enactment. The removal of federal troops from the South by President Hayes in 1877 had eliminated the last real barrier against North-South economic or political cooperation. Henry W. Grady would soon leave Atlanta, taking his message from the "New South" to northern sympathizers. Congress was thus granted a possible alternative to the complete federal abandonment of southern blacks and one that would least offend the South. That promising alternative to southern insistence on federal "noninterference" was the Blair Education Bill.

Although the Blair measure was couched in racially nonpartisan language, e.g., the spending of federal monies "equally for the education of all the children, without distinction of race or color," it was not surprising that the most vocal and enthusiastic support came from southern blacks. The controversial Hayes-Tilden election compromise of 1877 had been a serious blow to the aspirations of the millions of blacks left landless, poverty-stricken, and illiterate in the southern states. Growing disillusionment with Republican party politics was leading more and more blacks to the pessimistic conclusion that they could expect nothing from the Republicans or the federal government. Hayes-Tilden signaled the northern abandonment of southern black problems. However, the Blair bill raised new hopes. It offered something blacks wanted and needed— education—and it was difficult to find a black leader, educator, politician, minister, writer, journalist, or literate worker who did not fervently support the Blair bill. T. Thomas Fortune wrote in 1884 that no bill before Congress was so vital to Americans generally and blacks in particular. Although no black spokesmen had been consulted by Senator Blair on the particulars of his bill, it was a foregone conclusion that blacks would support it if only out of sheer desperation. This, despite provisions that would have allowed *segregated public schools*. But within the frame of racially segregated schools the recipient southern states would have been required to allocate both federal and state money "equally" for the education of all children. Thus, the Blair bill, if enacted, would have entailed strict adherence to the principle of "separate but equal." That such a provisional debate on such a substantive issue as federal aid to education took place more than ten years prior to the Supreme Court's *Plessy* v. *Ferguson* separate-but-equal doctrine, adjudicated in 1896, was significant. More significant, most southern blacks were willing to accept the separate-but-equal dispensation of the rewards of education, which was the main concern. Although doubts were raised as to how the federal power could guarantee that federal (or state) funds would be allocated "equally" among blacks and whites should the Blair bill be enacted, blacks, in the main, ignored these arguments on the premise of "Nothing ventured, nothing gained."

Despite wide public support for the Blair bill among whites and blacks, North and South, this crucial piece of social legislation failed to be enacted into law. The bill passed the Senate again in 1886 and 1888, but never reached the floor of the House. The Blair bill was killed, it was said, by the "parliamentary intrigues of northern and border state Democrats, who dominated the House leadership." Thus, after ten dramatic years, this bill disappeared from the national scene in 1890.

The Blair bill represented a unique political manifestation of the post-Reconstruction transition, when the southern states were impelled by a self-generated political logic to seek "redemption" through a perverse and antiblack rationalization of "states' rights." In other words, "when some compromise between federal authority and state prerogative remained a practical possibility,''[8] the South obstinately, and to its own developmental disadvantage, refused to compromise. Obviously, the "parliamentary intrigues" of Democrats—North, South, or in between —could conveniently resort to constitutional technicalities regarding federal power to camouflage the racial sentiments behind congressional opposition to the Blair Bill: In 1880 everyone knew that any Republican-sponsored legislation of this sort was heavily motivated by a desire to eradicate, as quickly as feasible, the badge of illiteracy that was the slavery inheritance of southern blacks. But here, even the withdrawal of federal troops in 1877 was not enough of a guarantee of southern political autonomy to allay southern suspicions of any gesture that smacked of federal interference. Actually, the idea of federal assistance for southern public education originated during Reconstruction, and then it was openly recognized by both supporters and opponents as "a radical instrument designed primarily to benefit the freedmen."[9] However, by 1880 Reconstruction was all but dead, and the Blair bill was designed so that southern whites would benefit as much as, if not more than, southern blacks. Black leaders, such as Alexander Crummell, the important religious and intellectual figure, pointed out that although the Blair bill was not ideal in all aspects, "its failure would be a disaster to the whole country, especially to the black race."[10] Few white spokesmen, other than Blair, protested that the failure of the Blair bill would be a disaster for whites as well. But even the most superficial awareness of the magnitude of the southern racial tragedy following the demise of Reconstruction reveals the scope of the ensuing disaster. From 1890, when the Blair bill was finally defeated, onward into the twentieth century, what was described as "educational lethargy" settled all over the South. Millions of illiterate whites were sacrificed by southern leaders whose main objective was to keep millions of illiterate blacks ignorant, impoverished, and politically impotent by denying them education. "I do not consider the education of the lower masses in the South a cure for all the ills of Southern society," said George W. Cable, "but I fail to see how they can be cured without it. . . ."[11]

In political terms the Blair bill was tailored to appeal to the "Redeemer Democrats," who represented the new southern ruling class in Congress and who, at that moment, were not at all ill-disposed to state support for black education. From 1880 to 1890, blacks were receiving an equitable share of school tax funds under Redeemer governments in such states as South Carolina, Mississippi, North Carolina, Alabama, and Kentucky. Thus, "federal aid to southern public schools became a genuine possibility during the 1880's because a substantial number of northernors agreed to certain conditions demanded by the new ruling classes of the South. Senator Blair believed that government officers should supervise the expenditures of funds, but when he discovered that southern congressmen would not support such federal interference, he capitulated."[12] The recalcitrance of Redeemer politicians on such questions as federal implementation of the Blair bill pushed northern Blair supporters to compromises such as the maintenance of segregated schools. For their part, *the overwhelming majority of blacks did not make segregated classrooms an issue with regard to the Blair bill.*

Of course, sporadic objections to "separate" classrooms were raised by a few black leaders such as T. Thomas Fortune and David A. Straker. Straker asked whether blacks would willingly "accept this strong inference of inferiority without a single protest."[13] Fortune, after strongly supporting the Blair bill's implied separation of the races in public schools, denounced "the manifest injustice" of a system that assumed that "one child is better than another" and noted that the "double expense" of maintaining two systems was an absurd policy for the impoverished South. Significantly, neither Fortune's nor Straker's antisegregation sentiments aroused any discernible response in the black community—*"Many blacks apparently preferred segregated schools. Separate churches and schools became symbols of racial achievement and they provided about the only avenue of opportunity for black professionals. During the 1880's many blacks opposed school integration in the North because it often resulted in the loss of black jobs (just as it happened in the South during the 1950's and 1960's)."*[14] (Italics added.)

In the midst of heated debates among northern black leaders over perceived "flaws" in the Blair bill at the Chicago convention of the Afro-American League in 1890, a southern black leader, Joseph C. Price, argued:

> I am opposed as much as anyone can be to discriminations. . . . But gentlemen from New York and Pennsylvania and Illinois must consider our position.

Observing that northern blacks would not be greatly affected by a lack of federal aid, Price pleaded that southern black schools needed every bit of assistance they could get, even if on less than ideal terms. "Our people are hungering and thirsting for education. . . . If we can't get the whole loaf don't in heaven's name withhold the half loaf that is offered us."[15] Southern blacks did not get the half loaf.

During the ten-year congressional debate that led to the defeat of "federal aid to education," northern liberals retreated from their initial approval of Blair to almost unanimous opposition. Their reasoning affords insights into the curious and retrograde politics of post-Reconstruction. Exactly one hundred years later, in the 1980s, one hears, almost word for word, a replay of the Blair verdict in the Reagan doctrine on social legislation.

The northern liberal retreat from support of Blair was one of the last actions in the northern ritual of "washing its hands of the Southern Negro." In 1883 the Supreme Court had succeeded in emasculating the series of civil rights acts passed by Congress between 1866 and 1875, all designed to "protect all citizens in their civil and legal rights." The moving finger of the judiciary was already pointing northern liberals away from any federal intervention into the resurgent Confederacy while preparing the legal sanctions for *Plessy* v. *Ferguson* thirteen years later.

As a way of getting around the anticipated charge of "unconstitutionality," the Blair bill framers recommended that *all* the states would "share in the appropriations, while the expenditures of the largest share in the South was to be insured by making the amount allowed each depend upon the number of illiterates."[16]

The Nation, which once favored the bill out of a sense of generosity because it was plausible, in 1886 called it "fallacious."

> Illiteracy is a bad thing for a community, but it is not the worst thing. It is important for the South that its present ignorance should be dispelled as soon as possible, but that is not the most important thing for the South. The vital element of any success that is worth achieving in this world is self-reliance.[17]

In 1884 *The New York Times* had supported the Blair bill:

> It is by no means a perfect measure, but it is in the right direction, and if passed it will do good. These are not very strong arguments for the bill in the House, but they are strong with the people, and the House will neglect them at its own peril.[18]

However, the House did neglect to heed the voice of the "people," and *The Nation* stepped up its attack on the Blair bill by calling it "A

Bill to Promote Mendicancy." The refusal of the House to vote favorably on the bill did not imperil the electoral status of a single member. It was the opinion of *The Nation:*

> The majority of the Republicans [voted for the bill] . . . because they had become satisfied that the measure would be defeated in the House, and thought it would look better for them to vote the same way as they had done before and then leave the Representatives to defeat the bill, than to be honest and confess that they made a mistake in supporting it two years before.[19]

By 1886 *The Nation's* attitude toward the Blair bill had changed from coolness to such intense opposition that it condemned it as a "Vicious Way of Legislating." What a curious and significant change in political orientation for a publication founded in 1865 to be *"Especially devoted to the interests of the Freedman."* Obviously Reconstruction and its aftermath had considerably cooled editor Edwin Godkin's ardor for the welfare of the freedman. Although the freedmen and their appointed leaders overwhelmingly favored the Blair bill, *The Nation's* opposition ignored their sentiments. While deftly skirting the issue of the bill's "constitutionality" as politically unarguable, *The Nation* resorted to painting a grossly overoptimistic picture of southern economic recovery from Civil War devastation:

> It was easy to show that the claim of Southern incapacity to maintain a decent school system was untenable, being based upon exaggerated representations of that section's poverty and backwardness in a period from which she has now emerged.[20]

Citing comparative statistics showing that in the 1880s states such as Arkansas, South Carolina, Louisiana, Florida, West Virginia, and Georgia were educating children using allocations of state funds that nearly matched the allocations of, for example, Maine, Vermont, and New Hampshire, *The Nation* concluded: "The truth is that the Southern States are already proving their capacity to grapple with this problem alone:"[21]

> Let not the nation make the fatal mistake of teaching the South to depend upon the Federal Government for the maintenance of its schools, and thus lose that quality of self-reliance which no amount of education of short order can make up for.[22]

Lurking behind these arguments was, of course, not merely the controversial issue of federal subsidies for education per se, but specifically federal subsidies for *black* education. On this matter, *The Nation* used a quasi-constitutional argument that objected to taxing "the people of the United States heavily for the purpose of helping to educate colored children in the sixteen old slave states, which were represented as too poor to do the work itself." But the Blair bill, while patently aimed at black illiteracy, made it clear that millions of white southerners were also growing up illiterate.[23] Yet *The Nation* concluded that illiteracy, though a bad thing, was not the worst thing. In the final outcome, as a matter of liberal consensus, the blacks were not consulted, but then neither were those southern whites, whoever they were, who ardently supported the bill. In courting white opinion everywhere against the bill, *The Nation* stated that in taxing all whites everywhere, "a more circuitous way of reaching the ostensible end, of educating colored children where the States could not do it, it is impossible to imagine." And to bolster this argument, *The Nation* quoted, significantly, an ex-slaveholder and Confederate soldier:

> You know my deep interest in the public school system. Hence I am opposed to national aid. You cannot plaster the South with this system. It is a growth, and its certain and healthy growth can only be secured by each community providing for its own schools. The Blair Bill is simply, in another form, the old hallucination, "fifty acres and a mule," which has caused more briers and sassafras bushes to grow in Southern fields than all else.[24]

The defeat of the Blair bill was *also* accompanied by the defeat of the Henry Cabot Lodge "force bill," which would have provided for federal supervision of national elections to protect black voters in the South against state measures designed to deprive them of the vote. It was passed by the House but defeated in the Senate. Interestingly enough, *The Nation*'s adamant opposition to Blair was not matched by any forthright alarm over the obvious fact that the defeat of the force bill doomed black voting rights guaranteed by the Fifteenth Amendment. In the face of these two congressional defeats, *The Nation* and its northern liberal constituencies were betraying southern blacks by pretending to believe that the South, if left to its own resources and initiatives, would treat black and white educational needs equally within the separate-but-equal doctrine. By 1900 southern deterioration in race relations proved that the defeat of Blair was, in fact, the disaster for blacks that had been predicted by black leaders. Southern optimism of the 1880s that Redeemer governments would underwrite efforts toward "racial equality" evaporated in the 1890s as legally enforced segregation and discrimination were adopted in all southern states in all spheres of economic, political, social, and *educational* life. In 1896 the Supreme Court doctrine of *Plessy* v. *Ferguson* gave federal sanction to legalized inequalities within the separate-but-equal frame which the South never intended to make "equal."

What happened during the fifty-eight-year interim between *Plessy* v. *Ferguson* of 1896 and the *Brown* decision of 1954 in American race relations was the inevitable result of the lost opportunities for "forgotten alternatives." What happened in the southern states did not *have* to happen, but *did* happen. However, it allows one the prerogative of asking, the question, conveniently fortified by informed hindsight, *How would race relations have evolved had the Blair bill, in some form of accepted compromise, been passed?* C. Vann Woodward, our outstanding interpreter of the southern historical experience, cites the failure of passage of the Blair bill as one of a number of forgotten alternatives that could have fundamentally altered the social direction of southern destiny.

Of all the forgotten alternatives, in addition to others actually pursued among the "forked roads" encountered along the way to "reunion," the Blair bill is among the least discussed. The low priority our historians give to the Blair bill in a long list of "revisionist" or "consensus" reinterpretations of Reconstruction is peculiar. Sixty-four years after the final defeat of Blair, it was public school education that touched off the explosive elements of reform versus revolution and counterrevolution in American society. It was not the Fair Employment Practices Committee (FEPC), the poll tax, segregation in interstate transportation, fairness in elections, segregation in the military, "white primary" or "higher education," etc., that fired the deepest public emotional involvement and the most violent public confrontation around the theory and practice of "racial democracy." It was racial democracy in public education at the primary and secondary levels that was the catalyst. Contrary to all established theories of radical dispensations, it was not the "labor-versus-capital class struggle" potential that fueled the "American movement," as Woodward described it, but a constitutional verdict by the most conservative branch of the federal power that reintroduced such unfinished business of the first Reconstruction era. Not until after the *Brown* decision did King appear and new militant leaderships follow in rapid succession. Here a recrudescence of the historically primordial elements of a racial and political character spoke to unanswered questions regarding the intended or implied evolution of American society. If perchance the southern states had helped the Blair bill become law, *Plessy* v. *Ferguson*'s separate-but-equal doctrine could still have been rendered, since southern blacks were willing to accept separate-but-equal public school facilities as not being incompatible with "segregation" (read: separateness) in all other areas of southern social life then evolving. Thenceforth, *ceteris paribus,* judicial decisions pecking away at the segregated southern social structure could have ruled unconstitutional, legal segregation in all areas of public life that the courts achieved up to 1950, including segregated public education as per *Brown,* with pretty much the same results we witnessed in public school "integration" in 1986. For all intents, and despite the *Brown* decision, as of 1986 legal segregation has been almost universally replaced by *de facto* segregation in public schools; and in both South and North, most black and white schoolchildren are as "separate" as in 1954, *if not more so.* Yet in 1952 when South Carolina and several other states attempted to compromise, in anticipation of *Brown* and to "equalize" the separate school systems by way of massive appropriations, the NAACP rejected this compromise. C. Vann Woodward described the event as follows:

> Acknowledging that time was running out, Governor James F. Byrnes of South Carolina admitted that *"To meet this situation we are forced to do now what we should have been doing for the last fifty years."*[25] (Italics added.)

The good governor should have been more historically specific and declared, "The South, led by my state, should have fought for the passage of the Blair Education Bill in the House of Representatives sixty-two years ago in 1890." In retrospect, and in view of southern sensibilities on regional autonomy, better that Congress should have intervened through Blair into the states' education prerogatives rather than the Supreme Court's judicial extremism in *Brown* in 1954.

Woodward, in his rather time-serving conclusions regarding these events, raised the legitimate question whether "the injustice of half a century or more could be repaired before the courts would close forever the separate-but-equal loophole for segregation."[26] He concluded that "chances were slight at best," yet several states initiated last-minute attempts to equalize the black schools. "Thirteen Southern states spent about eight times as much for school construction and maintenance in

1951–52 as they had in 1939–40.'' These states *should* have made that allocation gesture in 1890, which would have precluded the much later shocks of the *Brown* decision, or else softened the evolutionary processes toward the inevitable racial adjustments within the context of southern racial mores. However, Woodward, in his response to these belated southern attempts at so-called equalization, tendered the following historical value judgment:

> They were attempting the impossible task of maintaining two equal school systems with the lowest per-capita income of any part of the country. While they narrowed some gaps, the disparities between white and Negro education continued to yawn wide in many areas.[27]

In the 1980s the question remains, What educational "gaps" were really narrowed by the *Brown* decision? In 1986 most southern public school children (not to mention those in the North), were still attending racially separate schools, under the resulting jurisdiction of *centrally* controlled public school administrations. These were the unavoidable consequences of urban and rural demographics and the built-in tendencies toward a democratic group pluralism (not "democratic" racial integration), constitutionally espoused by the *Brown* decision. While Woodward and a legion of other white liberal and black leadership advocates of the *Brown* decision claimed that maintaining two equal school systems was an "impossible task," racial neighborhood demographics in the South (and North) have led to the maintenance of predominantly black schools and predominantly white schools that no amount of busing has altered. In the South, having the "lowest per-capita income" had little to do with the demographic results of racial distribution within the school systems except that the "equalization" of the two systems eliminated untold numbers of black schoolteachers, principals, and administrators from the formerly segregated schools, sending them into the ranks of the displaced and unemployed. Thus, the implementation of the *Brown* decision on the "integration" of the segregated school systems, while achieving the much desired goal of outlawing legally imposed segregation (which was the basis of the Supreme Court's decision), did *not* achieve the full integration of white and black schoolchildren, or the elimination of racially separate public school districts, which have become the rule rather than the exception in every major urban center anywhere in the country.

From a number of divergent points of view that at the outset questioned the judicial wisdom of the *Brown* decision (excluding of course the advocacy of the NAACP), the practical outcome of the societal processes within public school systems are not to be either morally or ethically deplored except for one important caveat. When the NAACP and its host of social science advocates of "full integration" rejected the southern states' compromise gestures toward the belated "equalization" of the racially separate school systems, they, in effect, did blacks a disservice; the potential rewards under the evolutionary rubric of an equal, biracial administration of public schools were destined, with or without the *Brown* decision, to evolve into the separate-but-equal biracial school system we see today. In the process of implementing *Brown,* the black teachers and administrators eliminated from the public school systems represented a loss to black communities. Despite their "lowest per-capita" state income, the southern states managed "integration" of the schools in line with southern "class" interests. By eliminating scores of black teachers and administrative personnel, the South was saved from allocating state funds for maintaining a *de facto* biracial school system that *should* have absorbed and financially supported all of those black teachers, principals, and administrators who were fired in order to implement the *Brown* decision. Thus, from the standpoint of *Brown,* blacks paid a price for "integration" insofar as the public school system was concerned. The question remains, Was the long-range price of "integration" worth it if measured by the cumulative results achieved by blacks as a minority group at the primary and secondary levels of education? Has the admittedly "inferior" status attained for blacks in public school education been remedied via "integration"? If so, how? If not, why not?

If the *Brown* decision's social consequences were limited to the confines of the school systems, it would be easier in the 1980s to measure the results cogently. But such was not the case. The *Brown* decision impacted upon far more institutional, racial, ethnic, class, and other educational areas of American life than public school administrative and instructional systems. In historical retrospect, when the evolutionary social and racial aspects of American society are refracted within the limits of the Blair bill's prognosis, the southern states paid an unnecessary price for their delay when forced by the federal power to ameliorate an educational situation in 1954 that could have been (and should have been) tackled in the 1880s with the aid of the same federal power. Hence, a profound question remains in the Eighties as a consequence of *Brown:* Would the passage of the Blair bill have rendered the *Brown* decision either judicially unlikely or irrelevant, or would the Blair bill's passage have resulted in another kind of constitutional lawsuit being argued based on other perceived violations of the Fourteenth Amendment's equal protection and due process clauses? What significance would such hypothetical arguments have with regard to the post-World War II civil rights court decisions and legislation leading to *Brown*? Although *Brown* purported to overthrow the separate-but-equal doctrine in terms of legal justice, it only hastened the growth of a different form of separate-but-equal dispensation in social practice. "Separate but equal," due to demographics, group psychology, economics, and class interests, is transformed into the social practice of group pluralism in public school education. What are the implications of this pluralistic trend for other groups in American society?

The general outcome of the *Brown* decision in extended areas of interracial, intraracial, interethnic, interminority existence in the 1980s poses critical problems for black leadership as it has evolved as a consequence of *Brown* from 1954 to the 1980s. The National Afro-American League first posed the seminal post-Reconstruction imperatives for the need of a civil rights philosophy for blacks in twentieth-century America. The National Association for the Advancement of Colored People (NAACP), which ultimately emerged as a result of the failed pioneering efforts of the Afro-American League, carried out its civil rights protest mission from 1909 to its culminating achievement of *Brown* in 1954. The NAACP achieved its aims, especially from the 1930s, governed by the social, racial, constitutional imperatives and civil libertarian assumptions most amenable to the functional legitimacy of its assumed role. Historically, however, the program of the NAACP, "both in its objectives and methods," was essentially the program that T. Thomas Fortune and others had conceived for the Afro-American League twenty years before.[28] In fact, Fortune himself pointed out that during the formative years of the NAACP, its leadership had co-opted the declaration of principles laid down by the Afro-American League in 1890. These principles related essentially to the urgent problem of the constitutional legalities underscoring the rights and privileges of black citizenship that were being undermined by the restoration of white supremacy in the southern states. Although the league during its life debated other important programmatic issues of a political, economic, and profoundly ideological nature, the NAACP was launched on such a watered-down version of what the league had attempted to outline that many of Fortune's allies rejected the NAACP principles on ideological grounds at the very outset. Thus was the NAACP launched out of the clamor of a grievously embittered and divided group of black leadership hopefuls.[29] T. Thomas Fortune lived until 1928, long enough to witness some early NAACP civil rights victories, but his prediction that the civil rights struggle assumed by the leadership of his generation in 1890 would "exhaust the best intelligence of the race for the next century" looms in the 1980s as a trenchant prophecy.

In 1954 the leadership of the NAACP exaggerated the civil rights implications of the association's most celebrated success—the *Brown* Supreme Court decision. That the decision would generate more civil rights problems than the Court mandated was not foreseen. Not until the 1980s would these new civil rights issues become manifest in their challenging complexity. The internal organizational crisis that would emerge within the NAACP's leadership in the 1980s had its roots in founding principles of the association that reach back to the years of civil rights programmatic transition from the National Afro-American League to the National Association for the Advancement of Colored People.

P ART TWO

I

The day following the historic Supreme Court decision of May 17, 1954, *Brown* v. *Board of Education, Topeka, Kansas*, certain members of the legal counsel for the NAACP were quoted by reporters on the future significance of that momentous ruling. When asked how long they thought it would be before segregation in education would be eliminated, one counsel replied that it might take "up to five years" for the entire country.

He also predicted that "by the time the 100th Anniversary of the Emancipation Proclamation was observed in 1963, segregation in all its forms
would have been eliminated from the nation."[1]

The civil rights vistas that sweeping decision immediately opened
for the NAACP were unprecedented for the public at large, both black
and white. Under the euphoric spell of victory, the NAACP, and many
of its most fervent liberal constituency, interpreted *Brown* as a mandate
to set more goals in the legal struggles against racial segregation and
discrimination. For a number of complex racial, economic, political,
cultural, legal, and regional reasons, civil rights strategies had, since the
World War II era, become more and more intensely concentrated on
segregation in the public school systems, especially in the South. By the
1950s it appeared to leading civil rights strategists that the real touchstone
for the more complete extension of racial democracy in America lay in
the democratization of public school education. This had not always been
the case, because high on the NAACP's agenda had been such pressing
issues as the eradication of discrimination in employment, both public
and private, residential housing, and higher education, and segregation
in the nation's military establishments—the most salient of civil rights
issues. Thus, for those blacks (and whites) who were of a dubious cast
of mind, the *Brown* decision, like the thunderclap of an approaching
storm, foretold social change of unknown scope and breadth. Today,
because of the absence of any definitive poll-taking among blacks in
1954, it is not possible to review exactly what *all* blacks really thought
about the *Brown* decision. Although most likely a minority, a considerable
if unknown number of blacks did not share the optimism of certain
members of the NAACP. Because the *Brown* decision would impact on
many more areas of social life than just public schools, the prospects
were hazardous and unclear. But for a black to criticize *Brown* meant
siding with die-hard southern segregationists and attacking widely shared
black ideals. Thus, it was impolitic to question *Brown* either for its legal
wisdom or mandated goals.

Those blacks who questioned the *Brown* decision did not object to
the implicit "moral imperative" to outlaw discriminatory practices against
members of the black minority. Rather, they were troubled by the implication of the term "racial integration," which during the 1940s had
been imperceptibly introduced into the lexicon of the NAACP as a synonym for "racial democracy," "racial equality," and "civil rights."[2]
While a Supreme Court decision bearing on any controversial racial issue
in the United States in 1954 would cast an oracular spell, as if the deity

had spoken through a tribunal of juridical vicars, ordinary people knew from living experience the true essence of American racial mores and beliefs. Racial attitudes fashioned racial customs, and the etiquette of racial contacts was as old as the Republic. Would a high court decision, either immediately or gradually, alter these customs? More than that, the *Brown* decision spoke specifically to segregation in public school systems in the South, and in certain "border" states, that involved the social world of children, not the adult world of extensive, interlocking organizational networks—social, cultural, economic, and political—that comprise the intricate web of society. What was startling about *Brown* was the immediate inference by the NAACP and its liberal constituencies that the Court had singled out public school segregation only as a convenient way of deferring a judgment on race relations beyond the classroom that would be pronounced later on. The immediate reaction of the tnen "Solid South" was massive resistance to *Brown,* both in the narrow scope as it related to public schools and in its broader implications as it impinged on institutionalized racial separateness in all of its forms.

An enduring question about the *Brown* decision in all probability will never be satisfactorily answered. Despite the dramatic unanimity of the nine judges, *who among them really believed in the ultimate implications of that decision*? How many shared the expectations of the NAACP strategists as pronounced by their legal counsels? It was natural that the civil rights leadership of that time would entertain an almost absolute faith in the "law," especially when the highest tribunal in the land promulgated a decision which was to be interpreted as the "law of the land" insofar as long-suffering blacks were concerned. But to what degree did Americans really respect the law when it came to race? American history had demonstrated, not very much. Yet the Supreme Court had unequivocally spoken on that matter. From then on, the uncommon word "integration" would be added to common lexicon of daily discourse as the media synonym for optimum race relations. During that time, the place-name "Korea," almost unknown in America before 1950, would enter the lexicon as a symbol of political and military travail, but far, far away. "Integration" was close to home and even more perturbing than Korea in terms of race, although the Korean conflict was in many respects a race war.

The Eisenhower Republicans were in power in 1954, and the civil rights forces led by the NAACP had progressed through the Harry S. Truman–Democratic party era buttressed by the executive weaponry bequeathed by Truman—whose Civil Rights Commission, established in

1946, had inquired into the condition of civil rights and made recommendations for their improvement. In 1948, Truman had initiated a study of blacks in the United States military, opening the way toward the integration of the armed forces that was fully attained during the Korean War. Also in 1948, Truman placed the full support of the executive office behind the civil rights leadership in federal employment. Truman's Fair Deal was but the post-World War II extension of Franklin D. Roosevelt's New Deal, which, with the watershed impact of World War II, had created the economic bases for black social and economic advances. This way social, political, and economic precedents were established for the *Brown* decision. On leaving office, Harry S. Truman had declared that there should be a civil rights program backed "by the full force of the Federal Government." The "full force" of the federal government meant, ultimately, the power of the Supreme Court. It was what civil rights leaders had been demanding, with high moral justification and indignation, ever since post-Reconstruction had ushered in the era of *Plessy* v. *Ferguson's* separate-but-equal doctrine of race relations in 1896. The *Brown* decision upset *Plessy* v. *Ferguson*.

The legal determination of the separate-but-equal doctrine of *Plessy* v. *Ferguson* had never been achieved in real social life. "Legal" separation of the races had never allowed blacks in the South anything resembling equal dispensation of social, economic, and political rewards. Specifically, the separate-but-equal doctrine had never mandated equal facilities in public school education. *Plessy*, however, when first adjudicated by the high court, dealt specifically with public, intrastate railway transportation at a time in southern history when blacks, generally, were struggling for education—*any* degree of public education—with a general agreement that black education would be segregated, i.e., *separate*, or there would be none at all. Unlike most liberal, historical civil rights doctrine of the *Brown* era, the *Plessy* verdict did not initiate racial segregation, but gave legal support to a segregationist social policy already in the process of being institutionalized since at least 1890. In the same way that the *Plessy* verdict gave blanket endorsement to *all* segregation after the fact, *Brown* was calculated to eliminate *all* segregation (i.e., separateness) with blanket application. The fact that public transportation, in the first instance, and public education, in the second instance, represented critically different areas of racial, cultural, political, and applied social policy was conveniently ignored by the high court's reasoning, which was as facile and pragmatic as it was of questionable intellectual probity. To strike out *Plessy*, which legitimized segregation (that is, separateness) in all areas of social life, the high court in 1954 mandated "integration," first in the public school systems. Carried away by the implications of this simplistic decision, the NAACP envisioned the total eradication of segregation in all its forms in less than ten years. If the NAACP had specified the total eradication of all *legally* mandated segregation, such optimism would have not been inconsistent with the dynamics of race relations in the United States, or with the distinctions between enforced segregation and inherent racial differences that no laws can monitor with careless disregard for race psychologies. Certain social scientists and democratic idealists might claim that the concept of race is a dangerous myth, but when blacks, whites, and other nonwhites in America *believe* in the concept of race, then race, myth or not, *is* a reality and a social fact and must be dealt with as such.

Yet, the peculiarities of the evolution of race concepts in the United States have caused a number of constitutional vagaries to arise. The outstanding legal vagary that emerged out of the political, economic, military, and social vortex of nineteenth-century American history was the Fourteenth Amendment. *Plessy* v. *Ferguson* arguments saw the Fourteenth Amendment one way in 1896 and concluded that "separate but equal" was not inconsistent with racial democracy, or equal rights, or equal protection. But the *Brown* decision of 1954 saw equal protection in a new contemporary light as if to imply that the legitimacy of race concepts of 1896 had changed to such a degree by 1954 that the American Constitution's pristine "color blindness" could be reinvoked by Court mandate. All of which was, of course, a matter of (Court) opinion. Social, legal, and racial history in America had fixed the range of legal reasoning available to civil rights jurists to the Fourteenth Amendment, one of the most vague amendments ever to be ratified by congressional procedure. The *Brown* unanimous decision said in part:

> We conclude that in the field of public education the doctrine of "separate but equal" has no place. Separate educational facilities are inherently unequal. Therefore, we hold that the plaintiffs and others similarly situated for whom the actions have been brought are, by reason of the segregation complained of, deprived of the equal protection of the laws guaranteed by the Fourteenth Amendment. This disposition makes unnecessary any discussion whether such segregation also violated the Due Process Clause of the Fourteenth Amendment.[3]

The tangled and contradictory logic accrued over the years *in stare decisis* regarding the meaning and intent of the Fourteenth Amendment unavoidably pushed the Supreme Court to the sweeping mandate of *Brown*. On the legal level, it led the NAACP to believe that an absolute victory had been won in its long forty-five-year struggle for justice. What loomed ahead was the problem of implementing the Supreme Court's 1954 decision, which shortly thereafter caused a modicum of restraints on hopes and great expectations. The following year, the executive secretary of the NAACP, the late Walter White, stated in his book *How Far the Promised Land?* that:

> This, then, is the balance sheet on the status of the American Negro in 1955, as I see it. It is not, of course, the final account of a job that is completed. Far from it. The alterations in the pattern of thought and action by both white and Negro America, though measurable and heartening, represent in many instances outward reform and not inner conversion. There are many barriers to rapprochement between white and non-white people in the United States because of tradition and enforced segregation. . . . As this is being written, twenty-nine of the forty-eight states still bar intermarriage. Far too many white Americans yet cling to exploded notions of racial superiority and inferiority, and many too many Negroes are convinced that all white people are incurably prejudiced.[4]

Social and racial realism made it necessary for the NAACP's executive secretary, within a year of *Brown,* to temper the civil rights exuberance that had greeted Justice Warren's grand opinion. And it is important here to cite the opinions of such spokesmen as Walter White because a running critique of similar leader types of the *Brown* era is a main theme of this essay. In 1954 it did not require law school erudition to deride an unseemly naïveté on the part of supposedly perceptive and experienced individuals working in civil rights. "Free by '63" became a rallying slogan inspired by civil rights leaders that carried a strong emotional appeal but that also discouraged any serious thinking about race. Today, it is permissible to ask: *How could anyone black have taken that slogan seriously in 1954?* Answer: In 1954–1955 such a question would have been derogated as the most negative pessimism. Surely, none of those "incurably prejudiced" white people cited by Walter White cared to believe it, which means that few, if any, of the cynical Negroes White mentioned actually believed in the NAACP's "Free by '63" mirage on the far horizon of American race relations.

Assuredly, the Supreme Court did open the floodgates to a protracted period of black mass actions and black revolts across the land that came

to organized fruition during the historic black Sixties. Already fully documented on the library shelves, those incipient and uniquely variegated
"Black Revolutions" need no specific recounting here except that, taken
together, they add up to a confused, discordant medley of contradictory
agendas—integrationist sit-ins, boycotts, protest marches, ghetto uprisings, Black Power separatism, aggressive black nationalism, Marxist-
Leninist radicalism—to mention the most prominent and media-augmented
trends. A galaxy of outstanding black leadership personalities came to
the fore—names that will be long remembered by the historically
conscious—Martin Luther King, Jr., Malcolm X, Medgar Evers, Rosa
Parks, James Farmer, Stokely Carmichael, H. "Rap" Brown, Eldridge
Cleaver, Huey Newton, Bobby Seale, Angela Davis, Jesse Jackson—
these were outstanding spokesmen for a multiplicity of black trends that
tried to translate a legal mandate for evolutionary social change into a
Black Revolution. For a quarter of a century following *Brown,* the pro-
tagonists and antagonists spawned by that decision engaged in extended
thrusts and parries, delays, advances, retreats, stratagems and obstruc-
tions, victories and defeats on numerous political, social, economic, and
cultural fronts. The profusion of social actions almost defies an activist's
compendium broader in scope than public school systems.

But by the end of the Seventies, the anti-*Brown* sentiments, waxing
stronger in a waiting game of tactical delay, brought to an end an era of
civil rights dreams while a number of hopes were deflated in the mired
quandaries of plaintiffs. The *Bakke* decision of 1978 signaled the cyclic
resurgence of interpretive argument on the meaning of the equal protection
clause of the same constitutional guarantee that swayed the Supreme Court
in favor of *Brown*—the Fourteenth Amendment. What the Supreme Law
giveth, it taketh away! The vagaries of the Fourteenth Amendment were
taking on the semblance of a legal trap, and not for the first time in its
controversial history. In 1954 the equal protection clause was cited by
judicial decree in ruling that the separate-but-equal doctrine was prejudicial against a specific racial minority (blacks), and thus had no place
in public education. In 1978 the Supreme Court cited the same equal
protection clause to rule in favor of a plaintiff, Allan Bakke, who claimed
that preferential treatment extended toward blacks in public education
discriminated against *him* in his quest for advanced degrees. It should be
noted that Allan Bakke had not, prior to his filing of suit for "due
process," experienced a lifetime under the onus of ethnic, racial caste,
or class oppression, nor had his ancestors. He was as near to the racial
ideal of "Nordic" perfection as any white racist could dream. Was the

Fourteenth Amendment ratified in 1868 *specifically* to establish and protect the citizenship rights of the blacks, or was it not? Beginning with
the *Slaughterhouse Cases* of 1873, through a wondrous maze of legal
argumentation, down to the *Bakke* decision, the Fourteenth Amendment
has been bowdlerized by judicial reiteration and reinterpretation, and also
whitewashed by conservative biases to such a degree as to cleanse the
equal protection clause of its political origins in the issue of black slavery.

In the first test of the Fourteenth Amendment, the *Slaughterhouse
Cases* of 1873, neither the plaintiffs nor the defendants were black, nor
did the points of argument have anything to do with the race question.
The issue at hand was whether the state of Louisiana had the power to
grant exclusive charter rights to one corporation to maintain a monopoly
on slaughtering cattle for public sale. The plaintiffs charged that such
state power was forbidden by the Thirteenth Amendment and by the first
section of the Fourteenth Amendment. In retrospect, it is of some interest
even now to quote from the case notes that summarized the majority
opinions in the *Slaughterhouse Cases:*

> . . . An examination of the history of the causes which led to the
> adoption of those Amendments and of the Amendments themselves
> demonstrates that the main purpose of all the last three Amendments
> (13th, 14th, and 15th) was the freedom of the African race, the security
> and perpetuation of that freedom, and their protection from the oppres-
> sions of the white men, who had formerly held them in slavery.[5]

Counsel for the plaintiffs argued that:

> The 14th Amendment is not confined to any class or race. It compre-
> hends all within the scope of its provisions. The vast number of laborers
> in mines, manufactories and commerce, as well as laborers on the
> plantation are defended against the unequal legislation of the State. . . .[6]

But well before Allan Bakke was to have certain arguments of
Slaughterhouse echo in his favor in the law chambers, court-ordered racial
integration in the public school systems, in the North and South, and also
the West, had encountered scattered success mixed with widening opposition, legal difficulties, and a faltering pace of implementation. To be
sure, legal segregation and separation had been outlawed, which was all
to the good for the whole society. If the NAACP's chief legal counsel
had clearly stated in 1954 that the outlawing of *legal* segregation and
discrimination was the express limit of the Supreme Court's power and

left it at that, *far more positive social and racial achievements might have been possible*. However, the NAACP, with the backing of the Court, equated all forms of segregation with all forms of separation. No one's "law" can eliminate *all* forms of social or racial separation in a multiracial or multiethnic society. That the Supreme Court justices did not comprehend this fact, or pretended not to, caused much psychological and emotional stress on both sides of the racial divides. Consequently, the optimistic "Free by '63" slogan was to become a joke in its sanguine expectations. *(What is freedom?)* By 1963 the social outcome of the *Brown* decision in areas *outside* the public schools was more segregation (i.e., separation of the races) than there was in 1953!

Yet from constitutional and racial standpoints, the *Brown* decision, theoretically flawed as it was, represented a landmark in the forced march of American social history toward its manifest *domestic* destiny. From a legal point of view, *Brown* was but the latest of a long series of judicial decisions stemming from the moral imperfections that had marred the American Constitution at its birth. The fatal flaw in that most historically advanced document on human liberty was its justification of human slavery. But this fact has by now become a rather superannuated historical misfortune of humankind in its millennial struggle toward "social progress." In this age-old enterprise, man's inhumanity to man has been a fateful exchange item in the catalogue of social evolution of human values. In this "onward" and "upward" struggle, men have waged wars, murdered, kidnapped, tortured, sold, bartered, raped, exploited, conquered, stole, plundered, laid waste, and enslaved. Men have also pioneered, invented, developed, built monuments of all kinds to secular pride, and destroyed in the name of special deities. Ancient civilizations were built on human slavery, and if it was the fate of New World civilizations to have inherited the institution of slavery to use as a footstool in their climb to "advanced stages," there remains no further need, as we approach the twenty-first century, either to defend or bemoan the moral misdemeanors of American slavery. *American civilization, as we know it, could not have been built without African slavery*. Because of this uncomfortable fact, the framers of the American Constitution had to legitimize slavery (like it or not). In this more than casual fashion was the slave written into the body politic as a labor adjunct, albeit as a helot without civil rights. Although the Founding Fathers, that celebrated club of self-serving, English-heritage worshipers, founded a "nation," what they really had in mind was the establishment of an *all-white* nation of English ex-subjects. Thus, not until historical circumstances *forced* the ratification of the Civil War Amendments was it admitted subjectively that an all-white American nation had been an absurdity long before the Declaration of Independence. Latter-day constitutional arguments about what the framers of the covenant *really* meant about such things as the "separation of powers," etc., can conveniently overlook an absolute certainty of intent: *They really wanted an all-white nation!* But the presence of considerable numbers of Africans in the colonies (plus the presence of aborigines) rendered the all-white ideal an impossibility. Institutionalized black slavery had negated the all-white ideal at the very outset.

However, the time-honored liberalistic retroactive *mea culpa* over the moral sin of slavery, in conjunction with the habitual black burden of historical shame and self-pity over the alleged irremovable stain of plantation degradation, have effectively obscured many of the real implications of the Fourteenth Amendment. We are blind to its essential evasions and ambiguities. This led inexorably to such a Court decision as *Brown,* based on an ambiguous constitutional amendment. *Brown,* the result of the *forced* march toward *de jure* "equality," could not but fail to result in a mismanagement of *de facto* racial, social, cultural, ethnic, and political elements in the body politic. By the early 1970s instead of racial integration advancing toward a progressively "open society," racial polarization advanced. With or without *Brown* and its unwarranted expectations, the outcome might have been the same, or different, but only in a matter of slight sociological degree. However, by 1980, in the midst of the Reagan political shift to the right, in keeping with the marked conservative mood enveloping the society, a more objective assessment of the racial situation was possible. The print media, true to their appointed form, vividly reported the twenty-five-year outcome of the *Brown*-inspired civil rights "revolution," to wit: *The Blacks Were Losing Ground in the Struggle for Equality.*

II   In Much of the South, Separation of the Races Still Is Key Fact of Life. . . .
        Despite New Laws, Old Ways Linger On, Particularly Outside a Few Big Cities. . . .

. . . So reads the caption to a "Minority Report" on page 1 of *The Wall Street Journal,* November 17, 1980. Although this situation generally prevailed also in the North and the West, the report began with an account of a black army sergeant who, upon returning to his hometown of Laurel, Mississippi, after an absence of fourteen years, discovered that he was unable to buy a house in Laurel's white sections. More than that, his black wife, with a college degree in mathematics, couldn't find a job. These evidences of lingering racism were only a few of the revelations the sergeant was to experience that proved him wrong about the heralded "changes in the South" during his absence; he had "assumed that the changes were for the better."

Racial conditions in Laurel *had improved,* but not to the degree that the sergeant had hoped. The sergeant's expectations mirrored the NAACP's 1954 belief that by 1963 segregation in all its forms would be eliminated from the nation. In 1966 the sergeant would not even have attempted to buy a house in the white sections of Laurel; and a real estate dealer would *not* have felt it necessary to resort to the kinds of subterfuge reported in this case to circumvent antidiscrimination legalities or formalities. But in other areas of Laurel's biracial existence, *things had improved:*

> Blacks and whites shop together, black clerks work in stores, and members of both races eat in fast-food restaurants. . . .

Such interracial conviviality over hamburgers is assuredly "integration" of a sort, and it was to win just this degree of integrated "freedom" that the black student sit-ins in Greensboro, North Carolina, courted jail and academic expulsion, if not worse, in 1960. Yet it was not full integration. However, the reporter pointed out that elsewhere in the South: "Well-dressed blacks now mingle with whites at expense-account restaurants and otherwise live middle-class lives. Blacks work alongside whites in stores, offices and factories across the South, attend the same universities and play on the same football teams. Separate washrooms and lunch counters are gone. Seats in the front of the buses are available to all."

Yet, the article continued: ". . . Talks with blacks and whites throughout the [southern] region show a wide division of opinion about black progress . . ." One of the most contested areas was, of course, housing. In Laurel (and elsewhere in the changed South), the reporter wrote:

> Except for one neighborhood that . . . is changing to black from white, residential segregation is complete. There are one large all-black public-

housing project and several all-white apartment complexes that accept
federal subsidy payments for low-income tenants.

The head of the local housing authority has a straight-forward
explanation why the public housing project is all black. *"You'll never
get whites to move into it.".* . . . The manager of an all-white apartment
complex is less direct. . . . "Blacks have applied for openings in the
building but they somehow all seem to find other housing before a unit
becomes available." (Italics added.)

The reporter pointed out that, generally, "social mingling between
young blacks and whites is rare, and it is discouraged." And specifically,
"there is very little social contact among Laurel adults either." In Laurel
the local NAACP leader asserted:

> Things will never change here. The whites said in the beginning they
> weren't going to do anymore than we made them do. If they comply
> with one [court] order, they get back into doing something else.

The white mayor of Laurel said that "while some bias remains in
the minds" of some of Laurel's blacks and whites, he knows of "no
discrimination because of the color of the skin. . . . I can look back and
easily find where a lot of discrimination existed unfairly and detrimentally,
but I can see tremendous changes now, not only in acts but in thought
processes." Moving eastward to rural Alabama, to a much smaller town
than Laurel, Mississippi, the reporter quoted the white mayor:

> I think it's similar to the way it's always been. . . . It's still a segregated
> society. If a white wants to have dinner with a black family, let him
> do it; nobody's going to stop him. But it just isn't done.

But if the black sergeant and the Laurel NAACP leader were dissatisfied with the rate of "progress" and cynical about the future, the
white attitudes, noted the reporter, reflected a sobering and paradoxical
view: "Whites often express surprise that blacks are anything but satisfied
and wonder what is left for blacks to want."

It is high time that some serious new thought be given to just what
the racial and sociological outcome of *Brown* (and all the civil rights
legislation that followed) might mean for the 1980s and beyond in the
United States. Why had it been so difficult in 1954 to foresee this outcome in readjustments in race relations in most of its general outlines?
Given our knowledge of the social psychology of race in America, given

the dramatic events reiterated and reassessed by the history profession, given the cultural contours of racial-group thinking, beliefs, prejudices, sentiments, etc., the racial situation *The Wall Street Journal* reported in 1980 could, *at best,* have evolved no other way. Fortunately for both blacks and whites, it could have been worse. Blacks (and minorities) who decry the current lag in economic and other social and political gains, the conservative defaults, the proliferation of antiblack, anti-minority right-wing extremists must understand that the promises and expectations of the *Brown* decision were both legally and sociologically improbable. Why?

Because first, the Constitution was conceived as a political covenant for an *all-white nation.* The Fourteenth Amendment, on which *Brown* was reasoned out in 1954, was monitored through congressional ratification in 1868 for mainly political reasons after much tortured argument. The original intent of the radical Republican supporters of the amendment was to confer legal citizenship on black ex-slaves; and with the Fifteenth Amendment this citizenship was fortified with all the civil rights privileges normally accruing to all American-born citizens without regard to race, color, or "previous condition of servitude." The ratification arguments in Congress reflected a political consensus that the hallowed Bill of Rights that had been added to the original articles in 1791 was both insufficient and unreliable for the constitutional protection of ex-slaves. However, the final version of the Fourteenth Amendment as ratified permitted such a degree of interpretive elasticity as to whose equal protection was actually defended that ultimately all types of citizens and interests were due as much, and even more, equal protection than the blacks. "Equality" was promised in the most ambiguous terms, with the intrinsic proviso that certain races, classes, individuals, and interests were "more equal" than others. In fact, by 1896 judicial as well as public opinion was so averse to including blacks as equal citizens in both the southern and northern state constituencies that the Supreme Court interpreted the Fourteenth Amendment to mean that blacks were due "legal equality" only within a segregated state of social existence—the *Plessy* v. *Ferguson* separate-but-equal doctrine. But there was no possibility or practicality of "equality" for blacks within a legalized framework of racial segregation, especially not in 1896.

From a constitutional premise, the *Plessy* doctrine should have demonstrated that the Fourteenth Amendment was a rather hollow instrument for the equal protection of black citizenship; but the American citizenry, black and white, was then, as now, stuck with the provisions of the

Constitution, as both written and amended. Thus fifty-eight years later, in 1954, the Supreme Court was forced out of circumstances to reverse the *Plessy* doctrine. But we are faced, admittedly or not, with the fact that *neither* of these extreme interpretations of equal protection is sociologically feasible or legally enforceable. The failure of *Brown* was already evident by the early 1960s; what *The Wall Street Journal* reported in its 1980 "Minority Report" was informative of the ultimate outcome of *Brown*, but it was also late.

The Fourteenth Amendment, cited by the high court in 1954 to support the *Brown* decision, does not, cannot, guarantee or enforce what *Brown* mandated. Hence, neither white nor black society in the main acquiesced willingly or voluntarily to *Brown*. Compliance came only when it was convenient to conform under duress, or ill-advised to resist or defy the decision under various social and geographical circumstances. Beginning with the public schools, and in the southern states, there *has* been integration, but the two races are generally as separate as ever. Before the *Brown* decision, racial segregation was due not only to segregationist laws, as in the southern states, but *also* to racial custom, racial economics, racial politics, and racial culture. Birds of a feather *will* flock together especially if, and when, the climate, prevailing winds, and feeding grounds make it feasible to do so. The *Brown* decision (backed up by prior Court decisions in the post-World War II era) purported, by implication, to eliminate all forms of legally enforced racial segregation through a sweeping order for full integration. But in its aggregate response, the society spontaneously balked at full integration, stalled in agreement, opposed the implementation of integration wherever possible. Why?

Because the society did not want to, did not have to. No law could make it. The more the society became integrated, the more it became "separate" on other levels. What desegregation did in fact accomplish, above, beyond, and outside the law of the land, was to bolster and encourage the spontaneous movement toward racial pluralism. When *The Wall Street Journal* cited the increased "separateness" of the races in the South, the description should have read increased "racial plurality." *The United States is racially, ethnically, and culturally a plural society. The legal and judicial problem is that the American Constitution was never conceived, written, amended, or otherwise interpreted either to reflect, accommodate, or otherwise acknowledge the pluralistic composition of American society.* As a judicial conception, what was questionable about the *Brown* decision is that while it legally and morally banished segregation, it did so on the premise that America is, was or ought to be ". . . one nation, indivisible, with liberty and justice for all," which was always a myth and continues to be a myth; but for all legal purposes—let it be called the "democratic imperative." Thus, the democratic imperative implicit in the political philosophy of the American Constitution prompted the courts, beginning with World War II, to undermine in piecemeal fashion or by peripheral envelopment the separate-but-equal doctrine of *Plessy* v. *Ferguson*. A series of indirect attacks on *Plessy* finally culminated in *Brown*, and mandated integration became the instrument for eliminating separatist restrictions imposed on blacks' efforts to achieve democratic racial equality in their life pursuits. Nevertheless, the racial-, ethnic-, cultural-group nature of American society implied a transitional step from *de jure* and *de facto* "separate but equal" (i.e., in theory) to *de jure* and *de facto* "plural but equal" through legally enforced desegregation. For this reason the sweeping mandate imposing the procedural instrumentality of integration ran into serious difficulties. How and why did the concept of integration evolve?

The *Brown* decision—aside from the economic, demographic, political, international, and other compulsions that pushed the harassed Supreme Court to render it—was strongly supported by a cumulative consensus of liberal social science interpretations of racial developments in the United States. Just as World War II was drawing to a close, the most trenchant assessment ever of American race relations was published. Compiled under the direction of Gunnar Myrdal, the renowned Swedish social scientist, *An American Dilemma* became the most widely read study of the historical outcome of American race relations and also the most controversial. Myrdal brought to bear on the race problem the observations, findings, and conclusions of more than seventy-five prominent and lesser-known sociologists, anthropologists, social psychologists, economists, political scientists, educators, and various social science researchers under the sponsorship of the Carnegie Corporation. A number of these social scientists were later enlisted in the Supreme Court hearings leading up to the *Brown* decision. The late sociologist, Arnold M. Rose, one of Myrdal's chief collaborators, wrote that Chief Justice Earl Warren, in delivering the opinion on *Brown*, "broke precedent and cited a few of the studies which influenced the court's thinking," and declared, "And see generally Myrdal, *An American Dilemma*, 1944."[7]

The choice of a foreign social scientist to conduct such a study lent much weight to the conclusion ascribed to Myrdal himself, that the race issue posed a dilemma for Americans. Etymologically, a "dilemma" describes a situation that has no satisfactory solution, that is a situation involving a choice between equally unsatisfactory alternatives. For many years, certain schools of Anglo-Saxon racial thought saw only two alternatives: assimilation, which was undesirable and biologically improbable; and expulsion, i.e., forced or voluntary emigration (to Africa or elsewhere), which was not only improbable but also so impractical as to be virtually impossible. Thus the dilemma. In the minds of many, this had been translated to mean there was no solution for the race problem in America. For many people the aggregate assessment in Myrdal's vast study did much to fortify the residual pessimism, particularly in the minds of many blacks, that the race problem promised little in the way of a democratic resolution. In 1945 the kinds of civil rights uprisings that occurred fifteen years later in the southern states were quite unthinkable. Liberals and leftists saw such an eventuality as leading to a "shooting affair." However, the groundswell of cumulative social change was already beginning, moving like a subterranean geologic shift toward the ultimate upheaval of *Brown,* and the fateful Sixties. Social perceptions about changing racial factors lagged behind the advance of material conditions pushing for superstructural alterations in social relations. The anticlimactic gloom of the postwar economic recession was mitigated only by such optimistic effects as were inspired by the doughty political career of a victorious Harry S. Truman, or by the glorious drama of a Henry A. Wallace rising only to fall in inglorious defeat and political extinction.

Such developments during the immediate pre-*Brown* era did much to lighten the pessimistic quandary surrounding American race relations. Truman's Civil Rights Commission demonstrated that at least the executive and the legislature were prepared to confront the "American Dilemma." When the southern anti-Negro political bloc struck back against its renegade southerner, Truman, with Strom Thurmond's Dixiecrat party movement, the pre-*Brown* battle lines were drawn for the civil rights struggles to come. The NAACP up to World War II had operated primarily in the broad field of "civil liberties," in defending black legal rights— the poll tax, antilynching laws, the franchise, etc. Then under Roosevelt and, later, Truman, the civil liberties field was extended into the economic area with the Fair Employment Practices Committee (FEPC), which sought to broaden job opportunities in various fields, especially in federal employment. But the FEPC, which was established to implement Roosevelt's Executive Order 8802 banning racial discrimination in government-financed defense industries, was not a victory won by the NAACP's efforts. The FEPC was the result of a threatened march on Washington by 100,000 blacks led by A. Philip Randolph, the black labor leader, in June 1941. This militant grass-roots mobilization was actually opposed by the NAACP leadership. After the war, Truman supported the efforts to establish a permanent peacetime FEPC. The NAACP had always been weak on the all-important bread-and-butter issue of jobs and the place of blacks in the economic order, which accounted in part for the notable lack of grass-roots support by blacks for the NAACP. In addition, the World War II integration of the armed forces was carried over into peacetime and was backed solidly by Truman. Democratic party politics, in dealing with blacks, was wedded to the Roosevelt New Deal heritage, which it could not disown and which carried the obligation to support black demands that it could not deny because of growing black "balance of power" leverage in presidential elections. Ironically, though, it took another war, the Korean conflict, to eliminate segregation in the military by way of a Truman executive order. The achievement of integration in the armed forces in the Fifties was a signal event. Not very many blacks, not to speak of whites, believed it would be brought about. At least on the international front, through "good" wars and "bad," the nation could pretend that the integrated military was a true reflection of the inner state of domestic racial accommodation. But the military was *not* civilian life in New York, Washington, D.C., or Laurel, Mississippi. The authoritarian structure of the military can enforce whatever it wants to enforce. Thus, the practical application of integration, especially in the crucial field of public and private housing, was cloudy. Nevertheless, Harry S. Truman ended twenty years of continuous Democratic party rule in Washington with the declaration that civil rights programs should be backed with *"the full force and power of the Federal Government"* in order to end discrimination against *minorities*. Already the pre-*Brown* era of civil rights programming was broadening the mainly *black*-inspired struggle for democratic equality to include, by definition, all other *minorities*. To what extent the inclusion of the term "minorities" in the developing civil rights framework actually qualified the meaning of integration as it applied to blacks was not clarified, since integration was still a foggy issue. Enter here the social scientists of the coming *Brown* persuasion.

In 1953 the NAACP and its legal corps organized a hundred or so lawyers and social scientists to support oral arguments to be presented before the high court in favor of the *Brown* lawsuit. Among the small contingent of black social scientists, social psychologist Kenneth B. Clark was to emerge as one of the most convincing presenters of "scientific" data purportedly demonstrating the deleterious psychological effects that segregation had on black children (and white) in separate public school systems. The prominence of Clark in these oral proceedings was significant. For one thing, Clark, although a rising star in the field of social psychology, was by no means the most prestigious black social scientist then known on the question of integration. In his preface to the first edition of *An American Dilemma* (1944), Gunnar Myrdal listed Kenneth Clark as an assistant to the staff in charge of various research tasks preliminary to initiating the difficult and absorbing labors that went into the finished study. However, Clark's name and/or specific contribution were not mentioned at all in the 1944 index. By 1952–1953, however, Kenneth Clark had risen in the ranks of the social science experts mobilized by the NAACP's corps of scientific advisers through his intensive studies on the educational problems of minority-group children. His famous Doll Test purported to show the effects of segregated education on black children's "self-image." In the 1951 trial proceedings of *Briggs* v. *Elliot* involving school segregation in Clarendon County, South Carolina, Clark first utilized his Doll Test findings in court testimony on behalf of integration. Later, the *Brown* decision made Clark an academic celebrity.

But prior to *Brown*, the leading black social scientists on the question of integration were W.E.B. Du Bois and E. Franklin Frazier, both sociologists. According to Arnold M. Rose, despite Du Bois's outstanding role in the civil rights struggle for forty years (before the NAACP was even founded), he "was in no way associated with the Myrdal research project" for *An American Dilemma*. Neither was Du Bois enlisted by the NAACP legal counsel to testify in the Court hearings leading up to *Brown*. The main reason was that Du Bois, despite his long devotion to civil rights, either did not favor integration or had serious reservations about it. His stand had resulted in his split with the NAACP executive board in 1934 during an internal debate over the merits of segregation versus integration. The essence of this crucial debate will be explored later. At the time of the debate, E. Franklin Frazier was a thirty-nine-year-old sociologist who during the late 1920s had graduated from the University of Chicago's premier school of sociology under the renowned Robert E.

Park and Louis Wirth. During his early years as a sociologist, Frazier became interested in investigating the social role of the black bourgeoisie, though he was not emboldened to publish his trenchant and sardonic criticisms until 1957 (i.e., after *Brown!*).[8] However, in 1949, Frazier had published his classic study *The Negro In the United States,* a remarkable accomplishment in the then not very advanced scholarly art of combining sociological methodology with historiography. In this study Frazier devoted his conclusions to the "Prospects for Integration of the Negro Into American Society." In a later edition (1957), Frazier revised these conclusions, obviously in response to certain empirical results in race relations stemming from *Brown*.

Considering the prospects for racial integration, Frazier cited the era of Social Darwinism and its ultimate legal support as exemplified in the *Plessy* v. *Ferguson* doctrine. However, Frazier pointed out that the Social Darwinist tenor of American racial thinking had, of necessity, been tempered as American society pushed forward into the twentieth century:

> During the half century which has elapsed . . . many important changes have occurred in the Negro, in the relation of the Negro community to the larger American community, and in the relationship of the American nation to a changing world. In view of these changes, which were precipitated by World War I and accelerated during the following World War II, what are the prospects for the integration of the Negro into American life?[9]

In retrospect, these changes were in fact so startling that the American mind-set during the age of *Plessy* could hardly have conceived of them, so prevalent was the notion that the Negro had no future in America and was a hopeless cause. As an example, Frazier quoted part of a speech by Charles Francis Adams delivered in Richmond, Virginia, in 1908:

> We are confronted by the obvious fact, as undeniable as it is hard, that the African will only partially assimilate and that he cannot be absorbed. He remains an alien element in the body politic. A foreign substance, he can neither be assimilated nor thrown out.[10]

This was the grandson of John Quincy Adams, the sixth American president, greeting the twentieth century with a Social Darwinist swan song one year before the birth of the NAACP. Frazier, in his superb analytical fashion, then essayed the Negro's chances for integration. He was, in the spirit of scientific restraint, careful not to speak glibly of the

goal of full integration that became so distractingly the rhetoric of the
Brown-inspired enthusiasts of the late Fifties. He described the "wider
educational opportunities" that had opened up since the 1940s. He cited
the "mass migrations to the northern cities," the "New Negro" literary
renaissance of the 1920s, and the "less dramatic but steady migration of
Negroes to Southern cities":

> Although the folk Negro has become transformed through education
> and greater participation in American culture, the fact of his color has
> continued to retard his integration into American life.[11]

Here Frazier discussed skin color among American blacks. This has
always been a touchy point of genetic reference with the black leadership
and the usual pigmentation of that leadership:

> In the city the social mobility of mulattoes or Negroes of mixed ancestry
> has been increased. Because of the anonymity of city life, they have
> been able to pass for white or for southern Europeans or South Amer-
> icans.[12]

Did skin color, then, play any significant role in the degree to which
Negroes were, or would be able, to integrate into American society?
Moreover, to pass for white meant assimilating into the white world,
something that Charles Francis Adams said was out of the question for
"Africans," and a "race-mixing" process that none of the "scientific"
findings used to buttress *Brown* integration suits even mentioned as an
issue of sociological inquiry. Thus, if the real estate operator in Laurel,
Mississippi, had sold a house in a white neighborhood to a Negro who
could easily pass, but *not* to the black sergeant whom Frazier would have
categorized a "high visibility" Negro, would *that* have proven the work-
ability of integration? Definitely not!

However, Frazier discussed the enhanced social mobility of the Negro, and how heightened sophistication about life and about the world in
general gave him and her a new conception of self. Moreover, said
Frazier, "the new conception which the Negro has acquired of himself
has been paralleled by a change in the white man's conception of the
Negro":

> The Negro is being redefined through the theatre, the radio, and the
> television. Whereas forty years ago the Negro appeared in advertise-

ments only as a grotesque, ape-like figure, a Negro artist may be used today to advertise classical recordings or be given a leading role in an opera on television. . . . As the Negro is found in new occupations and new roles the association of a dark complexion and negroid features with an inferior social status is tending to disappear. This is even apparent in the South where there is still insistence upon a biracial organization.[13]

In the process during which blacks went through changes in self-conception and whites went through changes in their conception of blacks, noticeable alterations took place within the black community which, according to Frazier, were "the result of changes in the economic and social organization of the Negro community."[14] The most important changes were the increased occupational differentiation. From the 1920 census onward, this occupational differentiation was shown in successive censuses. Thus, in the thirty years from the 1920s to *Brown,* the heavy concentration of blacks in agriculture as poor farmers, and unskilled laborers, and in domestic service was gradually reduced as higher proportions began to move into semiskilled occupations, then more slowly into skilled occupations and such white-collar occupations as clerical workers and salesmen. Although, Frazier said, the *proportion* of blacks employed in the professional occupations did not change significantly, the *composition* of the professional class had changed qualitatively:

> Whereas formerly most professional Negroes were teachers, preachers, and doctors, at the present time they may be found in a majority of professional occupations. The most important consequence of the increasing occupational differentiation of the Negro population has been the emergence of a sizeable middle class.[15]

This expansion of the Negro middle class was, however, most evident in the North, where the color barriers to better employment were lowered more quickly than in the South. In the North "the increase in the size of the Negro middle class has enabled a large proportion of Negroes to conform to American middle class standards of living." This was reflected in their dress, housing, and in other aspects of their lives. As a result, changes occurred in the orientation of the Negro community to the wider American community. However:

> The Negro community still remains the social world in which the majority of Negroes live. Although Negroes have increasingly adopted

middle class standards, they still find in their own institutions, especially
churches, and social clubs and other associations embodying cultural
interests, the main means of self expression.[16]

These were Frazier's observations in 1957, three years after *Brown*.
Although he pointed out that blacks were integrated to a much larger
extent in the urbanized North, where blacks were more deeply involved
in associations and institutions of the wider community, he advised:

*The complete dissolution of the Negro community appears to be in the
distant future despite the fact that there are indications that the Negro
is being integrated into certain phases of American society.*[17] (Italics
added.)

Since this was a difficult sociological postulate to demonstrate with
any mathematical precision, Frazier had to explicate what precisely integration signified. He attempted to accomplish this by describing the
concept of integration—"From Secondary to Primary Group Contacts,"
which purported to "define the typical stages in the development of
relationships between immigrants or minority groups and the dominant
white group in the United States." Frazier did not define what this "dominant white group" was, but he utilized the "race-relations cycle" models
devised by Emory S. Bogardus and others.[18] According to these models,
roughly six stages, plus a final stage, characterize the integrative process
of nonwhite minorities into the larger American society. In the initial
stages, minorities encounter "curiosity" from the dominant group, which
allows them recognition as a cheap labor source. Next, the minority
outsider becomes the object of industrial antagonism as a competitor.
Next, legislation mandates the exclusion of the minority outsider and
restricts his civil rights. Then, fair-play movements arise to defend the
rights and privileges of the minority group. This stage is followed by one
in which antagonism to the minority group dies down and that leads to
the final phase, during which the minority group must face the problems
and challenges of assimilation.

In Frazier's view, following the *Brown* decision, blacks were found
going through the fifth, sixth, and final stages of the race-relations cycle,
"depending upon the section of the country." The problem, then, as
Frazier saw it in 1957, was to determine in "which areas of human
relations integration is progressing most rapidly, and in which there is

greater resistance to integration.'' Following the *Brown* decision, the greatest resistance to integration occurred almost simultaneously in public school education and in public transportation, specifically during the Montgomery Bus Boycott in Alabama in 1956. These integration efforts strikingly bear out Frazier's conclusion that "the process of integrating the Negro into American society may be represented by a gradient. . . . This means that the Negro is being integrated *first* into those areas of American life involving secondary contacts as opposed to primary contacts, or secular as opposed to sacred relations."[19] What are "sacred" and "secular" social relations between the races?

Secular relations are exemplified in the way people of both races relate or intermingle in the streets, in places of amusement, on streetcars and subways, on trains and buses, in restaurants, commercial establishments, stores, and other public places; these are also called "secondary" contacts, because they are rather *impersonal*. However, public school systems fall under the heading of "primary" or sacred interpersonal contacts (along with churches, clubs, associations, fraternities, etc., including the most sacred and basic social unit, the *family*). The gradients of integration that lie between the most primary or sacred and the most secondary or secular need not be examined at this point. But it is worth noting that integration made noticeable advances in precisely those economic, cultural, social, and political areas that are defined as secondary or secular. Beginning with World War II, blacks registered racial progress in labor unions and semiskilled and skilled occupations, in white-collar upgrading in industry and white-collar employment, in their entrée into the professions and professional associations, the theater and the stage, sports, and university undergraduate and graduate education. Frazier explained that "Negroes are being integrated first into those areas of American life in which contacts are more or less impersonal and secular."[20]

These black advances on the integration front preceded the *Brown* decision. Institutional and structural roadblocks against black advances had already been broken in economic, political, and social programs sponsored by the New Deal and stepped up by a global war. However, when the Supreme Court was pushed in 1954 to render its legal ultimatum, it bypassed, for the time being, Frazier's social arena of secondary and secular contacts, and aimed its ukase squarely at one of the most primary and sacred institutions. The results were dramatic and fateful. "The prospect of educating white and colored children together in the public elementary and high schools . . . has aroused considerable resistance on the part of whites in the South."[21] Everyone involved, inside or beyond the intimate confines of the courts, knew what was coming. Frazier explained in 1957 that the organized resistance to public school integration was possible because of "certain sociological reasons":

> The main sociological reason is that the public elementary and high schools are closer to the family. The existence of parent-teacher associations is evidence of this fact. Colleges and professional schools are further removed from the family. To even a greater extent, college students and students in professional schools are removed from the family, or have broken family ties.[22]

Years later, in the Eighties the objective accuracy of Frazier's general assessments of integration progress was graphically valid. Frazier died in 1962 and, like Du Bois, he was a thinker who would be sorely missed. Whether Frazier could have foreseen the full outcome of the post-*Brown* era in the 1980s is questionable. Although he did say the complete dissolution of the Negro community appeared to be in the distant future, Frazier did not deal with what might happen should resistance to integration stiffen at a certain point of maximum integration at the secondary and secular gradient levels (saturation points?), or should extended holding action restrict the Negro community and forestall the dissolution for an extended time, if not *in perpetuum*.

Despite Frazier's remarkable scholarship and his perceptively clear analysis of the evolution of race contacts over the years, he was unavoidably trapped in a conceptual wicket of conflicting definitions. Of course, he was not alone either among professionals or among people in general, most of whom had to wrestle with the meaning of "integration" once the *Brown* decision was rendered: *What did it really mean?*

In his pre-*Brown* writings, Frazier talked about "segregation," "discrimination," "assimilation," and "integration." Then he began to use more frequently the term "desegregation," meaning the social movements against segregation inspired by the *Brown* decision. In the revised ending of the study reviewed here, Frazier wrote: "The Southern faction of the Democratic Party supported the economic program of the Republican Party, predominantly a Northern party, while the Republican Party refuses to take a clear stand for a program of *desegregation* in the south. Thus both parties are committed to a program of *gradualism* in regard to the *integration* of the Negro into American life."[23] (Italics added.)

Here Frazier used the terms "desegregation," "gradualism," and "integration" in a political rather than a legal juxtaposition. Expanding on this political note, Frazier added:

> The Manifesto of Southern Congressmen and Senators who defied the Supreme Court Decision of May 17, 1954 outlawing segregation in public education went unchallenged by the Republican leadership. Nevertheless, the laws of the land commit the nation to a policy of integration of the Negro into American society.[24]

Or so Frazier and many of the black elites thought following *Brown*. Aside from whether the laws of the land at the time of *Brown* meant all that Frazier said it meant, the above political assessment throws much contemporary light on Republican "civil rights" policies under Reagan as well as on the Republicanism of yesterday. Was it not Eisenhower Republicanism that sent the National Guard into Little Rock, Arkansas, in 1957 to endorse the law of the land in what Frazier called a most primary and sacred institution? Yes, it was; but then how could it be argued that the Republican party refused to take a "clear stand"? Would the southern Democrats have sent troops into Little Rock to uphold the law? Hardly. Yet in the face of the political temper of the times, how could Frazier claim that *both* parties were "committed to a program of gradualism" in regard to integration? *And what is gradualism in this regard?* Gradualism could conceivably take a century!

In retrospect, it is not difficult to understand why the fervent integrationists among both the black civil rights strategists and their white liberal supporters believed (or pretended to believe) that the Supreme Court had committed the American nation to the eventual complete integration of the races. Blacks who did not believe this were either ignored or forced to represent various shades of "anti-integration," "separatist," or "nationalistic" opinion, or else assumed critical stances outside the mainstream of social opinion. Frazier represented the sociological legitimacy of the integrationist school of thought represented by the NAACP. Yet contradictorily, he was not very popular with the NAACP, not as popular as Kenneth B. Clark, for example. Frazier's provocative *Black Bourgeoisie* (1957) was the most pungent criticism leveled at the black middle class ever published. Curiously, Frazier criticized the very class that was most supportive of the NAACP and its pro-integrationist policies. In 1957, Frazier sounded much like W.E.B. Du Bois who in 1934 had

broken with the NAACP's leadership over integration. Du Bois could
not accept Walter White's and Joel Spingarn's commitment to integration
as the NAACP's official policy.[25] In this regard, Frazier characterized
the association as follows:

> Even the NAACP, which has stood for "racial radicalism" and has
> received a large part of its support from Negroes, has been influenced
> by the middle-class outlook of its white supporters and has sought
> support primarily from Negroes with a middle-class outlook. . . . The
> "integration" of Negro intellectuals into both public and private schools
> and colleges has generally confirmed the faith of these intellectuals in
> the soundness of the middle-class way of life. "Integration" has thus
> tended to increase the size and influence of the black bourgeoisie, since
> their *social* life continues to be centered in the Negro community.[26]

Yet Frazier himself was most clear and unequivocal in his sociological justifications for the full integration program of the NAACP. No
black social scientist had written more persuasively regarding the need
for unqualified integration. But he did not figure as prominently in the
pre-*Brown* Court hearings as did Kenneth Clark, whose social science
testimony dealt specifically with the impact of race prejudice on children
in the public schools rather than with integration in the broader adult
social life that concerned Frazier. Intellectually, Frazier was pretty much
of a hero-model for many of the young-generation black radicals of the
1960s, mainly for his attacks on the "black bourgeoisie" in 1957. But
his system of analysis contained some unsatisfactory conclusions. When
he dealt with the process of desegregation, he was true to the social facts,
but to juxtapose the process of integration with desegregation confused
a legal construction of a problem with the manner in which the problem
was being resolved in real life. What Frazier the sociologist did not, or
could not, see was that desegregation would remove a number of discriminatory restrictions of *imposed* segregation *releasing blacks as a
racial minority into an advanced stage of group plurality. The United
States is a racially and ethnically plural society.* For this reason, Frazier
had to conclude that, despite integration, the ultimate dissolution of the
Negro community would be postponed.

Frazier, true to the post-*Brown* civil rights mood, implied that the
Supreme Court mandated that the laws of the land "commit the nation
to a policy of integration." Integration where? In the public schools of
certain states. But the public school system was the only primary and

sacred institution to which the Court specifically spoke in the *Brown* decision. The other institution, the family, which was more sacred than a public school and the most primary of primary institutions, was not, and could not have been, integrated by anybody's law. In consonance with Frazier's own terminology, it would have been more true to the social fact to have said that the Court committed the nation to a policy of desegregation, inasmuch as most of the progress made through integration has been (and was) desegregation in the social arena of "secondary group contacts," such as public places and travel accommodations. In clarification of the precise distinctions to be made between primary and secondary group contacts, Frazier wrote:

> Because of the predominantly rural character of Southern society, social life is still based largely upon primary or personal relations. With the growing urbanization of the South social control has become more impersonal as it becomes institutionalized in law. . . . [27]

True, but the same could be said for the more extensively urbanized sections of the North where primary and personal relations would still predominate even in the face of the desegregation of the secondary arena. For example, the white flight to the suburbs in response to integration and its urban impacts can well be construed as a white strategy to defend many primary or sacred areas of life as effectively as before the *Brown* decision. The institutionalization of the law can and does result in social control becoming more impersonal, and Frazier cited another example:

> Gradually, white policemen are becoming representatives of the *law* rather than conceiving of themselves as persons embodying certain attitudes towards Negroes. . . . The control of secondary relationships through the reign of law emphasizes the increasing importance of the government in the integration of the Negro into American society. . . . [28]

True enough, as experience has indicated since *Brown,* yet the reverse or converse was shown by the increase of police brutality against blacks and other minorities in carrying out the law in *both* primary and secondary areas of group contact. Thus, incontrovertibly, integration has been facilitated by law mostly in secondary group contacts by a process of desegregation, again by law, that has always been marked by gradualism in line with the Supreme Court's unspecific timetable of "all deliberate speed" stated repeatedly in implementing the *Brown* decision.

Nothing resembling the full integration the NAACP promoted in the 1950s is visible today. It is hard to believe that the civil rights leadership of the Fifties could have seriously believed that contemporary integration would turn out any different from what is seen today. *But they did*—which makes what is called "black leadership" in the Eighties a serious case of inherited incapacities born of a tradition of faulty strategies and limited social perceptions. The social policies of racial integration stemming from *Brown* have undoubtedly resulted in political, economic, and cultural progress for a definite *class* of blacks that existed before *Brown*. Integration has also resulted in the statistical increase in the dimensions of that class since the 1960s. But if it was ultimately the federal power that was most responsible for setting into motion those economic, social, political, and legal forces that aided and abetted the growth of this *new* class, these advances are now seriously threatened by the political alterations in the role of the federal power introduced by the new resurgent Republican conservatism of the 1980s. Where do blacks go from here—both the affluent *new class* and the vast economically poor majority that integration never touched?

Following the *Brown* decision, it became more and more fashionable for social scientists and critics to assess American blacks as a "minority" in an overly facile comparison with other "minorities," white and nonwhite. Some writers went further and implied that the black minority was classifiable with descendants of European immigrants who arrived in America as underprivileged, persecuted, or otherwise disadvantaged outsiders who had to fight their way up the social, political, and economic ladder in order to win equal citizenship. The post-World War II emergence of the civil rights crusade that appealed to the Constitution for its legitimate claims was not a movement of minorities, but of one minority, the blacks. By virtue of its own historical claim to constitutional verification (legally *sui generis*), the black movement led the way for the broader American minorities question to be reasserted in a fashion never before argued. Thus, what began as a black-versus-white civil rights encounter, sponsored by the judiciary, wound up in the Seventies as a black *and* minority issue leavened by the "woman question," which took *center stage* on the domestic minority front. Constitutionally, the assertion of the minority and feminist issues reinterpreted the Fourteenth Amendment's equal protection clause beyond the original intents of its framers in 1868.

In America there are minorities, but then there are other minorities; some minorities are equal, but some are more or less equal than others. American descendants of European immigrant groups make up what are called today "white ethnics," who are in fact minorities. Unlike blacks, white ethnics possess no constitutional reinforcements of their citizenship status, for the simple historical reason that they were never chattel slaves, but wage slaves; there *is* a difference. More than that, white ethnics, of whatever European origin, are *de facto* "assimilables" by virtue of skin color and racial origins, and are therefore candidates for intermarriage into the dominant White Anglo-Saxon Protestant (or Catholic) group.

The first pre-Civil War immigrants to encounter the nativistic animosities of the Anglo-Americans were the Irish Catholics in the 1840s.[29] By that time, considerable numbers of blacks had been arriving in the then English colonies since 1619, ten years after the Plymouth Rock landings. In fact, Africans had accompanied the Spanish *conquistadores* to various parts of the mainland before the *Mayflower*.[30] Indians, of course, were already present to greet the English and European invaders. Thus, by constitutional law, "preferential" citizenship is historically as *de facto* for blacks and Indians as for the founders who were of English heritage. In addition, blacks (like Indians) did not *voluntarily* forsake the land of their birth for American citizenship. In other words, American blacks do not share the social history of post-Civil War European immigrants or their immigrant heritage, and thus cannot be described as descendants of immigrants. Blacks *are* a minority, but women as a class or sex, although presenting grievances that fall within the purview of constitutional equal protection, are *not* a minority. However, the liberal civil rights consensus of the Seventies compares society's treatment of women to society's treatment of blacks. Thus, subordination or discrimination based on sex differences is equated simplistically with subordination, discrimination, and segregation based on racial differences. That such an analogy represents a travesty of sociological facts of race and sex differentials is neither understood nor admitted in the present outcome of civil rights policy and practice.

As the civil rights movement entered the 1960s, legislation and executive initiatives were geared to federal sponsorship and defense of the civil rights of blacks in voting and the extension of the privileges of the franchise as per the Fifteenth Amendment. However, by 1964 and even before, in congressional arguments the equal rights provisions of the equal protection clause of the Fourteenth Amendment began to be cited with reference not only to race but also to sex. Thus, Title VII of the Civil Rights Act of 1964 began by outlawing discrimination based on determinations of "race, color, religion, sex or national origin." Actually, Title VII had to do with the *economic* issue of equal employment opportunities, which, in a strict constructionist interpretation of the Fourteenth Amendment, was not a civil rights issue. It was, of course, the black civil rights movement that had pioneered the Fair Employment Practices Committee (FEPC) platform, backed by Truman, in the late Forties. Thus, the women's rights movement of the Sixties and Seventies was able to ride in on the momentum of the black civil rights movement via Title VII, when, in fact, the women's movement could not lay claim to a purely civil rights demand. The Nineteenth Amendment, which gave women the right to vote in 1920, left women, as such, *without* a civil rights demand but with an *economic* demand. This demand, unless it refers to minority *nonwhite* women, was *not* what the *black* civil rights movement was all about with regard to minority status.

With Title VII of the Civil Rights Act of 1964, the sexual aspect of citizenship was legislatively conjoined with the modern civil rights question of women as women. Thus, the FEPC legislative strategies initiated by the black civil rights leadership in the Forties were absorbed by the new legislation of the Sixties. This stretched the economic demands of blacks to include not only other minorities but women as well. Thus did *Brown* in 1954 open up a new era. First the judiciary, then a succession of innovations by the legislature added more elasticity to the already tenuous doctrine of the Fourteenth Amendment. As time passed, the embattled Fourteenth had less and less special meaning for blacks. The legislative reasoning that followed *Brown* was reminiscent of the legal reasoning in the *Slaughterhouse Cases* of 1873 when, during the arguments, significant remarks were made, such as "The 14th Amendment is not confined to any class or race. . . ." and "It is futile to argue that none but persons of the African race are intended to be benefitted by this amendment. . . ."[31] At this early stage of judicial argumentation, especially with a liberal Republican President Grant still in the White House and Reconstruction governments still in power in the late Confederacy, it was not politic to attempt completely to purge the Fourteenth Amendment of its "African slavery" origins. But neither the justices, plaintiffs in error, or appellants chose to allude to either women or other minorities. Justice Samuel F. Miller did, in delivering the majority opinion, make a tangential reference to "Mexican peonage" and "Chinese Coolie labor" as forms of slavery that came within the purview of the "amendments" (meaning the Thirteenth and Fourteenth), but constitutionally Indians and nonwhite minorities simply did not exist.

It took some ninety-two years—until 1964—for blacks as a minority, in a long-deferred civil rights confrontation, to become officially linked with other minorities and then with minorities and women. Close on the heels of *Brown* came a burgeoning chorus of complaints from the heretofore quiescent, long-slighted white ethnics that blacks were perhaps getting too much "preferential" treatment from a constitutional redress of accumulated grievances. From the black vantage on our society, other minorities have to be viewed in terms of the extent to which they are assimilable into the dominant "White Nation" American ideal, both in accessibility to the social, economic, and political rewards of American citizenship, and also in the degree that these white minorities voluntarily assume the life-styles of the nearest possible approximation to the White Anglo-Saxon Protestant (WASP) cosmology. White ethnics, though a proliferation of religious, national, and cultural minorities, are nevertheless in fact as assimilated as they basically care to be, or strive to be, and only as separate and distinct as they consider it to their group advantage to remain. In the long social process of their assimilation, life has not been a bed of roses in which to recline, blissfully contemplating the materialistic rewards of the American Dream. For the ethnics, life in the land of American White Anglo-Saxon pride and prejudice was advantageous basically because, as a "land of opportunity," America was better than Europe. America, for the ethnics, was better than Europe because they were never denied the right to earn a living by hard work despite the often calculated exploitation that accompanied this right. Moreover, the door to unfettered participation in the rough-and-ready, highly competitive field of American politics was never so tightly closed against the European ethnic that he couldn't pry it open by concerted effort. In this regard, the white ethnic has, since the ratification of the Fourteenth Amendment, had it all over the native-born lowly American black who had to compete against the European immigrant in the labor market, which was constantly manipulated by the employers in favor of the immigrant worker. Moreover, when one considers that in the Americanization of the immigrant the problem of assimilation was never cast in constitutional terms, one must again be struck by the ability of the Fourteenth Amendment's elastic ambiguities to be stretched or contracted according to *whose* bid for social, economic, and political rights is under consideration. For the white ethnics, the Bill of Rights was sufficient to motivate a mass migration out of European poverty and class-ridden social subjection to the land of opportunity. After arrival in the new land, whatever hardships the immigrants suffered, though arduous, were quite beyond the ameliorative scope of the Thirteenth, Fourteenth, or Fifteenth Amendments to salve, worsen, or qualify. European immigrants remained, for the most part, socially distant if not hostile to blacks and mostly oblivious to Indians and other nonwhites. Their ambivalences toward the WASPs usually leaned toward the Americanization school of subservient conformity, so much so that one of the more outspoken ethnic intellectuals of the Seventies could write:

> It is so much easier in America to forget one's ethnic past, to climb upwards into an elite culture, to become a "new man" without connection to a past. Who wants to become known as a "Jewish" writer, a "Catholic" writer, a "Slovak" writer? Lurking in such epithets is a concession of failed generality.[32]

This was written in the preface to *The Rise of the Unmeltable Ethnics* at the height of the new "ethnic pride" revival that came to civil rights fruition about fifteen years following the initial shocks of the *Brown* decision. Further on in this revealing book, the author declared:

> Reformist bureaucrats have neglected ethnic diversity (it would wither away). The political resources of ethnic diversity were overlooked. The recent increase in Black, Chicano, and Indian consciousness left other ethnic groups in a psychologically confused state. They were unable to be WASPs; they have lost confidence in themselves. . . . [Moreover] major programs in the last decade had as their symbolic message: "for blacks only." Thus the Urban Coalition poverty programs, Head Start, Black Studies Programs, bussing, integration and other major initiatives seemed to exclude others, *despite their need*. This was true in the public mind, even if not in fact.[33] (Italics added.)

But, *it was in fact,* despite the author's disingenuous attempts to qualify his white ethnic envy. Designating the Seventies as the "Decade of the Ethnics," the author could not bring himself to declare that the ethnic revival of the Seventies historically followed on the heels of the "Sixties: Decade of the Blacks," much as days of hope follow the dawn after dark nights of despair. More than that, the author ignored the crucial fact that the "recent increase in Black, Chicano and Indian consciousness" was inspired by a *constitutional* decision based squarely on the new interpretation of a long-standing constitutional issue. Like it or not, for the "unmeltable ethnics," blacks were the unabashed catalysts behind the ethnic consciousness aroused in the Sixties. *Who was stopping the white ethnics from seeking constitutional redress of grievances before the* Brown *decision?* Nothing or no one but the plain fact that white ethnics had no real constitutional argument in the first place! One can, of course, criticize black and/or *Brown* legal rationales, black methods, black excesses, black infantile expectations, the questionable emphases of certain black leaders, the tactical confusions, and the vagaries of disputed ultimate goals of integration. But nevertheless, blacks had behind them the legal forces of social history and the *constitutional* legitimacy of due process, to which, on record, no single white ethnic group could lay claim unless one would care to cite the WASP miscarriages of criminal justice in the cases of Sacco and Vanzetti or Bruno Hauptmann—two legal lynchings of white minority representatives.

This is not to dispute totally the legitimate group grievances of white ethnics, but the better to sort out and analyze the litanies of grievances by various minorities. This is important because the white ethnic intellectual quoted above, Michael Novak, was cognizant enough of the racial factor in the minority equation to link black civil rights with those of Chicanos and Indians. In the feverish pursuit of the American Dream, groups were handicapped, but some were more handicapped than others. White ethnics did not need the Thirteenth, Fourteenth, and Fifteenth Amendments, or a hundred years of litigation and court decisions, to legitimize their social status. And when one examines the pantheon of American achievers in various fields and finds such names as Kosciusko, Schurz, Frankfurter, Brandeis, Dvořák, Cardozo, Baruch, Tesla, Bartók, Toscanini, Cermak, Veblen, Sikorsky, Pulitzer, Wittke, and numerous other decidedly un-WASPish luminaries, it means that the American Dream was not always the sleepless nightmare of nonrecognition that inspired Martin Luther King's "I Have a Dream."

Thus, the question follows: Exactly what are the needs that our author on white ethnics believes the reformist bureaucrats "seemed to exclude"? Did white ethnics really need poverty programs, Head Start, black studies programs, or integration? It is safe to conclude that white ethnics neither needed nor wanted integration. As for poverty, the question is relative. White ethnics never experienced the "ghetto pathology" ascribed to black and nonwhite minorities. They knew little of the South or Appalachia. If white ethnics had needed poverty programs, they could have had them. The welfare bureaucracy lives by feeding on poverty—the more poverty discovered, the better for the bureaucracy! White ethnics got ethnic studies programs when they wanted them, but it was the black studies movement that inspired ethnic studies programs. Busing and integration, of course, white ethnics would have considered unnecessary, superfluous, and irrelevant because they were perfectly content in their neighborhood schools, and were never gerrymandered out of WASP-dominated public schools. Of course, one can understand their anxieties over integration inasmuch as in that highly dubious exercise in public school education futility, white ethnics resented being forced to mix with blacks wherever ethnic-neighborhood consolidations were threatened by black invasions. As E. Franklin Frazier pointed out, there was considerable resistance to integrated schools because elementary and high schools fall into the category of *primary, personal,* and *sacred* contacts, of which the *family* was the most sacred of all.

It is perhaps true that no one holds the inviolability of the family more sacred than white ethnics in their struggle for survival and status under the WASPs, but beyond that, integration did not bear the same racial connotations for relations between white ethnics and WASPs as it did between blacks and whites. One of the most witless aspects of the integration campaign directed by black leaders was the purblind implication that the white population, with whom blacks were supposed to integrate on all levels, was a WASP monolith devoid of ethnics, especially in the North. The white ethnics' problems with integration (or assimilation) existed on another level of interethnic accommodation and rapport. When the Irish, Poles, Jews, Italians, Greeks, Slavs, Germans, or others married WASPs or across other interethnic lines in American society, the only objections, mild or strenuous, came, not from society at large, but from the relatives of the couples joined in assimilated bliss. However, the vast majority of Americans, which means society, is against the intermarriage of blacks and whites; this includes the *majority* of blacks, whites, and ethnics! Frazier verified this stubborn fact:

> Resistance to integration becomes greater in those associations where contacts are free and informal. But it is in family relations, where human relations tend to be sacred. . . . This is why the strongest barrier to the complete acceptance of the Negro is the disapproval of inter-marriage.[34]

This general disapproval of intermarriage of blacks and whites implies much more than an oversimplistic conclusion of race prejudice. When Walter White, cited earlier, declared, following the *Brown* decision, that "twenty-nine of the forty-eight states still bar intermarriage," the implication was that repealing those anti-intermarriage laws might remove a major barrier against full integration. Any perceptive social scientist or intelligent observer should have known better. As a matter of fact, during the twenty-seven years following *Brown*, all such laws have been stricken. Yet full integration is still a chimera, and racial polarization has increased. If the majority of whites are against intermarriage, so are the majority of blacks, which means that on that primary and sacred level, *both* are prejudiced.

On a more sociopsychological level, the intermarriage taboo in a multiracial, multiethnic society such as the United States is the ultimate defense for the maintenance of plural legitimacy. Remove anti-intermarriage laws and the psychological taboos will still discourage or block the full integration of blacks into American society. Thus, the very race-relations cycle model Frazier used in his conclusions on the possibilities of integration does not, in fact, fully support those conclusions. In the recent decades since *Brown*, intermarriage between blacks and whites *has* increased. However, the partners in these marriages are generally *not* fully accepted by the white group or the black group on the primary or sacred family level. Instead, these interracial partners become integrated participants in the expanding social range of what Frazier described as the secondary or impersonal or secular areas of race contacts made in certain professions, sports, the arts, etc. "Negro and white professionals who marry across race lines are generally the more sophisticated members of the middle class, since there is as much opposition among the conventional members of the Negro upper and middle classes to intermarriage as among the same white classes," said Frazier.[35] All in all, the core primary and sacred sociological bases for racial and ethnic plurality are persistently maintained.

In the comparative sense, white ethnics are either already partially assimilated into American society or potentially assimilable. Hence, they are a group set apart from blacks basically because their problems with assimilation are problems of *class* not race. These considerations alone, of course, do not settle the issue or cover the full range of the challenges to black integration by the "rise of the unmeltable ethnics." What these ethnic and racial facts of American life have rendered more and more dubious was the 1954 claim by NAACP spokesmen that segregation in all its forms would be eliminated from American society by 1963.

But with the close of the turbulent black Sixties, the white ethnics were not the only WASP rejects to claim the oncoming Seventies as their age of redemption and long-deferred recognition. Out of the vast south-western bloc of states comprising Texas, New Mexico, Colorado, Arizona, and California emerged another minority phalanx, unfurling its banners of long-simmering communal pride into the national consciousness -the Chicanos:

> Unlike the ·fforts of the Negro people in America—who in past decades sought equality of treatment and opportunity in an Anglo-dominated world on the Anglo's terms and only recently sought anew a black identity and cultural separateness—the Chicano from the earliest phases of his uprising in the 1960's has sought equality and respect for his way of life, for his culture, and for his language.[36]

So reads a significant passage from the introduction to the *Chicano Manifesto* (1971). In the post-World War II era, blacks in the South, North, and East were hardly acquainted with the West Coast and Southwest minority issue of "Chicanismo" (Mexican-American nationalism). Blacks on the West Coast were, but then these blacks were predominantly newcomers to the West Coast, having been members of extensive black migrations from Louisiana, Mississippi, Texas, Oklahoma, and Arkansas during World War II. In the East the only nonwhite minority of immediate importance to blacks were the Puerto Ricans (if we leave out the West Indies as a minority). However, the black Sixties sparked anew the embers of ethnic pride everywhere, and Spanish-speaking Puerto Ricans and other "Hispanics" began to echo the political sentiments of an extensive subworld of Spanish-speaking Americans. The most vocal are the Chicanos, whose main population base is the Southwest but who claim thousands more scattered through Florida, Illinois, Indiana, Kansas, Michigan, Missouri, New York, Ohio, Utah, Washington, and Wisconsin. Says the *Chicano Manifesto:* "The current revolt of Chicanos against the Anglo system of life and thought is essentially a prophetic statement of purpose. We Chicanos are convinced that it is our destiny to carry out a major role in the coming decades not only in the United States but in all the Americas."[37] It is not surprising that the author of the *Chicano Manifesto* traces the Chicano revolt's earliest phases only as far back as the 1960s, despite historical grievances against the Anglos that date back to what for the Chicanos is a year of infamy, 1848, and the signing of the Guadalupe Hidalgo Treaty between Mexico and the United States. As a result of this treaty: "Lands and property were stolen, rights were denied, language and culture suppressed, opportunities for employment, education, and political representation were thwarted."[38] For American blacks, the history of the politics of race and war is Appomattox, Sherman in Georgia, Grant at Vicksburg, or Lincoln and the Emancipation Proclamation. But for the Chicanos, it is Santa Anna and The Alamo in 1836, and the military annexation of Mexican territories launched by the Americans in 1847. Yet it was not until 1965 that "the suppressed anger, resentment, and frustration of the Chicano broke out in the first radical thrusts of our movement toward liberation."

The *Manifesto* pinpoints the first of the radical Chicano actions as "the strike of the grape pickers in Delano, California, which began in September, 1965." However, more significant in terms of civil rights was that President Johnson's Civil Rights Act of 1964 had set up the Equal Employment Opportunity Commission, outlawing discrimination on grounds of, among other things, national origin. Thus was more bite given to Chicano protest by civil rights legislation first inspired by blacks on a national level. When Johnson's War on Poverty reached into the Southwest, the Chicanos, like the blacks, were drawn into that economic thrust of the civil rights movement. Yet the *Chicano Manifesto* admits that: "For all its good intentions, the Economic Opportunity Act of 1964 caught the Chicano relatively unprepared in terms of the sophisticated strategy plotting, lobbying, and deceit required for the pursuit of program approval and funding. . . . We did not have the knowledge of the labyrinthine ways of Washington that the Indian tribes, the Negro organizations and the foundations had. The Chicano had to learn gradually, and more often than not he was left holding an empty bag or at most a few crumbs."[39]

The emergence of the Chicano protest was significant in that, in addition to blacks and Indians, it brought within the civil rights purview another important nonwhite ethnic component with the potential of being an ally or competitor. The main difference between the Chicanos and the blacks, aside from civil rights experience on a national level, was that, unlike the blacks, the Chicanos did not have an initial constitutional *rationale* of a hundred years' legitimacy with which to litigate. For all intents, The Alamo is history and the Guadalupe Hidalgo Treaty, like the Indian relocations, are *faits accomplis* of national expansion. Historically, the thirteen colonies that ratified the Constitution contained three basic racial components—ex-Englishmen, ex-Africans, and Indians. The Chicanos, then, represent a new and increasingly viable component of the American plurality, especially since the civil rights outcome of the *Brown* decision eventually brought all minorities under the equal protection of the Fourteenth Amendment.

However, the emergence of Chicanos as a nonwhite minority reflects a uniquely different racial ideology vis-à-vis the Anglo-American that, on the face of it, contrasts significantly with the black-white encounter. Prior to the *Brown* decision, and for a decade or so during its implementation, the main ethnic allies in the blacks' civil rights cause were American Jews, at least in terms of formal Jewish *organizational* support. Officially, Jews were decidedly pro-integration until their defection from the civil rights agenda over strong objections to the implied quota provisions of "affirmative action." American Jews are traditionally known as having a high stake in the fields of public and private education, and since Jewish organizational support of civil rights departed over the issue of preferential treatment proffered blacks in graduate school admissions, the defection of Jewish liberalism on this issue was highly significant. This is especially true since the modern civil rights movement was launched by the *Brown* lawsuit precisely in the field of public education. One could infer from Jewish liberals objections to black quotas in higher education that integration at elementary and high school levels and integration at college and university levels were two different things sociologically, academically, and politically. This was, of course, what E. Franklin Frazier implied in his analysis that elementary and high schools belonged to the sacred areas of American life, while schools of higher education fall into the category of secular areas:

> That Negroes are being integrated first into those areas of American life in which contacts are more or less impersonal and secular is confirmed by what happened in the South with reference to the admission of Negro students to publicly supported educational institutions. Negro students were admitted first to the professional and graduate schools, and later to the undergraduate schools . . . without any serious racial friction.[40]

Hence, integration into elementary schools is one thing, but into graduate schools is something else. In fact, integration at college and university levels began *before Brown* and despite *Brown*. Integration at these secondary areas could therefore not be cited as a bona fide indicator of the full integration of blacks into the larger American society. If nothing else, the *Bakke* decision plus the opposition of Jewish liberalism to the threat of quotas show that when power enclaves are threatened, sociologically and psychologically the dominant white society will instinctively oppose, limit, and restrict integration even at the secondary areas of life. In such a manner are the avenues to social and economic power effectively guarded and the social and institutional forms of group pluralism effectively maintained. Thus, Jewish ethnic liberalism, in this instance, saw no real threat to the ultimate strongholds of privilege and power as a consequence of the *Brown* decision, but was alarmed by the possible consequences of the later affirmative action. There are deeper intellectual, cultural, political, and economic reasons for this opposition that need to be explored. However, the Chicano outlook on integration and education, as it was expressed in the *Manifesto*, was a significant departure from the prevalent black point of view. Said the *Chicano Manifesto:*

> While we Chicanos owe a great debt to the black people of America for striking out into untested ground, the Chicano can boast of his own personal history of rebellion and rejection of oppression. He has now reached the breakthrough point of personal liberation through a revolt of his own making.
>
> It is true that the black revolution has guaranteed that the minority peoples of the United States get a certain amount of attention from the dominant society, whether it is pro or con. The actions of the minority groups of the nation are now front-page news, whereas only a generation ago there were rarely any activities reported. *However, the current frustration and distrust within the black community concerning the progress that has been made, ostensibly by the old leadership and through old channels, illustrate to the Chicano that he cannot now simply copy the black movement; he has to surpass the effort by the blacks if he is to endure as a Chicano and somehow contribute to the rehabilitation of the whole country.*[41] (Italics added.)

Moreover, said the *Manifesto:* "Black people display a cultural perspective and philosophy little different from what the Anglo desires and demands. We Chicanos see the Negro as a black Anglo:

> Because we are interiorly integrated, the integration syndrome of black-white America has no relevance to the Chicano. For example, we do not believe that our Chicanitos must attend classes with Negroes and Anglos in order to attain an adequate education. If there must be integration, we say, let it be in terms of cash, curriculum, and control. Let the Chicano enjoy a just share of funds so that his barrio schools

can hire the most qualified teachers, purchase the best equipment, and give the young people the finest education possible. Integrate the history books, the literature books, the languages spoken in the classroom, so that the Chicano can identify himself there and feel pride in his being Chicano. The Anglo must let go of the total control he has maintained over the educational system.[42]

In other words, the Chicanos prefer autonomous control over the administration of their community public schools. This is the area Frazier cited as meeting the most resistance from dominant social groups, and yet where the modern civil rights movement launched its initial phases by legal mandate. The dubious social, racial, and political wisdom of the *Brown* decision was perceived by many blacks, whites, and Chicanos long before the *Chicano Manifesto* was conceived. The *Manifesto* did not object to the integration of Chicanos, blacks, or others into the secondary or secular levels of racial contacts—the colleges and professional schools—this implied agreement with black efforts on *that* level. Yet this does not negate Chicano criticism of the Black Revolution's strategies on other primary levels. And it raises a number of critical questions which, in view of the contemporary outcome of *Brown* and its progenitive movements, must be reassessed.

When the Supreme Court in the *Slaughterhouse Cases* of 1873 interpreted the Fourteenth Amendment's equal protection clause (conceived in the social interests of blacks) as a legal rationale behind which to defend the police power of the state of Louisiana unilaterally to allocate public resources to benefit a single private corporation, equal protection became an open-ended constitutional guarantee. It accrued to any public interest that had the temporal prerogative to sue for or defend against whatever overriding interests the Court decided to favor.

Later, in 1896 the same Court, deciding a civil rights case (*Plessy* v. *Ferguson*) in the same state of Louisiana, could reinterpret the same amendment to mean that racial democracy was not inconsistent with separate-but-equal intrastate railroad facilities for blacks and whites. This legal view had a definite validity in theory, but not a scintilla of truth in fact. Then through an attenuated series of decisions over a period of fifty-eight years, the Supreme Court either qualified or invalidated *Plessy* by way of *Brown*. Now "separate but equal" in public education was inherently unequal and therefore unconstitutional, and therefore illegal. To the satisfaction of the liberal school of democratic racial idealism, blacks were ostensibly anointed with the true blessings of racial democracy in action. But in doing so, the courts also absolved the southern states of the political and economic obligation to implement the equality of separateness, leaving blacks, after a quarter-century, still racially separate (in most things social) and also still *unequal*.

But the Chicano minority thrust, at the time of the publication of the *Chicano Manifesto*, had not completed the post-Sixties Hispanic evolution. The Spanish-speaking (or Spanish-surnamed) population is not homogeneous in terms of a minority ideology. Often Chicanos speak of themselves as "Latinos." By the 1980s, the Latino or Chicano population had arrived at a new consensus in which the designation "Hispanic" was used to include all Spanish-speaking populations from Mexico, Puerto Rico, Cuba, and parts of Central America. Included were Californians of Spanish ancestry that extended far back into the nineteenth century before the "Capitulation of Cahuenga," the final capture of Los Angeles, and the conquest of California from Mexico by the Americans Frémont, Stockton, and Kearny. This aggregate Hispanic population, next to the blacks, is the second-fastest-growing nonwhite minority in the United States, approaching 14.6 million. It is now being predicted that Hispanic census count might catch up to the black census count in perhaps a decade. This growing Hispanic population represents a new political dimension seeking a measure of political power through voting strength that would either match, complement, or even outstrip the supposed political power of the blacks. In the Eighties, despite Chicano reservations about identifying with the "integration syndrome" of the blacks, the new Hispanic front talks about the possibility of a black-Hispanic political coalition. But aside from a lack of clearly defined political goals for such a black-Hispanic coalition, the Hispanic minority involves a rather muted racial factor. A considerable number of Hispanics are properly classified as white. The Chicanos prefer to regard the blacks as "black Anglos," apparently unmindful that the blacks view the Chicanos as "brown Spaniards" (or Hispanos) and a large number of Hispanics as "white Spaniards" (or Hispanos). Thus, a possible political coalition involving blacks and other minorities only injected into the black-white civil rights involves a number of unresolved racial and ethnic contradictions.

V Finally, the entrance of minorities—white, nonwhite, and women—into the civil rights contest on a national scale had to qualify the social consequences of the *Brown* decision, which legally outlawed the separate-but-equal doctrine of *Plessy as it applied to race.* But the constitutional reinterpretation of the sociological evolution of race differences in the body politic prompted the introduction of ethnicity and gender into the civil rights fray in such fashion as graphically to qualify the intent and thrust for the full integration ideals of the NAACP and its supporting civil rights trends. Because these other minorities (white and/or nonwhite) do not assess their group situation in American society in the same fashion as the NAACP with its integrationist concepts, the 1960s civil rights revolution posed questions of the kind that no one (least of all white liberals) cared to answer: *What and which minority, ethnic group, or gender is going to be integrated by the blacks, and for what reasons?*

Except for economic or political advancement, these other minorities or genders do not seek integration as an overriding economic, political, or cultural principle. Whatever the social disabilities of these minorities, they had not been subjected to the kind of legally imposed discrimination or segregation that the blacks had endured since the end of the Civil War. Therefore, whether or not these other minorities had integrated, assimilated, or separated it was the result of the *laissez-faire* principles of the American "open society"—*each to his own and for its own.* However, the political and economic accommodations of these minorities to the dominant White Anglo-Saxon Protestant group status in American society (Anglo-conformity) was never an issue involving constitutional amendment guarantees. That is, not until the Nineteenth Amendment, and later the Equal Rights Amendment regarding the status of women. The Equal Rights Amendment questioned, for the first time since the Civil War Amendments, the contemporary relevancy of the American Constitution. The implied question becomes, How democratic *is* the American Constitution? Not in the light of what the United States was as a nation in 1781 or 1883 or 1920, *but into what manner of pluralistic racial and ethnic democracy did the American nation evolve?* Moreover, the introduction of the Equal Rights Amendment raised another startling and unprecedented constitutional question: *If the Bill of Rights, the Fourteenth and Nineteenth Amendments are not sufficient guarantees for the full economic, political, and social equality of women as women, then neither are the Fourteenth and Fifteenth Amendments, and their judicial reinforcements, sufficient guarantees for the full economic, political, and cultural equality of nonwhite minorities.* For a number of historical, economic, racial, cultural, and social reasons, coincident with the original racial and ethnic composition of the American nation at its inception, American blacks and American Indians assume *a priori* legal claims to the constitutional readjudication of their economic, political, and cultural status in American society. The subsequent failures of the Civil Rights Acts of 1964 and 1965 to satisfy the black-Liberal consensus expectations of "full racial equality" for blacks highlights the implications of this unresolved constitutional question. *Where* does the absence of civil rights equity begin and *where* is civil rights parity achieved? At what point in the legalization of civil rights parity does a racial, ethnic, minority, or gender demand for equity cease to be "civil" and becomes economic, political, cultural, educational, etc.?

Even without arguing the comparative assessments of the minority-group status of blacks versus the status of other minorities, the impact of these minorities on contemporary civil rights processes makes it obligatory to reassess the former separate-but-equal doctrine. A reexamination is required not in the light of *Plessy* or even *Brown,* but in the light of actual racial and ethnic *pluralism* as an American reality. Philosophically, "separate but equal" is, in the normative sense, "unequal" only if in social practice it is the governing intent to make separateness politically, economically, and socially unequal, which of course makes such practices immoral. Thus, separateness, which is not immoral, became segregation, which *is* immoral because it was not the intent to make separate equal. However, because it was not within the putative intent or within the economic and political capability of the state of Louisiana in 1896 to make separate facilities equal, this does not ipso facto absolve the state of some future obligation, under changed conditions, to render separate equal when, and if, it becomes feasible to do so. The *Brown* decision, in effect, absolved the state(s) of that obligation as a consequence of a legal analysis that separateness is inherently to mean inferior. Intrinsically, it means no such thing. Legally imposed segregation was what rendered separateness implicitly inferior. Remove the legal sanctions of imposed segregation, and separateness has the potential of achieving equality in its own right.

The *Brown* decision purportedly banished legally mandated segregation to the historical netherworld of discredited Social Darwinist doctrines of the late nineteenth century. At the time of *Plessy,* hardly *any* educational facilities existed in the South for either blacks or whites to be equalized for anyone's benefit. In basing the *Brown* doctrine in a sweeping decision purely within the purpose and function of public school education, the courts committed a beneficent act analogous to freeing long-term convicts from prison without adequate resources to survive in the free world. This was, of course, what the civil rights leadership demanded and got—the implicit Americanization of the Negro, which was extended to legally endorsed racial equality in all social areas beyond the public schools. The fetishistic belief in the transcendent democratic legacy of the Constitution led to a misreading of the Constitution's applicability to the sociological realities of race and ethnicity. Thus, even before the *Bakke* decision, not only did the implementation of *Brown* begin to falter and fade, but professional opinion in education, law, and legislation entertained muted doubts regarding the enforceability of *Brown* beyond a minimal integration in places where racial and ethnic demographics favored racial integration. But racially integrated public schools existed long before *Brown* as educational models.

The great majority of blacks and whites did not want busing for school integration. This meant clearly that enforced school integration was generally not accepted as a remedy for essentially flawed educational philosophies. Nor was integration a consensual priority in education. The entire busing issue highlighted in the most graphic fashion that if quality education could not be achieved for black children in their neighborhood schools, then neither could busing for integration achieve such a goal. Hence, as the busing-for-integration issue began to lose heat and momentum, antibusing referenda would proliferate in some localities and be pursued for the first time in others. Elsewhere, busing closed public schools and placed them under military guard. Racial tensions flared in many classrooms. Under many of these circumstances both blacks and whites adjusted to what they did not like and strove to comply with the law. In order to make schools racially mixed for the first time, curriculum diversity was sponsored for viability; in other situations the busing issue was quietly dropped and ignored. By 1978 even the most ardent southern liberal opinion fully in favor of the democratic ideal of improving the opportunities for black quality education had to concede the failure of busing. One southern writer on the issue summed up the growing consensus with the remark:

> *But the ultimate question is how a policy so consistently opposed by great majorities of Americans, including many blacks, ever came to be the law?*[43] (Italics added.)

Brown was, morally, an idealistically "good," transcendent, and redeeming legal decision, but, empirically, it was poor sociological jurisprudence. In 1983, findings by sociologists, educators, and other social scientists connected with the National Institute of Education (NIE) prompted a leading sociologist to suggest: "The assumption that integration would improve achievement of lower-class black children has now been shown to be fiction." The author of this statement, sociologist James Coleman, was during the Sixties post-*Brown* period a prominent advocate of the educational aims of the *Brown* decision.[44]

Part Three

I

To assess the *Brown* decision, as the majority of liberal reviewers have done, as an unqualified act of justice is to oversimplify. That simplistic judicial decision overlooked an exceedingly complex mix of racial, cultural, and institutional questions. The tangle of political, economic, cultural, class, and legal views that coalesced in the process that led to the decision was both contradictory and highly disputed. Consequently, a great deal of the expert sociological and psychological opinion marshaled in defense of *Brown* amounted to a crudely pragmatic negation of the allegedly "scientific" applicability of social science to any social phenomena comprehensible by empirical observation. Even legal opinion that was, in 1954, in sympathy with the Supreme Court's unanimous rendering in favor of the plaintiffs, was not fully convinced that the *Brown* decision, whatever its legal merits apropos the Fourteenth Amendment's equal protection clause, should be allowed to ". . . rest on any such flimsy foundation as some of the scientific demonstrations . . ." offered by the social scientists.[1]

The specific "scientific" demonstration alluded to was the controversial Doll Test, which offered as proof that segregated classrooms per se inculcated a negative self-image and a sense of racial inferiority in the minds of black elementary pupils.[2] In one of the pre-*Brown* hearings, the scientific witness, citing this test, concluded that as a result of segregation in Clarendon County, South Carolina, black schoolchildren—"Like other human beings who are subjected to an obviously inferior status in the society in which they live, have been definitely harmed in the development of their personalities; that the signs of instability in their personalities are clear, and I think that every psychologist would accept and interpret these signs as such."[3] But the question was raised: Should such conclusions be accepted as objective truth? The friendly legal dissenter, in this instance, argued: "Perhaps the main point is that this test does not purport to demonstrate the effects of school segregation, which is what the court was being asked to enjoin. If it disclosed anything about the effects of segregation on the children, their experiences at school were not differentiated from other causes. Considering the ages of the children, we may conjecture they had not been long at school."[4]

Had the elementary public school system been mainly responsible for implanting the negative self-image or the psychology of racial inferiority in the minds of black children, or had causes outside of the classroom been more decisive? Even *before* a child of a nonwhite minority group is born, its social status has already been categorized in a descending scale predicated on how America rates the status of its minorities. The extent to which the elementary classroom per se would influence self-image would depend on whose instructional values are dominant within that classroom. If the child's home and family-parent influences, plus the community climate outside the immediate home environs, impart a negative self-image to the child, then it is unlikely that the classroom could make a salutary difference. Especially was this the case in the southern school ambience of pre-1954. As an institution, a public school is created by and reflects the dominant values of the surrounding adult society, not the other way around. (Moreover, parenthetically, the obligatory evaluation of the pedagogical influence of the black schoolteacher was noticeably absent in these arguments.)

But in the case of *Brown,* a branch of social science was enlisted to prove that the public school was or could be the primary inculcator of social and individual values. But social psychology, said the friendly critic of *Brown,* "will need, above all things, the use of scrupulous logic in its internal, intermediate processes. If the premises are loose, the reasoning from them should be much tighter. . . . It is meticulous standards that bring respect and credence to scientific testimony."[5] The inference here was that the scientific testimony was, to a great degree, blind to objective sociological facts. Obscured were the webs of causative processes behind public school developments that could not be explained by simplistic methods of historical summation. As a revolutionary strategist once remarked, "Facts are stubborn things." The persistence of *de facto* segregation in public schools today should reemphasize that the advocates of *Brown* did not invent public school integration. Though public school integration had existed in numerous northern localities for decades, it had never brought about any millennial alterations in the quality of race relations either inside or beyond the integrated classrooms. Black and white pupils studied together, often played together, fought together, and dreamed together, up to a point. But usually somewhere during the junior high and high school years, blacks and whites began to relinquish these idyllic contacts, and finally went their separate ways at the threshold of graduation. Given these empirical educational facts of life in the liberal racism of the North, it is incredible that social scientists (black or white) could infer that the consequences of public school integration would be qualitatively different in the southern states, where *legal racism* prevailed.

Of course, *Brown* came during the post-World War II era of racial "enlightenment." The 1950s were not the Forties or the Thirties or the Twenties. The leaders in social psychology were basically liberal and egalitarian in outlook. Prior to World War II, American racism was not considered an abnormal or pathological ingredient in the democratic psychology of the nation. An everyday occurrence for blacks on the racial-endurance front was merely an annoying test of forbearance for the average white forced to deal with that troublesome black presence. When Ilya Ehrenburg, the renowned Russian journalist, visited the United States during the Forties, he remarked that in Russia before the Revolution, the intelligentsia did not buy the anti-Semitism of the masses and did not support the pogroms. But in the United States, he made the disturbing discovery that antiblack racism had fully permeated the intelligentsia. It was not until the Sixties that a ranking American intellectual, Charles E. Silberman, could unreservedly declare that "America is a racist society in a sense and to a degree that we have refused so far to admit, much less face." Refusal to face the ingrained racism was one of the reasons, among others more political, that an antilynching bill was never passed in the American legislature in the pre-*Brown* era. However, by the 1950s racism had become a negative blot on the American image in international relations. The United States could no longer tolerate legally sanctioned racial oppression and also parade a democratic national image before the world. Indirectly, this was one of the many causative factors behind the *Brown* decision, but there were several others.

An early causative factor leading to *Brown* was the disastrous impact of the Great Depression. As it penetrated deeper into the economic fabric of American society generally, the Depression affected, specifically, civil rights programming. As a result, the NAACP bogged down in a programmatic crisis. With its finances drained and membership declined, the NAACP found itself, after twenty-four years of meritorious existence, without an all-important economic platform for American blacks. The Depression laid bare this glaring deficiency. During the Roaring Twenties, the NAACP did not need an economic program to prove its legitimacy. Calvin Coolidge's guiding dictum that "the business of America is business" and Hoover's gastronomical refrain of "a chicken in every pot" fostered the illusion of an ever-expanding prosperity. The tens of thousands of blacks who had left the South and thronged into the burgeoning northern ghettos also clung to the mirage of expanding prosperity.

Even the NAACP had reason, during the 1920s, to believe that widening prosperity would be synonymous with widening civil rights opportunities. Increased vigilance and agitation was all that would be required. The several "Negro Meccas" of Harlem, Chicago, Detroit, and elsewhere were bursting with a newly found pride that assuaged indigenous poverty and congestion. When the Depression struck these ghettos, it was like the advent of an invisible plague, an assault on the Promised Land by a malignant spirit, a visitation by the evil eye of despair. The bright lights and rhythmic pulses of the new northern freedom were dimmed and subdued as the threat of starvation and hopelessness stalked the black communities.

While after the collapse of the economy Franklin D. Roosevelt crafted an economic recovery plan for the nation in general, blacks had no supplementary economic program of their own. Or to state the issue more concretely, black leadership in the civil rights organizations had no economic program on behalf of its black constituency. *Whether or not a civil rights organization should have had such an economic program was then, and remains, debatable.* For at the very inception of the NAACP, the leadership split over the issue of the primacy of economic questions over civil rights questions, or vice versa.[6] Unable to resolve this conflict programmatically at the time of its founding, the NAACP dispensed with an economic program and projected a purely civil rights, or as it was then perceived, a "civil libertarian," program. In doing so, the NAACP embraced what the political scientists described as *"noneconomic liberalism"* as its guiding philosophy.

Noneconomic liberalism was the preeminent article of faith of the whites involved in the black–white liberal coalition that successfully launched what was to become the major American civil rights protest organization in the twentieth century—the NAACP. In terms of individual leadership personality, noneconomic liberalism was the expressed liberalistic civil rights ideal of Joel E. Spingarn, who began his association with the NAACP in 1911, became chairman of the executive board in 1914 and president in 1930. Spingarn's ascendancy to the presidency sparked the first real internal and external criticism of the NAACP's "white presidency" syndrome. Spingarn, a former Columbia University professor of comparative literature, social reformer, and onetime political aspirant, would reign for twenty-eight years as a dominant figure in NAACP affairs. It was said of Spingarn:

> The programs he advocated both as a politician and as a social crusader fitted well within the framework of . . . "non-economic liberalism"— strong reformist impulses in the realms of civil liberties, race relations, and foreign affairs *but not in the basic distribution of wealth and power.*[7] (Italics added.)

Undoubtedly, a consequence of Spingarn's influential role in the evolution of the NAACP's social policies regarding noneconomic liber-

alism was that his philosophy (and that of his brother, Arthur B. Spingarn)
would "receive its greatest test when applied to the race problem"[8]:

> *As Spingarn's tactical approach to the problem of racial adjustment*
> *unfolded over the years after his affiliation with the NAACP, it was to*
> *become apparent that this all-important problem was to be governed*
> *by the tenets of noneconomic liberalism; more specifically, that the*
> *black man's struggle for full civil and political rights must take pre-*
> *cedent over any program of economic advancement, for once color*
> *discrimination had been swept away, the black man would be able to*
> *compete successfully with his white counterpart in jobs, education, and*
> *other avenues to economic stability.*[9] (Italics added.)

That the Spingarns were of Jewish background would, from certain
angles, raise retroactively, the critical question, about the meaning of the
informal black-Jewish alliance that fell apart in the late Sixties over the
issue of black anti-Semitism and Jewish liberal defections from the civil
rights movement. Did the influence of the Spingarns justify attacks on
the NAACP from right-wing conservatives, northern and southern, that
the civil rights movement was a Jewish- and/or Communist-inspired plot?
At the outset, the NAACP was neither. For one thing, the official American Communist party, as it came to be known, did not come into existence
until 1929, although organized Marxist-Communist movements and parties were born in 1919. For another, the Spingarns were thoroughly
assimilated Jews, as evidenced by their noticeable lack of involvement
in specifically Jewish organizational affairs. Accredited biographical studies of Joel E. Spingarn do not reveal evidence of any "pro-Zionist"
connections. Joel Spingarn had absorbed the twentieth-century extension
of the "abolitionist" tradition of his WASP associates in the NAACP,
such as Oswald Garrison Villard, Mary White Ovington, William English
Walling, Charles Edward Russell, and others.

In any event, the civil rights of "racial adjustment" was destined
from the outset to be noneconomic. In a society where the making of
money, the eager search after profits, the entrepreneurial activity, the
superexploitation of labor and natural resources, the ownership of land,
the perfection of technology, the expansion of industry, and where the
apotheosization of every financial scheme imaginable for individual en-
richment (even organized crime) was worshiped as the highest of virtues,
transcending religion itself, the American Negro was being advised by
white liberals to waive any program of economic advancement as a matter

of priorities. When it is realized that not a single European immigrant, not even the most unfavored, was ever told that the land of opportunity held such restraints on his or her citizenship ambitions, then the real economic relationship between native-born blacks and immigrant whites is better understood.

Ironically, most black spokesmen involved in the NAACP's launching adhered to this staunch philosophy of noneconomic liberalism, including W.E.B. Du Bois himself. This particular leadership bloc was one of the consequences of the ideological split growing out of internal debates within the Afro-American League, in which the dominant figure was Booker T. Washington. Acceptance of noneconomic liberalism by this bloc resulted in rejecting Washington's basic philosophy, i.e., the primacy of black economic development over civil rights agitation. When Du Bois broke with Washington's leadership in 1903, his defection coincided with the decline of the Afro-American League (then called the "Council"). He said of Washington:

> Today he stands as the one recognized spokesman of his ten million fellows. . . .
> This is an age of unusual economic development, and Mr. Washington's programme naturally takes an economic cast, becoming a gospel of Work and Money to such an extent as apparently almost completely overshadow the higher aims of life. . . .
> He is striving nobly to make Negro artisans business men and property-owners; but it is utterly impossible, under modern competitive methods, for workingmen and property owners to defend their rights and exist without the right of suffrage. . . .[10]

In opposition to this "economic conservatism" of Washington's, Du Bois countered with the tenets of noneconomic liberalism, and demanded as a matter of programmatic priority three things:

1. The right to vote
2. Civic equality
3. The education of youth according to ability.[11]

Black education was not then the fighting cause it would become sixty years later, but in 1903 Du Bois projected it in critical opposition to Washington's advocacy of "industrial education" as more suitable or practical for blacks than liberal arts training. In those seminal years of the civil rights movement, the divisions over political, economic, educational, and cultural programs were more clearly etched in leadership propaganda. But as the decades passed, the real substance of these divisive issues would be dissipated and then absorbed in vestigial forms in new leadership tactics for changed conditions. Thus, by the time of *Brown*, noneconomic liberalism would be dressed in the legal garb of a Fourteenth Amendment certification of liberal social science findings in the field of race and public education.

However, the legal origins of the *Brown* decision are found in the 1930s decade of the Great Depression. And the legal process leading to *Brown* was a by-product of the crisis that struck the NAACP when it realized that its guiding philosophy of a civil rights program based on noneconomic liberalism faced bankruptcy. Since the association had never considered economics a priority, it had never cultivated a black economic program. Many of the association's longtime critics had denigrated its pallid and nonfunctional attitude toward the economic progress of blacks. But the association always defended itself with claims that its civil rights advocacy was for the present and future benefit of all blacks, including its harshest critics. In this sense the NAACP was justified, if not certified, as a black *social* progress organization. "The business of America [*was*] business," and although such fastidious terms as the "private sector" were not then in vogue, the consensus was that it was up to the business sector to manufacture prosperity for everybody, even to provide sufficient unskilled and service jobs to keep the blacks happy in the promised land. But when the Depression wrought economic havoc in the private sector in 1929, the NAACP was shorn of its thin but respectable clothing and, like the fabled emperor, left bare.

It was not adventitious that among the first NAACP leaders to react publicly to this situation was W.E.B. Du Bois, the renowned scholar and editor of the association's official organ, *The Crisis*. Since the 1920s, Du Bois had been rethinking his principled positions on civil rights, black economic issues relative to black labor, capital and business enterprise. Severely stung by the black economic implications of the Marcus Garvey "Back to Africa" movement (1919–1925), Du Bois was forced to reconsider a number of civil rights concepts growing out of the noneconomic liberalism philosophy that had taken on such a doctrinaire connotation since the NAACP's founding.

Marcus Mosiah Garvey, a Jamaican, had ridden the crest of black labor prosperity occasioned by the industrial demands of World War I that had inspired the great migration of black labor out of the southern states to northern cities. With adroit black nationalist sloganeering, Garvey had used the romantic Back to Africa idea to beguile black people and extract untold hundreds of thousands of dollars out of the earnings of uncounted thousands of black workers. The result was the United Negro Improvement Association (UNIA), a hastily structured, semicooperative economic organization that included the controversial Black Star steamship line. The spontaneously successful UNIA collapsed in less than five years, and Garvey departed from the American scene via prison and deportation.[12] Though it proved a failure, the Garvey movement had lasting impact on black leadership in the 1920s and into the 1930s. The essential fact was that the movement attracted masses of blacks whom the NAACP could never have reached. Moreover, there is much evidence to suggest that the Nation of Islam (the Black Muslims of Malcolm X) was founded in Detroit in 1932 by a certain ex-member (or members) of the Garvey movement. The year was significant: The 1930 census showed that major northern cities such as New York and Chicago had since 1910 increased their black populations by 235,977 and 189,800, respectively, for aggregate totals of 327,706 and 233,903. In 1930 the five great industrial centers to which blacks migrated—New York, Chicago, Philadelphia, Detroit, and Cleveland—had a combined black population of 973,173, or 8.2 percent of all blacks in the United States and 18.7 percent of the nation's urban black population.[13] These migratory blacks had fled the agricultural depression that had already struck the southern states by the 1920s, only to fall victim to the crisis in the industrial North. The result was unprecedented widespread urbanized black poverty. W.E.B. Du Bois, the redoubtable social thinker, knew there had to be a change in the philosophy of the black leadership. But if Roosevelt had practical answers to the national catastrophe, Du Bois had only questions, which he raised boldly within the confines of the NAACP's top leadership.

The economic disaster of 1929 had revealed clearly that the guiding white philosophy of noneconomic liberalism was an insidiously debilitating leadership ideal to have been imposed on a nonwhite minority group seeking racial parity under American capitalism. Worse than that, noneconomic liberalism was a seductive entrapment into a fixed psychology of dependency, underdevelopment of social intelligence, and intellectual subservience. At best, the free market of capitalist economic activity was free for whites only, and even then it was free only for those whites who controlled the ascending ladder of command posts in the class hierarchies of entrepreneurial advantage. At worst, when competitive access to entrepreneurial rights to the free market was wiped out by the economic collapse of 1929, a nonwhite minority with no power, such as the blacks, was reduced to a level of mendicancy lower than that of a helot. At least a helot, slave, or serf merits the right to be fed, but a freed serf without a master becomes the worst victim of the economics of scarcity. The Great Depression was an era of artificial scarcity in which the prize of civil rights was the freedom to starve without regard to race, creed, color, or national origin.

When Du Bois recognized this sobering fact, he also realized that the fallacies of noneconomic liberalism had social ramifications other than the purely productive attributes of the economic man. Related social, institutional, political, and cultural issues growing out of race differences had to be confronted to effect a leadership antidote to noneconomic liberalism. This was a tall order, especially when the NAACP had been founded on rigorous adherence to noneconomic liberalism. It meant a reassessment of the NAACP's program. Thus, Du Bois, realizing that he had been less than wise when he opted for noneconomic liberalism in 1909–1910, challenged the NAACP leadership to change course in 1934. The ensuing debate, coming with the advent of Roosevelt's New Deal policies, is historically important because it set the course for the strategic and tactical change in direction of black leaders that would dominate black affairs up to the *Brown* decision and into the 1980s.

III   The first item on the philosophy agenda raised by Du Bois was segregation. What *is* segregation? he asked. In view of the peculiar evolution of race relations, two kinds of racial segregation had become conventional practice: *de facto* (imposed by social custom) and *de jure* (also created by social custom but legitimized by laws, codes, and ordinances). In addition, segregation was rigidly maintained by extralegal measures, such as physical violence and less extreme methods of physical and psychological intimidation. Theoretically, the South had imposed the separate-but-equal doctrine as the southern law of the land. But since the 1890s, this doctrine had been rendered a travesty of due process and equal protection even though, and even when, blacks sought redress within the social limits of the doctrine. Du Bois opened the debate in *The Crisis* magazine by declaring:

. . . In earlier years we discussed Social Equality at a time when there was no unity of opinion within or without the organization, so this year we are going to discuss Segregation and seek not dogma but enlightenment. . . .

. . . There is a good deal of misapprehension as to the historic attitude of the National Association for the Advancement of Colored People on race segregation. As a matter of fact, the Association, while it has from time to time discussed the larger aspects of this matter, has taken no general stand and adopted no general philosophy.[14]

Today, anyone the least familiar with the NAACP's philosophy on integration, especially since 1954, would no doubt consider this issue, raised in 1934, as either capricious, rhetorical or, perhaps, rather disingenuous. Had not the leading civil rights organization *always,* since its beginnings, been in favor of integration? Perhaps certain members had always been in favor of racial integration since 1909, but not until the 1930s did the NAACP make racial integration its overall civil rights policy. It was the impact of the Depression that forced the association unequivocally to declare itself on the issue. Because the NAACP did not have an economic program, Du Bois, among others, charged that it should establish one or lose its already diminishing prestige and legitimacy among blacks. To clarify his own position, Du Bois cited the original statement of civil rights principles declared by the NAACP in 1911 and further refined in 1915: The NAACP ". . . Conceives of its mission to be the completion of the work which the great Emancipator began. It proposes to make a group of black Americans free from the lingering shackles of slavery, physically free from peonage, mentally free and politically free from disfranchisement and from insult." Du Bois pointed out that this statement of principle still expressed the NAACP's objective in 1934 because it had never been qualified.

The NAACP first confronted the legal issue of segregation in 1912, but only by implication, noted Du Bois. The Second Report of the association in 1912 dealt with efforts by Kansas City to restrict blacks to specified residential areas by force of law—that is, by establishing residential segregation imposed by municipal ordinance. The NAACP, as Du Bois noted, vigorously fought against legally imposed residential segregation by taking its arguments to the highest courts in the land, beginning in 1915. This led to the association's first court victory in 1917, the Louisville, Kentucky, *Buchanan* v. *Warley* case. But said Du Bois:

. . . It will be noted here that the N.A.A.C.P. expressed no opinion as to whether it might not be a feasible and advisable thing for colored people to establish their own residential sections, or their own towns; and certainly there was nothing expressed or implied that Negroes should not organize for promoting their own interests in literature or art. Manifestly, here was opportunity for considerable difference of opinion, but the matter was never thoroughly threshed out.[15]

Du Bois then reviewed the substance of the major civil rights campaigns that the NAACP had initiated from 1912 to the 1930s. Many of these campaigns were exploratory, aimed at developing and perfecting organizational techniques. As important as they were as protest actions, these campaigns would soon be forgotten by succeeding black generations. Du Bois mentioned the campaign waged by the infant NAACP against the racial segregation policies initiated in governmental departments during the Wilson administration. During the first Wilson years the federal civil service departments in Washington, D.C., were reorganized along racially segregated lines with separate dining and rest-room facilities. In addition, several black civil service jobholders were either fired or demoted, transferred, or otherwise humiliated.[16] Woodrow Wilson was by birth a southerner; in fact, he was the first southern-born president since Andrew Johnson. The Wilson administration's attack on blacks in government bureaus was organized and instigated by southerners who had flocked to Washington seeking patronage on the heels of Wilson's victory in 1912. Confederate vengeance against blacks, which began in the South in the 1890s when segregation and disfranchisement laws were put into force, was extended into the capital, where discrimination and segregation were either *de facto* or semilegal. Thus, legalized segregation came to the nation's capital for the first time. Thus, the old Confederacy achieved in 1913–1914 what it had failed to accomplish in 1861–1862 —it captured the District of Columbia! Wilson's policies represented a serious blow against Washington's black, brown, and beige community and the political hopes and aspirations of blacks all over the country, and the outcry was nationwide from blacks and the white liberal community.

It was a personal defeat for Du Bois, who in 1912 had led a black exodus from the Republican party in support of Wilson's "New Freedom" platform. In 1912 the fledgling NAACP lacked the political clout to counter the Wilson administration's antiblack purge of Washington's civil service.

During 1915–1916, however, the NAACP mounted its first successful protest action: It organized a determined congressional lobby against passage of H. R. 6060, an immigration bill carrying a Senate amendment aimed at barring the entry into the United States of all persons of "African descent," meaning blacks from the Caribbean and Latin America, as well as Africa. Known also as the "African Exclusion Amendment," it was defeated and the bill itself voted down in the House. The NAACP lobbied strongly against the amendment on several grounds, one of which was "The Amendment operates against Christianity and Civilization by excluding African students from the benefits of American schools and colleges."[17] This bill's defeat dramatically increased the entry of black West Indians into the United States. One of these West Indians was Marcus Mosiah Garvey, who arrived in 1916. Ironically, the first organization Garvey attacked on ideological grounds was the NAACP![18] Had it not been for the NAACP's participation in the defeat of this bill, Marcus Garvey would not have had the necessary volume of West Indian immigrants in New York City with which to launch his sensational Back to Africa movement in 1919. Considering the ideological abuse Du Bois had to take from Marcus Garvey from 1919 to 1925, it was curious, if not understandable, that Du Bois in 1934 failed to mention this early programmatic success of the NAACP. Originally, *The Crisis* had proudly reported the bill's defeat as a great achievement, in fact as the greatest victory that the NAACP had won on its own organizational merits since its founding.[19]

Du Bois did review the NAACP's efforts on the labor front, such as fighting the "full crew" bills which led to the downgrading and firing of so many black railway employees when traditionally "black" railroad jobs (such as locomotive engineer fireman) were changed into exclusively "white" jobs. He reviewed the long struggle against Jim Crow laws on railway trains and streetcars, institutionalized in the South by 1896. But in his review of the association's program up to the 1930s, Du Bois rehashed what was to become twenty years later (1954) the centerpiece of the NAACP's civil rights program: the problem of public school segregation in both North and South. Said Du Bois:

Very soon, however, there came up a more critical question and that was the matter of Negro schools which the Association had avoided from the beginning any thoroughgoing pronouncement on this matter. In the resolutions of 1909, the conference asked: "Equal opportunities for all in all the states, and that public school expenditure be the same for the Negro and white schools." This of course did not touch the real problem of the schools. Very soon, however, definite problems were presented to the Association: the exclusion of colored students from the Oberlin dormitories in 1919; the discrimination in the School of Education at the University of Pennsylvania; and the Cincinnati fight against establishing a separate school for colored children, brought the matter squarely up front. Later, further cases came; the Brooklyn High School, the matter of a colored High School in Indianapolis and the celebrated Gary case.[20]

In other words, not since the NAACP's founding in 1909 had the association advocated a clear and definitive policy on the institutionalized system of segregated public schools for black students in southern, border, or many northern and western states. However, as Du Bois pointed out, the impact of the school cases mentioned (Oberlin, Indianapolis, etc.) forced the NAACP gradually to confront this reality by declaring that "further extension of segregated schools for particular races and especially for Negroes was unwise and dangerous, and the Association undertook in all possible cases to oppose such further segregation." This position on public school segregation represented expediency, a legalistic holding action because, as Du Bois explained, the NAACP

did not, however, for a moment feel called upon to attack the separate schools where most colored children are educated throughout the United States and it refrained from this not because it approved of separate schools, but because it was faced by a fact and not a theory. It saw no sense in tilting against windmills.[21]

The NAACP was unequivocally opposed to all forms of segregation and discrimination. Given the social realities, however, such a position was more idealistic than substantive because it was seen, Du Bois argued: "That in all these cases the Association was attacking specific instances and not attempting to lay down any general rule as to how far the advancement of the colored race in the United States was going to involve *separate racial action and segregated organization of Negroes for certain ends*."[22] (Italics added.)

The NAACP was founded just in time to confront the massive migrations of southern blacks into northern industrial centers inspired by the outbreak of World War I and prompted by unabated racial oppression and growing agricultural poverty. Just as long as the "race problem" remained in American public opinion a "southern problem," the predominantly agricultural South would be the prime focus of the NAACP's legalistic civil rights approaches. As late as the 1910 census, roughly nine tenths of the black population were still residing in the southern states, but the ensuing population shift recorded in 1920 and 1930 reflected a northern black urbanization of unprecedented proportions. With northern urbanization came alterations in both the economic and political (and cultural) status of American blacks. But for the unexpected advent of the Great Depression, it was conceivable that the NAACP would have had the flexibility to adjust its program gradually to changing conditions as it had already been doing, especially on segregation. As Du Bois revealed: "The overwhelming and underlying thought of the N.A.A.C.P. had always been that any discrimination based simply on race is fundamentally wrong, and that consequently purely racial organizations must have strong justification to be admissable. On the other hand, they faced certain unfortunate but undeniable facts. For instance, War came."[23] One of those "undeniable facts" following the war was, of course, the Garvey movement, based on the philosophy of racial separateness (i.e., voluntary self-segregation). The social and racial philosophy of racial separateness, the NAACP had to oppose emphatically. But by 1934 the Garvey movement was dead.

When the United States entered World War I in 1917, the NAACP faced the drafting of blacks into the segregated military. This posed a difficult problem for the association's antidiscrimination program. In the first place, certain members of the executive board were opposed to America's involvement in the war, thus bringing the NAACP under federal scrutiny for possible "sedition." On the other hand, an entrenched antiblack opinion surfaced within the War Department. One extreme opposed having blacks in the military in *any* capacity, while the moderate view maintained that they should be used only in strictly segregated and menial functions. When the NAACP requested that blacks be trained as commissioned officers on the same basis and proportion as whites, the War Department refused. To counter this refusal, the NAACP compromised and asked for a racially separate officers' training school. This they won. "There arose a bitter protest among many Negroes against this move," said Du Bois. "Nevertheless, the argument for it was absolutely unanswerable, and [the] chairman of the board supported by the students of Howard University, launched a movement which resulted in the commissioning of seven hundred Negro officers in the A.E.F."

"In all the British Dominions, with their hundreds of millions of colored folk," said Du Bois, "there was not a single officer of known

Negro blood. *The American Negro scored a tremendous tremendous triumph against the color line by their admitted and open policy of segregation.''* (Italics added.) This did not mean, however, that:

> Any of the members of the N.A.A.C.P. thought it right that there should be a separate Negro camp, but they thought a separate Negro camp and Negro officers was infinitely better than no camp and no Negro officers and that was the only practical choice that lay before them.[24]

The ravages of the Great Depression had accentuated the consequences of the racial and interracial dilemmas inherent in the blacks' *group* position in American society. This group position was contradictory to all the democratic principles written into the American Constitution. But if white society's racial practices were contradictory, so too were the American blacks' defensive and offensive responses to white racial policies. Or, to be more specific, the general black leadership policies were the most contradictory of all, which Du Bois was then forced to point out. As he noted, in 1920 the NAACP began to organize the black vote and cast this vote in opposition to the open enemies of blacks who were running for office. "This was without doubt a species of segregation. It was appealing to voters on the grounds of race, and it brought for that reason considerable opposition" said Du Bois. "Nevertheless, it could be defended on the ground that the election of enemies of the Negro race was not only a blow to that race but to the white race and to all civilization."[25]

During the 1920s, the final significant segregation problem that engaged the NAACP was the issue of Harlem Hospital. During this decade, blacks numerically captured that considerable stretch of prize Manhattan real estate that barely twenty years before had been a thoroughly white residential area known as Harlem. In taking it over, blacks appropriated an important institution—Harlem Hospital. For a number of years, Harlem Hospital had not admitted a single black physician or intern to its staff. Finally, through protest and political power, Harlem blacks obtained representation on the hospital staff in considerable numbers and also membership on the Board of Control. Du Bois called it a great triumph, but it was accompanied by a reaction on the part of whites, and also some blacks, "who opposed this movement, and an attempt to change the status of the hospital so that it would become a segregated Negro hospital, and so that presumably the other hospitals of the city would continue to exclude Negroes from their staffs. With this arose a movement to establish Negro hospitals throughout the United States." Here was an exceedingly difficult problem, Du Bois said:

> On the one hand, there is no doubt of the need of the Negro population for wider and better hospitalization; and of the demand on the part of Negro physicians for opportunities of hospital practice. This was illustrated by the celebrated Tuskegee [Alabama] hospital where nearly all Negro veterans are segregated but where an efficient Negro staff has been installed. Perhaps nothing illustrates better than this the contradiction and paradox of the problem of race segregation in the United States, and the problem which the N.A.A.C.P. faced and still faces.[26]

The NAACP had opposed the establishment of the Tuskegee Veterans Hospital on the grounds that it would be segregated, although it was doubtful, said Du Bois, "if it would have opposed such a hospital in the North. On the other hand, once established, we fought to defend the Tuskegee hospital and give it widest opportunity."

Later on in the 1930s, a prominent black critic of the NAACP's anomalous position on the Harlem Hospital issue wrote:

> Perhaps nothing could be more efficacious in relieving the overcrowding of Harlem Hospital and benefitting the entire Negro minority locally and nationally than the establishment of a large first-class all-Negro hospital in Harlem. The Negro group has more than enough first-rate doctors to staff such a hospital. There was a project to found a Negro hospital a few years ago, but before it was launched the idea was killed by an obstreperous and extremely vocal and effective group of Negro intellectuals who style themselves "anti-Segregationists." They maintain that a Negro hospital would be an incentive to the greater segregation of Negro doctors.[27]

"Preposterous is the situation in which the entire Negro minority is placed by its irrational intellectuals and their canny 'radical' white supporters," said this critic. "I predict that nothing could be more effective in breaking down the barriers of Segregation and compelling white doctors to recognize the merits of colored colleagues than the establishment of a great Negro hospital in Harlem." This kind of criticism, which was aimed at the NAACP by indirection, could have been voiced only in the 1930s. The rapid growth of northern black communities such as Harlem had obviously skewed the development of an urban ideology with exaggerated and unrealizable interpretations of the meaning of applied freedom. The resulting "irrationality" was, and has since been, most evident in the ranks of the black intelligentsia, or the educated elite. But W.E.B. Du Bois, as one of the most prominent representatives of this class, was able to apply his profound sociological insights and keen social perceptions to the reasons behind the growth of the peculiar quality of irrationality evident in civil rights leaders. Hence, in that crucial debate with his NAACP colleagues, only a Du Bois could have rationally delineated the irrationalities that lay camouflaged behind their civil rights pronouncements.

In practice, Du Bois said, "the NAACP had never officially opposed separate Negro organizations, such as churches, schools, and business and cultural organizations. It had never denied the recurrent necessity of united separate action on the part of Blacks for self-defense and self-development. It had, however, insistently and continually pointed out that such action was, in any case, a necessary evil often involving a recognition from within of the very color line which we are fighting without. That race pride and race loyalty, Negro ideals and Negro unity, have a place and function today, the N.A.A.C.P. never denied and never can deny." He then said:

> But all this simply touches the whole question of racial organization and initiative. No matter what we may wish or say, the vast majority of the Negroes in the United States are born in colored homes, educated in separate colored schools, attend separate colored churches, marry colored mates, and find their amusement in colored Y.M.C.A.'s and Y.W.C.A.'s. Even in their economic life, they are gradually being forced out of the place in industry which they occupied in the white world and are being compelled to seek their living among themselves. Here is segregation with a vengeance, and its problems must be met and its course guided. It would be idiotic simply to sit on the side lines and yell: "No Segregation" in an increasingly segregated world.[28]

Du Bois granted the ever-present danger of easily yielding to the promptings of *imposed* segregation without reason or pressure. "We segregate ourselves. . . . We herd together," he said. The Jim Crow galleries of southern moving-picture houses were filled with some of the best black citizens, both as law and social custom. Separate schools and other institutions had been established by black citizens in the North when the whites had made no such demand:

Such are the flat and undeniable facts. What are we going to do about them? We can neither yell them down nor make them disappear with resolutions. We must think and act. It is this problem which the _Crisis_ desires to discuss during the present year in all its phases and with ample and fair representation to all shades of opinion.[29]

With this opening critique, which was temperate in tone and reasoned in polemic, Du Bois set off a debate that seethed inside the NAACP's upper echelons and reverberated throughout the association's nationwide elite network, the _Crisis_ readership, and the black press. Coming from Du Bois, it was like a pronunciamento from the ranking Elder Statesman but was not fully received in the spirit of words of wisdom. It grated on the sensibilities of convinced integrationists, rankled the consciences of many of the educated elites, and cast into doubt a number of the black leadership's strongly held convictions. In effect, it questioned the social values of that leadership. The reaction was immediate, the debate heated and tension-filled.

Du Bois had anticipated devoting the entire year of 1934 to debating the complexities of racial issues, but the arguments lasted barely six months. Then the great Du Bois, the consummate scholar, social critic, writer, and thinker, was forced to resign his twenty-four-year tenure as editor of _The Crisis_ at the age of sixty-six. The Great Depression had brought the NAACP to an unexpected crossroads. The association had to make a turn; the turn had to be made without Du Bois. As was his congenital style, he was too rational for the unavoidable irrationality that suffused all thinking about race and racial issues by _both_ blacks and whites. The entire black position in American society was sociologically irrational, and the Great Depression had but deepened that crisis of irrationality in a national economy that had almost slipped beyond rational control.

What Du Bois was actually attempting in 1934 was to heal a breach—an ideological division that he himself had helped create in the black leadership ranks in 1905 between Northern and Southern blacks. At that time, southern black leadership centered around the personality of Booker T. Washington, who emphasized, among other essentials, _black economic development as the first priority_ in any program of black social uplift. In taking that position, Washington had downplayed and deemphasized civil rights protest as a temporary expediency. Thirteen years Washington's junior, Du Bois emerged in 1903 as a civil rights "radical" who criticized Washington's policies of accommodation. Du Bois accused Washington of asking that "black people give up, at least temporarily, three things:

> First, political power,
> Second, insistence on civil rights,
> Third, higher education of Negro youths—
> And concentrate all their energies on industrial education, the
accumulation of wealth, and the conciliation of the South.[30]

In revolting against this Washington philosophy, Du Bois had asked:

> Is it possible that nine millions of men can make effective progress in economic lines if they are deprived of political rights, made a servile caste, and allowed only the most meager chance for developing their exceptional men? If history and reason give any distinct answer to these questions, it is an emphatic NO.[31]

In 1905, Du Bois broke unequivocally with Washington and attempted to organize a civil rights protest group of his own.[32] This movement led four years later to an alliance with a vanguard of white liberals and socialists who founded the NAACP. From thence to the 1930s, Du Bois, as editor of the association's *Crisis*, played a dominant role in molding the NAACP into the major twentieth-century civil rights protest organization it became. *But in doing so, Du Bois had, perhaps reluctantly, accepted the noneconomic liberalism ideals of the white liberals and also the white socialists*. In the meantime, however, his thinking went through a metamorphosis, finalized by the shock of the Depression into a fundamental shift in position. The collapse of the capitalist economy in America and in the world graphically exposed *American blacks as having no group program or plan for economic survival or even a concept of one*. This was disastrous. Since Du Bois's fight against Washington, blacks had continued to remain a servile caste, deprived of political rights in the South. However, it could *not* be claimed in 1934 that (black) colleges were not graduating an increasing number of exceptional men (and women!) Thus, Booker T. Washington and his philosophy were no longer available as civil rights protest whipping boys in the black leadership contest. Yet Washington's rejected argument about the programmatic priorities of black economic development vis-à-vis civil rights protest had returned to haunt Du Bois. The NAACP's program up to 1934 of "organized opposition to action and attitude of the dominant white group" included "ceaseless agitation and insistent demand for equality: the equal right to work, civic and political equality, and social equality. It involves the use of force of every sort: moral suasion, propaganda and where possible even physical resistance." However, Du Bois concluded:

> *There are, however, manifest difficulties about such a program. First of all it is not a program that envisages any direct action of Negroes themselves for the uplift of their socially depressed masses; in the very conception of the program, such work is to be attended to by the nation and Negroes are to be the subjects of uplift forces and agencies to the extent of their numbers and need. Another difficulty is that the effective organization of this plan of protest and agitation involves a large degree of inner union and agreement among Negroes.*[33] (Italics added.)

Du Bois's remedy for this defect in the NAACP's program was to call upon blacks to unite around the idea of an *"economic cooperative commonwealth"* that would offset the exploitative consequences of class development under free enterprise. Because, he said: "We have lived to see the collapse of capitalism" and, therefore, the Negro must "by carefully planned and intelligent action [fit] himself into the new economic organization which the world faces."[34] Moreover, said Du Bois, racial segregation "will persist for many decades," despite anything blacks attempted to do about it. This, of course, raised the challenging question of what precisely would be the future of the NAACP's crusade against segregation. More than that, Du Bois clearly suggested that to unite around a program for the economic cooperative commonwealth, blacks would have to assume a stance of "voluntary self-segregation." Consequently, he was implying that the NAACP should reorient its program and support this stance of voluntary self-segregation in the economic sphere.

That, the NAACP's leaders were *not,* by any stretch of social imagination, about to do. The concerted rebuke they handed Du Bois was stunned, angry, and emphatic. Among other charges, he was accused of reverting to Booker T. Washington's economic position, which was only partially true. But any hint of programmatic "voluntary self-segregation" carried the Washington stigma of conservative accommodation. The very idea of a separate black economy even in theory, aside from its dubious feasibility, carried the notion of racial separatism.

The problem was that Du Bois had seen the light! He was not *really* talking about racial separatism, but about internal racial economic co-operation. Under the emotional stress of dissecting what was wrong with the NAACP's program in 1934, Du Bois did not have the dispassionate latitude fully to spell out his concept of the economic cooperative commonwealth. More than that, the economic cooperative idea had been placed on the civil rights agenda much too late. In retrospect, it is clear that any such program *should* have been initiated around 1900 or, at the latest, by 1909 when the NAACP was founded. Such leadership foresight in black economic matters was discouraged by the acrimonious competition and controversies that raged within the Afro-American League and the "Council" over the dominant role of Booker T. Washington's ideas of racial progress. Although Washington was understandably echoing the economic free-enterprise religion of twentieth-century American capitalism in black terms, it did represent a rather limited panacea for the minority-group survival of American blacks. Even a relatively viable black business class fostered by Washington's National Negro Business League[35] would not have gone very far in alleviating the economic disabilities of the black rank and file in the industrial, agricultural, and service sectors. This same problem exists in the 1980s in the efforts of Jesse Jackson's Operation PUSH, which is but an updated version of Booker T. Washington's black economic ventures.

However, between 1900 and 1909, black leaders were not in a position to examine the methods of economic cooperation brought to the United States by North European immigrants, principally by the Finns and Scandinavians. Economic cooperative ventures of the type Du Bois tried to promote in 1934 had been established in the United States as early as 1845.[36] The United Cooperative Society, organized by Finnish immigrants in 1907, for example, in Maynard, Massachusetts, competed successfully "not only with the independent merchants of the town but with the chain stores as well." A report published in 1941 on the progress of the Finnish United Cooperative Society stated that:

> This cooperative, still mainly directed by Finns and their children, has achieved a larger and more varied volume of business than any other local cooperative society in the eastern part of the United States. Its annual sales averaged $485,000 in the years 1936–38. Through the cooperative's facilities Maynard families can supply all of their food requirements, the coal and other fuel needed to heat their homes, gasoline and oil for their cars, and several other commodities such as range oil, ice, hardware and electrical appliances. The association also pro-

vides a line of farm supplies for its farmer members. Taken altogether, a working-class family can probably make two-thirds of its retail purchases directly from the cooperative society.[37]

Farmer-cooperative labor councils similar to this Finnish cooperative enterprise were established in Minnesota and other midwestern and eastern states during the same period by Poles, Italians, Irish, Danes, Norwegians, Swedes, Lithuanians, Russians, and Germans. These cooperatives came into being because "of the pressure on certain groups in the [United States] to improve their standards of living, and because, in certain cases at least, private agencies for distribution were not satisfactory."[38]

Noticeably absent in the whole history of the economic cooperative movement in the United States is that most economically deprived minority group, the blacks. Significantly absent also is any extensive practice of economic cooperative principles in the southern states, where the bulk of the black population resided up to the end of the 1930s. What blacks sorely needed were the kinds of cooperative economic, agricultural, and consumer enterprises that conceivably might have served as organizational bases for Du Bois's ideas in 1934. *The failure by early twentieth-century reform (and also socialist and labor) leaders, both black and white, to cultivate and encourage the principles of cooperative economics among blacks was a serious sin of omission.* However, given the semifeudal character of southern agriculture and labor relations between the end of Reconstruction and the 1930s, the absence of economic cooperative programs is understandable. Permeated as the region was with the racism of color, caste, class, and white supremacy—with the blacks at the very bottom rank of the labor scale—it is doubtful that any cooperative ventures attempted by blacks would have been permitted. It was not for nothing that upon launching the New Deal's economic centerpiece, the Agricultural Adjustment Administration (AAA) in 1933, Roosevelt dubbed the South the "Nation's Number One Economic Problem."

Du Bois was on the right track, but he and the NAACP had arrived at the crossroads of economic planning too late. Economic cooperative behavior had to evolve from a free and democratically nurtured labor situation, which the southern states had never had. As a result, the disruptive and socially uprooting character of black migrations out of the region had had pathological results in many instances. It had created northern urban enclaves of blacks whose social and economic backgrounds had placed them beyond the disciplines of economic cooperation on any but the most elementary level of personal survival in the catastrophe of the Great Depression. This, Du Bois's colleagues in the NAACP's top leadership most likely understood very well. But Du Bois was an idealistic seer, with a rational faculty for social comprehension—they were less so. To them, he appeared to be espousing an abhorrent racial separatism, which he was not.

When Du Bois countered that blacks worshiped in separate churches, were educated in separate schools and colleges; that blacks established separate racial societies, fraternal groups, sororities, clubs, professional groups; that blacks herd together wherever and whenever it is congenial, his opponents countered that such actions were a "necessary evil." White liberal opinion on the NAACP executive board supported this view. When Du Bois pointed out that there was "a larger movement on the part of the Negro intelligentsia toward racial grouping for the advancement of art and literature . . . for reviving ancient African art through an American Negro art movement . . . to use the extremely rich and colorful life of the Negro in America and elsewhere as a basis for painting, sculpture and literature," these developments were also seen as a necessary evil. Since Du Bois, like most other leaders, recognized the economic fact that American blacks were primarily consumers with limited experience in business enterprise, he did not elaborate on "separate Negro businesses." That is, neither he nor his debaters argued whether separate black businesses were a "necessary" or an "unnecessary" evil.

Throughout this extended debate, Du Bois pressed the NAACP to state a clear position on the meaning of segregation. He asked, Did the NAACP support or oppose the existence of separate black churches, schools, colleges, fraternities, professional groups, institutions of any kind, black literature, art, culture, etc.? The consensual response was best summed up in the reply of Walter White, executive secretary, supported by Joel E. Spingarn, chairman of the board:

> The Negro must, without yielding, continue the grim struggle *for* integration and *against* segregation for his own physical, moral and spiritual well-being and for that of white America and of the world at large.[39] (Italics.)

The full extent of internal ideological conflict and confusion that the Du Bois critique engendered within the NAACP hierarchy will never be known. Fleeting glimpses into the turmoil have been allowed through a limited number of scholarly investigations.[40] In his decision to resign his post, Du Bois *did* have supporters for his views inside and around the association's ruling factions, but they counted as a decided minority. Faced with leadership obligations to reexamine and readjust the NAACP's program to adapt to changed racial, social, economic, and political circumstances, the majority view refused to bend. In his letter of resignation, Du Bois said, in part:

> I owe it, however, to the Board and to the public to make clear at this time the deeper reasons for my action, lest the apparent causes for my resignation seem inadequate. . . .
> . . . Today this organization, which has been great and effective for nearly a quarter of a century, finds itself in a time of crisis and change, without a program, without effective organization, without executive officers, who have either the ability or disposition to guide the National Association for the Advancement of Colored People in the right direction.[41]

But if this was the true state of affairs with the NAACP in 1934, just how did the association manage to survive? By stubbornly hewing to the line of what had become conventional civil rights wisdom of the ruling black middle-class elites. These elites were, in fact, Du Bois's own intellectual progeny. They were prominent representatives of Du Bois's "Talented Tenth," that class under whose guidance and tutelage (and leadership) rested the black masses' own chances for survival and uplift, Du Bois had once proclaimed. But now the Elder Statesman of the Talented Tenth was calling into question the civil rights values of his progeny. Most of them were outraged at his critique. One of them, William H. Hastie, then a Washington attorney who would later be appointed the first black governor of the Virgin Islands, attacked Du Bois's arguments as "just about what Booker T. Washington would write if he were living." He charged further that Du Bois had become just another of those "abject, boot-licking, gut-lacking, knee-bending, favor-seeking Negroes [who] have been insulting our intelligence with a tale that goes like this: 'Segregation is not an evil. Negroes are better off by themselves. They can get equal treatment and be happier too, if they live and move and have their being off to themselves.' "[42]

Although Booker T. Washington had been dead for nineteen years, his influence had not abated; but even the shattering blow of the Great Depression had failed to inspire a reasoned reassessment of his message among the black educated elites. They had forgotten nothing, and had learned nothing. What they failed to appreciate was that Du Bois was attempting to conceptualize the economic basis and justification *not* for segregation, but for a *racial and ethnic pluralism within the context of the American racial, economic, political, and cultural reality as it was then evolving under Roosevelt's New Deal dispensation*. Because the timing was both awkward and late, Du Bois could not fully spell out his ideas. The history of black progress in the twentieth century had, circumstantially, moved beyond the scope of pre-1929 economic organization. More than that, in his first autobiography, *Dusk of Dawn* (1940), he managed to give only a rhetorical elaboration of the racially plural implications of his economic critique. Later, Du Bois seemed to have abandoned those economic premises when, under the pressures of personal associates, World War II, and intensified international Cold War tensions of the late 1940s, he veered toward the Communist left. Still later, he espoused socialism as the only practical solution to the economic plight of black America. To many, this represented a rather strange political shift for Du Bois, especially in view of his stinging criticisms of the Communist party's competition with the NAACP in the Scottsboro Case of 1931.

However, the challenge of the socialist doctrine *had* to be taken seriously in any discussion of black economics, especially in the 1930s. The Communist party's attack on the NAACP's "reformist legalism" was inspired by concerns similar to Du Bois's—the economic imperatives of the Great Depression and its political consequences. However, Roosevelt's New Deal deflated the Communists' political balloons on economic issues by saving the capitalist system for the capitalists, while at the same time relieving the NAACP of the immediate need to take Du Bois's criticisms seriously. The NAACP was saved by Roosevelt's New Deal. Now the changed role of the federal power absolved black leadership from either the necessity or the responsibility of heeding Du Bois's call for a black economic program. With the advent of Roosevelt's NRA, AAA, PWA, WPA, TVA, FERA, CCC, NYA, etc., black leadership immediately grasped the new option of criticizing the New Deal for its early failures to remedy the appalling economic plight of blacks when it excluded them from the administrative scope of the economic recovery program. In his criticism of the NAACP's civil rights philosophy, Du Bois charged that this approach assumed that the uplift of the black "socially depressed masses" was to be "attended to by the nation" and sundry "uplift forces and agencies to the extent of their numbers and needs." By 1934–1935, these "agencies" had become by implication the New Deal agencies.

Not since 1876, when the federal power abandoned southern blacks to the unmerciful control of the southern ruling classes, had blacks, North or South, placed any hopes in the beneficence of the federal power to grant them anything but cold indifference. How could a federal power that could not or would not exert its authority to stamp out the crime of lynching black males be viewed as a bountiful dispenser of black uplift? From the Republican administration of Hayes to the Republican regime of Hoover, neither blacks nor their leaders expected anything much from the federal government, nor did they get anything. Yet they still remained, for the most part, black Republicans with a black version of the free-enterprise mentality.

Roosevelt's Democratic party New Dealism changed all that. Moreover, the New Deal brought into prominence a new black leadership generation—or at least a corps of hopefuls who could, independently, ignore both the NAACP and Du Bois, and the latter's critique of the former, by assuming the role of chastisers of the New Deal as *their* new program. The new federal dispensation had provided a programmatic escape hatch for the black leadership. In lieu of creating at least the outlines of the kind of black economic program Du Bois had called for, black leaders were able to shun this obligation as unnecessary and irrelevant.

Within a year following Du Bois's resignation, *The Crisis* announced what was, in effect, a new programmatic approach to the economic problems of blacks in an article, "A Black Inventory of the New Deal." Just about two years into the New Deal recovery program, black economic conditions were going from very bad to worse. Then it became obligatory and expedient for the new advance-guard leadership to take up the slack of the old guard in the NAACP and guide the association through the worst years of its crisis. Said the above article: "It is highly important for the Negro citizen of America to take inventory of the gains and losses which have come to him under the New Deal. The Roosevelt administration has now had two years in which to unfold itself. . . . We can now state with reasonable certainty what the New Deal means for the Negro."[43] The article was an indictment—"The increase in the number of Negroes in relief families is an accurate indication of the deepening of the economic crisis for black America." Roosevelt's New Deal showpiece, the Agricultural Adjustment Administration (AAA), was actually enforcing poverty on black farm workers and driving them off the land, leaving them without income and unable to secure work or relief. The "code-making process" of the National Recovery Act (NRA), the attempted enforcement of minimum and maximum wages and maximum

hour codes, effectively ruled black workers out of the labor market because the bulk of them were unemployed. "Thus from the beginning
relatively few Negro workers were even theoretically covered by the NRA
labor provisions." The Tennessee Valley Authority (TVA), laying plans
for the creation of model towns for construction workers in Tennessee
electrical power projects, openly admitted that no blacks would be allowed. The Public Works Administration (PWA) was permitting construction project contractors to refuse to hire either skilled or unskilled
black workers. In a word, neither the AAA, the PWA, nor the TVA had
benefited blacks in the least. Thus, the time had come for a serious
reassessment of "the social and economic condition of the Negro at this
time," said the article:

> It was a realization of these conditions which gave rise to the proposal
> to hold a national conference on the economic status of Negroes under
> the New Deal at Howard University in Washington, D.C., May 18, 19
> and 20. At this conference sponsored by the Social Science Division
> of Howard University and the Joint Committee of National Recovery
> a candid and intelligent survey of the social and economic condition of
> the Negro will be made.[44]

Out of this conference was born in 1935 the National Negro Congress
(NNC), which, for a spell, was seen as an organization that would supplement, if not supplant, the NAACP. This threat to the NAACP was
short-lived, however. Not only was the NNC's life brief as an effective
new organization, but also, being a black-labor-radical coalition brought
the NCC under Communist party control, causing internal dissensions
between conservative, moderate, and radical blacks. Within four years,
the National Negro Congress began to disintegrate. More significant, with
Du Bois out of the way, the NAACP's top leadership had other plans.
Even during the high point of the internal debate with Du Bois, a new
civil rights phase was being sketched that would lead to the *Brown* decision.

Even before Du Bois's break with the NAACP, ground had been laid for a new departure in civil rights programming within the association's top leadership. The formulation of this program, plus the fortuitous launching of the New Deal's economic recovery program, combined to maintain the NAACP's viability. These factors allowed the NAACP to weather the Depression intact as a leadership organization.

This new civil rights program would eventually evolve into a legal strategy that lawyers would sum up later as the *School Segregation Cases*.[45] In brief, prior to the 1930s, legal attacks on segregation had not been fruitful in challenging the *Plessy* v. *Ferguson* separate-but-equal doctrine in what was seen as "the main categories of social activity in which civil rights problems arise—housing, earning a living, public accommodation, the armed forces, voting and so on."[46] But a keen analysis of the Supreme Court decision affecting these categories concluded that public education in the primary, secondary, and higher levels presented the most vulnerable sector of the legal bulwarks of segregation's separate-but-equal doctrine. This new legal tack would ultimately lead to the *Brown* decision.

Prior to 1938, little NAACP litigation had seriously challenged the concept of "separate but equal," which had been "entrenched in federal jurisprudence."[47] (This was, of course, the basic motivation behind Du Bois's demand that the NAACP clarify its position on the meaning of segregation.) However, within the historical purview of civil rights high court decisions, a number of these opinions contained examples of "egalitarian language"[48] usable as precedents for new strategies in a legal assault on *Plessy*. Among such high court decisions were *Strauder* v. *West Virginia* (1880), *Yick Wo* v. *Hopkins* (1886), *Buchanan* v. *Warley* (1917), *Gong Lum* v. *Rice* (1927), *Nixon* v. *Herndon* (1927), and *Nixon* v. *Condon* (1932). The significance of these decisions turned on the issue of "state action," that is, could the state or any governmental authority have the constitutional right, given the Fourteenth Amendment, to impose racially discriminatory laws, ordinances, statutes prejudicial to the due process or equal protection guarantees of any party. *Strauder* involved the right of blacks to serve on juries. *Buchanan* invalidated the attempt of Louisville, Kentucky, to establish racial zoning ordinances for housing. *Nixon* (1927 and 1932) invalidated Texas state laws barring blacks from primary elections. The case of *Gong Lum* saw the Supreme Court uphold the right of Mississippi to assign an Oriental girl to a segregated black public school against the wishes of both parents and pupil. In *Yick Wo* the Supreme Court invalidated the city of San Francisco's efforts by municipal ordinance to prevent a Chinese from operating a hand laundry.

The new strategy of the NAACP was to build on the egalitarian language expressed in the "elementary structure of *Strauder-Buchanan-Nixon-Yick Wo*" civil rights precedents.[49] In *Strauder*, for example, the Supreme Court had deplored "the very fact that colored people are singled out and expressly denied by statute all right to participate in the administration of the law, as jurors, because of their color. . . . ."[50] Around 1930 the American Fund for Public Service, otherwise known as the Garland Fund, in conjunction with the NAACP, initiated an effort to foster the new strategy. This new strategy was encouraged by the change in social and political climate brought on by the Great Depression. As one legal reporter in civil rights law later described the situation: "The development was not based entirely on chance; there was a planned legal program . . . the far-reaching social changes which coincided with and created a climate conducive to new legal and social relationships cannot be ignored."[51] These "far-reaching social changes" were a reflection of New Deal policies. The genesis of the new legal strategy devised by the Garland Fund and the NAACP was summarized in the 1934 Annual Report of the association:

On November 5 the American Fund for Public Service forwarded to the N.A.A.C.P. a check for $10,000, to be used exclusively for a campaign of legal action and public education against unequal apportionment of public funds for education and discrimination in public transportation. Expenditures in these efforts and direction of the campaign was vested in a joint committee representing the American Fund for Public Service and the N.A.A.C.P. composed of the following members: Morris L. Ernst, Lewis S. Gannett, James Weldon Johnson, James Marshall, Arthur B. Spingarn, Roger N. Baldwin.[52]

The Garland Fund collaborated with the NAACP to foster a doctrine more favorable to civil rights. If this aim implied that the NAACP did not *already* possess such a doctrine in 1934, this assumption lent considerable force to Du Bois's critique of the same year. Specifically, the American Fund for Public Service observed that the NAACP had not "made a coherent effort to develop a well-articulated body of precedent in this field [of civil rights]."[53] The implication was that the previous involvement of the NAACP in the evolution of legal rulings made in favor of plaintiffs or appellants in *Corrigan* v. *Buckley* on restrictive covenants, 1926; *Grovey* v. *Townsend* on the Texas white primary, 1935; *Nixon* v. *Herndon*, 1927; *Nixon* v. *Condon*, 1932, again on the legality of the white primary, was not sufficient to put the NAACP unequivocally on record against the legality of the *Plessy* v. *Ferguson* separate-but-equal doctrine.

What this development indicated was that Du Bois, even before his critique of the NAACP's overall program, was already being bypassed by a white liberal bloc aimed at reorienting the association's legal direction, and it is to be noted that he was not a member of the joint committee in this enterprise. Though it is doubtful that Du Bois was not aware of the new legal turn in the association's affairs, in his autobiography, *Dusk of Dawn*, he makes no reference to this important program development beyond one scant mention of the Garland Fund when he wrote that "James Weldon Johnson, our secretary, raised from the public and the Garland Fund nearly $80,000 for a civil rights defense fund. We continued winning court victories, but somehow despite them, we did not seem to be getting far."[54] Even six years after his break with the NAACP, Du Bois still claimed that its basic policies and ideals must be modified and changed.[55]

James Weldon Johnson, gifted poet, writer, lawyer, former American consul in Nicaragua and Venezuela under President Taft, was one of the few voices in the NAACP hierarchy to which Du Bois listened with much respect. However well-intentioned was Johnson's linking up with the new legal shift to public education as the prime civil rights arena, it was apparent to Du Bois that this shift would not basically alter the noneconomic liberalism incubus that had from the beginning restricted the NAACP and brought it to the verge of disintegration in 1934. In the same Annual Report of 1934, the NAACP elaborated further on the significance of the Garland Fund:

> It will be remembered from previous annual reports that the American Fund for Public Service, more generally known as the Garland Fund, had voted a much larger appropriation to the N.A.A.C.P. for a comprehensive campaign against the major disabilities from which Negroes suffer in American life—legal, political and *economic*. (Italics not in the original.)[56]

But the new legal campaign initiated here was not in the least economic in scope or conception. The report specifically explained that "because of the importance of the matter and the wide extent of the problem, *it has been agreed that the major emphasis shall be placed upon educational inequalities.* It should be made clear that the campaign is a carefully planned one to secure decisions, rulings and public opinion on the broad principle instead of being devoted to merely miscellaneous cases."[57] (Emphasis not in the original.)

To be sure, this was exemplary and legitimate lawyers' phraseology necessary in the inauguration of a new legal campaign. But into what would it translate educationally, politically, economically, culturally, and sociologically? What was really meant by "broad principle" as opposed to "merely miscellaneous cases"? If it was true, and it was, that the *Plessy* separate-but-equal doctrine was still entrenched in federal jurisprudence, into what would this new legal campaign translate in racial and, especially, in *economic* terms? In effect, it was the same noneconomic liberalism of the founding ideals of the NAACP carried over and extended into another legal dimension.

More than that, the miscellaneous cases in which the NAACP's legal corps professed to discern precedents for the kind of egalitarian language usable in developing the *School Segregation Cases* (the new campaign against educational inequalities), while legally useful and apropos, were also more broadly debatable from other points of view. In other words, the *Strauder-Buchanan-Nixon-Yick Wo* precedents were conceptually too limited for the kind of legal analysis the black situation required, and also ahistorical even within the context of public education inequalities insofar as blacks were concerned. For example, even though the *Strauder* v. *West Virginia* and *Yick Wo* v. *Hopkins* decisions took place during the 1880s, the lawyers mentioned nothing of the ten-year legislative debate over the Blair Education Bill, which had to do with federal aid to education, specifically involving southern blacks. Inasmuch as the entire legal debate over the constitutional intents of the Fourteenth Amendment turned on the state's role in applying the separate-but-equal doctrine, in administering due process and equal protection, the implications of the Blair Education Bill deserved to be reviewed. It had to be a foregone conclusion in 1930 that the future legal course of the *School Segregation Cases* could not avoid the intervention of the federal power—i.e., the state—in affairs of public education inequalities. For example, four years after *Brown,* "a proposed civil rights act of 1958 . . . sought to give affected districts the incentive toward desegregation of supplying federal funds to study and implement desegregation and of assuring them of federal monies to replace state aid which might be withheld for having desegregated."[58] Following *Brown,* civil rights lawyers could easily remember the *Civil Rights Cases* of 1883 that promulgated the "state action concept" and decided that "the Fourteenth Amendment applies to governmental but not to private conduct" in areas of racial discrimination.[59] They did not remember, however, that congressional advocates of the Blair Education Bill during the 1880s did not go so far as to promise federal monies for southern public schools in defiance of the states' rights prerogatives of states that did not want such federal aid for the education of blacks. In this sense the historical, and also the geographical, presentations in the study of law and race relations in search of usable precedents were often insufficient.[60]

In the *Strauder* v. *West Virginia* jury case, the Court decision favorable to blacks serving on juries was prima facie just and legitimate even within the concept of the separate-but-equal doctrine, which in 1880 had not even been pronounced. However, *Yick Wo* v. *Hopkins* was a decision of another genre, the deeper meaning of which civil rights lawyers involved with the NAACP only superficially compared with the evolution of the *School Segregation Cases*. In citing the equal protection or due process precedent in *Yick Wo,* civil rights lawyers sloughed over a crucial point from the black *economic* point of view. In the words of an NAACP lawyer, *Yick Wo* was a case of "arbitrary discrimination against a class (class in the sense of owners of laundries in wooden buildings, to take an example) constituted of Chinese subjects. . . . "[61]

Yick Wo had been operating a hand laundry in San Francisco for twenty years. San Francisco passed a laundry licensing act pointedly designed to rid San Francisco of Chinese laundries. When Yick Wo applied for a license, he was refused and later arrested and fined ten dollars for operating his laundry. Refusing to pay, Yick Wo carried his case to the Supreme Court, where it was upheld. Fifty years later, the NAACP legal corps would agree that the San Francisco licensing ordinance was racially biased and in violation of the Fourteenth Amendment in denying Yick Wo due process and equal protection. Another source explained *Yick Wo* v. *Hopkins* this way:

> This case helped to define the 14th Amendment. . . . It's a landmark case among other reasons because the court did a sociological investigation. They took a look at San Francisco's laundries; they counted all the laundries in San Francisco and noted that several hundred of them were run by Chinese and only a few by whites. But every time a Chinese man asked for a license he didn't get it. The Court asked, what is the purpose of San Francisco's laundry licensing ordinance? . . . The intent, the Court went on, is to drive a whole people out of a business, . . . that is an impermissible thing in law.[62]

In retrospect, it should be noted that Yick Wo was an immigrant, not a full citizen. All American blacks had been granted citizenship by the Fourteenth Amendment in 1868. However, the *Yick Wo* case involved more equal protection ingredients than were implied in the Civil Rights Acts of 1866 and 1875, which the Supreme Court had revised and nullified in 1883 as unconstitutional. Not only did the Supreme Court rule that a government body—i.e., the state—could not legislate a racially biased ordinance, it also implied that a governing body could not use its police power to prevent a *nonwhite minority group from earning a living by operating a legitimate business*. Thus, in the *Yick Wo* case the *economic* aspect was more crucial than the kinds of racial discrimination issues that would later dominate civil rights doctrine applied to blacks. Civil rights lawyers emphasized that "the main categories of social activity in which civil rights problems arise" for blacks were housing, earning a living, public accommodations, the armed forces, and voting. However, the noneconomic liberalism that guided the philosophy of the NAACP and its legal corps limited the earning-a-living rights of blacks to being employed, not operating an economic enterprise.

Patently this was the reason the celebrated case of *Moore* v. *Dempsey* (1923) could not be cited by civil rights lawyers as establishing any legal precedents usable in the evolution of the *School Segregation Cases* as was *Strauder-Buchanan-Nixon-Yick Wo*. However, in black civil rights —*economic* terms, *Moore* v. *Dempsey* had more in common with the sociological factors surrounding *Yick Wo* than *Yick Wo* had in common with *Strauder-Buchanan-Nixon*. Because the NAACP did not consider a black economic program *a priority*, civil rights lawyers could not and did not cite *Moore* v. *Dempsey*. The Supreme Court decision handed down in *Moore* v. *Dempsey* overruled the improper selection of jurors in a criminal trial in which the defendants were all black, and where the trial was conducted in an intensely prejudiced atmosphere. *Moore* v. *Dempsey* grew out of a race riot occurring in Elaine, Arkansas, in 1919. However, the underlying cause of the riot was economic.

In October 1919, a race riot erupted in Elaine, Phillips County, Arkansas, after black tenant farmers and sharecroppers tried to organize a cooperative farmers' association called the Progressive Farmers and Household Union of America. Through pooling their meager resources, these black tenant-farmers, sharecroppers, and independents organized to "*secure relief through the courts from vicious economic exploitation*."[63] White landlords and white farm workers, in collusion with the sheriff and deputies of Phillips County, organized a mob to terrorize the black farmers into abandoning their attempts at organization. This mob had the support and encouragement of most of the leading industrial and commercial spokesmen in Phillips County. A shoot-out resulted in which two white men and an undetermined number of blacks (reports varied— from two to three hundred!) were killed. The blacks were accused of a plot to "massacre white people." In retaliation: "A large number of white men armed themselves and rushed to the scene of the trouble and to adjacent regions and began the indiscriminate hunting, shooting and killing of Negroes." Twelve black farmers were jailed and quickly sentenced to death by an all-white jury in a courtroom "crowded with a throng that threatened the most dangerous consequences to anyone interfering with the desired result. The counsel did not venture to demand a delay of change of venue, to challenge a juryman or ask for separate trials."[64] In addition, sixty-seven other blacks (all black males) were sentenced to long prison terms for what the Arkansas press propagandized as a plot to massacre white people.

Similar racial atrocities had been occurring in the South since the 1890s, but 1919 was not an ordinary year. It was the year of the infamous "Red Summer" when all over the nation, constitutional guarantees of due process and equal protection were abandoned in order to stem threats of what public opinion viewed as subversive radicalism. Labor leaders and organizers, Socialists, Communists, and "revolutionaries" of all persuasions were hounded, persecuted, and jailed. Two hundred and forty-nine aliens suspected of so-called Bolshevik sympathies were deported to Europe. In July 1919, in a bloody Chicago race riot, sixteen blacks and fifteen whites were killed and over five hundred others injured. In five and one half months, from April 4 to October 1, 1919, there were race riots in twenty-two cities and towns throughout the nation; seventy-four blacks and at least one white member of the International Workers of the World (IWW) were lynched. This occurred in the immediate aftermath of World War I. After having served overseas in the United States military and supported the "War for Democracy," blacks, and especially black ex-servicemen, were demonstrating a well-merited racial assertiveness in pursuit of their citizenship rights. No doubt the Elaine, Arkansas, race riot had its roots in the general white southern reaction to black assertiveness. Still, it was extraordinary and had unique legal consequences. So much so that the NAACP took extraordinary steps to intervene in defense of the convicted men.

As a result of this intervention, what came to be called the "Phillips County Massacre" dragged through the state and federal courts until

February 1923, when the *Moore* v. *Dempsey* Supreme Court majority decision was delivered by Justice Oliver Wendell Holmes. This decision overruled the Arkansas Supreme Court's earlier decision not to reverse the verdict of the Phillips County Circuit Court of December 1919 that the twelve men should die. The NAACP stated in April 1923 that:

> For three and a half years, at a cost of more than $14,000, and in the face of relentless and bitter opposition on the part of the Arkansas authorities and the whites of the state, the N.A.A.C.P. has fought to save the lives of the twelve men who were condemned to death, and to release from prison the sixty-seven others who were sentenced to long prison terms for alleged connection with the so-called Phillips County, Arkansas "massacre" of October, 1919.[65]

The Phillips County Circuit Court had condemned the twelve black men in December 1919. "Lawyers employed by the NAACP appealed to the Arkansas State Supreme Court in their behalf and that court reversed the conviction of seven of the men and remanded them for retrial in the Phillips County Circuit Court. In the cases of the other five men the convictions were approved. It is this group of cases on which the United States Supreme Court has just rendered its verdict. . . . "[66] Why were these cases so important? the NAACP asked in its summation of the arduous appeal process. The federal court in Arkansas had remanded the conviction to the Phillips County Circuit Court. The county court had demurred, and the federal court had upheld the demurrer of the state of Arkansas that the defendants *"had no legal remedy."* However, the NAACP was able to report that:

> The United States Supreme Court reverses that decree and the case is sent back to the [federal district judge] to hear the facts. If he finds that the facts are as alleged in the petition, he will grant the writ of *habeas corpus*, and that will mean that the defendants are improperly held by the keeper of the penitentiary, must be brought before the court, and there discharged on the ground that they are not held by any legal process. Under the constitution no man can be deprived of life or property without the due process of law, and the Supreme Court has held that upon the facts alleged in the petition, if they are true (in filing a demurrer to these facts, the State of Arkansas does not deny they are true), these defendants are deprived of their liberty without due process of law. It is therefore highly probable that these men who have been under sentence of death since November 3, 1919, will soon be free.[67]

Under the conditions that prevailed in race relations in the southern states at that time, the NAACP was forced to hail the Supreme Court's decision in *Moore* v. *Dempsey* as a "great achievement in constitutional law." Liberal lawyers around the country, including those of the American Civil Liberties Union (ACLU), hailed the decision as one of "the most far reaching on habeas corpus ever made."[68] And so it was. However, unlike the Supreme Court decision in *Yick Wo*, the high court was not called upon to render a verdict on the essential, underlying economic factors involved in the Phillips County Massacre. The original aim of the black farmers' cooperative organization was to *secure relief through the courts* from vicious economic exploitation. In *Yick Wo*, the Chinese plaintiff was upheld in his right to operate a business enterprise for pecuniary gain. The Supreme Court ruled that the intent of San Francisco's licensing ordinance was to drive a whole people out of business, which was an unpermissible thing in law. That was precisely what mob rule did to black agricultural workers who tried to organize a farmers' economic cooperative in Arkansas, but the *Moore* v. *Dempsey* verdict had to evade the underlying economic issue. The "law" could not be used on behalf of these black farmers in an economic organizational effort. It is true that *Yick Wo* arose in California, which despite its anti-Chinese and anti-Japanese exclusionary politics was more "liberal" in its relations with Asians than was Arkansas in its black-white confrontations. Even so, the ongoing implications of the economic issue at stake in *Moore* v. *Dempsey* were not lost on the NAACP despite the association's obligation to praise highly the habeas corpus ruling of Justice Oliver Wendell Holmes.

Insofar as the civil rights position of the NAACP in 1923 was concerned, the Supreme Court's ruling in *Moore* v. *Dempsey*, despite its fervent reiteration of the constitutional right of due process, was still *ex post facto* a legal justification for maintaining the NAACP's guiding principles of *noneconomic liberalism*. So overwhelming were the conflicting points of view in DUE PROCESS OF LAW IN ARKANSAS, the caption under which the liberal *New Republic* magazine commented on the case, that the Supreme Court—even had it understood the economic issues, which *it did not*—was not even obliged to consider the underlying economic issues. The *New Republic* found Justice Holmes's version of the facts surrounding the Phillips County riot so shocking that the publication was moved to comment: "The story told by Mr. Justice Holmes, based on the statement of the petitioners, is so astonishing and, if true, throws such a glare of light on social conditions in Arkansas that we reproduce [the opinion] in full."[69]

In this opinion, Justice Holmes had succinctly described the events that led to the "killing on October 1 of one Clinton Lee, a white man, for whose murder the petitioners were indicted. They seem to have been arrested with many others on the same day. The petitioners say that Lee must have been killed by other whites, but that we leave to one side as what we have to deal with is not the petitioners' innocence or guilt but solely the question whether their constitutional rights have been preserved."[70] In other words, the fundamental constitutional issue was the Fourteenth Amendment's due process. However, Justice Holmes stated the following legal disclaimer:

> *They say that their meeting was to employ counsel for protection against extortions practiced upon them by the landowners and that the landowners tried to prevent their effort, but that again we pass by as not directly bearing on the trial.*[71] (Italics added.)

"Not directly bearing on the trial . . . !"—which was to say that constitutional guarantees of due process under the Fourteenth Amendment did not include guarantees of the rights of blacks, under any circumstances, to defend themselves organizationally *against the economic inequities imposed by the system of free enterprise when the administrative, corporate, and proprietary control of the economy was in the hands of members of the dominant White Anglo-Saxon Protestant group.* This was not what the Supreme Court implied in *Yick Wo* v. *Hopkins.* But, then, the economic issue involved in *Yick Wo* did receive a high court hearing on its merits while in *Moore* v. *Dempsey,* the economic issue, for which the defendants originally sought legal counsel, never got to court. In summing up the legal and economic aspects of the *Moore* v. *Dempsey* decision, the NAACP explained as follows:

> The decision opens up the entire question of economic exploitation of colored and white farmers alike under the share-cropping and tenant-farming systems of the South. According to Albert Bushnell Hart of Harvard University, the Negro forms two-fifths of the population of the South but produces *three-fifths of the wealth.*[72]

In this relationship, black farmers and landowners in all the cotton-producing states entered into a contract under which an equitable division of the crops and profits produced was supposedly guaranteed. But under the racial intimidation that ruled a South backed by mob law, black farmers were seldom given itemized accountings, were seldom allowed to know the price at which the crops they raised were sold by the landlords, were forced to accept the landlords' figures for supplies received, and dared not question the honesty of the accountings. Bills for supplies were padded, prices received through the sale of crops were whatever the landlord chose to tell his tenants. Thus, black farmers usually found themselves deeper and deeper in debt every year regardless of how few supplies they used or how high the price of cotton or corn. The NAACP continued:

> Under the system no Negro is allowed to leave a plantation as long as he remains in debt. Thus, the landlord cannot only take by force and intimidation all of the crop but he can assure his labor supply for the coming year. It was against such a system as this that the colored men in Phillips County, Ark., organized.[73]

Later on, in the aftermath of the riot, a "Committee of Seven" was appointed by the governor of Arkansas to adjudicate what the press called an *"insurrection"* in Phillips County. This Committee of Seven stated in no uncertain terms that all white citizens in Phillips County and surrounding areas were of the opinion that the "law should take its course" and that there should be no talk of commutation of sentences or otherwise interfering with the verdict for the execution of the prisoners. In nearby Helena, Arkansas, a meeting was called by the Rotary Club to demand that the prisoners either be executed by the state or be lynched. *This meeting of the Helena Rotary Club was attended by seventy-five representatives of the leading industrial and commercial enterprises of Helena, members of the American Legion Post and the Lions Club.* In effect, this was a case of localized *class war and race war*, which had it spread throughout the South would have amounted to a *revolutionary* situation. But the irony of it all was that the implications of the Arkansas race riot were lost not only on the Socialists and the northern radicals, but on the *entire American labor movement of the 1920s,* none of which demonstrated the least public interest in the Arkansas tragedy; nor did any official voice in the American labor leadership make the gesture of an *amicus curiae* brief in the *Moore* v. *Dempsey* decision.

So struck by the racial impact of the Supreme Court's due process opinion in *Moore* v. *Dempsey* was the ultraliberal *New Republic* that its editorial board pondered whether Arkansas's states' rights had been unconstitutionally overruled by the federal judiciary in nullifying the Arkansas County Circuit Court's convictions of the blacks. The liberals found due process so "astonishing" that, like the Supreme Court, they lost sight of what they had no comprehension of in the first place—the underlying economic causes of the Arkansas race riot. Yet one month later, the same *New Republic* could editorially criticize the Supreme Court for striking down the law establishing minimum wages for women in the District of Columbia in the case of *Adkins* v. *Children's Hospital,* a decision that cast doubt on the legality of all minimum-wage laws. Said the *New Republic:* "One road to economic justice has been closed up by the Supreme Court. The state may recognize that whole classes of women workers are subjected to starvation wages, but the state may not intervene." Further:

> *The Supreme Court does not know that democracy and wage-slavery are incompatible. The unions do. The Supreme Court does not know that every worker must feel his moral position weakened by the fact that his death or disability may thrust his wife or daughter or sister into a position where she has to make a choice between slow starvation and moral degradation. The unions do. The Supreme Court does not know that the degradation of one class of labor is a menace to all labor. The unions do. . . .*[74] (Italics added.)

The liberals were arguing a legitimate labor issue that the Supreme Court refused to understand. Significantly, the Supreme Court rendered this minimum-wage decision more than two years after the Nineteenth Amendment, giving women the vote, had been ratified. Thus, the constitutional civil rights of women were not seen as including the right to economic equity, as would be the case forty-one years later in the Civil Rights Act of 1964. However, in 1923 while the economic rights of women *(which meant white women)* were better understood by the unions than by the Supreme Court, it did not follow that either the liberals, or the Supreme Court, or the unions understood the significance of economic exploitation of black labor as exemplified in the Phillips County situation. On *economic* issues the Arkansas case demonstrated that black labor had no recourse to relief through the courts. Thus, it did not matter to the *New Republic* that the brutal exploitation of black farm labor was also an issue in which the federal power would not intervene because of states' rights. In the early 1920s, organized labor was consumed in fighting for its own legitimacy against the onslaughts of an antilabor federal power. Thus, the first line of defense for American labor was the economic security of white workers (male and female), *not* black workers (male or female). In this racial, economic, and political context, the new frontier for civil rights achievement was (white) women's suffrage; for blacks it was *Moore* v. *Dempsey,* a Supreme Court decision that said, in effect, that the rescue of twelve blacks from sure death by execution, and sixty-seven others from long-term incarceration, was more than sufficient in the way of civil rights reinforcements for black survival—even in the face of supereconomic exploitation of black labor. But the economic implications of the Phillips County defense were not lost on the NAACP. *Moore* v. *Dempsey* made it crystal clear in 1923 that the NAACP's civil rights program required some semblance of a *black economic component.*

In the same issue of *The Crisis* in which the legal outcome of the Arkansas case was summarized, the NAACP argued the challenging economic problem of "Cooperation and the Negro," an article written by none other than the young E. Franklin Frazier, the upcoming star sociologist. He wrote: "The recent impulse given to Cooperation through organization on the part of the farmers and the removal of legal barriers is sure to affect the Negro. . . . The types of cooperation in which the Negro will possibly engage are: Cooperative Marketing Societies; Cooperative Supply Associations; and Credit Unions."[75] Frazier then described sporadic attempts at cooperative marketing that were taking place among black farmers. Obviously, the Phillips County project was one such effort, but just how extensive these efforts were remains difficult to determine. Recorded economic history of these developments is scant. Moreover, the extralegal opposition to cooperative enterprises were not remedied by the courts. In Phillips County legal counsel obtained by black farmers were driven out of the county with threats of violence.[76] Unlike the small pecuniary significance of Chinese hand laundries in the surrounding economy of San Francisco, attempts by black farmers and agricultural workers to organize cooperative marketing enterprises represented a clear threat to the entire foundation of the southern agricultural system, based as it was on naked racial exploitation.

In describing this situation, Frazier, then only twenty-nine, had to be temperate and circumspect in considering the harsh facts of life in southern agriculture. Realistically, he had to point out that most of the black efforts at cooperative farm marketing were ephemeral and had usually failed, adding: "They have failed partly because of the ignorance of the Negro farmer and partly because he, under necessity, has been compelled to sell prematurely. The absence of any organization to bind him to his promises and the economic domination of the white landlord have had a share in these failures." Successful cooperative marketing enterprises among black farmers, Frazier explained, could be achieved only when they were placed on a cash basis in renting and were organized under intelligent leaders according to their mode of production and area of the market. More than that, areas organized as logical units would naturally contain black and white farmers. Thus, the question arose: Would black farmers enter these societies on an equal basis with white members: *"It should be the duty of rural [black] leaders to see that Negro farmers enter on equal terms or form independent societies. In an organization where the size of one's holdings do not count in voting power the accident of color would certainly have no place. Certain social consequences implied in these organizations merit more consideration than can be given them here."*[77] (Italics not in the original.)

In any event, Frazier had to admit that in many rural communities in the South, the black consumer was absolutely powerless to free himself from the white landlord commissary. Moreover, white landlords resented teaching scientific methods of agriculture to black tenants, and white neighbors would not tolerate the organization of a system to eliminate their stores. Nevertheless, wrote Frazier, a great step toward economic emancipation could be achieved through developing cooperative enterprises in many centers of the black population. And he concluded that if the black people, especially the farmers, were to avail themselves of the economic and social advantages of cooperation, in spite of the large percentage of illiteracy, the following program was necessary:

1. To disseminate among them literature on the principles of co-operative enterprises;
2. To get rural leaders, after studying the mode of production and the market of different communities, to organize consumers and farmers; and
3. To liberate the Negro from the present share-crop system of farming.

Thus, despite the NAACP's non-economic liberalism, the association could not avoid making a gesture in recognizing black economics as a crucial issue. But it was only a gesture. In summarizing his arguments in favor of a concerted approach to the "principles of cooperative enterprises," Frazier shifted the responsibility for such an effort to Booker T. Washington's Tuskegee Institute's annual Farmers' Conference in Alabama. Although Washington had been dead for more than seven years, the annual Tuskegee conferences of black farmers and agricultural workers that Washington had originated were still being held in 1922. Regarding these farmers' meetings, Frazier wrote:

It is to be regretted that such an occasion as the recent Farmers' conference at Tuskegee Institute was not utilized to disseminate among Negro farmers the principles of economic cooperation. The incidental references to spontaneous attempts at cooperative marketing by the farmers attending the conference not only should have invited an investigation of the progress of the movement among Negro farmers, but should have been the basis of a discussion of the problems connected with this new era in agriculture. With the proper information and encouragement the farmers could have used their initial undertakings as the foundation for further efforts.[78]

However, this article by Frazier was symptomatic of the NAACP's shirking its leadership responsibilities and obligations on the black economic front. No doubt the brutal suppression of the Progressive Farmers and Household Union in Arkansas, and the tortuous legal battle that followed, were cause for restraint. Thus, with the old anti-NAACP nemesis, Booker T. Washington, no longer on the scene, it was more expedient to shift the responsibility for black economic leadership onto Washington's heirs at Tuskegee Institute. What exactly transpired at the Tuskegee conference to which Frazier referred is difficult to determine. But a clue to the 1922 program can be gleaned from a report of the Tuskegee Farmers' Conference of 1920 that was published in an issue of *Survey* the same year. *Survey*, a liberal social welfare publication of the time, reported that:

For the first time in the history of the South, prominent white and colored leaders brought together in a great public meeting attended by twenty-five hundred prosperous Negroes at Tuskegee Institute, Alabama, last week, spoke out with coolness and tolerance on such matters as lynching, the proper accommodations of Negroes on railroads and other public carriers, the establishment of impartial justice in the courts and proper handling of colored prisoners, the reasons for considering the ballot as a means of protecting men's families and property, equitable distribution of public school funds and other problems on which there has been serious diversion of opinion. The discussion of the Negro in industry was second only to the frank discussion by both white and colored leaders of the problems of race relations, race improvement and race cooperation.[79]

Three thousand blacks attended this Tuskegee conference, including the white governor of North Carolina, T. W. Bickett, who "spoke out emphatically against lynching." Dr. Robert R. Moton, Booker T. Washington's successor as principal at Tuskegee, emphasized that: "All that the colored people of this country want is a square deal in all human activities, that Negroes do not ask for special privileges, but they ask for impartial justice." No doubt the Arkansas massacre was considered, but the white-black economic conflict, if discussed, was not reported. Thus, five years after the death of Washington, Tuskegee Institute spokesmen were beginning to sound just like the NAACP. So it was predictable that at the annual NAACP convention held in Kansas City in August 1923, five months after the appearance of Frazier's discussion of black economic cooperation, the issue occupied no prominent place on the convention agenda. True to its founding ideology, the NAACP would sidestep the leadership imperatives involving black economic organization. The NAACP would perpetuate a flawed civil rights policy that from the 1920s to the 1980s, would mar its effectiveness, haunt its future, and compromise its legitimacy. But this was not all.

During the NAACP's four-year legal campaign on behalf of the Arkansas victims, the American Fund for Public Service, which seven years later would donate funds to the NAACP's joint committee to help finance the legal costs of preparing the *School Segregation Cases,* had already established a special fund for the benefit of the labor movement. The gift, of an unknown amount, was made by Charles Garland to the American Fund for Public Service with the proviso that the income and principal be spent for the "benefit of the American labor movement." A statement issued by the Fund's trustees declared: "The American Fund for Public Service, Inc., in its support of labor education shall favor those organizations and institutions which instill into the workers the knowledge and the qualities which will fit them for carrying on the struggle for the emancipation of their class in every sphere."[80]

Amid the concerted antilabor onslaught that disrupted the nation, these were indeed noble prolabor ideals. But there is no record that these labor education funds found their way into the hands of black farmers whose economic struggle had generated the racial strife and legal struggle leading to *Moore* v. *Dempsey.* The dismal plight of black workers and farmers represented an even more serious threat to the sanctity of the labor movement than attacks by the enemies of labor. Yet when black workers and farmers attempted to help their own cause they got no help from either organized labor or the liberal or socialist friends of labor.

Controversy arose over the labor politics of the American Fund for Public Service. In 1923 the Workers' Education Bureau, a subsidiary of the American Federation of Labor (AFL), under the leadership of Samuel Gompers, applied for a subvention from the American Fund for Public Service and was turned down. Gompers responded by vilifying the Garland Fund and its trustees. The *New Republic* responded to Gompers's attack by asserting: "From the Gompers standpoint, there is only one way for a worker or an 'intellectual' to promote the interests of American labor; and that is to swear loyalty to the A.F. of L. and support without question the policy of its management." The American Fund for Public Service responded by declaring: "We do not see our way clear to financing any enterprise except those definitely committed to a radical program of the character indicated. . . ." in Charles Garland's original purpose.[81] But what would constitute a "radical" labor educational effort? In the eyes of the American Fund for Public Service, seemingly nothing at all in the struggles of black labor was radical enough for its support. It is a well-known fact that the American Federation of Labor neither respected nor cared about the plight of the unskilled, semiskilled industrial, or agricultural workers—even white ones. If this was the AFL attitude toward unskilled white workers, it requires no extended imagination to understand what the AFL thought about black unskilled industrial or agricultural workers. Because the American Federation of Labor was interested only in the economic status of white workers involved in craft unions made up of highly skilled labor, it became a victim of the antilabor crusade in the 1920s. "Between 1920 and 1924 membership in all labor organizations declined from 5,110,000 to 3,600,000, and the A.F.L.'s membership dropped from 4,078,000 to 2,866,000."[82] The American Federation of Labor harbored little or no sympathy for black workers, considering them a cheap labor source and a strike-breaking threat to white labor in general. The liberal *New Republic's* rebuttal of Samuel Gompers's craft-union conservatism was principled, but as in the response it gave to the labor economics issue behind *Moore* v. *Dempsey*, the magazine refrained from getting to the core of the AFL's racial policies.

The other major liberal organ, *The Nation,* had gone further two years earlier in 1921 by publishing an "Open Letter to the Governor of Arkansas,"[83] spelling out both the transgressions of constitutional rights of black defendants in the Phillips County case with regard to due process, and the "iniquities of the peonage system," i.e., the basic economics issue that spawned the racial shoot-out. The publisher-owner of *The Nation* was Oswald Garrison Villard, an influential member of the NAACP executive board. There is no record of a response from the Arkansas governor. Also, of course, the NAACP pursued no policy of encouraging blacks themselves to organize in the struggle against economic exploitation. Any organized support of black labor either from the NAACP itself, or from the white liberals of the Garland Fund, was less than verbal. Like the liberals among the Supreme Court justices, and those on the *New Republic* and *The Nation,* the social uplift ideals of white liberals vis-à-vis blacks did not encompass the realities of black economic conditions on the industrial, agricultural, or professional labor fronts. Consumed with the conviction that constitutional legalities represented the magic formula for the transformation of civil rights guarantees into racial equality in all spheres of life, white liberals refused to assume that real democracy was possible without strong economic reinforcements. Hence, the celebration of *Moore* v. *Dempsey.* Forced to do so out of circumstances of the "slow wheels of justice," the NAACP had no choice but to allow a legal victory for liberalism to conceal a black defeat in the economics of self-advancement.

A fable:

> A poor family attempts to build a homestead. Enemy oppositionists attack the family and destroy the homestead. The family retaliates and some of the enemy are killed. The family is arrested by law enforcers and convicted for murder. But "justice" later prevails; the family is freed because of mitigating circumstances. Their lives are spared, but no one is forced to pay for the homestead.

What was even more questionable about the labor–civil rights orientation of the American Fund for Public Service was that some of the executors, such as Roger N. Baldwin, were also active members of the League for Industrial Democracy (LID). The LID was composed of fervent socialist and allied liberal groups whose interests were workers' education, workers' health, workers' cooperative enterprises, consumer cooperatives, workers' housing, etc. Beginning with its founding in 1921, the LID worked to support, popularize, and develop the ideas of economic cooperative enterprises among various ethnic groups. A massive two-volume *Documentary History of the League for Industrial Democracy* was published in 1980. Volume I, 998 pages, records only one scant reference to black workers, and that in connection with the problem of integrating black workers into the southern factory system. In the 1920s the future of blacks in labor unions was, indeed, dim. White workers' opposition was intense, especially in the South. The slow spread of cotton and textile manufacturing was introducing the factory system into the agricultural South, but the southern attitude toward blacks was "Negroes are for heavy labor. Negroes for farming, most certainly, yes. But Negroes in the cotton factories most emphatically, no! The Negro is alright in his place. But let him stay in his place. The Negro is too lazy and shiftless for the factory system." In other words, the implied attitude of the pro-labor, pro-union, socialist-liberal concern for all aspects of black labor was a delicate hands-off approach because the problem was too hot to handle.

Thus, it is not difficult to understand why the NAACP backed off from confronting the black economic issues behind *Moore* v. *Dempsey*. It is even less difficult to understand the liberal logic that motivated the American Fund for Public Service to avoid funding economic education for black workers in favor of funding the NAACP's *School Segregation Cases* as a *priority* in the cause of racial equality seven years later. What was shown was that if the American Federation of Labor's politics was not radical enough, black labor's economic politics was *too* radical. Taking the implied position that racial discrimination against blacks on the *higher education* front had priority over racial discrimination on the *economic* front was a curious inversion of the theory of class roles in the history of radical politics. It would mean in the long run that the degraded economic position of the black minority as a whole would not be touched no matter what civil rights victories would be won on the higher education front. But even this was not all.

There were even more societal, racial, and constitutional spin-offs from *Moore* v. *Dempsey* than civil rights history has so far taken into account. The black group's societal relationship to "other minorities," which would not emerge as a full-blown issue until well after the *Brown* decision, had its first meaningful public exposure as a consequence of *Moore* v. *Dempsey*. With regard to constitutional guarantees of due process and equal protection, by 1923 *Yick Wo* v. *Hopkins* was the oldest retroactive legal precedent available to the lawyers of the American Fund for Public Service when it funded the NAACP's legal initiatives in the area of discrimination in higher education. When the lawyers cited *Yick Wo*, they did not cite *Moore* v. *Dempsey*, which had a constitutional relationship to *Yick Wo* that they would not admit. Moreover, *Moore* v. *Dempsey* had a due process relationship to an earlier case that, for a number of touchy legal and racial reasons, civil rights lawyers relegate to a cautious legal anonymity. That case was *Frank* v. *Mangum* (237 U.S. 309) 1914.

In 1913, Leo M. Frank, a northern Jewish industrialist, was convicted in Atlanta, Georgia, for the murder of a fourteen-year-old white girl who was employed in his pencil factory. As in the Phillips County, Arkansas, murder trial of the blacks six years later, Frank was sentenced to death in a courtroom dominated by a mob bent on a lynching if the court did not convict. During the trial, anti-Semitic sentiment reached an all-time high point in Georgia. Frank's death sentence was later commuted by the governor of Georgia to life imprisonment. As a result, mob rule took over, wrested Frank from prison control, and lynched him by hanging. The murder of the white girl, Mary Phagan, remains to this day an unsolved mystery since the guilt of Leo Frank was never proven. That the leading witness against Frank was a black worker in Frank's factory lent a note of invidious notoriety to what were then perceived as the social, racial, religious, economic relations between blacks and Anglo-Saxon whites; Jews and Protestant whites; and the social relationships of blacks to the intimate ties between Jews and Protestant whites, especially in economics, business, and industry. In his conviction in a Georgia courtroom, Leo Frank was blatantly denied his constitutional rights to due process.

The noted lawyer who argued Leo Frank's appeal before the Supreme Court was Louis Marshall, an eminent authority on constitutional and corporation law, and also a prominent Jewish communal leader, the president and founder of the American Jewish Committee, and intimately associated with a wide range of Jewish civic, philanthropic, labor, and educational affairs. Louis Marshall argued Leo Frank's case on February 25, 1915, and lost. The Court ruled by majority opinion against Frank's appeal petition; it upheld states' rights to the effect that "state process had determined Leo Frank had a fair trial. If the courts of Georgia certified Frank's equity, the Supreme Court required nothing more." Dissenting were Justices Oliver Wendell Holmes and Charles Evans Hughes. Said Justice Holmes: "Mob law does not become due process of law by securing the assent of a terrorized jury. We are not speaking of mere disorder or mere irregularities in procedure, but of a case where the processes of justice are actually subverted. . . ."[84]

Marshall lost the appeal, but the Frank legal problem remained. The due process issue of *Frank* v. *Mangum* surfaced again in the case of *Moore* v. *Dempsey*. Louis Marshall hailed the *Moore* v. *Dempsey* due process victory. The NAACP wrote Marshall thanking him for the *Frank* v. *Mangum* habeas corpus proceedings, which had been used in *Moore* v. *Dempsey*. Marshall replied, in part:

I am in receipt of yours of the 9th instant with enclosed copy of the opinion of the Supreme Court of the United States in Moore v. Dempsey, which is exceedingly gratifying to me, especially in view of the fact that it has given the Supreme Court an opportunity to adopt the principle for which I contended in Frank v. Mangum 237 U.S. 309, and which was advocated in the dissenting opinion rendered in that case by Justices Holmes and Hughes. . . . . The stone that the builders rejected has now become the chief of the corner, I regard it as a great achievement in constitutional law. .   85

The *Moore* v. *Dempsey* verdict later motivated Louis Marshall to join the NAACP as a member of the executive board. Moorfield Storey, then the NAACP's white liberal president, extended a personal invitation for Marshall to join. Apparently, at first Marshall was not avid about accepting. But after thinking it over, he replied on November 30, 1923:

I must apologize for not having answered your kind letter of the 5th instant, in which you have requested me to become one of the directors of the National Association for the Advancement of Colored People. If by accepting the honor I am making amends for my apparent neglect, I shall be very glad to consent to serve. I agree with you that, now that the Ku Klux Klan is sowing the seeds of discord throughout the country, it is the duty of those who believe in the maintenance of America's best traditions to unite in counteracting that evil influence.[86]

In later years, certain Jewish writers cite the period of *Frank* v. *Mangum* and *Moore* v. *Dempsey* (1915–1923) as the time of the bonding of what in later years came to be called the "black-Jewish alliance." For example, one writer's study of this particular minority-group collaboration opens with the observation:

To the casual observer in 1915 there was little similarity between the status of Jews and blacks in America. Jews, mostly immigrant workers from central and eastern Europe, clustered in northern cities. Some had attained wealth and prominence in the years preceding World War I. Blacks, on the other hand, lived predominantly in the rural South and most remained trapped at the bottom of the American social and economic ladder. Yet when Leo Frank, a young Jewish entrepreneur in Atlanta, was lynched in September 1915 by a mob of white southerners, many Jews began to wonder how dissimilar their positions really were.
      After the Frank lynching the leaders of American Jewry and the elite of the Jewish world became acutely conscious of the similarities

and differences between themselves and blacks. While Jews had been involved in black affairs for years before the Frank murder, and since the beginning of the twentieth century had participated vigorously in efforts to change the racial status quo in America, that affair precipitated an upsurge of Jewish interest in blacks. They recognized that both identifiably separate groups were profoundly affected by their marginal status in the society.[87]

The assertion here that Jews "had been involved in black affairs for years before the Frank murder, and since the beginning of the twentieth century" was, of course, an inaccurate generalization because it was not explained just how Jews *as a group* were involved in contrast to certain *individual* Jews being involved like Julius Rosenwald, the millionaire philanthropist, or Joel E. Spingarn, the assimilated white liberal, neither of whom espoused the kind of organizational Jewish communalism Louis Marshall did. Nevertheless, this initial bonding, brought about by the coincidence of two important high court decisions, placed the social position of minority groups within the purview of constitutional interpretation for the first time. After the *Brown* decision, thirty-one years later, the position of blacks versus that of other minorities would be extended to include other distinctive groups, including women, numerically not a minority. Significant, at the time of the emergence of the black-Jewish alliance, the Nineteenth Amendment granting women the vote was ratified; this implied that the civil rights aspect of equal protection had been consummated for women. By "women" was meant white women inasmuch as blacks, male and female, remained effectively disfranchised in the southern states. However, as a civil rights measure, the Nineteenth Amendment did not satisfy the demand for economic equality, which would become an issue in the women's rights movement after 1920. Thus, behind all of the civil rights issues confronted by the Supreme Court or by constitutional amendments of the period loomed the basic, unresolved problem of economic equity. While *Frank* v. *Mangum* and *Moore* v. *Dempsey* juxtaposed the social status of Jews and blacks, neither legal opinion was even remotely concerned with the relative *economic* positions of either blacks or Jews in American society.

The Jewish writer quoted above asserted that the lynching of Leo Frank forced American Jewry to recognize that blacks and Jews, as identifiably separate groups, "were profoundly affected by their marginal status in society." But if in fact some Jews had attained wealth and prominence prior to World War I, then there had to be a qualitative difference in the marginality of blacks and Jews. No doubt, Louis Marshall was more than aware of these differences when he accepted the NAACP's invitation. Marshall, unlike Joel E. Spingarn, chairman of the executive board, was not an assimilated Jew. As founder and president of the American Jewish Committee, Louis Marshall was a strong proponent of Jewish communalism, the maintenance of Jewish group identity and integrity. He was not an "assimilationist" or an "integrationist" in the sense that a number of NAACP leaders, such as Walter White, were integrationist in black terms. He stated at one point that he was not a "Zionist"[88]; another time he declared that he had been unable to convince himself that "the nationalistic movement represented by the Zionists possesses any element of practicability."[89] Yet Marshall was deeply committed to the work of the Jewish Agency, the organization most devoted to developing the Jewish homeland in Palestine. But above all, he was one of the great humanitarians in spirit, a man of broad learning, of manifold accomplishments and personal interests. As an expert in constitutional and corporation law, he possessed a highly disciplined legal mind, profoundly interested in the juridical aspect of the civil liberties of disadvantaged minorities in American society. Thus, his legal outlook coincided with that of the NAACP on questions of constitutional legality. Like the white Protestant liberals who ran the NAACP, his preoccupation with the constitutional implications of the Fourteenth and Fifteenth Amendments compelled him, as a consequence of *Moore* v. *Dempsey*, to identify with the association's civil rights program. On the broad subject of "Discrimination and Bigotry in the U.S.," Marshall wrote and expounded with zeal on questions of law and social morality. Yet with all that, Louis Marshall's membership on the executive board of the NAACP was something of an incongruity. In terms of his own social and intellectual outlook, Marshall's only comparative counterpart on the NAACP executive board was W.E.B. Du Bois, whose own points of view on civil rights would eventually alienate him from the NAACP and force his resignation. Louis Marshall died in 1929, which precluded the possibility that he might have also resigned, if indeed he had not already done so intellectually, before his death. For it was on the essential meaning of the black-Jewish alliance, its racial, political, economic, and cultural implications, that the presence of the leader of a Jewish organization on the NAACP's executive board should be judged.

What little correspondence Marshall carried on with NAACP officials concerned only the fine points of the legal rendering of briefs, lawsuits, and Supreme Court decisions. For example, a number of his

published letters were analyses of the strategies used by plaintiffs in
lawsuits against the Democratic State Committee of Texas, which barred
blacks from voting in Texas primaries. Although the Supreme Court had
ruled in *Nixon* v. *Herndon* that such actions were unconstitutional, the
Texas Democratic Committee proceeded to devise other schemes of barring blacks from voting, in violation of the Fifteenth Amendment. In this
regard, Louis Marshall, unreservedly and consistently upheld and pursued
the legal enforcement of the civil rights of blacks and other minorities
expressed in the Fourteenth and Fifteenth Amendments. Yet Marshall
publicly revealed nothing of what he thought of the NAACP's general
policies beyond the scope of purely legal issues. He had thrown his legal
expertise into collaboration with a civil rights organization whose guiding
philosophy was governed by the social and racial outlook of white Protestant liberals (and sociologists). One of the most prominent among these
white liberals was Joel E. Spingarn. What Marshall, the Jewish com-
munalist, actually thought about Spingarn, the assimilationist, does not
appear in his published papers; there does not appear a single letter
addressed to the chairman of the executive board on those all-important
legal matters such as the Leo Frank case. Significantly, Spingarn's biographer does not reveal that he expressed any interest in the Leo Frank
case.[90] Even more inexplicably, no published record exists of any mutual
exchange of civil rights views between Louis Marshall and W.E.B. Du
Bois. Here was a case of the linking of the two major civil rights organizations then extant, the NAACP and the American Jewish Committee,
each represented by a leadership personality of extraordinary prominence
in the affairs of blacks and Jews, and yet they did not correspond and
exchange views. Something was profoundly amiss here.

The American Jewish Committee was founded in 1906 fundamentally "to prevent the infraction of the civil and religious rights of Jews
in any part of the world," and "to secure for Jews equality of *economic,
social,* and *educational* opportunity."[91] (Italics added.) The list of the
American Jewish Committee's extraordinary accomplishments and the
broad range of its activities is beyond the scope of this limited inquiry;
however, one endeavor should be mentioned because of its relevance to
the issues being argued here: The American Jewish Committee *"has led
in the systematic application of the social sciences to the study of anti-
Semitism and other forms of prejudice."*[92] The truth was (and is) that
the American Jewish Committee and its intellectual adherents pioneered
in ways *never equaled* by their white liberal Protestant allies *in the scientific study of anti-Negro race prejudice.* The NAACP never succeeded

in replicating such a controlled, ongoing, and systematic study of race prejudice in all of its *political, economic, and cultural implications from an American black perspective*. One reason the NAACP could not accomplish this is traceable to the association's programmatic approach to black education in general, and was implicit in the evolution of the *School Segregation Cases*, and in W.E.B. Du Bois's arguments on problems of black education. The irony here was that Du Bois's pioneer investigations in race prejudice and its institutional consequences were neither supported nor encouraged by white liberals, nor emulated by succeeding generations of his Talented Tenth. Du Bois's social science findings have been imitated, but have not been conceptually enlarged upon since 1900 except in a few rare instances. For example, the very crucial area of *the economics of race prejudice is a social science field that has never been thoroughly and systematically investigated in the United States*. In 1913, Du Bois participated in formulating a proposal for President of the United States Woodrow Wilson to appoint a national race commission to "engage in a non-partisan, scientific study of the status of the Negro in the life of the nation, with particular reference to his economic situation." No one in the NAACP understood more thoroughly than Du Bois how vital the underlying economic factor was in any consideration of black civil rights programming. In the evolution of the civil rights movement over succeeding years, race prejudice and economics would be reduced to the problem of "race discrimination" in employment. *Moore* v. *Dempsey* revealed that race prejudice and economics had a deeper significance in the economic culture of American society than the secondary market activity of hiring; the primary factor was (and is) ownership and proprietorship in free-market enterprises. In 1913, Woodrow Wilson, because of what he described as the adverse anti-Negro sentiments of senators from the South and elsewhere, backed off from and refused to give his approval to a national race commission.[93]

It was the crucial disparity between the economic status of blacks and Jews that qualified the meaning of any alleged social significance of the black-Jewish alliance. The American Jewish Committee's founding for, among other purposes, securing for Jews "equality of economic opportunity," implied that American Jews did not already have such equality in 1906. America was not Russia, Poland or Spain, where Jews had a history of being *de facto* barred from participation in certain economic areas. If American Jews did not possess such equality of economic opportunity, then Moses Frank, Leo Frank's uncle, would not have had the opportunity to establish the National Pencil Company in Atlanta,

Georgia, in 1907. Moses Frank offered Leo Frank the position of su-
perintendent in this factory. This Jewish-sponsored business activity took
place in Atlanta, the "Heart of Dixie," the scene in 1906 of one of the
most shameful and bloody race riots ever to occur in the post-Reconstruction South. However, at that moment, where was the southern Anglo-
Saxon Protestant anti-Semitism? It was assuredly not operative against
Jewish economic initiative. But where *was* it operative? Leo Frank had
married into a prominent, well-established Atlanta Jewish family. "The
Jews of the South," wrote one author, "even into the 1940's, were a
single proprietary and self-employed class of retail merchants, peddlers,
traveling salesmen, brokers, agents, and manufacturers. There was a small
professional class and almost no 'intellectuals.' "[94] Leo Frank married
into this class. Thus, as far back in American economic history as the
early nineteenth century and beyond, American Jews had been highly
visible in proprietary and entrepreneurial economic activity. A study
published in 1924 detailed the participation of the Jews in laying the
"economic foundations of America," pointing out that "the Jew has
truly made himself part and parcel of American life. He is inextricably
connected with its very warp and woof. . . ."[95]

     Thus, how could Jewish "marginality" in American economics be
claimed? And with reference to the black-Jewish alliance, how could
"black marginality" and "Jewish marginality" be two sides of the coin
of racial prejudice and/or bigotry flipped in the American game of social
ostracism and persecution? Unlike the American Jewish Committee's aim
to secure equality of economic opportunity for Jews, the NAACP pursued
a policy of noneconomic liberalism whereby blacks had to *forswear any
program for economic advancement* as a matter of civil rights principle.
For themselves, with or without the blessings of democratic citizenship,
of American freedom from European class-ridden persecution, Louis
Marshall and other founders of the American Jewish Committee would
have denigrated such a restriction for Jewish immigrants as an absurd
insult. For all of its barbaric racism, uncivilized bigotry, and systematic
genocide practiced on the Indians, the United States offered any immigrant with a white skin open access to the pursuit of whatever economic
ambitions the immigrant aspired to and was willing to work for. Jewish
immigrants were no exception. Only the paternalistic outlook of white
liberals, their disregard for black intelligence, made them oblivious to
the black perception of the economic advantages European immigrants
were offered in the expanding American capitalist economy. One of the
causative factors in the cultivation of the ideology of Du Bois's black

Talented Tenth was crude materialism. In describing the social mentality of the blacks in the NAACP's leadership, Du Bois wrote:

> In the organization whose leadership I shared at the time, I found few colleagues who envisaged the situation as I did. The bulk of my colleagues saw no essential change in the world. It was the same world with the problems to be attacked by the same methods as before the war. All we needed to do was to continue to attack lynching, to bring more cases before the courts and to insist upon our full citizenship rights. They recoiled from any consideration of the economic plight of the world or any change in the organization of industry.
>
> My colored colleagues especially were deeply American, with the old theory of individualism, with a desire to be rich or at least well-to-do, with suspicion of organized labor and labor programs; with a horror of racial segregation. My white colleagues were still liberals and philanthropists. They wanted to help the Negroes, as they wanted to help the weak and disadvantaged of all classes in America. They realized poignantly the dislocation of industry, the present economic problems; but most of them still believed in the basic rightness of industry as at present organized. . . .[96]

However, Du Bois's Talented Tenth most clearly perceived that every white European immigrant came to the United States for the freedom to earn a livelihood and, if possible, to get rich.

In 1920 the reaction of the NAACP's radical wing against the leadership's conformist submission to the civil rights legalities of white liberalism was so embittered that the situation after World War I was summed up as the "Crisis in Negro Leadership." This "crisis" was engendered by the intense ideological friction between what was then called the leadership "left" and the leadership "center." One participant declared: "That the fight is between the Center and the Left Wing we agree." The center forces for the most part supported the NAACP orientation, claiming that:

> The Center has these points in its favor: The spirit of equality running through American legislation; the capacity of the nation to respond to high ideals in national crises; the active support of many fair minded whites in their fight to secure justice for the Negro; a splendid record of achievements in the race's behalf in securing legal nullification of the Grandfather Clause, residential segregation and peonage. It has successfully opposed segregation of Negroes in Federal employment and discrimination in civil service . . . it has carried on strong propa-

ganda against lynching and mob violence; it has given strong support
to the race in industry, education, religion, politics, and culture, and
had built up effective organizations in all parts of the country, to promote
the welfare of the race and the nation.

The left-wing spokesman responded: "We do not intend to engage
in satire. . . . It is elementary that the spirit of equality runs through
neither the letter nor the administration of American law. And this is true
in every part of America, and especially so where most Negroes reside
—in the South." Moreover, said the left wing, surely the center apologists
are aware of:

The Jim Crow car laws, the disfranchisement in the South, the laws
against intermarriage in 37 states, and THE UNEQUAL ADMINIS-
TRATION OF THOSE LAWS in all the different states when applied
to the Negro. Does [the center] not also know that the Sumner Civil
Rights Law was declared unconstitutional years ago, while the Thirteenth, Fourteenth and Fifteenth Amendments have been dead letters
since 1876? So far, from the spirit of equality running through American
legislation, we find the spirit of inequality, injustice and prejudiced
administration running through the entire warp and woof and fabric of
American law.[97]

The left wing challenged "any number of the Center to show a single instance in which this [American] nation has responded to high ideals
in a national crisis." Consequently, said the left wing, the blacks
are rejecting the center and the "Right Wing, led by Du Bois and [the
NAACP] . . . ," creating a "Crisis in Negro Leadership." But the left
wing, of course, could not have known in 1920 that this "crisis" would
continue as an endemic condition for the next sixty years. The social
mentality of the center leadership, so aptly described by Du Bois, would
become a self-perpetuating outlook which could not change or adapt.
Trapped in the net of liberal civil rights legalities, unable to maneuver
within the economic restrictions imposed by free-enterprise capitalism
(which the liberals upheld) against racial democracy, the center was
immobilized.

But the "Crisis in Negro Leadership" did not fail to inspire an
organized attempt at a leadership alternative. In 1924 three hundred black
delegates from sixty-three organizations met in Chicago to formulate the
elements of a new program. The aim was to create a "representative

national council to be known as the Negro Sanhedrin." Explaining the motivation behind this move, Alain Locke, a Howard University professor of philosophy, wrote:

Negro leadership and organizations, unfortunately, have not been an exception to the rule that groups under adverse social pressure, with imperative need for unity, seem always to exhibit, nevertheless, a superabundance of factionalism. They are thus unwilling collaborators with their oppressors. An effort to coordinate the organized agencies of race work is therefore a noteworthy symptom of progressive thought and action. Such an effort has been successfully made in an all-race conference of Negro organizations at Chicago out of which has come . . . the Negro Sanhedrin.[98]

That little has been written about this Negro Sanhedrin testifies to the intrinsically flawed programmatic tradition of the black civil rights movement. If the political, economic, and cultural approaches of the movement have been functionally flawed since the movement's inception, *so has the historiography of the civil rights movement also been flawed to such a degree that contemporary critics and chroniclers can only pretend to understand how, where, when, or why the civil rights movement failed to achieve this or that end, and by whom.*

In this sense the Marcus Garvey Back to Africa movement (1919–1925) has been poorly interpreted by historians, especially since this black nationalist movement occurred at the same time the black-Jewish alliance was in bloom. The ideological rhetoric of the Garvey movement aside, what held it together for its brief life was its *economic program,* the crucial aspect of black survival that civil rights leaders would not touch, thus forfeiting the support of the "masses." Since the American black masses had neither the possibility, nor the genuine desire, nor the means to return to the African continent, the Back to Africa rhetoric served only to cover up that Marcus Garvey and his chief lieutenants were simply incompetent managers of the money gleaned from the earnings of unsophisticated black workers. American Jewish fund raising for the Zionist "Back to Palestine" endeavor would never have been guilty of the gross, almost criminal mismanagement of hard-earned funds as was the Garvey movement's "Black Zionism." The money Garvey and his chief lieutenants collected from black workers was a form of "primitive capital accumulation," which demonstrated above all that lower-class blacks *could* be organized if given an effective leadership. Such a rate of capital accumulation by blacks could not have been achieved in the West Indies or in any other geographical sector of the black world that was industrially backward and poverty-stricken or under colonial administration like Garvey's Jamaica. These funds were squandered in such a negligent and vainglorious fashion that the Garvey movement dug its own grave. However, Garvey's personal contacts with Jewish spokesmen during his meteoric sojourn in the United States is worth a concise study in its own right, since much of what is reported about Garvey and the Jews is conjectural or unverified.

Another offshoot from the black-Jewish alliance period that deserves more interpretive investigation is the Negro Sanhedrin movement, which *might* have been inspired by people *outside* the NAACP rather than by those Du Bois described as his "colored colleagues."

The Negro Sanhedrin was an attempt by dissident black lower-middle-class professionals, educators, and a smattering of "intellectuals," to establish a leadership organization patterned after the ancient Jewish Sanhedrin. The Jewish Sanhedrin was the supreme rabbinic court in Jerusalem during the Second Commonwealth era. The term was a Hebraization of the Greek *synedrion,* meaning "assembly." At first, sanhedrins were trial courts judging criminal violations of Jewish law. Later, they evolved into bodies governing either strictly religious or wholly secular areas of civil authority. Still later, the Great Sanhedrin was instituted to interpret Jewish law, and also to enact decrees for religious observances, laws for universal education, for the rights of women, and for the administration of trial courts. The Great Sanhedrin was reportedly dissolved in 66 C.E., four years before the destruction of Jerusalem by the Romans in 70 C.E. During the early sixteenth century, a number of rabbis attempted to reinstitute the Sanhedrin after the expulsion of the Jews from Spain. In 1806, Napoleon attempted to organize a sanhedrin to "decide the conduct of laws for the French Jews." A "Paris sanhedrin" met in 1807 and "agreed that the principles of a liberal, secular state were compatible with the laws of the Jewish religion." With the establishment of Israel in 1948, some Orthodox Jews wanted to revive the Great Sanhedrin, but were opposed by "many groups within Orthodoxy and outside its ranks."[99]

The "Crisis in Negro Leadership" motivated Kelly Miller, the well-known dean of Howard University, to issue a call for a conference. The conference was conceived to establish a Negro sanhedrin. Miller stated in the call that:

The Sanhedrin was a Jewish assembly or council. The Great Sanhedrin was composed of seventy-one members, and sat at Jerusalem with supreme jurisdiction. The Lesser Sanhedrin, composed of twenty-three members, sat in each province with local and limited jurisdiction.

The use of the term in its present application grew out of the circumstances surrounding the Jews in Europe under the domination of Napoleon Bonaparte. The Emperor found that the relation between the Jew and the Gentile world was a fruitful source of antagonism, persecution and race friction. In order to compose this troublesome situation he called a Sanhedrin of all of the Jews under his jurisdiction, which assembled upon his invitation and perfected a scheme of working relationship between the two groups that has operated with more or less success and satisfaction down to the present time. Similarity of situation suggests a like conference of the Negro peoples of the United States today under the ancient designation. The Greater Sanhedrin with nation-wide function, and the Lesser Sanhedrin limited to city and local jurisdiction, also suggest a happy comparison.[100]

The intimate facts behind this organizational attempt are not generally known, except that the guiding spirit was Dean Kelly Miller in collaboration with others, such as Alain Locke. In reporting on the initial proceedings of the Negro Sanhedrin, Locke wrote "The Negro Speaks for Himself," which carried the clear message that blacks needed a leadership organization free from the ideological and financial control of liberals, in contrast to the NAACP. In other words, it was a bold attempt at black leadership autonomy that harked back to the original aims of the Afro-American League during the 1890s. Thus, in implied opposition to the organizational approach of the NAACP, the Negro Sanhedrin had to propose a different program that, if somewhat duplicating the NAACP program, had to pose a contrasting set of priorities. Alain Locke described the Sanhedrin as *"an agency that may speak for the Negro on his own interests, problems, and activities in a much more authoritative and unpartisan way than any that has hitherto existed. . . .The published program may be regarded as representing what the Negro wants and wants unanimously at this stage of the race situation."* Moreover, "we are a group of ten million in the midst of ten times that number. The welfare of one must not be sought at the expense of ten. While we can surrender no rights, inalienable and conferred, all of our policies must be patriotic and considerate of the whole equation of which we constitute but a factor." The following were recommended as cardinal principles and the salient points of attack:

Public Health: The imperative need of improving and safeguarding the physical stamina of the race, and of enlisting the full cooperation of Negro organizations in public health campaigns.

Education: The necessity for equal school facilities based upon equal per capita distribution of all public funds available for the maintenance of public school education; for a large share of administrative participation by the Negro in the control of his education, public and private; and for all forms of higher education—professional, technical, and liberal, to produce, in the public interest, intelligent leadership for the race.

Labor: Protesting the exploitation of Negro labor in the conflict between capital and organized labor as unfair and detrimental, and declaring for the principle of the standard wage and the recognition of Negro workers in fields where Negro labor is organized; endorsing community assistance to Negro workers, especially recent migrants, in industrial centers; and recommending organized financial relief to the Negro farmer for the alleviation of direct and indirect peonage and the increasing of farm productivity.

Politics: Maintaining the necessity of political activity as necessary to race welfare, and the protection of the right of franchise and all civil and common citizenship rights as the only safeguards of democratic institutions.

Women's Movements: The endorsement of equal rights and equal participation of women as necessary and more favorable to the advance of the race situation.

Public Utterance: The necessity of reserving the right of protest and of maintaining free and untrammeled public utterance as the chief resource against discrimination and injustice.

Inter-Racial Relations: The stressing of the increasing need for local effort and community adjustments because of the recent changes of distribution in the Negro population; endorsement of the system of inter-racial committees, and the recommendation of the extension of this plan to communities where they have not yet been established; recommending that Negro organizations assume financial responsibility for their fair share in the support of civil and social projects.

Alain Locke explained that at the Sanhedrin conference, "there was determination to transform the liabilities of the enforced separatism of [the] race life into group assets of spiritual, social and cultural autonomy. Overtopping the sense of limited resources and restricted opportunity, there was a prevailing practical optimism that in these aspects the assets of the Negro, well administered, were equal to the task of meeting the

heavy liabilities of his status in this democracy and the grave responsibilities of maintaining a life necessarily separate in some respects from
that of the older elements in the population." And, "in the words of the
sponsor of the movement":

> This conference is destined to inaugurate on the large scale a new phase
> of race life which has been developing for a decade or so with the
> improved economic and educational condition of the Negro
> population—namely the period of self-help and organized cooperation
> toward discharging our share of responsibility, direction, and effort in
> the solution of the race situation in America.

In support of this declaration by the chief sponsor, Kelly Miller, the
conference unanimously recommended the following six points of internal
policy:

> *Business:* The concentrated development of business enterprises, co-
> operative and private, toward the development of financial prosperity
> and economic independence; and, as necessary to the success of these,
> the supplementing of industrial and technical training with professional
> business training.
> *Fraternal Organizations:* The importance of combining, through
> inter-fraternity organizations, the considerable and growing resources
> of the Negro fraternal and benevolent associations for the financing of
> social projects in education, business and community betterment.
> *Public Press:* The importance of maintaining a race press higher
> than the average standards and freer from the commitments of parti-
> sanship and the policy of commercialized news, in the interests of greater
> race unity and more dignified and representative race publicity.
> *Race Movements:* The desirability of building up cooperative con-
> tacts between the Negro peoples of America, the West Indies, and
> Africa, and of a development, both as a responsibility and opportunity,
> of the movement for help in the economic, educational and spiritual
> redemption of Africa.
> *Negro Youth:* The development of organized cooperation between
> the organizations of the Negro college youth and the whole body of
> race organizations, and the endorsement of the constructive program of
> the committee of the Negro fraternities and sororities.
> *Cultural Program:* The desirability of promoting and extending
> journalistic and educational contacts between all bodies of Negro peo-
> ples, of promoting scientifically collected information about the history
> and achievements of the race, and of stressing the study of African

civilizations and of the capitalizing of the undoubted spiritual assets of
the race in all forms of the arts as perhaps the most immediately available
and promising path to world service and recognition.

As a definitive new plan for social action in terms of leadership
principles, the Negro Sanhedrin was, in its general outlines, exactly what
American blacks sorely needed. It was a graphic illustration that the
National Association for the Advancement of Colored People was a pale
and insufficient organization for reasons other than those imposed by the
restrictive paternalism of white liberals. Proof that a serious "Crisis in
Negro Leadership" existed was the attendance at the Sanhedrin by representatives from six small and regionally based civil rights groups, plus
delegates from the NAACP itself. However, the Negro Sanhedrin struggled for a few years and finally collapsed without having gotten beyond
the planning stage. Why such a necessary and timely organization failed
has never been seriously explored. A. Philip Randolph's *Messenger* magazine, the main source of the radical left-wing attack on the black leadership center of the NAACP (and Du Bois), was soft in its editorial
criticism of the Negro Sanhedrin meeting:

> The All Race Conference has come and gone. All in all, it was a success,
> that is, from the point of view of stressing, in a big way, the idea of
> race unity, cooperation. For this, all credit to Dean Miller. If it serves
> as a sort of clearing house through which the varied Negro agencies of
> all types and interests can be mobilized when crises arise in the life of
> the race, then it will become of great constructive value to the Negro.
> If not, it is useless, for the program of the Permanent Findings Com-
> mittee is a mere repetition of the old programs of the past. The con-
> ference made its first big, grave mistake in not setting aside a day for
> the discussion of Negro labor, just as it had a day for the Negro church,
> business, education, etc. Withal, the press, church, fraternal, civil and
> economic movements of the race should co-operate with Dean Miller
> with a view to making the Sanhedrin a truly useful instrument of race
> thought and action. Our own thought is that the Dean needs more of
> the dynamic, aggressive, militant spirit of the young Negro, armed with
> scientific, economic and historical knowledge in the councils of the
> body than he does of the hesitant, cautious elder statesmen.[101]

What was meant here by "scientific, economic and historical knowledge" was "scientific socialism." Radical left-wing blacks in the 1920s
believed that black people could not solve the race question under cap

italist free-enterprise arrangements. But if economic democracy for blacks was unrealizable under capitalist free enterprise, the NAACP, despite its leadership flaws, was committed and destined to pursue racial equality in all spheres within the capitalist system. Through all the bitter but spirited debates, tribulations, attacks, adjustments, defeats, and minor victories, the NAACP would survive, intact, through the turbulent Twenties' economic prosperity only to witness the catastrophic collapse of capitalist free enterprise in the 1930s.

In the meantime, the fruits of the black-Jewish alliance would be programmatically edible, if not fully tree-ripened in the natural sweetness of a more thorough intergroup understanding. Thus, the failed attempt to establish the Negro Sanhedrin, while an intriguing statement to have been made in the light of the black-Jewish alliance, added a new dimension of thought but not of civil rights practice. A curious outcome was that not a single Jewish leader went on public record with an opinion about the significance of this attempted organizational departure from the leadership program the Jews were supporting. Jewish writers would claim that Jewish involvement in black causes was an obligation that transcended mere *noblesse oblige*. The "bonds of empathy" were based on a conviction that "the Jews had a peculiar ability to understand the problems of blacks. That understanding sprang from a similarity of experience, from a shared history of discrimination and oppression." But if Jewish leaders understood all of this so empathetically, they did not understand that they might have been supporting the wrong kind of black leadership. Their attachment to the tenets of white liberalism prompted a strong support of black civil rights causes because a fight for the civil rights of blacks was ultimately a long-range civil rights defense of the status of Jews in American society. They did not, however, take into account that the vast majority of blacks were not loyal to the leadership of the NAACP. Jewish leaders, well known for a very acute sense of social perception, did not ask why? Even when disaffection with the NAACP leadership showed up in an attempt to establish a Negro sanhedrin, Jewish philanthropy apparently evinced little if any interest. *This lack of interest was all the more significant because the Negro Sanhedrin, as a leadership expression, was copied directly out of the Jewish experience in history*. On paper, item for item, the proposed program of the Negro Sanhedrin was a blueprint for a duplication of the Jewish organizational approach to every political, economic, cultural, and educational aspect of Jewish life, both in the United States and abroad. Of course, it was true that centuries of experience had taught the Jews the crucial lesson that without strong, purposeful internal organization there was little chance for survival in a hostile world. To this very day, American blacks have not learned that lesson.

By the 1920s, Jews in America did not need a great sanhedrin revisited; they had already imbibed such leadership principles to the extent that they became instinctual, an artifact of the group psychology, an ethnic trait, a religious dictum, an *a priori* educational rule of thumb. Thus, Jewish success in the United States was almost ordained. No doubt, the reincarnation of the Great Sanhedrin "in blackface" in 1924 must have appeared to Jewish leaders as an unseemly black leadership aberration that did not merit their philanthropy. But some American black social thinkers were persevering to bring order out of the social chaos and disintegration that followed the mass migrations of blacks from the South to the urban North. In response to the "Crisis in Negro Leadership" brought about and exacerbated by this mass population shift, came the idea of the Negro Sanhedrin. All else having failed, it appeared that blacks needed a "council of the elders" patterned after the tradition of the Great Sanhedrin, revealing the strong black Christian experience of combining religious conviction with secular social goals. Given the strong conviction by the organizers of the Negro Sanhedrin that their program was timely and relevant, why did they fail to implement the leadership plan? Fundamentally because of a lack of financial resources coupled with a failure of collective will on the part of the organizers. Why did not the NAACP attempt to incorporate the Sanhedrin program in the spirit of collaboration? Basically because, on paper, the Negro Sanhedrin was implicitly a pronounced deviation from the noneconomic liberalism to which the NAACP was irrevocably committed. More than that, white liberalism was conditioned not to sanction any effort by blacks toward autonomous self-determination. Yet if scholarly Jews in the black civil rights movement were aware of the significance of the Negro Sanhedrin as an attempted reincarnation of leadership-council principles from the Jewish past, they did not reveal themselves. On the other hand, the radical black left wing was critical of the Sanhedrin conference and equally dubious about its prospects, claiming that both "the Sanhedrin and the U.N.I.A. [meaning the Garvey movement] are almost equally valueless and visionary, although we are a little inclined to award to the Dean [Kelly Miller] for keeping his feet nearer to the ground of reality."[102] Later, Kelly Miller summed up his views on the meaning of the Negro Sanhedrin: "After all, the Negro Sanhedrin is an influence rather than an organization. Principles must be laid down and programs outlined.

The plans must be constructive, remedial, ameliorative and inspirational. It will fail of its essential aim if it does not hold up an ideal to Negro youth which is worth striving for, and, if need, worth dying for." However, from the 1920s to the 1980s no such constructive, remedial, or inspirational black leadership organization was ever put together. Successive generations of black youth would be born, evolve, hesitate, ponder, persevere, and flounder into the blind anonymity of deferred dreams and frustrated hopes—without a functional philosophy for coping with American realities.

Whatever the real intensity, the quality of rapport Jews had for the black cause, such sentiments would not erase the consciousness that Jews had all the economic privileges incident to being white. The black-Jewish encounter was one of the consequences of the World War I mass migrations of blacks to the North. By 1920 Jewish immigrants in large numbers had preceded this black in-migration into some of these cities by at least thirty years. New York City, of course, was something of an exception in that there was a pre-Civil War history of blacks in New York. The full range of the black-Jewish encounter in labor, politics, civil rights, economics, and culture has not been fully explored for the period 1915 –1935, the time span in which the black-Jewish alliance was nominally operative. Immigrant Jews, especially those from Russia and other Slavic countries, brought with them an intimate experience of anti-Semitic persecution. What they saw in the United States was a reenactment of the infamous pogroms of Russia now perpetrated against the blacks. To many of these East European Jews, the American blacks became the "Jews" of the United States, the native American analogy to the victims of the Russian White Hundred, the "organized anti-Semitic shock troops" of the Russian czars. After the East St. Louis race riot of 1917, in which scores of blacks were killed, the Jewish-language press called East St. Louis "Kishinev," the name of the Russian town in which over fifty Jews were killed in 1903.[103]

Similar to the interest shown by Jewish leaders in black civil rights, Jewish critics and writers would acclaim black accomplishments on the cultural front. This cultural response was of course typical of the white liberal press in general, especially in New York, where the bulk of the Jewish population lived. Between the end of World War I and 1930, blacks had arrived on the cultural scene as personifications of a "new Negro vogue." Thus, the black *arrivistes* could not escape the attention of the Jewish press, inasmuch as the black "New Negro" vogue impacted strongly on the artistic, literary, theatrical, musical, and entertainment fields. During this period, liberal (and not so liberal) magazines and newspapers were full of critical and laudatory reportage on the unique impact of blacks on the musical, theatrical, dance, literary, and entertainment culture of the United States. To this day, American "culture" studies have not seriously examined the critical significance of this phe nomenon. Sadly, to this day, black intellectuals, educators, and scholars themselves have not fully accomplished this review. Latter-day Jewish writers cite the Jewish reaction to the phenomenon of the Twenties known as the Harlem Renaissance. Jewish magazines believed that "Jews were able to serve as cultural bridges between the white and black world because they understood both. As whites, they moved with greater freedom in elite circles than blacks, but as members of a marginal group with a history of oppression, they better understood the tensions, anxieties, and moods of American Negroes. They firmly held that Jews and blacks drew their inspiration and values from the same sources. The Old Testament origin of the black spirituals and the biblical themes dramatized in *The Green Pastures* only confirmed their faith in the existence of a close bond between the two peoples. Historic parallels of segregation and discrimination strengthened this bond. Without being facetious or naïve, the magazines sincerely declared that Jews, more than any other group, could and did empathize with black Americans."

Thus the Jews, similar to the entire white liberal cultural *avant-garde* of the 1920s, paid homage to black jazz music, dance, literature, blues, theaters, and entertainment, to dramatic representations and graphic arts displays. In most respects the Jewish aesthetic response to the black artistic ferment was the same as the general white liberal response, but from a different ethnic perception. The general response was that the artistic gifts of the blacks were "raw and elemental"; the original Negro jazz was "puerile," "shapeless and chaotic." It was left to Jewish musicians and composers to polish up this pristine black music and render it sophisticated enough for presentation to the general public. This interpretive function was a reflection of the role that Jews "sought to make themselves the interpreter of the Negro to American society":

> In a subtle and indirect manner they used the themes of black suffering, black achievements, and black cultural life as a vehicle to explore the meaning of their own experiences in America.[104]

But during the same period of the black cultural "coming-of-age," Jews were also intensely involved in every branch of the creative arts and striving for recognition. In fact, by 1923 American Jews had achieved domination of the theater as a corporate institution. In an article titled "The Jew in the Theater," *The Nation* magazine declared:

> During the season now drawing to a close something around 2000 actors have been engaged in the various legitimate productions in the New York theater. Of these about 10 percent have been Jews. The task of artistic direction has been in the hands of about twenty-five professional stage directors, of whom less than one-third are Jews. The original American plays produced would run to something more than sixty, of which about 40 percent were written by Jews. The plays eventually produced were brought onto the stages of theaters considerably more than half of which are either owned or controlled by Jews. And when after a New York run these plays sought for booking on the road this was secured from organizations which were practically 100 percent Jew.

The article then declared that if the above figures were made into a diagram, the curve would run through "actor, director, author, owner, national booking agent," beginning at 10 percent and rising toward 100 percent, which would indicate, according to *The Nation*, a "comparative neglect on the part of the Jew of the artistic in favor of the commercial factors of the theater." *The Nation* then posed a question: "Do these figures, admitting they are approximately true, give a faithful picture of the contribution of the Jew to the New York theater? Answer: They do not." In explanation of this conclusion, *The Nation* observed that "the American theater has during the last generation moved out of a state of personal management and control into a state of corporate management and control. . . ." However:

> In the process of change from the old individual to the new corporate organization the Jew has been an active agent. Indeed he has practically dominated the change and he dominates the corporate institution created as a result.[105]

Aside from the tantalizing question of the quota system by which WASPs were constantly accused by Jews of limiting the scope of Jewish participation in this or that field of intellectual endeavor, it is interesting that this assessment of Jewish participation in the theater was published in one of the most liberal of liberal publications. The owner and publisher of *The Nation* was Oswald Garrison Villard, who was on the NAACP executive board. The associate editors included two prominent Jews (there

were, of course, no blacks), hence this assessment of the corporate power
of Jews in the American theater could not be interpreted as anti-Semitism.
What was pointed out here was merely a fact of corporate life among the
competing cultural groups and economic groups in the 1920s. Thus, *where
was the anti-Semitism*? More than that, as a consequence of the black-
Jewish alliance, just where did the black minority group fit in the context
of corporate power control in the cultural fields among the dominant and
subordinate racial, ethnic, or cultural groups? What was called the "New
Negro" vogue was, in fact, accompanied by a "new Jewish" vogue in
the cultural arts. If these two minority-group vogues brought about sympathetic celebration and collaboration via the black-Jewish alliance, it
also ended with cultural group competition, imitation, exploitation, subordination, and patronization coupled with creative suppression and negation. The blacks contributed the raw aesthetic ingredients of the cultural
vogue in music, dance, theater, and entertainment, but ended up on the
short end of the material rewards, having no economic and corporate
control over the vogue, while exercising an autonomously creative function that was next to negligible.

However, the less than favorable and amicable outcome of the black-
Jewish alliance was not the fault of Jewish leadership involvement in the
black civil rights cause, nor the fault of WASP leadership, nor that of
black leadership taken singly. The fault lay in the philosophy of liberalism
itself, in its application to the emergent twentieth-century problems of
blacks as the largest nonwhite racial minority in the United States. All
three leaderships—WASP, Jewish, and black—retroactively share a por-
tion of the blame for the failures of black leadership under the circumstances that prevailed. A black leader such as Du Bois could see and
understand that the social outlook of his "colored colleagues" was not
of the quality that the contingencies of the black situation demanded. A
Jewish communal leader of the Louis Marshall type would never have
tolerated other Jews with the kind of social outlook described by Du Bois
to occupy a commanding position over the Jewish group as a whole. It
goes without saying that Jews, in general, harbored no animus against
the "desire to be rich or at least well-to-do," but the Jewish rich were
never guilty of the unforgivable sin of ignoring the economic, political,
and cultural interests of poorer Jews while gaining wealth. The organizers
of the Negro Sanhedrin were mindful that for blacks to run after riches
(as scarce as they were for blacks) to the extent of forgetting the dire
poverty, both material and spiritual, of the great majority of blacks was
not an example of representative leadership. They stated in their platform:

"The welfare of one must not be sought at the expense of ten." But if Louis Marshall, in joining the NAACP executive board, became aware of this philosophical contrast between black and Jewish group leadership, he did not publicly reveal it. No one as perceptive as Louis Marshall could been unaware of this seriously flawed approach to the citizenship advancement of numerically the most economically disadvantaged minority in American society. But Marshall was not on record as having said so. This discrepancy made Louis Marshall's membership on the NAACP board a minority-group incongruity. In fact, because of the liberally inflated social significance attached to it, the black-Jewish alliance, could—from a political, economic, and cultural point of view—be characterized as a functional misalliance, laudable in its liberal humanitarianism, but misapplied in terms of the pursuit of a genuine goal of racial democracy in a plural society.

In connection with his membership on the NAACP executive board, Marshall's essentially humanitarian role had a dual character. On the one hand, he was an accomplished constitutional lawyer; on the other, he was the leader of a minority-group civil rights organization of a very special kind—the American Jewish Committee. He was inspired to complement the program of the NAACP by virtue of the legal ax he had to grind with the Supreme Court over constitutional principles when the Court turned down his appeal arguments in favor of Leo Frank. When *Moore* v. *Dempsey* vindicated Marshall's previous point of constitutional law in the Leo Frank appeal, he was moved to join hands with the NAACP legal corps in what he perceived as a joint effort in the fight for social justice according to constitutional legalities. If a concordance of views on constitutional principles symbolized a black-Jewish alliance on one plane of an interminority agreement, on other levels it was flawed and lacked validity because of the juxtaposition of two dissimilar sets of minority-group values. Jews in America, despite regional and geographical differences, were molded by one religio-philosophical tradition—Judaism. This tradition afforded them what one writer described as the "book of books which contained for them the totality of human wisdom." It gave them "their powers of endurance and their tenacity in the face of all obstacles." The tenets of Judaism inculcated in Jews the individualism, the self-discipline, the love of learning, the intellectual ideals, and the necessary austerity of life-style and all the other mental attributes necessary for the achievement of success in all aspects of social endeavor—economic, political, cultural, and educational. Due to the circumstances of their particular brand of Americanization, blacks, as a group, were woefully lacking in black versions of these salient Jewish attributes. It necessarily followed that Jewish approaches to such problems as civil rights, education, social equality, politics, economics, culture, philanthropy, group cooperation, etc., were dissimilar. The spokesman for the American Jewish Committee, Louis Marshall himself personified the dissimilarities.

Marshall's personal views on public and private education vis-à-vis Jews were at variance with those of the NAACP vis-à-vis blacks. This was especially clear after 1930 when the Garland Fund–NAACP joint committee began to formulate the legal strategies for the *School Segregation Cases*. Marshall, of course, died in 1929. But in 1926, he spelled out his views on the relationship of Jewish education per se to public and private schools operated by Christians. It appeared that the Adelphi Academy, a private school, had raised objections to enrolling Jewish students. In response to a letter of inquiry on the matter, Marshall wrote:

> I must confess that I cannot get unduly excited over it so long as the school is not a public but a private school. I participated actively in the fight against the Oregon Compulsory Public School Law in the Supreme Court of the United States, for the purpose of establishing the principle that parents should have the right to control of the education of their children and to send them to private schools as well as to public schools. It would seem to follow from that principle that if any persons desire to establish private schools for the purpose of educating the children of their own religious faith or of their own social class, they would have the right to do so. . . .[106]

Marshall argued that the founders of and contributors to the Adelphi Academy were Christians and conducted Christian services at the opening of classes. The Adelphi Academy had made it plain that it preferred students of its "own religious beliefs" but had allowed a few Jewish children to enter the academy. However, the academy had lately raised the question whether *any* Jews should be admitted, or if a quota should be established. Marshall continued:

> . . . What right have we, as Jews, to criticize them for acting in accordance with their convictions and their prejudices in that regard? What right would they have to criticize us as Jews if we established private schools and indicated that we did not consider it desirable that non-Jews should attend?

Marshall explained that he believed in public schools, since the great mass of American children get their education in such schools. But those who desired parochial schools did so because of their conviction that religious education was all-important. "It is only since people have become materially prosperous and socially ambitious that this question of admission or exclusion from private schools has arisen," he said. He admitted that he had sent his own children to a special school that was neither fully private nor fully public, because "the public schools in our neighborhood were not as good as they should be." Personally, Marshall said, he had no objection to the suggestion offered by the administrators of the Adelphi Academy that "Jews establish private schools of their own if they do not desire to have their children educated in public schools, and if they find difficulty in having their children admitted into private schools maintained by Christians. I certainly would not send my children to a private school conducted, as most of them are, as adjuncts to churches and in which the Christian doctrines are openly taught. . . ." Marshall further observed that he did not consider that Jews, in general, were having any serious difficulty in seeking adequate education for their children, and ended by saying: "I have no patience with Jews who are willing to subject their children to such anti-Jewish or non-Jewish influences merely because they would like to have their children enrolled as pupils in a school which may give more or less social prestige."[107]

If one took Louis Marshall's discourse on public and private education and substituted the words "race" for "Jews," or "black" for "Jewish," his views coincided almost completely with those of W.E.B. Du Bois on the then current arguments about the institutional direction of black public education. Du Bois would often pose the question, Do blacks need separate schools? And his leadership colleagues would answer emphatically in the negative. The one difference, however, was that blacks were also Christians—of the same religion as their American oppressors. Thus, the religious factor was one of the qualifying elements in the marginality of Jews and blacks within the context of the indigenous American plurality. For Jews in America, religion was the badge of a plural honor within the Judeo-Christian tradition; for blacks, race was the stain of social ostracism and the marginality of the outcast, and Christianity did little to soften the contempt of their white co-religionists. For the Jews, as reflected in Marshall's views on education, discrimination in public or private education would never have led to a Supreme Court decision in which the price for the alleged benefits of "integrated education'' was relinquishing control of the education of their own children. For the Louis Marshalls, "self-segregation" posed none of the horrors of the negation of group self-esteem as was the case with the Walter Whites of the NAACP. Jews understood the real value of separate (Jewish) institutions of all kinds; the NAACP leaders, generally, did not.

On the higher-education front, Louis Marshall carried on a lengthy correspondence on the public and parochial missions of the Jewish Theological Seminary of New York—a separate institution of higher education. At one point, he discussed the necessity of merging Hebrew Union College and the Jewish Theological Seminary. He wrote that "while the latter leans to orthodoxy and conservatism, to a greater degree than the former, that fact should not stand in the way of placing both under one management. The fundamental purposes of both are identical. They are intended to foster Jewish learning and scholarship, to teach the principles of Judaism, to promote the study of the Bible and the Talmud, and the great literature which they have called into being."[108] Lest anyone concluded that this institutional interest in specifically Jewish education was rigidly parochial, or that it favored the doctrines of Orthodox Judaism over those of Reform Judaism, or vice versa, Marshall explained that through this merger, "the best Jewish scholarship could then be enlisted toward the advancement of our cause. The interests of all classes of Jews throughout the country would be concentrated."[109] Although various Orthodox and Reform factions argued, conflicted, and competed over what *style* of Jewish institution of higher education was more appropriate in the United States, there was broad consensus favoring the *need* for Jewish institutions of higher education. Marshall himself was opposed to the existence of Yeshiva College because it had hopes of becoming a secular Jewish university which Marshall believed was inappropriate to the cause of Judaism in America. Yet he believed that "Judaism and Americanism can go hand in hand." Thus, despite his differences with other Jewish spokesmen on the problems of Jewish higher education, his was the transcendent voice that monitored and moderated the debate in the broad community over Jewish separatism and parochialism, as opposed to Jewish integration in higher education.

But while the program of the American Jewish Committee aimed to secure equality of educational opportunity for Jews, charges of discrimination against Jews in higher education, similar to charges of economic discrimination, were overexaggerated in the liberal consensus. Jews increasingly had the options of having the intellectual fruits of higher education both ways—separate or parochial, or universal and integrated.

Leo Frank, born in Texas in 1884, graduated from Cornell University in 1902 as a mechanical engineer and immediately received employment in what appeared to be two different White Anglo-Saxon Protestant companies who needed his expertise. In the non-Jewish institutions of higher education, it was reported in 1924 that at least twenty-one Jews held professorships and chairs in the following universities: Chicago, California, Michigan, Detroit, Wisconsin, Clark, George Washington, Harvard, City College, Columbia, Yale, and Smith College. Sixteen others had made distinguished careers in medicine, psychology, and anthropology within or without the universities. Eleven Jews had attained high posts in the legal profession, including the Supreme Court. W.E.B. Du Bois, a product of Fisk, Harvard, and the University of Berlin, truly a pioneer social scientist in the United States, would never in his entire life be recognized with even a visiting professorship in a major white university or small college. Thus, the comparative marginality of blacks and Jews had no real functional relevance to the racial, religious, or minority-group realities in twentieth-century America. As for Du Bois he had a genuine cause for complaint against the oppressive consequences of racial and social discrimination, but he remained strong, proud, creative, and intellectually durable to the age of ninety-five.

In 1922, in a spirited response to a judge in Iowa who had made public utterances of an anti-Semitic tone, casting aspersions on the dealings of a Jewish firm involved in a lawsuit, Marshall wrote: "I had never dreamed it would be possible for a judge of an American court to refer in this manner either to the faith or to the race of any person whose acts were the subject of judicial consideration." The Iowa judge had laced his written opinion on the lawsuit with references like "the Jewish gentleman," "the race of Israel," "the three Yids." Marshall agreed that the firms in question had been involved in gross stock frauds, but that the judge's remarks had the intent of doing injury to the collective character of all Jews. "When you cast obloquy on the name of the Jew and upon the race of Israel, have you considered whom it hits?," Marshall wrote:

In many of the States of the Union there are distinguished Jews upon the bench who are the sons of the ancient race to which I belong. You undoubtedly know some of them by reputation. Let me enumerate them. Mr. Justice Brandeis of the Supreme Court of the United States; Judges Mack, Alschuler and Mayer of the United States Circuit Court; Judge Sloss of the Supreme Court of California; Judge Cardozo of the Court of Appeals of New York, one of the greatest jurists of our time; Mr.

Justice Greenbaum of the Appellate Division of this State; Judge Marcus of Buffalo; Judges Lewis, May and Lazansky of Brooklyn; Judges Lehman, Bijur, Erlanger, Newburger, Platzek, Wasservogel, of the Supreme Court of New York County; Judges Rosalsky and Koenig of the Court of General Sessions; Judge Horace Stern of Philadelphia, and his eminent and venerable predecessor, Judge Mayer Sulzberger of the same city, one of the greatest jurists of America, are but a few of the judicial officers in courts of superior and supreme jurisdiction. There are thousands of Jewish lawyers throughout the country who enjoy in their several communities the respect and confidence of their fellow-citizens and who rejoice to render gratuitous service for the public welfare. Some of the leading physicians of the United States belong to this race. The man who is at the head of the Rockefeller Foundation, Dr. Flexner, is a Jew, as are several of the leading members of his staff. In works of philanthropy we have men like Julius Rosenwald of Chicago, Felix M. Warburg of New York, the late Jacob H. Schiff, and thousands of others, who give regardless of race or creed and who deem it to be their duty as men and as human beings to help wherever there is need.[110]

In the United States, anti-Semitism had little to do with race but was an inherited superstition and, like all superstitions, had its origins in ancient religious beliefs, frictions, and competitions based on fundamentalist doctrines. Within the social, cultural, and religious contexts of the American democratic imperative, anti-Semitism (similar to anti-Catholicism) would not escape being part of the intellectual and folk baggage of European immigration, but it would be modulated and kept at bay by the American democratic imperative. There would be no anti-Jewish pogroms in the United States, but there would be lynchings and massacres of blacks motivated by racist beliefs. In the face of these racial assaults, blacks could retaliate only on pain of death.

In retaliation against anti-Semitic discrimination in public and social life—in hotels and public places, for example—American Jews had the options of building and owning such accommodations both for their own separate social life and for the use of non-Jews. In the fight against the anti-Semitic *Protocols of the Learned Elders of Zion* campaign instigated by Henry Ford, the automobile magnate, Jews responded with well-publicized rebuttals plus a boycott against the purchase of Ford cars. Thus, it was in this spirit that Louis Marshall could respond to a letter written to him by a Jewish "Discouraged Scholar," a "Bachelor of Philosophy and a Doctor of Jurisprudence," who was employed in the actuarial department of a major insurance company at a hundred dollars a week (in 1929!). Marshall's correspondent's letter was a litany of complaints about discrimination and a list of grievances growing out of his failures since graduating from the University of Chicago with a law degree even *before* he became an American citizen. Marshall replied as follows:

> Apparently you entertain a grievance against society, because you are under the impression that you have not been appreciated and because you have not been able to proceed on a path strewn with roses. From my point of view, the fact that you have had to encounter difficulties had afforded you an opportunity, if properly regarded, to strengthen your character. The vast majority of the men who in this country have attained any position have been those who have struggled with the odds apparently against them and have overcome what appeared to be insurmountable difficulties. Compared with many you have been very fortunate in that you have had educational advantages both in Europe and in the United States far greater than come to the lot of the average man.
>
> You complain of poverty, of having worked while at college in fifteen different capacities—from a cab driver to a tutor in mathematics. What of it! Others have had a similar experience. When my father came to this country, unable to speak the language, friendless and alone, he worked on a farm. He worked as a track-hand in railroad construction. He was a porter. He was a peddler. He tried his hand at a dozen different occupations. Yet he always rejoiced in his work and gained the respect of all who knew him. I never went to college for a single day. As a boy I did hard manual labor, which is now prohibited under the Child Labor Laws; salted hides and calfskins, and did other work of a kind which to most people would be unattractive. But I gloried in it and was happy that I was enabled to help my parents in their days of struggle. It was always my endeavor to idealize whatever I did. I never sat down and wept.[111]

Marshall apologized to his beseecher of fraternal sympathy for the brutal frankness of his response. He told the would-be lawyer that his attitude toward life was indefensible for a man of his age with the advantages he had had. Marshall advised him that if adding and subtracting figures had no meaning for him, then the contempt he had for his work with the insurance company indicated a flabbiness of mind and an absence of backbone. He advised him that it was his own fault if he did not understand at the very outset that his law degree from the University of

Chicago did not permit him to practice law unless he had gained American citizenship, and that it was deplorable that he had not stated what efforts he had made to become a bona fide citizen. Marshall explained that the ranks of the legal profession were overcrowded and that even if he were admitted to the bar association, it might be wise to hang on to the actuarial job he had by improving his status and making himself indispensable to the insurance company. Do not imagine, Marshall told him, that because you are a Jew that promotion is impossible, and finally advised him:

> There undoubtedly are cases where Jews are discriminated against, but there is too much whining on this subject by those who are seeking a royal road to wealth and advancement. There is only one sure road to success—that of hard work and perseverance, which is paved with optimism. . . .

"Cut out the tears," Marshall advised. "If you have in mind to pursue the legal profession, read law, read history, familiarize yourself with American institutions and with those subjects which enter into one's daily life, and you will have no cause for regret."[112]

On the issues of anti-Semitic discrimination in economics, the professions, politics, education, employment, etc., a Louis Marshall could speak to Jews in this fashion and he would be taken seriously and with due respect, if not with full agreement. A W.E.B. Du Bois responding to blacks, especially to the black elite—the Talented Tenth—in this spirit, would have been branded an accommodationist Uncle Tom, after the image of Booker T. Washington. Whatever Louis Marshall might have thought inwardly about the black-Jewish alliance, or the black-Jewish connection symbolized in the legalities of *Frank* v. *Mangum* and *Moore* v. *Dempsey*, he and his Jewish communicants understood well enough that anti-Semitic discrimination in the United States bore little essential comparison with racial discrimination and segregation.

On a number of occasions, Marshall had to criticize evidences of anti-Negro sentiments among Jews. In 1907 the Educational Alliance, a Jewish group, held a debate on the question of black voting rights in the southern states. The Educational Alliance, taking the position that the disfranchisement of blacks was justified, had invited Louis Marshall to participate in the debate. Marshall responded:

> I must say that I am rather surprised at the subject chosen—"Resolved, that the South would be justified in disenfranchising the Negro"—and

to learn that the Educational Alliance is to argue the affirmative of the proposition. It seems incredible to me, that a body of Jews who have just emerged from virtual slavery, and who are seeking in this country the privilege of voting, which was withheld from them in the land in which their ancestors have lived, should for a moment consider the propriety of arguing in favor of the disfranchisement of any citizen of this country.[113]

This incident raises some doubt as to just how extensive and deeply felt was the Jewish support of the social, racial, and political implications of the black-Jewish alliance. There was no way of gauging just where within the broad Jewish consensus lay this fount of empathy for the plight of blacks. On the other hand, there was no way of gauging to what extent blacks reciprocated with empathy toward Jews. Jewish writers, much more so than black writers, have investigated these intergroup issues. The Jewish motivation for supporting black civil rights causes to a more public degree than any other disadvantaged minority has been explained by Jewish writers, one of whom asserts:

Participation in the struggle for black rights may have been useful to Jews in several other ways. Jews were constantly in search of allies. They occupied, according to their own perceptions, a precarious position in the United States and Europe. Their constant anxiety, while not always conscious, made them believe that they must solidify and ensure their lot in America by building bridges to liberals with power, like those established white Protestants who made up much of the NAACP leadership. The Jews undoubtedly realized that blacks possessed no power, but it was not among them that they were casting about for friends. They were attempting to forge an alliance with the Moorfield Storeys, the Oswald Garrison Villards, the Jane Addams, the Mary White Ovingtons. While they met many of these same people in other progressive reform activities, the black civil rights movement was one more place where they could try to solidify their relations with powerful liberal whites.[114]

While this adequately explains the motivations of Jews to participate in black civil rights causes, it only partially explains the response of the black leadership to this Jewish involvement. If the black-Jewish alliance signaled any such thing as a socially functional interminority-group collaboration, black civil rights leaders did not attempt to profit from this alliance by emulating the techniques American Jews used to elevate their group status in American society. What nullified the potential of this alliance was the gross imbalance between the comparative *economic* status of blacks and Jews. Even if a "community of interests" existed between blacks and Jews, even if anti-Semitism and anti-Negro racism were viewed as factors legitimizing a black-Jewish alliance, the organized Jewish methods of overcoming civil rights disabilities were not being emulated by the black leadership. Although black migrations were disruptive and made effective black organization difficult during the 1920s, demonstrative efforts should have been made by black leaders. Such efforts were not made because the black leadership had been committed to the civil rights philosophy of noneconomic liberalism even before the black-Jewish alliance. It was precisely over the issue of *economics* (Jewish versus black economics) that the black-Jewish alliance collapsed in 1935 and entered a stage of disintegration leading to the 1960 era with its rise in vocal black anti-Semitism. In 1935 the Harlem racial uprising directed at white economic exploitation, white shopkeepers, white landlords, and white organized crime was also directed at Jewish shopkeepers, businessmen, and landlords. From the end of World War I to 1930, the NAACP was unwilling to reorient its program to include the all-important issue of economic organization. Yet in 1929 *The Crisis* commented on the meeting of the Sixth National Cooperative Congress, held by the Cooperative League of the United States of America in Waukegan, Illinois. The Cooperative League, said *The Crisis,* is a federation of about 329 of the most progressive consumers' stores, bakeries, restaurants, apartment houses, credit societies, creameries, and various other types of business undertakings:

> The membership of these associations is made up of farmers, big and little, factory workers, miners, railroad men, office employees, professional people of every class who know that they are exploited as consumers and are trying to find a remedy in cooperative organization.

The Cooperative League reported, said *The Crisis,* a total of 155 societies with a membership of 77,826, and annual sales totaling $14,000,000 (not including the figures for credit and insurance societies). Since no blacks were reported to have participated in this congress, *The Crisis* found it necessary to add: "The achievements of co-operation are worthy of the study of those who are considering an economic program for the Negro."[115] The NAACP could say this, from a lofty position of civil rights guardianship, and blandly imply that the economics issue was *not* the association's business. Moreover, it was not even the business of the National Urban League, the sister "social uplift" organization of the NAACP, founded in 1911. A product of the social reformism of the "Progressive Era," the National Urban League was established specifically to lend social welfare aid for the adjustment to city life by the newly arrived blacks from the rural and small-town South. In this regard the National Urban League was even more relevant to the basic bread-and-butter needs of disadvantaged blacks than was the NAACP. But influenced (as was the NAACP), by white liberal reformism (and also by white liberal conservatism), the National Urban League was never able to overcome the programmatic limitations of its origins insofar as the purely economic problems of blacks were concerned.[116]

Louis Marshall, the legal ally of the NAACP in its civil rights philosophy, died in 1929. Five years later, Du Bois would resign from the NAACP on the grounds that the association, among its other failures, had not formulated an economic program for blacks. Whether Louis Marshall was aware of Du Bois's growing disaffections within the top echelons of the NAACP is not recorded. But had he lived until the mid-1930s, Marshall would have witnessed the Harlem racial uprising that shattered the idealistic but flimsy premises on which the black-Jewish alliance had rested. The Harlem uprising revealed that the civil rights philosophy based on noneconomic liberalism had borne its own seeds of diminishing returns. Given the remarkable minority-group success of American Jews in economics, politics, culture, education, statesmanship, etc., up to the Thirties, what would Louis Marshall have concluded? No doubt the rise of Hitler in Germany in 1933 would have marked the beginning of a change in his attitude, as it had affected many other Jews in their attitudes toward blacks following the Harlem uprising. But it would not have altered the fact that Jewish support for black civil rights causes, however humanitarian, was similar to the liberalism of the White Anglo-Saxon Protestants, just another version of noneconomic liberalism. Jewish writers have by implication spelled this out, as for example:

> Black Americans needed champions in a hostile society; Jewish Americans, on the other hand, wanted a meaningful role so as to prove themselves to an inhospitable one. Thus, Negro civil rights and philanthropy seemed proper spheres in which Jews could prove themselves, demonstrating their generosity, selflessness, and their importance.[117]

In the same vein, Jewish magazines such as *The American Israelite* and *Opinion* took special pride in that Jews were willing to fight the civil rights battles of blacks:

> Serving as intermediaries for blacks not only grew out of the Jewish heritage and tradition as defined by these magazines but also figured in a general Jewish campaign for a more positive public image. By proving how tolerant, broadminded, and non-ethnocentric Jews were, the magazines hoped that they could dispel many ancient and deep-seated prejudices and stereotypes of Jews.[118]

However, in assuming this role, Jewish leaders reasoned that the defense of black rights was a first line of defense on behalf of the group status of Jews in American society:

> The role of Jews as the special friend of blacks, the Jewish religious precepts which called for social justice and equality, the Jewish history of suffering and oppression, the writers felt all laid the basis for the retention of a distinctly Jewish culture within American society. The problems of American blacks provided an ideal medium by which Jewish leaders could emphasize and expound upon the relevance and virtues of the culture, within the American context.[119]

In addition, the Jewish defense of black rights would ultimately redound to the enhancement of the Jewish image by combating anti-Jewish stereotypes:

> Jews also used the crusade for black equality as a forum to dispel certain prevalent stereotypes about Jews. For centuries Jews had been plagued by the image of the greedy, clannish miser, always out for himself. In the movement for black legal rights, Jews could prove themselves generous, selfless, tolerant, and humanitarian. These possibilities begin to explain the large Jewish contribution to the movement to grant equal political and legal rights to blacks. In the final analysis, however, the majority of Jews in the NAACP sincerely believed that their commitment to the crusade sprang from a special sympathy and a unique ability to understand the suffering of America's blacks.[120]

Here, the theme of retaining a "distinctly Jewish culture" within American society through the defense of blacks posed several intriguing questions in the 1920s that were never really investigated or fully interpreted. Jewish culture was essentially a biblical tradition transplanted in the United States after centuries of Roman, Greek, and post-Renaissance European conditioning. Black, or Afro-American culture, which Jews would discover in places like New York City, was distinctly an American group-cultural phenomenon. The black-Jewish commitment on the civil rights front was but one level of group relationships; the cultural encounter was on another social and secular level. Here, the outward, secular contacts between Jewish culture and black culture took place in the creative fields, especially in literature, theater, and music. The implications of this cultural encounter have only been superficially explored.[121] And a Louis Marshall would not prove a very likely source of critical introspection on such intellectual matters as group-cultural functions in the creative arts. Despite the prevalence of the voguish notoriety of such artistic issues during the 1920s, whatever personal interests Marshall might have had in such matters are not revealed in his published papers.

But the main proposition here is that if the motivations of Jewish leaders for supporting black civil rights causes went beyond normal eleemosynary humanitarianism, it also cast an uncomfortable light on the mentality of black civil rights leaders who avidly sought out, pursued, and accepted every dollar proffered by Jewish philanthropy. Those who were powerless to finance their own institutions had to accept every philanthropic dollar freely given:

> The proclivity of Jews to give to charity, the use of Jewish members as contacts with other wealthy Jews, and the recognition on the part of the Association's non-Jewish officials that Jews gave more consistently than non-Jews were best illustrated in 1930 when William Rosenwald offered to donate $1,000 annually for three years to the NAACP, providing that four others agreed to do the same. Depression conditions had severely hurt the Association and officials desperately sought sources of revenue to keep the organization afloat. Walter White informed Jacob Billikopf of the financial straits of the organization and Billikopf put Rosenwald in touch with White. Herbert Lehman, Mary Fels, Felix Warburg, and Harold Guinzburg, publisher of Viking Press, all responded within several months. The only non-Jew to do likewise was Edsel Ford. Several other Jewish donors, stimulated by the Rosenwald offer, agreed to give smaller amounts. Altogether, as a result of the Rosenwald plan, the NAACP secured $16,350 for three of the worst years of the Depression.[122]

But it was mainly Du Bois who, among the NAACP leaders, appreciated that only the strength of Jewish communal resources permitted such a degree of financial support. Although Du Bois often cited the Jewish internal organizational skill, and exhorted the Talented Tenth and the insolvent 90 percent to attempt to emulate the Jews, his pleas fell mostly on deaf ears. Nothing was learned. The Jews, desperate for group recognition as bona fide champions of social justice for all people according to the American democratic creed, could pay money to enhance their own social position. What Jews, a thoroughly practical people, actually saw in the NAACP—its solvent leadership representing a tragically insolvent nonwhite minority group—beyond its moral and legalistic insistence on the rights of blacks is not easily determined. Louis Marshall himself once advised a correspondent about the unmanly hazards of philanthropy. Marshall's correspondent begged to be taken under the great lawyer's guidance and patronage. Marshall replied: "A young man with your training should be ashamed to make such a suggestion. In order to get along in the world one must depend upon himself. To look for a patron is to invite degradation."[123]

As a preeminently constitutional lawyer, Louis Marshall's interest in civil rights covered practically the entire range of discrimination and bigotry against not only blacks but other nonwhite minorities such as the Chinese and Japanese. His intimate tie with the NAACP was premised on the concordance of his own views with those of the NAACP on the fundamental legal questions of the basic rights of citizenship promised by the Constitution. He was in full support of what white liberalism essayed as "social justice." He did, however, entertain differences with certain guiding legal approaches of the NAACP. "Marshall respected the work of the Association, although he often disagreed with its stand. For example, he seriously questioned the constitutionality of the Dyer Anti-Lynching Bill which the NAACP pushed so vigorously in the 1920's," says one writer.[124] But a more complete documentation of all of his differences is not available. Black civil rights and the NAACP represented the legal instrumentalities by which Marshall could salve the bitter gall of defeat he had experienced in the Leo Frank case, *Frank* v. *Mangum*. "There has been perhaps no crime committed in our day that can compare in lawlessness with the lynching of Leo Frank, whom I represented before the Supreme Court of the United States," Marshall wrote in 1922, in the same letter in which he discussed the Dyer Anti-Lynching Bill introduced in Congress that same year. The Dyer bill was passed in the House by a vote of 230–119, but never secured favorable Senate action. The bill initiated the antilynching campaign of the NAACP that continued until 1940 without securing any antilynching legislation.[125] With reference to the lynching of Leo Frank, Marshall declared, "the fact of such a crime against the administration of justice caused me to form the resolution to do whatever it lay in my power to do, to assist in putting an end to so monstrous an iniquity as lynching."[126] Yet Marshall argued against the passage of the Dyer Anti-Lynching Bill. His reasons:

> Great as the evil is, it would not, however, equal that which would follow the usurpation by the Congress of the United States, of the power which it does not possess under the Constitution. An evil precedent is apt to lead to others until the Constitution itself may ultimately be destroyed by methods savoring on anarchy and mob action. Indeed the pursuit of such methods would amount to a lynching of the Constitution.[127]

Marshall defended this position on the premise that "under our dual system of government the police power is lodged in the States and not in the Federal Government." Although lynching was a crime against peace, order, and justice of the state where it is perpetrated, Marshall wrote: "The State has plenary power and jurisdiction to deal with this crime as it has with all infractions of the safety and welfare of its inhabitants. Congress cannot legislate as to matters which lie within the domain of the criminal jurisdiction of the States." Although his correspondent insisted that the power to deal with lynching is conferred by the clause in the Fourteenth Amendment that forbids any state to deny to any person within its jurisdiction equal protection of the laws, Marshall contended that:

> The murderers who took Frank from the prison where he had been lodged by the State, though punishable by the State whose sovereignty they had contemned, had committed no act forbidden by the Constitution of the United States.[128]

Thus, although Marshall had argued Leo Frank's appeal on the grounds that his conviction had been rendered in a state courtroom atmosphere which had been a travesty of the due process clause in the trial procedure, the federal power, according to Marshall, lacked jurisdiction over this type of violation of the right to equal protection inplied in the Fourteenth Amendment. According to Marshall's legal reasoning, the state of Georgia had the state sovereignty *right* to declare Leo Frank guilty even though Marshall opposed that verdict. For Marshall, Frank's appeal to the Supreme Court was a request that the federal court countermand a verdict rendered by state sovereignty exercised through a state court. However, for the Dyer Anti-Lynching Bill, Marshall reasoned that the legislation "does not undertake to proceed *against* the State, as such, assuming that it were possible. It is directed against public officers of the State who do not prevent lynching and against localities where lynching has occurred. It seeks to include in its condemnation those who conspire, combine or confederate with such officers on the theory, you suggest, that they are conspiring with the State itself to deny equal protection of the laws. This theory of bringing the case within the law of conspiracies is in my judgment far-fetched and reasons in a vicious circle, and if indulged [in] would open the door to all manner of perversions of 'the equal protection clause' "[129]

Marshall admitted the plausibility of arguing that when an officer of the state in the performance of his duties deliberately by *affirmative action* deprives a person of equal protection, such an act may be made punishable because it is that of an agent of the state, which can act only through agents. On the same theory, he said, "it may be conceded that if the Warden of the State Prison of Georgia had turned over Frank to the mob mad for his blood, or had at their instance, knowing its errand, admitted it into the prison such affirmative act could have been made a penal offense by Congress. . . .

> It is, however, a different matter to legislate with respect to non-action, to a mere failure or neglect to do what a court or jury might say, could or should have been done to prevent the consummation of the lawless purpose of the mob which lynched one who had aroused its passions. In my opinion the test lies in differentiating between affirmative action or non-action or failure to act.[130]

As a constitutional lawyer, Louis Marshall was indeed a most unbending "liberal constructionist." His legal brief for Leo Frank's appeal did not prevent either the "affirmative action" or the "non-action" on the part of the Georgia prison authorities who allowed Frank to be taken from the prison by a mob and lynched. This was the same mob that had negated Frank's due process rights when he was convicted in the state courtroom. Yet Marshall could reason, in his own "vicious circle," that Leo Frank's constitutional rights to due process had been violated during the trial, and that the victim's rights to equal protection had been (or might have been) violated when he was lynched, but that the actual lynching was *not* a violation of his Fourteenth Amendment rights because it was not an "act forbidden by the Constitution of the United States or which constituted an infraction of its sovereignty."[131] Thus, Louis Marshall had to wait for *Moore* v. *Dempsey* in 1923 to receive both his legal vindication and justification for arguing on behalf of Leo Frank's due process, which did not prevent the victim's fate because of the negation of equal protection. Such were the ambiguities of the embattled Fourteenth Amendment; such was represented the substantive hollowness of liberalism and its jurisprudence. The entire legal rationale of the NAACP hung on the assumption that the Fourteenth Amendment guaranteed equal protection in support of equal citizenship in all spheres—political, economic, and social—and was also enforceable by the federal power. However, Louis Marshall, as champion of the civil rights of the disadvantaged, said no.[132]

With respect to Louis Marshall's stalwart humanitarianism, it might be said that he did not really know the South of 1915 for what it really was. In one constitutional sense, he was prophetically right about the Dyer Anti-Lynching Bill. Despite the accumulated sentiments that gained ground up to World War II in favor of antilynching legislation, no such legislation ever got through the United States Senate.[133] On this question, the legitimacy of states' rights prevailed throughout. On the other hand, Marshall's strict liberal constructionism was also an indication of a legalistic blind spot in his perceptions of racial and minority-group realities and imperatives. On the lynching menace, Marshall would not yield to the more liberal (and equitable) construction that "expands the meaning of the statute to meet cases which are clearly within the spirit or reason of the law, or within the evil which it was designed to remedy, provided such an interpretation is not inconsistent with the language used." From 1885 to 1914, a tabulated total of 2,732 individuals was lynched in the United States, most of whom were black males. Everyone knew that even this was a conservative estimate. For 1915 Tuskegee Institute said the total lynched was fifty-two; the *Chicago Tribune* said fifty-four; *The Crisis* said seventy-four, of whom sixty-nine were black males, five were white men, and four were black women. In 1910 two Italians were lynched in Florida. The Italian government protested until it was found that the victims were naturalized citizens. *The Crisis* sardonically commented: "The inalienable right of every free American citizen to be lynched without tiresome investigation and penalties is one which the families of the lately deceased doubtless deeply appreciate."[134] Eleven Italians were lynched in New Orleans in March 1891; an unspecified number were lynched in Hahnville, Louisiana, in 1896. In the latter case, "Italy again became wrathful and demanded that the lynching of Italians cease and that an indemnity be paid to the families of the victims. Italy's claim was based upon the fact that all three men were subjects of King Humbert. The United States government this time paid $6,000 to the relatives of the victims.'' The New Orleans *Times-Democrat* took the position that Italy had no claim to indemnity because other assassin-lynchers of American citizens had not been punished. Questioning whether lynching the Italians had "a race implication" or was "directed against any nationality," the *Times-Democrat* observed:

> We doubt whether the United States would accomplish much if it lectured mobs and told them, "All right. Go on with your lynching, but confine it to natives. Don't interfere with foreigners what ever they do." A foreigner is just as safe in this country as a native, and there is no reason why he should be more so.[135]

When one of the leaders of the mob that lynched the Italians was asked what prompted him to participate, he replied: ". . . The foundation of American institutions is the will of the people. . . . They, in their sovereign might, have the power, if they will, to retake unto themselves the authority which they have delegated whenever they believe such authorities abused."[136]

No, Louis Marshall did not really know the South on the race, minority, and immigrant issue for what it was. Or he could never have sworn to do all in his power to fight against the heinous crime of lynching, and then back off from assigning the Fourteenth Amendment's due process and equal protection clauses as legal methods for combating the crime. Even if only time and the progressive amelioration of racial and minority-group friction would eradicate the crime of lynching, nothing in either constitutional or Judaic law forbade the application of the law toward moral ends. But then again, Marshall's interpretation of the Fourteenth Amendment was, in retrospect, a summation of the intrinsic substance of the amendment. Do the clauses on equal protection and due process *really* vouchsafe equality in every social, political, economic, and cultural condition? Thirty-two years after Marshall declared that the Dyer Anti-Lynching Bill threatened to "open the door to all manner of perversions of '[the] equal protection,' " came the *Brown* decision, which reinterpreted the Fourteenth Amendment in such a way as to embolden the NAACP leaders to believe that the millennium had arrived—full racial equality by way of equal protection was on the near horizon. The black-

Jewish alliance was by then a thing of the fading past, and one wonders if Louis Marshall would have called the *Brown* decision a "perversion."

One cannot say. By the time of the *Brown* decision's interpretation of equal protection, social evolution had wrought unprecedented changes in the temper of American race relations. The 1930s Depression and the New Deal had altered, for all time, the American "quality of life." World War II had brought about another quality of international and intranational relationships. The *Brown* decision's interpretation of equal protection was more a result of the changed social climate in America than any serious reassessment of the *Plessy* doctrine of separate but equal. *Brown* was simply a pragmatic, liberal juridical guilt trip by nine justices whose own honest, personal interpretation of equal protection was no different from Louis Marshall's in 1922. The Supreme Court justices of 1954 had a point of view on constitutional legality and equal protection that was essentially the same as the Supreme Court panel that voted the majority opinion in *Moore* v. *Dempsey*. If it was true, as the *New Republic* charged in 1923, that the Supreme Court did not understand that "democracy and wage-slavery are incompatible," the same was true of the Supreme Court of 1954. Which is to say that if Justice Oliver Wendell Holmes's majority opinion in *Moore* v. *Dempsey* was a due process decision in defense of equitable trial by jury in criminal cases, the decision had nothing to do with, in fact dismissed, the question of equal protection in the all-important area of *economic activity in race relations*. Constitutionally, the Supreme Court of 1954 indirectly inherited this Fourteenth Amendment equal protection rationale from *Moore* v. *Dempsey* without having to admit it as precedent. This omission was abetted by the fact that the Garland Fund–NAACP joint committee in structuring the *School Segregation Cases* cited the precedents of the "elementary structure of Strauder-Buchanan-Nixon-Yick Wo," *leaving out Moore* v. *Dempsey*. Hidden behind the liberal social justice veneer of equal protection in the *Brown* decision was that eliminating legal segregation and discrimination did not guarantee racial equality, racial democracy, or equal protection in group economic activity.

Thus, it was not at all accidental that Louis Marshall, while hailing the due process vindication of his constitutionalism in *Frank* v. *Mangum* and lending his legal expertise in support of the NAACP's civil rights program, is not on record as regretting that in *Moore* v. *Dempsey* (the due process victory notwithstanding) the legal right of the Phillips County, Arkansas, Progressive Farmers and Household Union of America to organize itself never got its day in court. This oversight (if it *was,* indeed, an oversight) was of course attributable to Marshall's rather rigid liberal constitutional constructionism. More than that, Marshall was also a prominent corporation lawyer, which, in the eyes of some liberal critics of the time, was a contradiction. It took a legal mind with a "split personality" to be a legal champion of the rights of underprivileged racial minorities while lending legal aid to corporations. This is, however, the "American" way of responding to the economics of free enterprise, and Louis Marshall said more than once that "Judaism is Americanism." Arthur Brisbane, a prominent publicist of the time, once publicly charged Louis Marshall with aiding and abetting the interests of large corporations. Marshall, as an elected member of the New York State constitutional convention, had voted to defeat a proposed revision of the New York constitution that Brisbane asserted would have proven "an admirable instrument of government, and that its rejection would be a positive misfortune." Marshall answered: "You hold me up to obloquy and ridicule, as a lawyer for corporations, thereby insinuating that I violated my oath of office as a member of the Constitutional Convention, by serving the rich and the prosperous, and ignoring the interests of the general public."[137] Marshall then defended his integrity by declaring that he had fought more corporations than he had defended, and had been instrumental in procuring more decisions adverse to corporations than many other lawyers had achieved. He cited the cases he had argued in the higher courts against the corporate interests of five major railroad companies, and a number of leading trust companies of New York, in all of which he sought to hold both companies and officers responsible for acts charged to be illegal. He complained to Arthur Brisbane:

> It is true that, among my clients, there are corporations, but since most of the business of this country, important and unimportant, including that of newspapers, not excepting your own, is conducted by corporations, you make it exceedingly difficult of a lawyer, and for that matter the great majority of our men of affairs, to earn a livelihood.[138]

All of which emphasized without a doubt that Marshall was on the side of social justice, and, from his strict liberal-constructionist point of view, supported the interests of the general public. However, he gave no indication that he was aware of the liberal-constructionist blind spot in the *Moore* v. *Dempsey* verdict. Seventy-five of the leading industrial corporations in Helena, Arkansas, banded together to mass their corporate weight against a group of defenseless blacks accused of instigating an organized plot to "massacre" whites.

In terms of the Fourteenth Amendment, it was enlightening and significant that the margin of difference between what the NAACP sought and what Louis Marshall thought lay in interpreting the meaning of equal protection. He parted company with the NAACP on the legislative propriety of the Dyer Anti-Lynching Bill. Yet he could write to Jacob Schiff, the wealthy German-Jewish financier, that:

As a result of many years of observation and study, I unhesitatingly say, that life, liberty and property owe their protection in this country to the Constitution as it has been interpreted by the courts, and that the success of those who are belittling the Constitution, who are creating a sentiment of distrust of the courts and of their judges, and who are blindly throwing themselves into the arms of the Socialists, would undermine the magnificent fabric which has made this country what it is. There is absolutely no reason for this demagogical procedure. Never in our history have the rights of the people been more thoroughly protected than they are today. Never has there been greater consideration and solicitude shown to the laborer, to the wage-earner, to the weak and the helpless, and to those who are struggling to better their conditions, than at the present moment. Our statute books are filled with salutary laws having these ends in view, adopted in the usual and ordinary course of legislation and in the natural process of evolution. To have enacted them forty years ago, would have arrested our industrial development. There was then no public policy which required them. Whenever the need arises, our legislatures will not hesitate to respond.[139]

As a liberal constructionist, Marshall was not militant. In his devotion to Americanism, Marshall could forget that the American Constitution was conceived and written by the militants of the Revolutionary era who, by force of arms, separated from the English Crown. His refusal to sanction legislative militancy against the lynch-mob menace was all of a piece with his refusal to sanction open opposition to the Ku Klux Klan. He strenuously objected to other Jewish organizations, like the Order Brith Abraham, which planned "to open a fight against the Ku Klux Klan and purposes to invite various other Jewish fraternal organizations to join in the movement."[140] Although he admitted that the Klan openly espoused a hatred of Jews, Catholics, and Negroes, he felt that it was not the business of Catholics and Jews to be in open opposition to the Klan, but the duty of the Protestant churches. "I cannot understand why the Jews should at once rush into print and accept the idea that there is an issue between them and those of other faiths, and regard themselves as being the objects of the attacks of the Ku Klux Klan.''[141] He said that the principal target of the Klan was the Catholic Church. "But we do not, however, find that the leading Catholics are rushing into print . . . . in a strident and vociferous manner. They exercise much better judgment by dealing with it quietly and not by thrusting themselves into the public eye." In this discussion of the Klan with other Jewish leaders, Marshall did not mention the NAACP or what stand blacks should take on the Klan. Thus, the crucial point here was (the lynching of Leo Frank notwithstanding) that it was blacks whom the Klan was lynching, not Catholics or Jews. Within the broad range of civil rights issues relating to blacks, there were a number of cracks and fissures in the black-Jewish alliance. At no time or place, on no issue or circumstance, in the duration of this alliance, were Jews of any parochial persuasion ever called upon to sacrifice Jewish interests on behalf of civil rights. Yet Louis Marshall, the constitutional theorist, was unsparing in his profound but liberal-constructionist legal analysis of the "Rights of Negroes." He broadened this legal inquiry to include the rights of the Chinese and Japanese, the rights of weak nations such as Haiti, minority rights in such European countries as Poland and Roumania, and the legal aspects of social and political questions of broad character. The scope of his legal-topical range was almost encyclopedic. It was interesting that except for his liberal-constructionist departures from the civil rights positions of the NAACP on antilynching legislation, the Ku Klux Klan, and equal protection, Marshall's legal reasoning complemented the NAACP's evolution toward the *School Segregation Cases*, which were planned after his death.

In his brief on the "Rights of Negroes," Marshall began as early as 1906 to draw some pertinent legal, social, and humanitarian comparisons with other causes. In that year, he advised a southern minister whose religious affiliation was not clear that it would be impossible to get the American government to intervene on behalf of the oppressed and tortured Jews of Russia in view of the prevalence of ugly race riots and almost daily occurrence of "wholesale massacres of Negroes by American citizens." Our government, he said, "which has frequently confessed its powerlessness to prevent these barbarities and atrocities, will cut a sorry figure if it should undertake to criticize Russia for the treatment of its Jews by the Black Hundred, or the Hooligani, or other miscreants, however named."[142] A bloody race riot in Atlanta, Georgia, had taken place in 1906. In 1908, Anna Strunsky, the Russian-Jewish wife of William

English Walling, one of the white liberal founders of the NAACP, declared that "America's treatment of the Negro was even worse than Russia's treatment of its Jewish minority."[143] But at least the Russian Jews could migrate to a better life in America; the blacks had nowhere to escape to. It seemed that the bedrock of Jewish sympathy for the persecuted American blacks came primarily from the Russian Jews.

Following *Frank* v. *Mangum*, Marshall's interest in Negro rights was reflected in his participation in preparing the "Reply Brief for the Plaintiff-In-Error, *Nixon* v. *Herndon*," (1927). The issue was the right to vote under the Fifteenth Amendment. Did this amendment guarantee the right of Texas blacks to vote in that state's white primaries? "The right of a citizen to vote, regardless of race, color or previous condition of servitude, is denied and abridged by a law which forbids him, on account of his race and color, to vote at a primary election held under the laws of Texas," said the opening paragraph of the brief. The Supreme Court findings in *Nixon* would later be used to structure the legal edifice of the *School Segregation Cases*. In this brief Marshall assessed *Nixon* v. *Herndon,* plus all the other state actions used, as in Texas, to bar blacks from voting in white primaries. The Texas legislature tried to infer that the Fifteenth Amendment did not expressly refer to voting at primaries, which, formally speaking, were not general elections. However, said the brief, "it is thus evident that in these states, including Texas, party lines are so drawn that a nomination in the Democratic primary is equivalent to an election," the general election being nothing but a gesture in which few participate. Thus, barring blacks from white primaries was a violation of the Fifteenth Amendment.

Marshall used another illustration—the Nineteenth Amendment— to prove that Texas was in violation of the Constitution in the use of the white primary. Wrote Marshall: "Its form and language are identical with the terms of the Fifteenth Amendment until we read the last words. Both begin:

> The rights of citizens of the United States to vote shall not be denied or abridged by the United States or by any State on account of . . .
>   The Fifteenth Amendment continues with the words "race, color or previous condition of servitude." The Nineteenth Amendment continues with the single word "sex."

The brief argued that a woman could take part in a primary without further authority than that conferred by the Nineteenth Amendment, so long as the woman possessed the other qualifications requisite to the exercise of the right of suffrage. In other words, she could not be prevented from voting at a primary on account of her sex. Of course, said the brief, "under the Texas statute, if she is a Negro, her sex would not save her from its discriminatory purpose." It was true, of course, that when the Nineteenth Amendment came into force on August 26, 1920, voting at primary elections, unknown fifty years before, had become familiar. "Yet, it would have been an absurdity to say that in 1920 the right to vote, so far as it related to women, included the right of voting at a primary election, whereas at the same time the right of the Negro to vote at a primary election did not exist because when the Fifteenth Amendment was adopted there were no primary elections." The provisions of the Nineteenth Amendment, said Marshall, could very well be included by an amendment to Article 15 of the Amendments to the Constitution, so that the article could read:

> The rights of citizens of the United States to vote shall not be denied or abridged by the United States or by any State on account of *sex*, race, color or previous condition of servitude.[144]

"Could it then have been contended that under such a provision of the Constitution the right of women to vote at primaries could not be denied or abridged, but that the right of Negroes to vote could nevertheless be denied or abridged, because the same words had two different meanings due to the fact that they originated in two different periods of our social development?" Marshall further contended:

> The history of the Thirteenth, Fourteenth and Fifteenth Amendments discloses that it was the purpose of the framers to make them self-executing from the moment of their adoption, and to confer upon the Negroes, *ipso facto*, political equality.[145]

Thus, in the interpretive legal context in which he argued *Nixon* v. *Herndon*, Marshall was equitable enough in his liberal constructionism to assert that the equal protection inferences of all three Civil War Amendments implied *full political equality* for blacks. He did not imply what limits might be set beyond which any claims or demands for equal protection might prove "perversions." The question of whether political equality was attainable without economic equality was not a constitutional issue at that juncture. In the black-Jewish alliance, economic equality implied, qualitatively, two different propositions. For American Jews, economic equity was never a serious problem. For women, the new force on the political scene in 1920, economic equity would be relative, depending on the class, race, or color of the women being discussed. For blacks, the question of economic equity was moot, if not verging on hopeless. In essence, blacks of all classes were being told by labor and corporate interests:

> You should be allowed to perform only agricultural labor.
> You shall not be allowed to function in the skilled labor trades in competition with whites.
> You shall not be allowed to work in the factory system above the rank of common laborer.
> You shall not presume to attempt to organize yourself into a collective corporate or cooperative economic enterprise against the interests of white corporate enterprises already in existence.

While force and persuasion told blacks they should not attempt to participate as equals in such economic activities, at the same time they were accused of being shiftless, lacking in thrift, lacking in industriousness, being lazy, eschewing the virtues of hard work and individual initiative, being of innate criminality, being unfit candidates for acceptance into the society of *men* endowed with the capacity to participate as free individuals in the America of democracy and free enterprise.

No white European immigrant group (including the Jews) was ever implicitly or directly advised that the privilege of economic self-advancement was not one of the promises of American citizenship. *America was the land of opportunity.* In Louisiana, where an undertermined number of Italians were lynched during the 1890s, the issue was not economic competition between the Italians (most of whom were Sicilians) and the Anglo-Americans. It was that the Italians did not understand the etiquette of Anglo-American racial attitudes toward blacks. Because the Italians more or less freely fraternized with Louisiana blacks, the Anglo-Americans accused them of being a threat to "white solidarity," especially in post-Reconstruction politics. However, immigrant Italians had been welcomed into New Orleans. In fact, it was recorded that "economically, the Italians were important in New Orleans." The city owed them a great obligation, the *Daily Picayune* pointed out in 1890, because they had developed "the fruit business to the point where the importation of fruits took on economic significance for the port." Because the Italians had begun as street peddlers, the fruit business:

> Had grown into an enterprise with the dignity and proportions of a great commercial interest employing a score and more of steamships and hundreds of thousands of dollars of capital.[146]

The native whites were somewhat amazed at the phenomenal growth of the fruit business in New Orleans in the brief period since the Italians had arrived. But Italians in the rural parishes of Louisiana did not fare so well. In the sugarcane fields, they were willing to perform tasks that Anglo-Americans considered suitable only for blacks. The Italians not only fraternized with the blacks, but allied themselves with blacks in the Populist political campaigns. In the political power struggles between the Republicans, the Populists, and the Democratic party of white supremacy, the rural Italians were caught in the middle and suffered retaliation from the Democrats, which was both repressive and violent.

The Anglo-American–Italian-immigrant–American-black political and economic encounter in 1890s Louisiana vividly highlighted the trapped economic position of the blacks in the southern (and northern) economy. Since the 1890s was the decade in which the South tried to drive blacks out of electoral politics through disfranchisement, the *economics* of the black position was frozen into noncompetitive submarginality. Vis-à-vis the European immigrant, this was the economic position into which the blacks were pushed all over the United States, north, south, east, and west:

> Italians, along with other immigrants, had been invited to Louisiana as early as 1865, when some planters were seeking "docile" whites to substitute for Negro laborers and to enlarge the white electorate of the black parishes. In September, 1865, the white and black Radicals of Louisiana united to found the Republican party of Louisiana. Many Democrats feared they might ultimately lose control of the black parishes unless the white population in those parishes could be increased by the attraction of immigrants.[147]

However, the lynching orgy in Phillips County, Arkansas, in 1919 that led to *Moore* v. *Dempsey* did not involve the intrusion of white immigrants into the white-black racial equation. In fact, writers in the 1920s pointed out that no immigrants risked the impropriety of settling in a territory which was "a belt of mud, a hundred miles wide in places," a geographical characteristic "which prevented Arkansas from having a port as well as a metropolis, a civilization, and a history." It was written that Arkansas was settled by a people "who were willing to foot it a hundred miles through muck to get nowhere, founded Arkansas and achieved their aim":

Mighty planters, greedy merchants, daring pirates with beautiful hot-blooded women—these came not to Arkansas, nor founded there an aristocracy of strength and cunning. But the kind of folk that pirates terrorized and merchants cheat, and planters impress into peonage were the wandering sheep that grazed their way into Arkansas to establish there a morons' paradise. No strong men arose to oppress them because the pirate-merchant-planter breed was not in them. They could not raise up strong-arm Caesars among themselves because there were no Caesar chromosomes in their blood. They were an infiltrate, and in seeping into Arkansas through a mud filter the Caesars had been strained out.[148]

It was said that while the great migration going "out West" moved along the Ohio River, the descendants of Colonial bond servants, Crackers, descendants of the Georgia convict colony moved into Arkansas. Hoosiers from the Great Smokey Mountains found their way into Arkansas, and "as no strong tribe followed them into this retreat they were never driven out again." Other mountain folk came later, proliferating in their beloved highlands till they crossed the Mississippi and peopled the Ozarks. But the writer added: "These people are not mentally dull nor physically inefficient. They are simply a highland race that loves solitude and scorns comfort, literature, and luxury":

These three strains, the mountain people, the Crackers, and the Piker numskulls, have united to make the Arkansas nation; for they are a nation, as distinct from the other peoples in America as is a Swede from a Dane.[149]

From this description of Arkansas, it can be surmised why the Phillips County race riot and orgiastic shoot-out was, even for the South, more wanton, more irrational, more bestial, more murderous in its "frontier" profligacy than any American race riot following World War I. But what made the Phillips County Massacre even more unique in its vigilante extremism was that it was the first of the major race wars that compelled the intervention of the federal courts on the issue of constitutional redress for civil rights violations of the most uncivilized temper. The singular consequence of the Arkansas affair was that the imperatives of due process dragged the case back and forth in the lower and higher court systems for four years until the *Moore* v. *Dempsey* decision. But considering all the elements involved in this tragic and bloody drama, it is strange that the affair was never written up in sufficiently lengthy form to divulge the intimate facts that are still unexplored.

Even Louis Marshall, with all his literary gift for argumentive detail on legal matters, refrained from reviewing the mass of detailed information on what happened in Phillips County. Despite its redemptive legal accomplishment, *Moore* v. *Dempsey* was and remained a judicial metaphor that closed the books on the full details of what had occurred. For Marshall the due process issue was settled. Leaving *Moore* v. *Dempsey* and *Frank* v. *Mangum* behind, he pursued the legal continuum having reference to the "Rights of Negroes" that took him back to *Yick Wo* v. *Hopkins*. Along the way, Marshall argued that a violation of Fifteenth Amendment rights of blacks to participate in primary elections, as in Texas, was also concomitantly a violation of the equal protection clause of the Fourteenth Amendment. "Independently, therefore, of the Fifteenth Amendment," he wrote, a Texas statute barring blacks from voting in primaries likewise offends against the Fourteenth Amendment, "because it denies to persons within its jurisdiction the equal protection of the laws." Citing the *Slaughterhouse Cases,* he took the position that it was evident that *Slaughterhouse* "recognized that the chief inducement to the passage of the [Fourteenth] Amendment was the desire to extend federal protection to the recently emancipated race from unfriendly and discriminating legislation by the States." While the principal purpose of the amendment was to protect persons of color, the broad language was used to protect all persons, white or black, against discriminatory legislation by the states. More than that, the amendment's equal protection clause also protects the rights of Chinese, who are not black or generally considered white:

A mere reference to *Yick Wo* v. *Hopkins*, 118 U.S. 356, and to the classic opinion of Mr. Justice Matthews in that case will suffice for the purposes of this argument, although in the ordinance there in question there was not the brutal frankness which characterizes the legislation now under consideration which expressly discriminates against the Negro. In the case cited, without reference to the fact that it was intended to discriminate against Chinese laundrymen, they were not named in the ordinance, although in its operation, as well as in its purpose, it was designed to differentiate between them because of their race and others who conducted laundries.[150]

Even though if the San Francisco ordinance was in fact anti-Chinese in the aggregate, "designed to differentiate between them because of their race and others who conducted laundries," Louis Marshall was not prepared to carry the legal analogy implied in *Yick Wo* to the full degree of equal protection consequences and/or logic. His sense of equity was acute enough to point out that in the anti-Chinese ordinance, "there was not the brutal frankness which characterizes the legislation now under consideration which expressly discriminates against the Negro." In other words, the state action against the Chinese in San Francisco was not as brutally frank as the state action of Texas against the blacks. But state action against the blacks in Phillips County, Arkansas, was even more brutal, to the extent of severe physical violence. However, Marshall, like the most liberal of liberals, could not draw the implied conclusions on how equal protection was dispensed depending on *who* the aggrieved minority was, nor under *what* political, economic, or cultural or social circumstances equal protection was parceled out. *Yick Wo* v. *Hopkins* implicitly stated that it was constitutionally illegal for State action to prevent a nonwhite individual, whether immigrant or citizen, from operating a *business enterprise* in a *de facto* white residential or business zone in San Francisco. Yick Wo, by winning in court, achieved *both* due process and equal protection on the specific issue of economic equity. When the black Progressive Farmers and Household Union of America sought court protection to defend its right to organize an *economic* activity, a lynch mob prevented the case from ever reaching the courtroom. Thus, on the question of economic equity the blacks got neither due process nor equal protection. Later, the due process won by *Moore* v. *Dempsey*, which Louis Marshall so zealously hailed, was *ex post facto* the original intent of the aggrieved parties in pursuit of equity.

Liberal jurisprudence, then, was in accord with the racial economics of the labor unions, the Liberal-Socialist League for Industrial Democracy, the Garland Funds (American Fund for Public Service), and the Supreme Court. The accusation by the *New Republic* that the Supreme Court did not understand that "democracy and wage slavery" were incompatible was rooted in the interpretive ambiguities written into the Fourteenth Amendment. Due process and equal protection were purely conditional guarantees, as limited in legal possibilities as they were open-ended as to whose rights were in jeopardy. Thus, constitutional protection leaned heavily in favor of economic power of corporations, industrial management, and land ownership. Liberal humanitarianism of the constitutional constructionist temper was extra careful to hold back at the water's edge of states' rights. Unless the state, through its courts, or the Supreme Court specifically mandated equal protection and due process for nonwhite minorities, especially in *economic* matters, liberal jurisprudence would uphold noninterference by the federal power by failing to question the absence of equal protection in matters of economic equity. This characteristic liberal default, which permeates the legal system in economic matters, works most heavily to the detriment of blacks—the most numerous minority among all the minorities, white and nonwhite.

This was further demonstrated in Louis Marshall's extensive analysis of the California Alien Land Law of 1920 in connection with the "Rights of Japanese." Marshall began:

> The Californian Alien Land Law forbids aliens ineligible to citizenship under the laws of the United States to lease real property in the State, although the right to do so has been conferred on all other aliens. The former are thus deprived of the equal protection of the laws within the meaning of the Fourteenth Amendment.[151]

This law was passed by the California legislature in 1920. Marshall argued against the discriminatory features of the law, pointing out that it contravened the General Laws of 1913, of California, Act No. 113, which permitted even aliens who were eligible for citizenship to lease lands in the state for agricultural purposes for a term of three years. Prior to 1920, Japanese who were eligible for citizenship, or were already citizens, could not only lease but also purchase land, *which they did.* Quoting from the brief offered in discrimination suits in California on this matter, Marshall cited the provisions of the Civil Code of California:

> Section 671 of the Civil Code of California provides:
> Any person, whether citizen or alien, may take, hold and dispose of property, real or personal, within this state.
> Section 672 reads:
> If a non-resident alien takes by succession, he must appear and claim the property within five years from the time of succession or be debarred. The property in such cases is disposed of as provided in title eight, part three, code of civil procedure.[152]

The California Alien Land Law of 1920 attempted to revise the General Laws of 1913 for the purpose of Japanese (also Chinese and Malayan) exclusion from the right to buy or lease California land. But this exclusion prompted Marshall to cite Section 2169 of the *United States Revised Statutes* of the Federal Naturalization Law, which reads: "The provisions of this Title shall apply to aliens being free white persons, and to aliens of African nativity and to persons of African descent." From this, Marshall concluded:

> The persons eligible to citizenship are, therefore, all aliens who come within the description of free white persons and all aliens of African nativity and of African descent. That would include, broadly speaking, the natives of every European country, without exception, all of the white and black people of North, Central and South America; Armenians born in Asiatic Turkey; Mexicans, Parsees; Syrians born in Damascus or at Beirut; all native-born Africans from the Mediterranean to the Cape of Good Hope. It excludes Chinese, Japanese and Malayans.[153]

In other words, since the *United States Revised Statutes* of the Naturalization Law confer inalienable rights of citizenship on all aliens from European and African countries (including people of African descent), the California Alien Land Law of 1920 was in violation of the equal protection rights of Japanese immigrants to buy or lease land according to the Fourteenth Amendment. Since the *United States Revised Statutes* did not specifically confer inalienable rights of land-buying citizenship on the Japanese, Chinese, or Malayans, the California Alien Land Law of 1920 was an attempt by the California legislature to bar such Asians from acquiring land. Since the California Alien Land Law of 1920 did not propose to bar from acquiring real property those aliens who were covered under the citizenship-test Section 2169 of the *United States Revised Statutes* as to color or country of birth, its attempt to debar Japanese, Chinese, and Malayans was a violation of their constitutional equal protection privileges. More than that, Marshall argued, to debar Asian aliens in such a fashion was even a violation of the intents of Section 1, Article XVII, of the California constitution, which, said Marshall, "is not prohibitive in its terms. So far as it goes, it is merely permissive. It excludes nobody. It reads:

> Foreigners of the white race or of African descent eligible to become citizens of the United States under the naturalization laws thereof, while

bona fide residents of this state, shall have the same rights in respect
to the acquisition, possession, enjoyment, transmission and inheritance
of all property, other than real estate, as native born citizens; provided,
that such aliens owning real estate at the time of the adoption of this
amendment *may remain such owners*; provided further, that the legislature *may*, by statute, provide for the disposition of real estate which
shall *hereafter* be acquired by such aliens by descent or devise.[154]

Marshall's legal reasoning objected to the fact that any alien who
fell under the classification described in Section 1 of the California legislation of 1920 were permitted to acquire title to and hold all the agricultural lands in the state, "even were the nations to which they may be
subject actually at war with the United States," while the Japanese were
not. He pointed out that the Japanese were subjects of a friendly and
honorable nation with which the United States was associated during
World War 1, and some of whom had fought side by side with American
citizens. Yet in California, the Japanese, because of their color and racial
stock, were debarred from rights that were freely bestowed on other aliens,
"who may have been arrayed against us in arms and who in every way
may be inferior to the Japanese."[155] But he added:

> Without in any way seeking to belittle the men of other races or na-
> tionalities, it is difficult to understand the basis of discrimination under
> this statute between the illiterate Portuguese, the inhabitants of Para-
> guay, Mexico or Venezuela, the Russian mujik, Slovenes and Hun-
> garians, Montenegrins and Croatians, Sicilians and Syrians, and the
> industrious, enterprising and intelligent Japanese, who while cultivating
> land occupied by them in California have converted burning deserts into
> smiling oases and regions infested with malaria into marvels of fertil-
> ity.[156]

Here, the liberal-constructionist sense of fair play pleads for constitutional equity among diverse immigrant groups, especially nonwhite
groups, on the American economic scene. At the same time, Marshall
argues that equal protection not only applies to such legal procedures as
due process, or to such democratic abstractions as social justice, or social
and racial equality, but applies also to equity in property matters—*real
property*, land. In short, equal protection can apply to the equitable
distribution of economic wealth. Marshall was even more specific in this
regard, using the *Yick Wo* v. *Hopkins* decision as precedent: Quoting
from the then recent decision of the California Supreme Court, based on

Yick Wo v. *Hopkins*, declaring legislation discriminatory of aliens invalid under the Fourteenth Amendment, and involving the California Alien Land Law of 1920, Marshall wrote:

> The meaning of "the equal protection of the laws" thus guaranteed by the Federal Constitution to every person within the jurisdiction of a State is not left in doubt by the decisions in so far as such an act as the one here involved is concerned. In *Yick Wo* v. *Hopkins, supra,* it is said that "the equal protection of the laws is a pledge to the protection of equal laws." . . . "That equal protection and security should be given to all under like circumstances in the enjoyment of their personal and civil rights; that all persons should be equally entitled to pursue their happiness and . . . enjoy property; that they should have like access to the courts of the country for the protection of their persons and property, the prevention and redress of wrongs, and the enforcement of contracts; that no impediment should be interposed to the pursuits of any one except as applied to the same pursuits by others under like circumstances; *that no greater burdens should be laid upon one than are laid upon others in the same calling and condition. . . .*"[157]

The *Yick Wo* decision was handed down by the Supreme Court in 1886. Yet Louis Marshall, in his learned and extended briefs on the "Rights of Negroes" and the "Rights of the Japanese" (and Chinese and Malayans), did not extend the *economic* dimension of this equal protection ruling as an anterior constitutional issue in his assessment of *Moore* v. *Dempsey.* In this regard, all that aroused his passion for justice was that the Supreme Court had vindicated his arguments regarding due process in *Frank* v. *Mangum.* More than that, his extended arguments about the manner in which equal protection was parceled out to the variegated collection of immigrant minorities from Europe, Africa, and Latin America implied that *"all aliens of African nativity and of African descent"* were blessed with constitutional preferential treatment compared with Asian immigrants, which was far from true. In the southern states, the obstacles thrown up by whites against the acquisition of *good land* by blacks was more formidable than the prohibition of Japanese land ownership in California. Also, his assertion that American citizens of African descent were allowed the same degree of constitutional equal protection as European immigrants "without regard to any differences of race, or color, or of nationality" was blatantly untrue.[158] Land ownership by blacks in the southern states, especially without onerous debt-free conditions, was extremely difficult. It seems also that Marshall in

his fervent espousal of land ownership by all immigrants, especially
European, did not investigate how many blacks actually obtained western
land, compared with the number of European immigrants, as a result of
the Homestead Act of 1862.[159]

The *Moore* v. *Dempsey* decision was the legal end product of race
conflict and land ownership in the southern states. The basic wealth and
capital accumulation in the southern region came from the products of
the land, where "the Negro forms two-fifths of the population of the
South but produces three-fifths of the wealth." Albert Bushnell Hart, the
Harvard historian who was one of the first to measure the economic
impact of black labor on the southern economy, made this estimate. His
study of southern race and economic conditions in 1912 was, and remains,
an ample illustration that the California land question vis-à-vis the Japanese was one thing, but the land question in the South vis-à-vis the
blacks was something else again. There was no *equitable* comparison.
Hart's study, in addition to being a social history of class, race, and
economics of the South, was also a plea for racial reconciliation in order
that the potential sources of wealth in the region could be developed for
the benefit of blacks and whites. Hart was unsparing in his assessment
of the effects of black illiteracy, unreliable work habits, shiftlessness,
petty criminality, and other negative traits induced by small-town and
city life. However, the solid core of the black labor force that was centered
in plantation agriculture was highly productive and hard working. White
proprietors or landowners knew that without their strictly controlled black
labor force, agricultural profits were not ensured. Hence, southern black
agricultural labor was, to a great degree, cheap forced labor. Under such
circumstances, opportunities for black economic progress and development were checked, discouraged, and prohibited by intimidation, decep-
tion, open force, legal and illegal opposition. The South justified its
treatment of its black labor force on the grounds of Negro inferiority.
But, as Hart argued:

> If the Negro is inferior, it does not need so many acts of the legislature
> to prove it. . . . If the Negro is unintelligent, he will never, under
> present conditions, get enough votes to affect elections; if he does
> acquire the necessary property and education, he thereby shows that he
> does not share the inferiority of his race. The South thinks about the
> Negro too much, talks about him too much, abuses him too much. . . .[160]

This was not the treatment handed out to Europeans and other immigrants, for whom American citizenship and hard work were the open

door to any level of economic well-being, and even affluence, their self-directed capabilities could take them. But as for the agricultural South, wrote Hart: "So far as can be judged, the average frame of mind includes much injustice, and unwillingness to permit the Negro race to develop up to the measure of its limitations."[161] This opposition, especially in the economic sphere, often took on a virulent form. One of the most extreme racist ideologists of the southern scene, Thomas Dixon, Jr., a writer and exponent of white supremacy and the subjugation of blacks, was described and quoted by Hart: *"Here, for instance, is Thomas Dixon Jr., arguing with all his might that the Negro is barely human, but that if he is not checked he will become such an economic competitor of the white man that he will have to be massacred."* (Italics added.) Hart expanded:

> He protests against Booker T. Washington's attempts to raise the Negro, because he thinks it will be successful. Part, at least, of the customary and statutory discrimination against the Negro which have already been described are simply an expression of this supposed necessity of keeping the Negro down, lest he should rise too far. All such terrors involve the humiliating admission that the Negro can rise, and that he will rise if he has the opportunity.[162]

Like many white southerners of his ilk, Thomas Dixon's second-in-rank-order objects of venomous hatred, next to blacks, were northern white liberal "meddlers" in southern racial affairs. However, these liberals, especially those connected with the high councils of the NAACP, had managed, in the name of racial democracy, to so disarm black leadership on the issue of black economic democracy that a Thomas Dixon would have no cause for fear. The northern white liberals' imposition of the leadership idea of *noneconomic liberalism* effectively took care of that problem. Hence, the outcome of the Phillips County Massacre in *Moore* v. *Dempsey*, and *all in the name of the Constitution.*

Up to 1930, the twenty-one years of the NAACP's existence stamped in the character of the association not only its positive social ideals but also its fatal flaws. Its programmatic mold was shaped for all time; its legal rationale, its interpretive constitutional philosophy, based on the *a priori* mandates of the Fourteenth and Fifteenth Amendments, was informed by the liberal-constructionist response to those amendments. Its dominant theme, orchestrated by white liberals, was that full equality for blacks in social life, politics, economics, culture, and education would eventually be realized once the temper and tone of American race relations were shaped according to the implied democratic intent of those amendments. Essentially a pragmatic, legitimate, idealistic, and well-intentioned point of view, it was, at the same time, naïve. Naïve because it reduced the concept of "civil rights" to a passive, acquiescent subordination to the socially limited possibilities of the Fourteenth Amendment's equal protection clause. By its acceptance of *noneconomic liberalism*, the association consciously deprived itself of the possible means of *political* leverage whereby the social range of equal protection might have been enlarged to mean much more than the phantom results of mere integrated racial equality. Following the economic collapse of 1929, even the perceptive members of the white liberal consensus began to understand the legal limitations of the constitution in the sphere of economic equity for disadvantaged minorities. In 1936 the League for Industrial Democracy came to the conclusion that:

> Under our federal system of government, most laws of a social and *economic* nature have been left to the states. Congress has assumed power over only those activities specifically delegated to it by the Constitution. *It has had to keep its hands off countless problems involving the regulation of industry and agriculture, problems that are national and international in scope and that cannot be solved through state action.*[163] (Italics added.)

In this constitutional context, the economic nature of agriculture was vitally crucial to the NAACP's black constituency in the South before the Depression. In its campaign to protect blacks against lynching by mob violence, the NAACP was blocked by the constitutional deference to states' rights. Even the leader of Jewish opinion in the black-Jewish alliance, Louis Marshall, upheld states' rights in this regard. The southern agricultural economy maintained not only the superexploitative institutions of sharecropping and tenant farming, but also *peonage* in violation of the *Thirteenth Amendment* (not to speak of the Fourteenth and Fifteenth). Yet the expert NAACP legal corps was forced to program its civil rights approach to a strategy of enforcing the equal protection clause of the Fourteenth Amendment, which was demonstrably incapacitated from the date of its ratification in 1868 to enforce racial democracy via its equal protection clause.

The constitutional and legal subservience of the NAACP legal corps (both black and white) was so conformist in its liberal constructionism that there is no indication they were concerned that by 1916, at least, thirty states had legislation governing the voluntary creation of industrial producer and consumer cooperatives, as well as agricultural producer and consumer cooperative societies. At least five southern states had either enacted such laws or were in the process of considering them for adoption—Alabama, Florida, Mississippi, Oklahoma, and South Carolina.[164] (Arkansas was a question mark.) Yet, so obsessed was the NAACP legal corps in tedious grappling with the implied restrictions of equal protection that there is no indication that they attempted to apply their legal expertise toward either enforcing the provisions of these laws on behalf of blacks where they existed, or pressing for enacting such laws where they were not in force, e.g., in Arkansas. Forced by such tactics to place an unrealizable hope in the federal backing of the Dyer Anti-Lynching Bill, it was not until the late 1930s that W.E.B. Du Bois was informed as to one of the main reasons why the antilynching legislation passed by the House was defeated in the Senate. Wrote Du Bois:

> The Dyer Anti-Lynching Bill went through the House of Representatives on to the floor of the Senate. There in 1924 it died with filibuster and the abject surrender of its friends. It was not until years after that I knew what killed that anti-lynching bill. It was a bargain between the South and the West. By this bargain, lynching was let to go on uncurbed by Federal law, on condition that the Japanese be excluded from the United States.[165]

Finally, for the decade of the 1920s, this egregious blind spot in the liberal-constructionist legal visions of equal protection led to invoking *Strauder-Buchanan-Nixon-Yick Wo* as constitutional rationales for the *School Segregation Cases*, and eventually to *Brown*. Politically and economically, it was a conceptually flawed legal continuum because it left out of the legal picture the defeated and unrealized economic factor in *Moore* v. *Dempsey*. In this regard, the black-Jewish alliance as a subminority factor within the broader black–white–liberal civil rights alliance added little beyond humanitarian philanthropy to the black cause that would have sufficed to transcend the limitations of the civil rights of noneconomic liberalism. Liberal civil rights humanitarianism and philanthropy had added up to what Du Bois called the "Old Liberalism." On leaving the NAACP, he described his mood:

> By 1930, I had become convinced that the basic policies of the Association must be modified and changed; that in a world where economic dislocation had become so great as in ours, a mere appeal based on the

old liberalism, *a mere appeal to justice and further effort at legal decision, was missing the essential need; that the essential need was to guard and better the chances of Negroes, educated and ignorant, to earn a living, safeguard their income, and raise their level of employment.*[166] (Italics added.)

 But the Old Liberalism would prevail. When the NAACP's leadership agreed in 1930 that the major point of attack in the civil rights of full equality would shift to institutionalized educational inequalities, it was still pursuing the vague promises of equal protection under the Fourteenth Amendment.

Perhaps certain anxious minds within the association thought that the perceived "egalitarian language" of *Strauder-Buchanan-Nixon-Yick Wo* contained the legal promise of eradicating *both* educational and economic inequalities. Just what justified such an extravagant expectation is today difficult to conjecture. Nothing in the black experience since World War I indicated any economic redress other than what private industry was willing to grant in exchange for access to the black cheap labor reserve. Not until 1936, with the advent of the Congress of Industrial Organizations (CIO), did labor unionism officially confront the race question in economics by setting out to organize the unorganized black workers. But even here, organized labor would barely impact on the accumulated black economic disabilities. Moreover, even 1936 was late in making up for the organizational backwardness of American labor. Forty-four years later, in 1980, unions would account for the organization of only about 20 percent of the total worker population.

The deepening crisis for black America had occurred under the most unlucky circumstances. The Great Depression struck during the tail end of the most massive migratory population shift the blacks had ever managed in their American experience. This northern shift resulted in a measure of economic prosperity for the unskilled and semiskilled, plus an escape from not only southern racial oppression, but the growing economic depression that had already struck southern agriculture. However, when the Depression struck the industrial sectors of the economy as well, the blacks were the hardest hit. It was then that the absence of an economic program in the civil rights movement of the 1920s became glaring. It was then that the crucial question of economic survival took precedence in the whole raft of civil rights issues. During the NAACP's annual convention of 1932, a contingent of delegates was led by George S. Schuyler, the well-known black critic and journalist, who made the following plea:

> I know of no better way for the National Association for the Advancement of Colored People (of which I am proudly a member) to really and fundamentally advance the colored people of this country than to endeavor to organize a consumers' cooperative society in every city where it has a branch. The opportunity is now and has long been at hand. The time may soon come when this opportunity is past. By all means let us do something economically constructive before our people succumb to the forces making for their destruction.[167]

But the time had already passed—such an economic program *should* have been introduced by the NAACP in 1920. By 1932 the Depression had already done its deadly work; the uprooting character of the great migration had left thousands stranded in congested northern ghettos in the grip of joblessness, nuclear (and extended) family disorganization, urban vice and crime, health hazards unknown in the southern agricultural region of landed poverty. The unprecedented prosperity of the 1920s had buttressed the belief that blacks' racial progress could inch forward aided by an expanding national economy. But that relative black prosperity had vanished in the social turmoil of the cyclical crisis endemic to capitalism. *The black populations, then newly arrived in the northern urban centers, would never fully recover from the sociological shock treatment experienced during the Great Depression even into the 1980s. From the 1930s through the Forties, Fifties, Sixties, Seventies, and Eighties, additional migratory waves would only aggravate the already existing urban pathologies introduced in 1929.*

Caught in the unexpected grip of a national emergency, the NAACP could not change program horses in the middle of a torrent. Time and the ingredients of adverse social evolution outran black leadership potential. Black leadership lost pace with social history in the making, *and would never catch up*. The economic underpinnings of whatever advances blacks had made in the Twenties collapsed in 1929. Like the frantic survivors of an overturned ship, blacks were rescued by the New Deal, under whose benign influence they, in the main, would become economic wards of the state. The noneconomic liberalism of the civil rights leadership of pre-1930 would be exchanged for the new liberal economic dispensation sponsored by the federal power. Thus, blacks born during the 1930s and beyond would become the "Children of the New Deal," indoctrinated with the psychology of dependency on the government. They would look to the state as the benefactor of all the rights and privileges of citizenship—of racial equality, health, education, and welfare, employment, housing and recreation, equal rights, of constitutional guarantees of equal protection by way of a governing document that was never written to guarantee any such equal protection. The Children of the New Deal would never have cause to remember, because they would never have known, that prior to 1930 such a minority-group psychology dependency expectation of the federal power's beneficence was not a factor in pursuit of their share of the American Dream, or even a figment in the social imagination.

From its very inception, the NAACP never had a program or a campaign of any sort that was not the result of a frantic adjustment response to meet a new and unforeseen contingency. The national emergency of World War I forced the NAACP to adopt an approach to black labor and blacks in the military. In 1931 the celebrated case of the Scottsboro Nine forced the NAACP to make good its hard-earned reputation as the leading champion of the elementary legalities of black civil rights. The Scottsboro Case was one of the most flagrant violations of the elementary ethics of social justice in Alabama since World War I. Sentenced to death on trumped-up rape charges, the nine youthful Scottsboro victims became the focal point of a nationwide protest. The case opened wide the door for the entry of the Marxist-Communist radical critique into black affairs for the first time.[168] New black ideologues began to speak of Communism as the only answer. Prominent literary personalities, such as Langston Hughes, joined the Communist left, while others, like George S. Schuyler, would evolve into prototypes of "black conservatism."[169] Critics who had put together the "Black Inventory of the New Deal" had Marxist leanings. This criticism of the New Deal, as an economic analysis, was the preannouncement of the National Negro Congress (NNC) in 1936. The NNC emerged out of a May 1935 conference sponsored by the Social Science Division of Howard University. At Howard a Joint Committee on National Recovery was formed for "a candid and intelligent survey of the economic condition of the Negro." The committee promised that:

> Unlike other conferences it will not be a one-sided affair. Ample opportunity will be afforded for high government officials to present their

views of the "New Deal." Others not connected with the government, including representatives of radical political parties, will also appear to present their conclusions. Not the least important phase will be the appearance on the platform of Negro workers and farmers themselves to offer their own experience under the New Deal. Out of such a conference can and will come a clear-cut analysis of the problems faced by Negroes and the Nation.[170]

But if the National Negro Congress was seen as a more radical substitute for the reformist NAACP, it would lack permanence. By 1940 the NNC, a broad coalition of blacks, labor, fraternal groups, churches, and Marxists, would begin to disintegrate over the "Communist" issue. But the NAACP would weather all of this 1930s stress and strain by quietly mapping out its strategies on the educational inequalities front. If the expanding prosperity of the 1920s had been shattered by the economic crash of 1929, it had been a boon to black colleges. The lasting effects of this new prosperity in black education would carry over into the 1930s. Thus, when the Garland Fund–NAACP joint committee laid its plans in 1930 to make black inequalities in education the main priority in the attack on *Plessy* v. *Ferguson,* a comparatively fertile base existed from which to launch this strategy.

The NAACP shift in civil rights emphasis to the education front had more than an expedient rationale. Following the collapse of Reconstruction, and the southern nullification of the Fourteenth and Fifteenth Amendments, socially pragmatic leaders had concluded that the only long-range hope for black "social uplift" lay in education. From 1920 to 1930, despite the struggling backwardness of black public school education in the South, black student enrollment in college had risen from approximately 2,132 in 1917 to approximately 13,580 in 1927. This estimate, reported for black colleges, included some two hundred to three hundred black students in white colleges and universities.[171]

Because of the unreliability of any form of censual reporting, especially with regard to blacks in the South at that time, black student counts had to be approximate. Thus, it was stated that "some thirty-nine" had won doctorates, without citing which institutions (black or white) had conferred these doctorates. By 1929 more refined counting methods permitted *The Crisis* to extract from a government *Survey of Negro Colleges and Universities* by the United States Bureau of Education in conjunction with the departments of education of nineteen states, with the cooperation of seventy-nine Negro colleges, the Association of Colleges for Negro Youth, the Phelps-Stokes Fund, and other foundations. The report revealed:

> In the 79 schools, the total enrollment of college students in 1922–23 was 6,684. In 1926–27, it was increased to 13,860.
> All the colleges except seven receive both men and women students. Four receive only men, and three only women. In 1926–27, of 12,090 students, 6,146 were men and 5,944 were women.[172]

Seventy-nine all-black colleges! Given that the entire black population in the United States was estimated at between twelve and thirteen million, seventy-nine colleges might seem a lot,—one college for about every sixteen thousand blacks. But census figures for blacks were notoriously unreliable in the southern states, where politicians used police power to prevent entire counties with high black population ratios from being counted. More than that, the academic and administrative caliber of many of these black colleges was far below accepted educational standards for institutions of higher learning. Measured by prevailing American educational achievement levels, the United States Bureau of Education report pointed out that: "It is estimated that in the United States for every ten thousand whites, 90 white students are attending college, and for every 10,000 Negroes, 15 students are attending college." Moreover, said the report:

> A study of the libraries of the 79 colleges included in the survey reveals one of the most serious present deficiencies. Of the 79 institutions, only 15 have libraries of 10,000 or more volumes. While laboratories are beginning to be equipped, very few institutions have yet made the necessary preparation for teaching biology, chemistry and physics. Biology is the worst off. *The colleges have done outstanding service in their contribution to musical art. Nevertheless, many schools are handicapped by poor instruments.*(Italics added.)

This emphasis on musical training in contrast to the retarded level of training in other areas in the humanities, or in the social or physical sciences, was one of the hallmarks of black college education. Music training had a high priority because it was the *one* field (other than theological studies for the ministry) where black excellence was eagerly accepted by both liberal and conservative whites. For many years it was standard practice in black colleges to impress white trustees and possible financial contributors by entertaining them with well-coached black students singing a repertory of Negro spirituals. Occasionally, black students in certain colleges revolted against being used for such practices. Moreover, given the cultural impact of the black idiom on American music by way of folk music, ragtime, blues, and jazz, black music possessed the ingredients of a distinct Afro-American school that had the potential of matching the creative accomplishments of any national European school. And given the exploitative politics and economics of the musical arts in the United States, black colleges failed to serve an obligatory function as *institutional* forces in the development of the black music heritage.

Overall, black colleges failed to produce Du Bois's hoped-for black intellectual leadership, particularly in the arts, humanities, and professions. Severe handicaps imposed by external social forces rendered black educational institutions weak in generating positive and socially effective educational values. W.E.B. Du Bois repeatedly devoted articles and editorial notes in *The Crisis* to "Advice to Negro Colleges," admonishing and scolding college administrators and teachers on the question of black educational deficiencies. However, civil rights leaders, most of whom were products of those black colleges, elected to blame the educational backwardness of black colleges, collectively, on *segregation*. Most of them were not in favor of the existence of all-black colleges, and this attitude motivated and rationalized the civil rights shift in priorities to emphasize educational inequalities.

But black educational institutions had positive aspects despite handicaps that were basically traceable to woefully insufficient funding. One advantage was the education of black women. In the earlier cited 79 black colleges surveyed for 1926–1927 by the United States Bureau of Education, 5,944 of the 12,090 students were women—a gender ratio not duplicated in white colleges and universities. This revealed an approximately 49 percent black female enrollment in black colleges, whether these were good, worse, or substandard. Although no reliable statistics show the ratio of female to male faculty in these black colleges, a conservative estimate is that at least one third of the black faculty were women. In the 1929 college report, *The Crisis* cited thirty-one "outstanding scholars" among the graduates of forty black colleges. Of these, eighteen were women. This high ratio of college-educated black women compared with black males has always been an important but overlooked factor in the professional and economic status of black females within the socioeconomic status of the black group as a whole. No disadvantaged minority group in the United States could boast as high a ratio of college-educated women as has been traditional in the black group. In fact, nowhere in the entire black world—in Africa, the Caribbean, or Latin America—has any black constituency had the degree of access to education that black Americans have had.

Yet black colleges have been demeaned not only by the white college establishment but also by many blacks themselves. Although institutionally black colleges did not measure up to forging the kind of Talented Tenth leadership espoused by Du Bois, their positive socializing influence has been unique. Given the educational context in which black colleges evolved in the United States, where educational values and standards per se were controversial issues, black college education was a remarkable achievement in quantity if not quality. And given the degraded economic, social, and political status of the black minority, it was notable that women were given practically *equal* access at the college level. Thus, the socializing influence of the gender role in black education was one of several factors in black life that belie the fallacies that equate female oppression because of sex with black oppression based on race. For example, educational statistics for the year 1930 reveal that a total of 139,752 degrees of all levels was granted in the United States. At the bachelor's level, 73,615 were awarded to men, 48,869 to women; at the master's level, 8,925 to men, 6,044 to women. At the Ph.D. level, 1,946 were given to men, 353 to women. These figures were taken from the national aggregates.[173] While it is doubtful that such sex ratios were matched in any society in the industrial West in 1930, the overall sex ratios in black colleges were higher and, therefore, more "democratic" based on sex.

How civil rights leaders viewed the educational status and social function of black colleges was important in the legal rationalizations that made them give educational inequalities *priority* in civil rights programming by 1934. The 1929 government *Survey of Negro Colleges* did not deny that gross inequalities needed attention. But, said the report, "the progress made in the development of Negro higher educational institutions in the United States during the last decade has been astonishing in its scope and almost incredible in its magnitude." With regard to the real-property factor, the survey pointed out that:

Ten years ago the annual income of the universities and colleges included in this survey totalled $2,283,000. For 1926–27, the annual income amounted to $8,560,000, an increase of 27.5 per cent. The financial support being accorded Negro higher education is nearly four times what it was in 1917.

Total capital investment in the real properties of these colleges had also increased at a precipitate rate, said the report. In 1917 the value of the physical plants of these institutions had been fixed at $15,720,000. In 1929 this value had risen to $38,680,000, representing a gain of 146 percent, due principally to the construction of modern school buildings and other physical improvements. Given the retrograde race-relations situation in the southern states at that time, such material advances in black education were truly phenomenal. Said the report:

> The most important advances made by the institutions, however, has been the large increase in their productive endowments, indicating the existence of a growing conviction that Negro higher education must be placed on a permanent basis through the provision of a stable annual income. In 1917, the productive endowments of the universities and colleges making up this survey amounted to $7,225,000 with an annual yield of $361,250. Since then additions have brought this total up to $20,713,000, the annual yield being $1,071,300. The gain over the period of 10 years in both endowment and annual yield, therefore, has been approximately 185 percent.

The 1929 survey committee was also "favorably impressed with the excellent preparation of the teachers":

> On repeated occasions teaching of outstanding quality was observed in college classes in literature, modern language, mathematics, science, and in many other subjects. Notwithstanding notable defects in the teaching at certain institutions, there is every reason to believe that proper encouragement and more adequate financial support will serve to develop the quality of teaching in Negro higher educational institutions to a high standard.

Though this was an assessment of black colleges in the aggregate in 1929, black education was not only separate but unequal (unequal compared with white colleges in the aggregate), and for Du Bois's Talented Tenth, the black elites, the rising middle class, and those who aspired—*there was the rub*! Moreover, except for professional education in medicine, dentistry, pharmacy, law, and theology, black colleges did not rate doctoral programs in the sciences and liberal arts. Even more demeaning for the standout black graduates with scholarly teaching ambitions were the low salaries: "The average salary paid the upper third of teachers in all the institutions is $2,263 annually. The average salary of the lower third is only $863.'' For white institutions in what was called the "South Central Division" of the southern land-grant colleges, the upper median salary was $4,958, the lower, $2,016.[174] Thus, after sixty-five years, beginning from the end of the Civil War, the education of blacks in predominantly southern black colleges, aside from being separate, was assessed as inferior.

As a reflection of the Du Bois intellectual persona, of being the transcendent product of a superior education, education for progress per se was, as several observers have noted, "the ideal that unified the Talented Tenth. This unity around the ideal of education transcended divisions of personality, politics, and ideology. Other civil rights efforts might fail—exercise of the ballot, protection under the law, inclusion in labor unions and professional bodies—it was the rare Afro-American bourgeois or elite member who faltered in the faith in higher education.'' But despite the demonstrable progress being registered in black education, it was still inferior and appeared doomed to remain so if far-reaching changes were not made within black colleges, or if other avenues to higher education for blacks were not opened up. Racial discrimination and segregation had imposed the stamp of inferiority on black education. Hence, the NAACP's shift in civil rights emphasis to institutionalized discrimination against blacks in education. Hence, the entry of the American Fund for Public Service (the Garland Fund) in 1934 with a financial contribution to be used exclusively for a campaign of legal action and public education against the unequal apportionment of public funds for education.

Viewed in retrospect, the reference to "unequal apportionment of public funds for education" could have implied the intent democratically to equalize public funding of black education, specifically black colleges, by legal action. Such a legal tack would have implied that the NAACP programmatically supported the legitimacy and the perpetuation of separate black educational institutions. This was one of the questions Du Bois put to the NAACP leadership in his critique of its ambiguous stand on segregation. However, subsequent legal tactics on the part of the NAACP clearly showed that the governing philosophy of the association was *not* to defend the legitimacy of separate black schools. Taking off legally in the *School Segregation Cases* with references to the "unequal apportionment of public funds for education" was only a legal ploy. The main intent behind it would not be openly declared until the *Brown* decision twenty years later, when the NAACP disavowed either the necessity, the desirability, or the legal justification for separate black public schools on the elementary and secondary levels. In the meantime, following the entry of the Garland Fund into the matter, the prime target would *not* be against "unequal apportionment of public funds" for black elementary and high school education, but the white university establishment, by filing lawsuits against graduate and professional schools in the South and Southwest that had traditionally barred eligible blacks.

When the American Fund for Public Service began its collaboration with the NAACP, Nathan R. Margold, then the Solicitor in the Department of the Interior, represented the Fund. At that stage, the Garland Fund memorandum proposed an initial attack on civil rights issues as follows:

> It is proposed that taxpayers' suits be brought to force *equal* if separate accommodations for Negroes as well as whites. . . . It is suggested that seven (7) suits in the worst states, as follows, be instituted: South Carolina, Georgia, Mississippi, Louisiana, Florida, Alabama, Arkansas. . . . Such taxpayers' suits, it is believed, will (a) make the cost of a dual school system so prohibitive as to speed the abolishment of segregated schools; (b) serve as examples and give courage to Negroes to bring similar suits. . . .[175]

But Margold was not in full accord with the Garland Fund memorandum: "Margold himself, however, would have preferred an all-out attack on segregation itself—based upon *Yick Wo*—which he believed would gain not only the improvements suggested by the memorandum, but probably more. . . " Margold felt:

> It would be a great mistake to fritter away our limited funds on sporadic attempts to force the making of equal divisions of school funds in the few instances where such attempts might be expected to succeed. At the most, we could do no more than eliminate a very minor part of the discrimination during the year our suits are commenced. We should not be establishing any new principles, nor bringing any sort of pressure to bear which can reasonably be expected to retain the slightest force beyond that exerted by the specific judgment or order that we might obtain. And we should be leaving wholly untouched the very essence of the existing evils.
>
> On the other hand if we boldly challenge the constitutional validity of segregation if and when accompanied irremediably by discrimination, we can strike directly at the most prolific sources of discrimination.

We can transform into an authoritative adjudication the principle of law, now only theoretically inferable from *Yick Wo* v. *Hopkins,* that segregation coupled with discrimination resulting from administrative action permitted but not required by state statute, is just as much a denial of equal protection of the laws as is segregation coupled with discrimination required by express statutory enactment. And the threat of using the adjudication as a means of destroying segregation itself, would always exert a very real and powerful force at least to compel enormous improvement in the Negro schools through voluntary official action.[176]

In terms of the legal strategy then being proposed, this reference to *Yick Wo* v. *Hopkins* was like returning to the scene of a crime in order to reconstruct what actually occurred, but then coming away leaving the most crucial evidence behind. Margold inferred that in some constitutional fashion *Yick Wo* was, by itself, more relevant than *Strauder-Buchanan-Nixon.* But how? The *Yick Wo* lawsuit was not about racial segregation in education or housing, or discrimination in transportation, public places, etc. For all anyone knows today, Yick Wo's family might have resided in a racially segregated "Chinatown in San Francisco." *Yick Wo* v. *Hopkins* had to do with the right of a nonwhite minority member to operate a business in an economic free-enterprise market activity. The right of a Chinese to operate a laundry had nothing to do with any equal division of state funds, nor did any administrative action by the state to prevent him, whether permitted or not by state statute, have anything to do with the "equal divisions of school funds." Thus, Margold's contention that basing *School Segregation* lawsuits on the principles of *Yick Wo* would be "establishing new principles" was a legal non sequitur. The real, self-evident principles of *Yick Wo* were not even identified by Margold, and not only because they were inapplicable to the issue of public school segregation. If, indeed, Margold had the full minority-group economic sense of the *Yick Wo* case in the back of his mind, he did not spell it out in his departure from the Garland Fund memorandum. If using "limited funds on sporadic attempts to force the making of equal divisions of school funds" was, indeed, a waste of resources, there was nothing in *Yick Wo* that offered any better option beyond a mere verbal, but empty, threat of adjudication. The lawyers, in this instance, were grasping at a legal straw that had several years before floated away through *Moore* v. *Dempsey.* The very fact that the Garland Fund lawyers could not cite it explains why the recall of *Yick Wo* left Margold dangling in the contemplation of seeing in *Yick Wo* something not there. His talk of using the *Yick Wo* "adjudication as a means of destroying segregation itself" was legal nonsense. Which, of course, explains why the joint NAACP–Garland Fund legal pact on public school segregation proceeded to bypass Margold's proposition:

> In fact, the aspect of elementary and high school education which Margold proposed to assail was not approached seriously by the participants in the campaign he helped to map out until about 1950.[177]

Why 1950 (the coming of *Brown*) and not 1934? First, because the 1930s were patently not amenable to a Supreme Court ruling on public school desegregation—especially a conservative and mean Supreme Court that was trying to kill Roosevelt's New Deal. Because of the judicial temper that prevailed, the NAACP decided to shift its focus so that "the actual casework was launched in the 1930's with suits against graduate and professional schools. The reasoning behind this tack appears to have been that inequality in higher education could be proved with ease. *There were virtually no public Negro graduate and professional schools in the South, and judges would readily understand the shortcomings of separate legal education, which some of the cases concerned.*" It was reasoned that:

> Since it would be financially impossible to furnish true equality—both tangible and intangible—desegregation would be the only practicable way to fulfill the constitutional obligation to equal protection. *Small numbers of mature students were involved, undercutting arguments based on violence and widespread social revolution. Finally, Negro leadership would be augmented whether there was desegregation or enriched separate schools.*[178] (Italics added.)

This strategical shift away from Margold's legal line was put under the direction of Charles H. Houston, vice-dean of Howard University Law School, and initiated in 1934. "While schools were the primary interest in this undertaking, cases involving restrictive covenants, public accommodations, interstate travel, recreation, the rights of criminal defendants, voting, and other activities were also brought or defended as part of a coordinated effort to create civil rights precedents in the courts." In 1936 Attorney Charles H. Houston, in an article, "How to Fight for Better Schools," gave this advice:

In every state both by legislation and judicial decision public school systems are made responsive to public control and demands. The difficulty is that the Negro in the South has been kept out of governmental and administrative affairs so long that he does not consider himself part of the sovereign public. The first item on any program for improvement of public schools for Negroes must be convincing the mass of Negroes themselves that they are part of the public which owns and controls the schools. They must be taught that strictly speaking there is no such thing as a Negro public school, or a white public school. There are public schools administered and attended exclusively by Negroes, and public schools administered and attended exclusively by whites. But both schools belong to one and the same system, and the system belongs to the public.[179]

While urging the "mass of Negroes" to become actively involved in the business of school boards, school budgets, and the public records of school administration, Houston was preparing the ground for the coming of *Brown*. However, at this stage, Houston did not mention the term "integration" of *de facto* and *de jure* racially separate public school systems. It was much too premature even to contemplate integration, since the strategies being mapped out had to avoid being viewed as instigations for "violence and widespread social revolution." The issue of desegregation in the public elementary and high schools was placed on the civil rights back burner, while Charles H. Houston directed attention to the *main* priority: desegregation in higher education. What followed from this strategy was a number of lawsuits involving black students seeking entry into graduate and professional schools in traditionally all-white southern universities. The three most important and prominent lawsuits were: *Missouri* ex rel. *Gaines* v. *Canada* (1938), *Sweatt* v. *Painter* (1950), and *McLaurin* v. *Oklahoma State Regents* (1950).

This decisive turn in the NAACP's civil rights strategy was already in process at the moment Du Bois embarked on his comprehensive critique of the association's overall orientation. Black education as a spearheading movement for social change was indeed a novel conception. Since the overwhelming majority of black people did not and would never go to college, what was in the offing was a program of *social reform elitism* that, in the eyes of its sponsors, would avoid dangerous dalliance with "social revolution."

Significantly, the NAACP altered its style in its annual summary on the progress of black education. Prior to 1934, this annual summary had

covered primarily the enrollment figures in black colleges, which up to
the 1930s numbered slightly over ninety. However, the NAACP's education report of 1934 covered only seventy-one colleges, of which only
forty-two were traditionally black schools. The total black enrollment in
these institutions was approximately 15,307. Of this total, the heaviest
enrollment was naturally in the black schools. However, the twenty-nine
northern white colleges and universities covered in this report enrolled
approximately 799 black students. Among these institutions were Harvard
with 4 blacks, Yale with 10, University of Illinois with 122, Wayne
University with 182, and Dartmouth with 1. Since this annual report was
geared to be highly selective, the enrollment of *all* the black schools was
not reported.[180] Thus, the enrollment estimate of 15,307, an undercount,
revealed that despite the economic collapse of 1929, and the deepening
of the economic crisis in the worst days of 1933–1934, *black college
attendance had increased.*

However, this quantitative expansion of black college attendance
only concealed that *qualitatively* black segregated education was not producing the intellectually and socially liberating results that education per
se had promised. Du Bois had popularized the elite ideal of the Talented
Tenth, men and women trained to be ''leaders of thought and missionaries
of culture among their people. The Negro race, like all other races, is
going to be saved by its exceptional men'':

> I believed in the higher education of the Talented Tenth, who through
> their knowledge of modern culture could guide the American Negro
> into higher civilization. I knew that without this the Negro would have
> to accept white leadership, and that such leadership could not always
> be trusted to guide this group into self-realization and to its highest
> cultural possibilities.[181]

But by the 1930s, Du Bois's educational ideal for blacks had been
turned from a noble theme into a tragicomedy. Despite the astonishing
increase in black enrollment in institutions of higher learning, exactly
what kind of higher education was necessary for the realization of the
intellectual role of Du Bois's Talented Tenth? How many of the black
college students of 1934 envisioned themselves as potential leaders who
would guide ''the American Negro into higher civilization''? In fact,
what constituted ''higher civilization'' for blacks in American society—
a society that was then looked down upon by ''civilized'' and ''cultured''
Europeans as ''uncultured'' and materialistic? For Europeans and others
scrambling to emigrate to the United States, America had only one thing

to offer in addition to freedom and democracy and that was the opportunity
to make money, earn a good living, and, perhaps, get rich. It would not
require much imagination to guess that the average black college student
in the 1930s was motivated by the same ambition. Thus, it was already
demonstrable that the NAACP's civil rights shift to the desegregation of
higher education might succeed in elevating the educational image of
black students in social status and prestige, but would not augment "Negro leadership."

    At the very moment when the Margold–NAACP–Garland Fund civil
rights shift was initiated, a spirited debate was going on within the black
student–academic community over the ultimate social and cultural consequences of black education. Specifically, the debate was an evaluation
of black colleges as viable institutions in the educational process of aug-
menting "Negro leadership." One debate, among several, that summed
up the issues was published in the NAACP's *Crisis* magazine after Du
Bois's departure and was titled "Which College—White or Negro?"
Written by a black student in a contest conducted by the NAACP, the
article said:

> In this period of changing social conditions in which the fate of the
> Negro fluctuates with every rising or ebbing tide of economic prosperity,
> this question is one of vast and profound significance, is the white
> college educating the Negro to the end that he will look at life more
> intelligently and cope with its bewildering problems more confidently
> than the Negro college; or is the Negro college more far-reaching in
> the complicated task of fitting the Negro youth for the proper social
> adjustment to an environment that is both discouraging to his most
> ambitious efforts?[182]

    In his prizewinning essay, the student described the social, academic,
and intellectual experiences of black students in white colleges in the
1930s as he saw it. He noted the isolation of the lone black athlete who
made the varsity football team, who must practice tact and diplomacy in
everyday contacts with teammates, coaches, professors, and students in
order to survive. He mentioned the serious black student doomed to bury
himself or herself in the dormitory room with books because most ex-
tracurricular activities on campus were closed to a black student. He
described the attitudes of the average white college student toward the
average black student: "They are polite, too polite, but they never thaw."
The student asked: What college channels were open to the black student
for the development of his/her latent talents, or some distinction in rec-

ognition of individual merit or ability? What about the dramatic club? he asked. Would the black student be eligible? In most cases, no. What about the fraternities? Even if the black student elected to "segregate" himself or herself, in a "Negro Fraternity," such a fraternity, wrote the student, would have had "just about as much influence and activity on the white campus as a dead man in the catacombs of Rome." Well, what about the college literary guild? If the black student was gifted with some literary ability and was accepted in the guild, he or she was told it would be a wonderful opportunity for the guild to hear some entertaining "Negro dialect" stories or poetry after the fashion of Joel Chandler Harris, Paul Laurence Dunbar, Irvin Cobb, and Octavus Roy Cohen.

With the possible exception of the college choir, wrote the student, and certain athletics, "the Negro's chance for demonstrating or developing personal initiative or group leadership is very poor. Go to any campus where the Negro is in the minority and observe how he is neglected by the majority group and how in his own group he is disintegrated by a thousand petty cliques and jealousies. If the white college succeeds in doing anything at all, it is highly successful in tearing down the attitude of friendliness between the Negro students. All of them vie for recognition by their white brothers and sisters; and when one in the crowd gets it, like a pack of wolves, the others pounce upon him for trying to 'betray the race.' The student concluded:

> Without hesitation and apology I answer that I believe the Negro college will be the saving grace of the Negro race until the fundamental attitude of the white man toward the Negro makes a radical change. The white college until that time, can never prepare the Negro for life.

Preparation for life meant, of course, preparation for gainful employment either outside the confines of academia or inside black educational institutions. After the black student graduates, the student asked, "Where is he to teach and what race of people?":

> Nine times out of ten he finds himself instructing black boys and girls in the delta of Louisiana or the foothills of some sunbaked Georgia town. And how does this Negro who has been taught with white students conduct himself? Does he come to the South with the feeling that it is not so bad after all; or does he still cling to the view that his education is something so greatly superior to his fellow teachers, graduates of Negro schools, that he is forever casting aspersions on his co-workers? Does he accept conditions as he finds them or is he constantly referring to the Negro's advantages in Columbus, Ohio?

Usually, wrote the student, the black products of white colleges cast aspersions on the general qualities of black educational institutions and the people involved. The black products of white institutions found it difficult to work with blacks because they had spent all of their college years trying to get away from blacks gracefully or in trying to approach them awkwardly and artificially. They were not prepared for life among their own people because they were unsympathetic to their aims and shortcomings, never having experienced the same group ambitions or despair:

> He cannot lead the people because he has not the initiative and he cannot follow a leader because he feels he is too superior. There is only one thing he can do successfully and that is to deride and criticize his associates who have been "victims" of a segregated school system. He is a tragic, haunted, incapable misfit, and usually finds his way across the Mason-Dixon line in search of a position commensurate with his opinion of his abilities, and finally consoles himself with a red cap blue uniform in the station of some metropolitan railroad terminus.

The student claimed that if any college prepared black youth at all for service and dignified work, it was the Negro college. In this view, the student in question had an army of supporters but also a multitude of detractors. His arguments were symptomatic of the raging debate within the ranks of black professionals, educators, and leaders over the positive and negative aspects of segregated black education. Faced with the existence of some ninety-odd black colleges with a growing enrollment and, in many cases, with an expanding range of facilities, the NAACP, in particular, had to conclude that black colleges contradicted its programmatic opposition to all forms of legal segregation. Thus, nonsegregated higher education became the civil rights alternative for blacks because it was seen as being of superior quality. More than that, only nonsegregated colleges (i.e., white colleges) granted doctorates in fields besides medicine, dentistry, pharmacy, and theology. Thus, in effect, in the evolution of the NAACP's involvement in *School Segregation Cases* as its new civil rights program, the association was forced to take the position of having it *both* ways by formally accepting segregated black education while seeking to eliminate it by legally campaigning for increased black enrollment in *de facto* all-white colleges. Contrary to the prizewinning student's estimate of the education of blacks in white colleges, the NAACP rationalized that *"Negro leadership would be augmented whether there was desegregation or enriched separate schools."* However, again it was Du Bois who pointedly disagreed with the NAACP on the issue of black education. He spelled out his views the following year in an article, "Does the Negro Need Separate Schools?"[183] His answer was an emphatic *Yes*.

Thus, the turn in the NAACP's civil rights strategies that evolved into the *School Segregation Cases* occurred amid a debate among the black elites on the educational value of separate black colleges. Of course, the seminal arguments relating to this issue had been voiced even before the NAACP was founded. In the *public* elementary and secondary school arena, the issue of racially separate facilities had been voiced during the arguments over the Blair Education Bill. Later, what was called the "Washington–Du Bois controversy" had its roots in Du Bois's criticisms of Tuskegee's "industrial education" philosophy being accepted as the preferred content for black education. At that time, hardly any black spokesman argued against the existence of separate black schools. As Du Bois had often pointed out, "the plain fact faces us, that either we will have separate schools or we will not be educated."

Having officially resigned from the NAACP, Du Bois not only expressed an unofficial vote in absentia against the association's new legal tack on black education, he also outlined into future perspective the eventual outcome of the *School Segregation Cases* twenty years in advance of the *Brown* decision. "The question I am discussing," he wrote, " 'are these separate schools and institutions needed?' And the answer, to my mind is perfectly clear. They are needed just so far as they are necessary for the proper education of the Negro race":

> The proper education of any people includes sympathetic touch between teacher and pupil; knowledge on the part of the teacher, not simply of the individual taught, but of his surroundings and background, and the history of his class and group; such contact between pupils, and between teacher and pupil, on the basis of perfect social equality, as will increase this sympathy and knowledge; facilities for education in equipment and housing, and the promotion of such extra-curricular activities as will tend to induct the child into life. . . .

"To sum this up, theoretically," said Du Bois, *"the Negro needs neither segregated schools nor mixed schools. What he needs is Education. What he must remember is that there is no magic, either in mixed schools or in segregated schools. A mixed school with poor and unsym-*

pathetic teachers, with hostile public opinion, and no teaching of truth
concerning black folk, is bad. A segregated school with ignorant place-
holders, inadequate equipment, poor salaries, and wretched housing is
equally bad.'' (Italics added.)

Implied here was much more than the functional problem of segregated education; it was the failed hopes of the great educator himself.
Despite the quantitative leap forward of black education up to the 1930s,
qualitatively, black education (segregated or otherwise) had proved a
consummate failure. Black education had produced a growing crop of
formally "educated" blacks, but it had *not* produced a representative
corps of *leaders in any field* either inside or outside academia. The reason?
Black education was not designed either by blacks or whites to accomplish
such an intellectual goal. By the 1930s, this dismal fact had become so
graphic that another prominent black intellectual leader, the historian-
educator Carter G. Woodson summed up the problem in *The Mis-Edu-*
cation of the Negro (1933).

Woodson argued that the Talented Tenth in whom Du Bois had
placed so much faith were actually products of institutionalized "mis-
education." Woodson opened his critique by outlining a history of
mistakes made and perpetuated in the education of Afro-Americans, and
admitted that as an educator he had committed some of the errors himself.
He declared that after forty years of experience of educating the "black,
brown, yellow and white races" in both hemispheres, it was his conclusion that the educational system that had developed in both Europe and
America was an antiquated process that did not even meet the needs of
white people: "If the white man wants to hold on to it, let him do so;
but the Negro, so far as he is able, should develop and carry out a program
of his own." This was the conclusion of an elite among the black elites,
a Harvard-trained historian who had once "never faltered in his faith in
higher education":

The "educated Negroes" have the attitude of contempt toward their
own people because in their own as well as in their mixed schools
Negroes are taught to admire the Hebrew, the Greek, the Latin and the
Teuton and to despise the African. . . . Practically all of the successful
Negroes in this country are of the uneducated type or of Negroes who
have had no formal education. The large majority of the Negroes who
have put on the finishing touches of our best colleges are all but worthless
in the development of their people.[184]

For this situation, Woodson placed the blame on both black and white educators, but mostly on the whites who had trained the blacks who had attempted to train other blacks. Was this indictment an exaggeration? A finicky discontent with the arduously slow pace of intellectual cultivation by an impatient Elder Statesman? In 1933, Woodson was fifty-eight, Du Bois sixty-three—both of them were castigating the then maturing generations of their highly touted Talented Tenth. Sixty-eight years out of the shackles of chattel bondage, the collective black mind was charged with having been crippled by the American education system of values! The Great Depression had shown up the most glaring deficiencies in the group existence of blacks, not only in the area of economics, but even more insidiously in the molding processes of the mind imposed by higher education, which, according to Woodson, was the root of the trouble. Whereas Du Bois presented a reasoned argument that courted both sides of a group approach to life (integration versus segregation), Woodson's remonstrance was unilateral, allowing no margin for rebutting his interpretation of what the goals of black education ought to be. If Du Bois called into question the values of the Talented Tenth, Woodson went further and illuminated the roots of those values in the very educational processes that were supposed to inculcate a more viable and constructive black *gestalt*. While a Du Bois was content to chide the Talented Tenth into reforming themselves *within* the context of the educational system that produced them, Woodson preferred to junk that system almost in its entirety and fashion a new one closer to his heart's desire. Among other disastrous results of the educational system, it had failed to teach blacks the basic arts of earning a living in a hostile economic and social environment. The educational system produced "educated Negroes" who estranged themselves from the "masses." Outside control of black education had succeeded in discouraging black professional education. In the face of the continued political disfranchisement of blacks, *political education* of the most elementary sort had been neglected, especially in black institutions. Woodson's disaffection with American education insofar as blacks were involved was well nigh total. He did not cite the NAACP by designation, as had Du Bois, but his reference to "social uplift" groups made the inference clear: "We have appealed to the Talented Tenth for a remedy, but they have nothing to offer. Their minds have never functioned. . . ." The "educated Negro shows no evidence of vision. . . . The Negro must now do for himself or die out as the world undergoes readjustment."

Actually Du Bois thought the same as Woodson, except that he, the sociologist par excellence, placed the problem of black education within the many-sided social, economic, and cultural contexts in which the educational process took place. Considering the then current attitude of white America toward black America, not only did blacks need to maintain and defend their separate schools, but it seemed certain that in the future they might need more of such schools: "It is of course fashionable and popular to deny this," he wrote. "To try to deceive ourselves into thinking that race prejudice in the United States across the Color Line is gradually softening and that slowly but surely we are coming to the time when racial animosities and class lines will be so obliterated that separate schools will be anachronisms."

Much as he would like to hope that one day American public education would "create the intelligent basis of a real democracy," he had to face the fact that "race prejudice in the United States is such that most Negroes cannot receive proper education in white institutions":

> If the public schools of Atlanta, Nashville, New Orleans and Jacksonville were thrown open to all races tomorrow, the education that colored children would get in them would be worse than pitiable. It would not be education. And in the same way, there are many public school systems in the North where Negroes are admitted and tolerated, but they are not educated; they are crucified.[185]

As a product of Harvard, Du Bois knew whereof he spoke regarding black students in northern universities, "where Negro students, no matter what their ability, desert, or accomplishment, cannot get fair recognition, either in classroom or on the campus, in dining halls and student activities, or in common human courtesy":

> It is well-known that in certain faculties of the University of Chicago, no Negro has yet received the doctorate and seldom can achieve the mastership in arts; at Harvard, Yale and Columbia, Negroes are admitted but not welcomed; while in other institutions, like Princeton, they cannot even enroll.[186]

Du Bois admitted that there had to be considerable difference of opinion among blacks as to just how far racial separation in schools ought to be encouraged. "No general and inflexible rule can be laid down." If, for example, public opinion was such that in certain localities black children could not receive decent and sympathetic education in the white schools, and no black teachers could be employed, there was no choice but to accept separate black schools. Where local conditions and favorable public opinion permitted racially mixed schools, they ought to be encouraged. However, where public opinion was manifestly against such policies, Du Bois believed that "the futile attempt to compel even by law a group to do what it is determined not to do, is a silly waste of money, time, and temper."[187] *Twenty years later this questionable waste of money, time, and temper was precisely what occurred in the implementation of the* Brown *decision.*

However, the legal route taken by the NAACP on the segregated school issue would lead inevitably to the "integration" debacle that followed the *Brown* decision. Not until after *Brown* could the black education issues argued by Du Bois in 1935 be clarified. Du Bois had charged:

> The NAACP and other organizations have spent thousands of dollars to prevent the establishment of segregated schools, but scarcely a single cent to see that the division of funds between white and Negro schools, North and South, is carried out with some faint approximation of justice. *There can be no doubt that if the Supreme Court were overwhelmed with cases where the blatant and impudent discrimination against Negro education is openly acknowledged, it would be compelled to hand down decisions which would make this discrimination impossible.*[188] (Italics added.)

Du Bois, though prophetic, would be disproved by future events. Under the prodding of the NAACP lawsuits leading to *Brown,* the Supreme Court did *not* hand down decisions compelling an equal division of funds "between white and Negro schools, North and South," but legitimized the position of Charles H. Houston that there should be "no such thing as a Negro public school or a white public school," hence "integrating" the Negro school, as such, out of existence. Thus did the Supreme Court deny the legitimacy of the important concept of the community or the neighborhood public school. In pursuit of the American democratic imperative, the liberal consensus had done its work without the least comprehension that in one of the most vital areas of public and societal responsibility—*public education, at the primary and secondary levels*—it was committing a disservice to society as a whole. In its efforts to erase the historic guilt-laden carryovers from *Plessy* v. *Ferguson's* separate-but-equal doctrine, *the Supreme Court's* Brown *decision was a mindless act of social irresponsibility.* Racial segregation was *not* the cause of the inferior education found in separate black public schools, and racial integration was no guarantee of the universalization of quality education for blacks or for any other nonwhite minority. If quality education for blacks would not be found in separate Negro public schools, it would, likewise, not be discovered in integrated school systems. The root of a lack of quality education was to be found not in segregated education, but in American educational philosophy as a whole. Essentially, American education was not geared to the intellectual and spiritual needs of nonwhite minorities.

But in keeping with the NAACP's legal timetable on the issue of black education, the *Brown* decision came as a postponement, since the elimination of discrimination in higher education had been the association's top priority. As a result of bypassing the Margold–Garland Fund strategy, the lawsuits launched in the late 1930s against the offending white graduate and professional schools began to pay off in the post-World War II period. Breakthroughs in higher education were made possible by the new civil rights atmosphere encouraged by the Truman administration. Truman's 1946 committee to inquire into the condition of civil rights specifically recommended the elimination of discrimination in higher education. By 1952 the NAACP's priority campaign on the higher education front, begun in 1938, had made successful inroads into the predominantly white bastions of colleges and universities to the extent that "there were perhaps twelve thousand Negroes enrolled in Northern and Western colleges in the Fall of 1950, with another 67,000 enrolled in colleges in the South; enabling one to guess that seven per cent of Negro children in the elementary schools, and ten per cent in the high schools, and fifteen per cent of Negro college students, are physically 'integrated' as part of the whole American educational complex."[189]

The prime goal of the NAACP had been achieved—the integration of black aspirants to higher education into the privileged, prestigious preserves of white graduates *four years before the* Brown *decision* without a *"social revolution."* There the legal agitation on the integration-education question should have stopped. Integration in higher education had its social, intellectual, and professional justifications. American institutions of higher learning *should be* open to the admission of *all,* irrespective of race, creed, color, or sex. But the primary and secondary public school system was a horse of another civil rights coloration. The administration of primary and secondary public school education should have been left under the guidance of community control, wherever feasible, practical, and possible, as a matter of local adult social responsibility—which was what Du Bois argued with such passion:

> But in the case of the education of the young, you must consider not simply yourself but the children and the relation of children to life. It is difficult to think of anything more important for the development of a people than proper training for their children; and yet I have repeatedly seen wise and loving colored parents take infinite pains to force their little children into schools where the white children, white teachers, and white parents despised and resented the dark child, made mock of it, neglected or bullied it, and literally rendered its life a living hell. Such parents want their child to "fight this thing out,"—but, dear God, at what a cost.[190]

The NAACP's ordering of civil rights priorities in the 1930s spoke unwritten volumes about the character of the association as a leadership organization. Its strengths and weaknesses were the logical endproducts of its origins—a set of questionable philosophical ideals, the social consequences of which the NAACP would never escape. Although justified and rationalized by the assumption that the quality and quantity of Negro leadership would be augmented by making integration in higher education the main priority, the new legal strategy would ultimately cancel out the NAACP's impact and leadership potential; *even more, it would cast into doubt any* raison d'être *for its continued existence after the Civil Rights Acts of 1964–1965.*

On the integration of blacks into American society, the judicial, executive, and legislative processes leading to the elimination of legally enforced and *de facto* segregation in public places and accommodations, public transportation, housing, employment, recreation, the military, had all been set in irrevocable motion before the *Brown* decision. Such civil rights were constitutionally legitimate and socially demanded for the racial democratization of society. *However, during the democratization process, black administrative control over the previously segregated and* de facto *racially separate schools within the public school system should have been fought for and maintained wherever feasible, at all costs, especially in the urban centers.* When the NAACP leadership rejected South Carolina's offer to equalize the racially separate public school system by massive increases in state appropriations in an effort to forestall the *Brown* decision, *the association negated in advance the possibility of black political bases being fashioned around the important state func-*

tion of public school funding and administration. Such was one facet, the *political* facet, of the midcentury outcome of the "Crisis in Negro Leadership" that emerged in 1920.

In the game of electoral politics, black leadership has had no issues of political leverage, only numerical voting strength. However, this voting strength has never been predicated on a political power base grounded in tangible economic, administrative, cultural, or social policy issues with the viability of forcefully influencing *public policy.* Hence, merely winning public office became the one and only tangible goal for black political leaders. Beyond that, black office holders possessed only the pretense of being backed up by substantive political power bases representing issues that would impact on public policy. Thus, the continuing emphasis on the mobilization of black voting strength; thus, the ongoing campaign for black voter registration; thus, the empty threat that the maximization of black voting strength would somehow alter the course of American political history in race and minority-group issues. However, the Civil Rights Acts of 1964–1965 promised no such grandiose affirmation of potential black political power. While the Voting Rights Act of 1965 did, in fact, speed up the mobilization of black voting strength, and opened the doors to the unprecedented growth in numbers of black elected officials (BEOs), these BEOs were catapulted into office as symbols of black civil rights coming-of-age. But, with rare exceptions, they brought nothing with them into political office that bore the least resemblance to a black economic, political, and cultural program that meant much to anybody, friend or foe, black or white, beyond the politically mundane business as usual stance of the liberal consensus. Following the Sixties, black politicians were suggestive of military leaders whose armies were forever in training (voter registration) but were never readied for participation in the field of battle for substantive goals worth fighting for. Carter G. Woodson had pointed out that one of the failures of the education of blacks in black colleges was *political* training. Under the heading of "Political Education Neglected," Woodson argued that:

> Negroes have been terrorized to the extent that they are afraid even to discuss political matters publicly. There must be no exposition of the principles of government in the schools, and this must not be done in public among Negroes with a view to stimulating political activity. . . .[191]

Thus:

In certain parts, therefore, the Negroes under such terrorism have ceased to think of political matters as their sphere. Where such things come into the teaching in more advanced work they are presented as matters of concern to a particular element rather than as functions in which all citizens may participate. . . . Negroes in certain parts, then, have all but abandoned voting even at points where it might be allowed. In some cases not as many as two thousand Negroes vote in a whole state.[192]

Woodson said this in 1933, at the moment when the NAACP's official policy of noneconomic liberalism was being put to the test by the onslaught of the Great Depression and Du Bois's attacks. But the leadership inspiration by the NAACP up to that time was so ineffectual that even the Talented Tenth were not politically responsive. Said Woodson:

Some of the "educated" Negroes do not pay attention to such important matters as the assessment of property and the collection of taxes, and they do not inform themselves as to how these things are worked out. An influential Negro in the South, then, is one who has nothing to do or say about politics and advises others to follow the same course.[193]

From 1933 to the Civil Rights Acts of 1964–1965, the social, political, and organizational outlook of the newly emergent black middle class and the educated elites did not change substantially. On the contrary, the Civil Rights Acts and the belated enforcement of the Fifteenth Amendment encouraged a wave of new-generation political aspirants to run for office with a minimal comprehension of the full potential of black political power and how it might be organized, mobilized, and managed. *The ongoing absence of an internally organized black community infrastructure of economic, cultural, political, social welfare, educational, self-help efforts would limit the range and effectiveness of the new black political leadership.* This absence, a historical condition, would become more apparent than ever before with the arrival of new black aspirants to political office in the Seventies. They would not be representative of the long-standing organizational influence of either the NAACP or the National Urban League. In fact, the Civil Rights Acts of 1964–1965 would not substantially deter either the NAACP or the National Urban League from continuing to downplay the community organizational supports that black politicians would require in pursuit of *real* black political power. In any era of civil rights advance, whether the Twenties, Thirties, Forties, Fifties, Sixties, Seventies, or the Eighties, the black leadership would remain distinctly middle class. However, as one perceptive social critic has pointed out, "whatever the exaggerations in [E. Franklin] Frazier's account of the 'black bourgeoisie,' there seems to be little doubt that the Negro's ability to organize has for the most part been confined to his social life."[194] Dominating all this evolution in black leadership styles was the NAACP's influence in discouraging and retarding localized community efforts toward self-generating, self-help organizations. The association's blanket integrationist priorities would render its legalistic civil rights victories as politically empty as the victories of black mayors over the economically devastated northern centers of urban decay.

The American societal limits to the implementation of racial integration, in both demographic and sociological theory, were amply demonstrated by E. Franklin Frazier, following the implementation of *Brown* I and *Brown* II. Hence, the racial democratization following the impact of *Brown* ultimately resulted in the hastening of *class stratification* within the black minority group as a whole rather than (plural) racial democracy in economics, politics, culture, and education for blacks. The stratified social elevation of roughly a third of the black minority group re-created a new, post-civil rights version of the earlier black middle class—an unavoidable consequence of the NAACP's essentially middle-class concept of racial equality. If the social organizations of the former black middle class did not extend beyond the particularist function of social club, social clique, class versions of the denominational church, *ad hoc* civil rights or political pressure group, elite fraternity or sorority, or other versions of black voluntary associations, the new black middle-class versions were just as ill-equipped in imagination to respond organizationally to the economic, political, cultural, or educational needs of blacks as a group minority. In this regard, the new black middle class, the upwardly mobile recipients of the Sixties' civil rights rewards, would transcend the organizational limitations of the earlier middle class only to a degree that would prove socially expedient. Such an outcome, however, was unavoidable. As a nation, the United States, which pretends that it is not a class-differentiated society governed by dominant-versus-subordinate class ideologies, is essentially predominantly middle-class oriented. So the ultimate civil rights achievements were the nearest possible approximations by blacks to the norms and standards of the American middle class. On the black political front, this elevation of the new black middle class meant that its political power would be effectively limited and restricted by the iron law of oligarchy. New black political aspirants, enlivened by the late 1960s evocation of Black Power, set out to repeal the iron law of oligarchy, which, as one political analyst observed, had made the old middle-class leadership "unresponsive to the needs of the masses." But lacking the backup of an ongoing organized community infrastructure, the new black political elites could only amend the iron law of oligarchy—they could not change it.

Thus, the black Children of the New Deal and their children, the generations of the Sixties and Seventies, inherited a civil rights legacy fostering the illusion that the civil rights revolution of the post-*Brown* era represented the coming-of-age of a new black leadership that would usher in the millennium in racial equality. Such a heritage of innocence had its social roots in the liberal dispensations of the New Deal—an age of economic recovery and truly a decade of hope. However, post-New Deal racial integration, constitutional equal protection, the reversal of *Plessy*, the reinterpretation of the embattled Fourteenth Amendment, etc.—these hard-won democratic reinforcements, while legally just, socially progressive, and democratically legitimate, lacked the potential to compel full political, economic, cultural, social, and educational equality for black aspirants through the integration process already undergone, a built-in societal saturation level beyond which minority-group advances are materially blocked. At that point, material and psychological realities remain impervious to laws, court decisions, protests, and legal manipulations. This fact would not become clear until the 1980s.

P ART FOUR

I

In the wake of the *Brown* decision, the air of an unprecedented emergency pervaded most of the large black communities. Judging from the general media coverage, the same was probably true for most of white America even though the Supreme Court's mandate on public school segregation was pointedly aimed at a uniquely southern education issue. Since the emergency proclaimed a quality of alert that had never before been sounded, few among the millions of whites and blacks, except those in the South, pretended to imagine exactly what it meant. More than that, if this alert heralded a new emergency for black communities, there was a disturbing absence of the quality of leadership one would expect to come to the fore to face the unanticipated contingencies certain to result.

Apart from the leaders associated with the NAACP who had labored so diligently to realize the era of *Brown,* few others were of the national stature of an A. Philip Randolph in his own field of labor. When the *Brown* era arrived, Afro-Americans could boast of numerous spokesmen, but scarcely any deserved the designation of "leader" of national stature. The NAACP leadership had matured into roles that were decidedly one-dimensional, operating under the lone functional banner of civil rights. But as crucial as civil rights was to the fortunes of black America in midcentury, it was still a one-dimensional approach to the goals of racial equality. For at the fateful, historical moment of *Brown,* it was barely recalled that thirty-four years had passed since the "Crisis in Negro Leadership" was acknowledged in 1920. Randolph, still active, had debated the political and economic significance of the crisis. That great man W.E.B. Du Bois, who had emphasized the almost complete irrelevancy of "Negro Leadership" in 1934, was surprisingly still active. More the social thinker and critic than a leader of mass influence, Du Bois in 1954 was far too old and much too unappreciated by the emergent *Brown*-era generation. In 1954, Du Bois could not boast of a recognizable "Du Bois School of Intellectual Thought," or even one outstanding intellectual heir to embrace the man's immense range of creative thought.

Thus, *Brown* was but one additional feature of the rapid social and legal transformation of American society, a historical process in which the important facts of the year before fade like popular fashions. There was little consciousness that since the 1920s—despite the Great Depression, a wrenching economic dislocation lasting ten years, a world war involving the nation for nearly five years, five years of postwar social and economic readjustment—"The Crisis in Negro Leadership" had not been remedied. In fact, there was in 1954 little if any recognition that such a crisis had ever existed. More to the point, this crisis had *not* been solved with the aid of the New Deal, *but had actually been confounded and deepened.* By virtue of its proxy federal role in the public sector, the New Deal scattered its limited social reform benefits among blacks in such fashion that the nascent leadership was transformed into a new class of spokesmen and spokeswomen whose function was to beseech the administrators of the white power establishments in the public sector for fair treatment on behalf of their black constituencies. Prior to the New Deal, the opportunities for such a leadership style were limited. Once the American celebration of capitalistic free-enterprise market relationships and the spirit of individualistic self-reliance were drowned out by the economic collapse, the New Deal ushered in a new era of federal power as a social and economic benefactor to the victims of distress. Du Bois, for one, did not believe that the New Deal would seriously alter the fringe position of blacks in the economic order in its pre- or post-1929 capitalistic form:

> We have reached the end of an economic era, which seemed but a few years ago omnipotent and eternal. We have lived to see the collapse of capitalism. It makes no difference what we may say, and how we may boast in the United States of the failures and changed objectives of the New Deal, and the prospective rehabilitation of the rule of finance capital; that is but wishful thinking . . . the whole organization and direction of industry is changing. We are not called upon to be dogmatic as to just what the end of this change will be. . . . What we are sure of is the present fundamental change.[1]

What *did* change for American blacks at that critical juncture was the concept of the nature of black leadership. In his critique of the leadership style of the NAACP, Du Bois had charged that this style did not *"envisage any direct action of Negroes themselves for the uplift of their social depressed masses."* Moreover, in the very conception of that program, the uplift of the black masses would *"be attended to by the nation and [blacks] are to be the subjects of uplift forces and agencies to the extent of their numbers and need."* In other words, according to this philosophy, black leadership would entail no social, cultural, political, or economic roles beyond the scope of a civil rights program narrowly defined by demands for constitutional legality. Few critics were willing to point out that this concept of leadership was, in effect, a rationalization that negated the social determinants of true leadership. Conveniently for this concept of leadership, the New Deal's uplift forces and agencies were a godsend: The implication was that handing over economic and other problems and making the black masses wards of the New Deal, *there would be no further need for any effort but civil rights by a declared leadership.* The "Crisis in Negro Leadership" of 1920 was thus qualified by a retreat in the face of social reality, and was to reappear under a new banner of spokesmanship.

By 1954 the "Crisis in Negro Leadership" had long been smoothed over by mollifying anointings of political liberalism and the institutionalization of black spokesmanship. In the secular political, economic, and cultural sense, a true leadership class had disappeared. What had blossomed in its stead was a fluctuating procession of black spokesmen and spokeswomen whose ranks were widely accessible and moderately remunerative, a career opportunity for the alert, the knowledgeable, the more ambitious, and the opportunistic. In any real sense, the only black leaders with real constituencies were preachers of various Protestant denominations. Rarely political or economic, black church constituencies were, however, strongly anchored in grass-roots community settings, serving both a religious and a social function. Despite exceptions, black preachers generally avoid civil rights protest activities and civic leadership roles. Yet they maintain the strongest "prestige" leadership roles of any political or civic spokesmen within the black communities.

Following the heyday of the New Deal, the welfare-state administrative apparatus became, for better or worse, the best of all possible worlds for the black underprivileged. Successful or would-be black spokesmen came and went, riding the popularity crests of every welfare-state innovation, exhorting, agitating, arousing, pleading, cajoling, condemning, or upholding. The ideological blanket of the politics and economics of whiteness would brook no elevation of black spokesmen to platforms of national prominence. A champion prizefighter or an Olympic medalist would be allowed recognition by the mass media as a "credit to his race"; a religious cult leader with a mass following would be sensationalized by the press, both as a curiosity and as proof that religion was the preferred opiate for the social and economic marginality of being black. But no secular black leader in the politics or economics of black survival would appear. Only when the international impact of World War II wrenched the American nation and its black minority out of a myopic, self-satisfied insularity, did the welfare-warfare state of affairs wipe the social history of the Twenties and Thirties from the pages of contemporary references. Civil rights issues took on a new gloss with the advent of Harry S. Truman. The Democratic party encountered the fact that, willy-nilly, black migrations had built up balance-of-power voting bases in key northern cities that could not be ignored by any White House occupant or hopeful. The growth of an unheralded black voting power became one of the new factors in the post-World War II period of readjustment. But this development in black political power, which played such an important role in the 1948 reelection of Truman, was not accompanied by a comparable enhancement of black leadership in politics or any other field. Among the definitions of the essential qualities of leadership, one is that it must make its followers more conscious of their innate potential. As one theorist has put it, leadership, to be effective if not great, "does not dictate; rather it engages the fundamental needs and wants, aspirations, and expectations of the followers." Moreover:

> Leadership is a process of morality to the degree that leaders engage with followers on the basis of shared motives and values and goals— on the basis, that is, of the followers' "true" needs as well as those of leaders: psychological, economic, safety, spiritual, sexual, aesthetic, or physical. Friends, relatives, teachers, officials, politicians, ministers, and others will supply a variety of initiatives, but only the followers themselves can ultimately define their own true needs. And they can do so only when they have been exposed to the competing diagnoses, claims, and values of would-be leaders, only when the followers can make an informed choice among competing "prescriptions," only when—*in the political arena at least*—followers have had full opportunity to perceive, comprehend, evaluate, and finally experience alternatives offered by those professing to be their "true" representatives. Ultimately the *moral legitimacy of transformational leadership, and to a lesser degree transactional leadership,* is grounded in *conscious choice among real alternatives.* Hence leadership assumes competition and conflict, and brute power denies it.[2] (Italics added.)

Not once in the twentieth century has the Afro-American minority group been allowed this quality of leadership. The stress and grinding strain of sheer survival within the grip of the most rapid social changes has frustrated its emergence since the 1920s. Since that time, much of the conscious struggle and subconscious striving on the part of hopeful, forward-looking blacks of whatever class, has been, as one observer has put it, "the politics of the 'Search for Leadership.' " Thus, given the specific ideological and political temper of the late Forties and early Fifties, the emergence of Martin Luther King, Jr., was both curious and significant. That a black leader of his style would not only appear but would subsequently grow in personal stature so as to be acclaimed by Afro-Americans as the *single* black leader in the twentieth century seemed then, a remote possibility. In fact, as we will see, the possibility had been raised—and demolished—by one of the more astute observers of the times. But the fact that King was a Baptist preacher emphasized an element peculiar to the black experience that could have been predictable.

The most authoritative black spokesmen have always been preachers rather than purely secular leaders. In the politics of race, the white power structures had little fear that preachers could not be trusted to exercise the social control of interracial accommodation.

In 1948, Oliver Cromwell Cox, a black sociologist of exceptional scholarship, published *Caste, Class and Race—A Study in Social Dynamics*. It was, and remains, a brilliant feat of analytic virtuosity covering a wide range of investigations into the phenomena of caste, class, and race as reflected in the social practices of a variety of world cultures. Beginning with the evolution of India's caste system, Cox moved on to the evolution of class, covering such facets as political-class struggle, democracy and class struggle, and class and caste. Finally, he tackled the subject that had motivated his book, the race problem in the United States. The specific compulsion behind Cox's study was to attack and invalidate the underlying thesis of Gunnar Myrdal's *An American Dilemma*.

Myrdal, as explained earlier, had created a stir by posing the race problem in terms of a dilemma, a choice to be made between alternatives of equal undesirability. Myrdal and his colleagues did not even essay any possible alternatives that might solve the dilemma. Explaining that his study was not a description, Myrdal said it was a presentation of "facts only for the sake of their meaning in the interpretation."

What grievously nettled Cox was that Myrdal posed the problem in terms of ethics and morality, in which the American nation faced the moral imperative of squaring the American democratic creed with its racial practices. To Cox, such an assertion bordered on "mysticism":

> Myrdal, as a confirmed moralist, is not concerned with the problems of power but rather with problems of "regenerating the individual" by idealistic preachments. If only the individual could be taught the morality of the Creed, then society would lose its fever of racial pathologies and settle down to a happy existence.

If the race problem in the United States is preeminently a moral question, it must naturally be solved by moral means, said Cox, "and this conclusion is precisely the social illusion which the ruling political class has constantly sought to produce."[3] Hence Myrdal, said Cox, was guilty of shying away from a discussion of the ruling class in the southern states as a political class that uses its power to maintain divisions between black and white workers by instilling racial hatreds and emphasizing the doctrines of white supremacy. To achieve racial democracy in the South, where it was most blatantly absent, political-class warfare against the ruling political class was inescapable.

In summing up his own arguments and conclusions about the race problem in the United States, Cox had to deal specifically with the "Crisis in Negro Leadership" in the immediate postwar era. On this question, Cox was as uncompromising and caustic as he was in dealing with Myrdal.

Cox, who was born in Trinidad in 1901, had the advantage of the unsentimental objectivity of the outsider. Like most West Indians, he had not been "socialized" with any of the accommodation ideas characteristic of some schools of black thought. As a representative of a world community that in the 1960s would come to be called the "African Diaspora," Cox's views on the American race problem were significant.

For Cox, the main thrust of the Afro-American should be, and was, for complete racial assimilation: "The solidarity of American Negroes is neither nationalistic nor nativistic. The group strives for neither a forty-ninth state leading to an independent nation nor a back-to-Africa movement: its social drive is toward assimilation. In this respect Negroes are like most other American immigrants; it is well-known that the social tendency toward assimilation is an American cultural trait. Therefore, the solidarity of Negroes is defensive and tentative only, while their social orientation is centrifugal. *For them social solidarity is not a virtue in itself.*" (Italics added.) Parenthetically it may be said that sociologist Cox's association with the great body of rank-and-file blacks was rather limited, since it was highly questionable and oversimplistic to equate black desires for equal inclusion with a social drive toward assimilation. Back in the 1920s another outstanding spokesman from the Caribbean, Marcus Garvey, had caustically condemned Afro-American leaders precisely because *they* were, in his view, committed to no racial goals but assimilation. Because of this, black leaders were, in Garvey's view, gross misleaders of black people! In this instance, he had of course made an implied distinction between those he viewed as "leaders" and those as "followers." His rise to leadership coincided with the growing "Crisis in Negro Leadership," the roots of which Garvey never completely understood was a uniquely American race problem (not a West Indian or an African one) that had to be solved *in* the United States and *not* in Africa. Because of this misreading of the race and class elements in the United States, Garvey never understood that his movement's ideology helped to confound and deepen the "Crisis in Negro Leadership." Thus, at least by the late 1940s, it had become increasingly evident that black leadership had a problem. It was not seen, for example, that with the coming of the *Brown* era, the relationship of the American black minority's status to that of the rest of the African Diaspora and also to that of other minorities would be redefined. Said Cox:

> One of the most persistent laments among Negroes in the United States is that the race has no great leader. There is a sort of vague expectation that someday he will arise. But Negroes will not have a "great leader" because, in reality, they do not want him. The destiny of Negroes is cultural and biological integration and fusion with the larger American society. Opposition by the latter society is generally directed against this aspiration of Negroes. Therefore, a great leader, whose function must be to bring about solidarity among Negroes, will facilitate the purpose of the opposition. The old-fashioned great leader of the post-slavery period, the almost unreserved appeaser of the Southern aristocracy, is gone forever. To develop a powerful leader Negroes must retract themselves, as it were, from their immediate business of achieving assimilation, and look to him for some promised land or some telling counterblow upon their detractors. At present, however, the most that the race can hope for is many small torchbearers showing the way upon innumerable fronts.[4]

Cox not only negated the possibility of the emergence of a black deliverer on the legendary white horse, or even of any role for the "many torchbearers . . . upon innumerable fronts," but he further wrote:

> *These leaders cannot give Negroes a "fighting" cause. None can be Moses, George Washington, or Toussaint L'Ouverture; he cannot even be Mohandas Gandhi—a Lenin will have to be a white man.*[5] (Italics added.)

Oliver Cromwell Cox was essentially an academic disciple of Karl Marx and an exponent of the latter's class-struggle prophecy as the eventual path to liberation for the oppressed blacks. He explained, by clear disavowal, that he was not a practicing member of any Marxist political movement: "If, therefore, parts of this study seem Marxian, it is not because we have taken the ideas of this justly famous writer as gospel, but because we have not discovered any other that could explain the facts so consistently."[6] Consequently, Cox was of the opinion that for the Afro-American the only practical path to liberation, especially in the southern states, was in a political movement aimed at the overthrow of the southern ruling political class: "If there is to be an overthrow of the system, it will be achieved by way of a political-class struggle, with Negroes an ally of white democratic forces of the nation. *It will not come by way of an open interracial matching of power. As a matter of fact, the struggle has never been between all black and all white people—it is a political-class struggle.* . . . But just at this point Negro leadership seems to be weakest. Today very few of those who have the ear of the public appear to appreciate the significance of the modern political-class movement. Some, like W.E.B. Du Bois, are frightened by the prospects of violence."[7]

This was published six years before the historic *Brown* decision and seven years before Martin Luther King, Jr., in striking contrariness to Cox's prophecies, appeared as a practicing disciple of Mohandas Gandhi.

King's advent seemed an unparalleled happenstance to those who had missed a number of subtle new indicators in the tense political clamor of the late Forties. Even with his unique social and political powers of observation, Cox saw nothing on the political or racial horizons of the Truman era that pointed to the King phenomenon. As an honorary member of the ruling southern Democratic anti-civil rights bloc in the Senate, Truman had become vice-president under Roosevelt as a result of the political power of that bloc. Cox failed to mention in his study that in 1946, Truman, as president, had taken unprecedented executive initiative in setting up two interracial commissions to investigate the racial situation in civil rights and in higher education. This omission revealed that Cox, like many others, having lost the captain (Roosevelt), was floundering in the open seas, unable to interpret the shifts in the prevailing winds.

The NAACP, however, was very much alert to the subtle executive moves of Truman, who, in his own disingenuous, political fashion, was picking up the Roosevelt torch along a civil rights path that Roosevelt could not tread. While the breakaway Dixiecrat party was attempting to oppose Truman's reelection in 1948, black spokesmen in Clarendon County, South Carolina, were preparing, with the assistance of the NAACP, to launch a court case against the county school board for its long-established policy of furnishing buses for white schoolchildren but not for black.[8] This initial school segregation case *was not for integration,* but for the equalization of school facilities under the separate biracial system. The petition was filed March 16, 1948, in the United States District Court in adjacent Florence County. By the time this case would reach the Supreme Court of the United States, it would be known as *Briggs* v. *Elliot,* one of the five cases subsumed under *Brown* v. *Board of Education, Topeka,*

Kansas, in 1954, but *Brown* was not filed until February 28, 1951. In consonance with the NAACP's integrationist orientation, the *Brown* lawsuit of 1951 became more crucial than the Clarendon County case. This was because the Clarendon County case retained the Deep South separate-but-equal doctrine, while in Kansas, a border state, the issue became unqualified racial integration in the public school system. A memo sent to Thurgood Marshall of the NAACP in support of *Brown* by a ranking NAACP lawyer, said, in part:

> . . . The more I think about this case, the more importance I think it
> will have on our main objective of securing legal support for our attack
> on segregation. . . . Our possibilities for winning here seem much better
> than they are in South Carolina.[9]

In other words, the outlook of the NAACP since the Du Bois debate of 1934 had not been for equalizing educational facilities, but for unqualified integration—come what may! The liberals (most of them) applauded. The long-range strategy was to peck away at the hard-core segregationist South by attacking public school segregation at the soft spots of border-state vulnerability.

When the Clarendon County case was filed, Martin Luther King was graduating from Morehouse College in the Deep South and preparing to enter Crozer Theological Seminary in Pennsylvania. At Crozer King, unconscious of what fate had in store for him, would begin the philosophical preparation for his role.

One can understand, in retrospect, why the late Forties atmosphere could not have presaged a Martin Luther King. As Oliver Cromwell Cox saw it (and he was not alone), the appearance of an American Gandhi was an implausibility. Any conceivable social change for the South had to assume the revolutionary semblance of political-class warfare, violent and bitter. Communists thought much the same. When William Z. Foster, chairman of the Communist party, was asked about the prospects of black racial equality in the South, he quipped, "That's a shooting affair!" The very idea of an organized civil rights protest movement originating in the heart of the South and premised on nonviolent methods of civil disobedience would have seemed absurd. In the late Forties the strains and stresses of postwar economic readjustments were enlivened by a resurgence of sporadic racial violence on the southern scene. In competition with the NAACP, and utilizing the initiatives gained in the Scottsboro Case of the 1930s, the Communists seized the initiatives of several civil rights violations of blacks during the late Forties.[10] However, these important black civil rights issues were overshadowed as the congressional anti-Communist crusade gathered momentum. While not as punitive and extralegal as the "Red Scare" campaign of the early 1920s with its Palmer Raids and mass deportations of radicals and "subversives," the anti-Communist crusade of the Forties, which led to the McCarthy era, was a clear signal that the American political and legal system was not about to tolerate any organized political movement seriously dedicated to "revolutionary" alterations in the social system. Of course, McCarthyism was itself an extremist outcropping of the conservative bipartisan political attempts to wipe out as many of the carryovers of Roosevelt's New Deal as possible—a reactionary swing of the political pendulum that got out of hand. Since the bulk of American organized labor collaborated in repressing political radicalism, and was retrenching into its traditional pro-capitalist–free-market Americanism, the race question remained the only potentially explosive threat to the status quo. But it was a threat that was still not recognized as such.

These Forties developments—the anti-Communist crusade, the Cold War orientation in foreign policy, the nationwide political reaction—said something significant about the American system. The political interplay encouraged within the folds of the separation of powers resulted in a dialectic of unpredictable contradictions. Wholly out of character with the postwar political reaction, the Truman administration, with the support of parts of the legislature, was debating and pushing civil rights initiatives. These executive efforts were a salutary departure from the political temper of the late Forties. This process would not only confound the radicals and "revolutionary" doctrine concerning class warfare, but would contribute to a political hiatus of restraint, a political vacuum in which all protest activity was reduced to the alarmist postures of self-defense—a style that was disarming for all pretenders to antiestablishment leadership. For black spokesmen, civil rights emerged as the one and only issue of transcendent importance, the only banner for leadership visibility, the only cause for demonstrating militancy.

A good example was the preacher-politician Adam Clayton Powell, Jr., a traditional black Democrat, a product of the militant Harlem of the 1930s New Deal dispensations. This heir to well-established but local community-based political power, once elected to Congress had but one issue of national significance—civil rights. Because the Democratic party under Truman had to be committed to civil rights gestures in order to control the executive, Powell's only course of congressional action was to prod the Democrats into hurrying their civil rights' pace by threatening to bolt the party in favor of the Republicans. There would be a long way to travel before the barriers of segregation and discrimination would collapse; and for all the show of civil rights militancy, nothing portended a "revolutionary" overthrow of any institutional barriers to full racial equality. Civil rights leadership would have to march to the tune and pace set by the federal establishment; the militants and radicals would have no options other than to harass the civil rights moderates into hurrying the pace.

The pressures of international realities were also promoting a favorable climate for the civil rights initiatives of the postwar Forties. The American race question had been internationalized as one of the graphic consequences of World War II. The entire world turned critical eyes toward the United States, where the capital city had to open its diplomatic windows for all the nonwhite world to peer into its secrets. When the first of the "colored" nations, India, gained its independence from Britain in 1947, America's most notoriously denigrating racial situation was the scandalous one in Washington, D.C. All the colonial and soon-to-be ex-colonial nations were aware of the race problem in the American South, but the national capital was not always understood as being, in essence, a southern city. Very soon, though, the nonwhite world began to understand Washington for what it was; it then became a political truism among the capital's ruling elites that for the good of the American image abroad, Washington had to change. Early in his administration, Eisenhower, the unlikely moderate conservative, without fanfare ordered first steps to be taken toward desegregating the capital. But even then, no one expected that changes in race relations in Washington would so soon thereafter be followed by the Supreme Court decision of 1954 that would impact on the entire nation. Neither Oliver Cromwell Cox nor very many others could have foreseen the *Brown* decision following Eisenhower's entrance into the White House. In fact, one of the most outraged of all political leaders at the *Brown* decision was Eisenhower himself.[11]

This evolutionary change in race relations was being fostered by presidents such as Truman and Eisenhower even against their own racial convictions. What would propel the politics of these changes was the enhanced power of the black vote, based in the expanded black urban ghettos. Here a contradictory fact of life ran counter to civil rights hopes and goals. One prominent white liberal put it: "The urban ghetto was at one time and the same time the force that constricted Negro life and aspirations and yet formed the base for black political power and the activities of civil-rights organizations. Because the black vote was often tied to Democratic city machines, it was not as effective a voice of protest as some believed it could have been."[12] Here a case of demographics worked in mysterious ways for civil rights wonders to perform. Only the segregated black urban ghetto could produce such political power. Yet the individual benefactors, the appointed and elected public officials and politicians whose status was predicated on the very existence of the segregated urban ghettos, would reject the legitimacy of the ghettos' existence. The general logic of this political leadership would be to eschew and disdain *all* social policy aimed at internal economic, social, and cultural improvements of the ghettos on the assumption that such improvements amounted to the perpetuation of segregation. The civil rights influence of white liberalism had, from the outset, played a dominant role in fostering this logic. By the 1950s, before the persistence of segregated black urban ghettos (i.e., communities) would render public school desegregation a mockery, a prominent liberal commentator had to admit:

> Without the urban base, the Negro protest movement would have remained small, and without the political leverage the urban masses provided, it would have remained impotent. Though no one realized it at the time, and though other factors were also essential in bringing about the events that were to follow, by midcentury the vote of the black ghetto in the North had reached the proportions that made possible the civil rights revolution.

Why this integrationist-versus-segregationist or separatist evolutionary civil rights contradiction had occurred was explained by this liberal observer:

> In politics, black power meant independent action—Negro control of the political power of the rural Southern Black Belt counties and of the black ghettos, and the use of this control to improve the condition of farm laborers and slumdwellers. It could take the form of organizing a *black political party or controlling the politicial machinery inside the ghetto* without the guidance or support of white politicians. Where predominantly Negro areas lacked Negros in elective office, whether in the rural black belt of the South or in the urban centers, black power advocates sought the election of Negroes by voter-registration campaigns, and by working for the redrawing of electoral districts. The basic belief was that only a well-organized and cohesive bloc of black voters would provide for the needs of the black masses. . . . In eco-

nomic terms, black power meant creating independent, self-sufficient
Negro business enterprise . . . but also by forming Negro cooperatives
in the ghettos and in the predominantly black rural counties of the South.
In the area of education, black power called for local community control
of the public schools in the black ghettos. Throughout, the emphasis
was on self-help, racial unity. . . . [13] (Italics added.)

Seen, however, in the context of the unfolding American national
phenomenon (and its race factors), it *was* as if the democratic imperative
were forcing its way to the front ranks of social evolution, slowly prompting and tentatively adjusting race relations gradually in consonance with
the American democratic creed. If this process were to continue, the
logical outcome would be complete racial democratization (or full integration, as the NAACP put it). Such a purview would not, however,
entail a social revolution. It would confound the revolutionaries, both
black and white. It would render irrelevant the Marxist prognosis of Oliver
Cromwell Cox, the Communists, and Socialists, even though all these
schools of radical or revolutionary social change were forced to jump on
the civil rights bandwagon as a matter of political morality. But not until
Martin Luther King appeared would the NAACP, the Marxists, or other
miscellaneous radicals imagine the social applicability of morality in the
politics of race. It was as if the democratic imperative were, through the
personality of King, assuming the conscious assumption of the moral
imperative, suggestive of Myrdal in its defiance of social illusions "the
ruling political class has constantly sought to produce." Then came the
Brown decision, and the NAACP leadership was inspired to view the
unfolding of the democratic imperative as so inexorable that the optimistic
slogan of "Free by '63" seemed warranted.

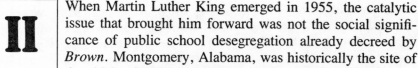

When Martin Luther King emerged in 1955, the catalytic
issue that brought him forward was not the social significance of public school desegregation already decreed by
Brown. Montgomery, Alabama, was historically the site of
the old Confederate capital, where the heart of the Old South
still palpitated in wistful recall of a lost cause. Montgomery was the

"Cradle of the Confederacy." Even *Brown* I and II of 1954–1955 did not present a "clear and present danger" to segregationist traditions in Alabama when King appeared, since few Alabamans believed the South would not successfully circumvent and ultimately defy the implementation of *Brown*.

However, like the Alabama segregationists, Martin Luther King was *also* a southerner—a black one. Not so ideologically fixed on race relations, he was not an accommodationist throwback to Booker T. Washington. Although born and bred in Georgia, King later matured as an intellectual product of northern university enlightenment, which during the 1940s and 1950s would produce a growing number of nonconformist native black southerners. In this regard, King was a unique southern product even before he was called to lead that uniquely southern movement—the Montgomery Bus Boycott. King had been the pastor of the Dexter Avenue Baptist Church in Montgomery a little over a year when Mrs. Rosa Parks committed her famous infraction of the Alabama race laws on public transportation. From that fateful moment, King's pastorship in Dexter Avenue Baptist would be augmented by preparation for his martyrdom thirteen years later in Memphis, Tennessee. The theological and intellectual product of Boston University, King had settled into what augured to be a prominently successful pastorate in a Deep South, black middle-class church. This church post launched him as first among a galaxy of black civil rights heroes of varying ideological styles who would emerge in the Fifties and Sixties. Subsequently selected by popular acclaim as the spokesman of a genuine grass-roots movement, King was inadvertently thrust into a commanding, brand-new type of black leadership role. He developed into the kind of leader no forecaster of black or white radical protest could have foreseen. But *who* and *what* Martin Luther King was (and was not) can be better understood in the clarity of retrospection.

Not until after the Montgomery Bus Boycott had persevered through a long siege of pain and peril to its successful conclusion did King speak in implicit, self-revelatory terms in his *Stride Toward Freedom* (1958). Numerous profiles of King had been written between 1955 and 1957, but the genuine essence of the man was disclosed for the first time in this book. In the opening pages King revealed an interesting personality sketch of the transformed native's return to his home, bearing an enlightened and intellectually detached point of view toward the stark realities of his native land. Under the heading "Return to the South," King described driving from Atlanta to Montgomery, where he was scheduled to deliver his invitational sermon at Dexter Baptist the next morning:

> It was a clear wintry day. The Metropolitan Opera was on the radio with a performance of one of my favorite operas—Donizetti's *Lucia di Lammermoor*. So with the beauty of the countryside, the inspiration of Donizetti's inimitable music, and the splendor of the skies, the monotony that usually accompanies a relatively long drive—especially when one is alone—was dispelled in pleasant diversions.[14]

Here was a man of an intellectual mold far removed from the more traditional "down home" profile of a black Baptist preacher. According to the conventional image, one might have expected his musical tastes to have veered toward the church hymn, or perhaps toward some version of gospel singing, which was part of the musical vogue among quasi-religious blacks in the 1950s. E. Franklin Frazier, writing on the "Negro Church," had described gospel singing as an outgrowth of the "secularization of Negro religion . . . an accommodation between traditional Negro religion and the new outlook of Negroes in the new American environment."[15] But from the outset, King embodied a degree of secularization of black religion the likes of which had been rarely witnessed before in black American terms. His acute awareness of who and what he was as a black Baptist preacher was in evidence when he wrote of how he chose the theme of his invitational sermon at Dexter Baptist:

> Since the membership was educated and intelligent, should I attempt to interest it with a display of scholarship? Or should I preach just as I had always done, depending finally on the inspiration of the spirit of God? I decided to follow the latter course. I said to myself, "Keep Martin Luther King in the background and God in the foreground and everything will be alright. Remember you are the channel of the gospel and not the source."[16]

King related nothing about the kind of music that was sung because the musical aspect of the Baptist church ritual is routinely predictable. His sermon topic was "The Three Dimensions of a Complete Life," which, no doubt, channeled the gospel word of God to the congregation in the kind of message his parishioners wanted to hear, which at that moment was *not* a secular message about civil rights issues. Until the Montgomery Bus Boycott began, King's obvious secular concerns were just how he, a native southerner, would adjust to the established patterns of segregation he knew so well. There was little advance indication that he saw his pastorship at Dexter overly involving his pulpit in the politics of race. Although King and his wife, Coretta, had seriously debated the disadvantages of abandoning the "cultural life [they] loved" in the North for the restrictive pressures of southern segregation, they decided that they had a "moral obligation" to return to the South "at least for a few years":

> Since racial discrimination was most intense in the South, we felt that some of the Negroes who had received a portion of their training in other sections of the country should return to share their broader contacts and educational experience in the solution.[17]

At that moment, however, this was a rather obligatory declaration of idealistic fealty to their southern heritage, since they had the feeling that "something remarkable was unfolding in the South," and they wanted to be on hand to witness it. (All black southerners know this sentiment well—they never cease to be black southerners in spirit!) Actually, the impact of the 1954 *Brown* decision issuing out of Washington, D.C., had engendered the feeling that something remarkable was unfolding in Alabama. Later on when the bus boycott was in high gear, King was to agree that *Brown* had been the impetus that galvanized the undercurrents of protest against entrenched segregationist doctrine, but it could not explain, he wrote, "why the protest occurred when it did, it cannot explain why it happened in Montgomery." King had observed earlier that "the United States Supreme Court decision on school segregation . . . appeared to have no effect." In Montgomery the schools were, of course, segregated, and the *Brown* decision had no apparent effect on "Montgomery's determination to keep them that way."[18] Thus, if the high court's decision had inspired nothing in 1955 but the manifest determination of the white South to oppose this decision by all means necessary, it only meant that some groundswell of grass-roots protest emanating from somewhere deep in the recesses of the black community's consciousness *had* to occur. If Montgomery could not be explained by any prior causation—social, material, or otherwise—then neither could King explain the ordering of any antecedent logic of effects that, for him, took on a rather indeterminate character. Certainly the long history of injustices in public transportation in Montgomery and the entire South was a partial explanation, wrote King, but not the whole. So, for King, since every "rational explanation" failed to explain Montgomery, there was "something about the protest that was supra-rational; it cannot be explained without a divine dimension.''[19] But if Montgomery could not be explained by any rational unfolding of empirical antecedents, how did King explain himself? He was self-centered enough about his personal role not to limit the explanation of Montgomery to a realm of pure voluntarism devoid of divine will. Thus, his elevation to leadership in the boycott by popular acclaim was *also* by divine will—the will of God.

Within the social confines of the Dexter Baptist congregation, King's intellectual and theological preparation well qualified him to attribute his leadership role to divine ordination. But by his transformation into leader of a secular social protest movement, King had, out of necessity, to pull the black church itself into secular social activism in a way it had never before been involved. If in the intimate confines of Dexter Baptist's rituals, King vowed to keep himself in the background and God in the foreground, once he assumed leadership of the boycott, he had to project both God *and* the black church to the foreground in company with his leadership presence before the nation. What manner of roles, then, would King, God, black religion, and the black church play in this brand-new feature in black social protest? Secular jurisprudence, secular social protest, secular social rebellion would combine with divine will, divine dimensions, and black consciousness to project another version of the social gospel movement from an earlier period in history.[20] But the social protest groundswell led by King was destined to assume other ideological dimensions, especially in the Sixties, that would put the "divine dimensions" of King's imprimatur on black protest to a serious test in the secular black arena. King would end up as "The King God Did Not Save," as one of the post-Sixties analyses of King's personal impact on the historic course of civil rights dispensations would put it.

The history of the last quarter-century has rendered a number of verdicts on the roles of King and the civil rights movement, and on the concerted impact of the various militant protest trends that either complemented or competed with King's ascendancy. From 1955 to 1968, King's unprecedented persona hovered over and above the panoramic dimensions of the clamorous black upsurge like a guardian angel both loved and rejected. When he died, that discordant army of black militant trends was also in the final stages of disarray. The tumultuous black Sixties were on the wane—SNCC was scattering in a score of directions; CORE had ousted the integrationists and turned separatist; Malcolm X had been martyred; the Black Panthers had left their natural environment of California on the assumption that they could become a national organization, had encountered the brutal, repressive reality of Chicago and

New York, and had thus been destroyed. Across the nation's campuses, enclaves of callow black students attempted to carry the torch as if they were the inheritors of SNCC of 1960–1965. These militants perpetuated the Sixties' radical enthusiasm not because of King's role but despite King. During his reign, King could not encompass all of these militant trends inasmuch as the great majority of these activists did not agree with his moral posture, and attempted to transcend him in an effort to expand their social and racial goals. In one way or another, these Sixties activists perceived their goals as essentially unmoral (not amoral), having less to do with the social ethics of any moral philosophy than with the pragmatic assertion of participatory rights in a racist society.

What separated most of the black militants from King was their lukewarm attraction to, if not outright rejection of, his guiding principles of nonviolence. As close to Thoreau's civil disobedience as King was, the militants had to part from him on the question of nonviolent resistance. An underlying cause of this younger generation's uncomfortableness with nonviolence was that King borrowed his resistance concept from Mohandas Gandhi, who practiced the philosophy of *Satyagraha* in a society in which the oppressed were the vast majority, while in the United States the oppressed blacks are the minority. Thus, in political, economic, cultural, and ideological terms, the goals of both King and the black militants were hindered and denied by a wide range of built-in societal barriers that King would be satisfied and morally righteous enough to confront with a purely moral posture.

This moral posture unquestionably appealed to the majority of older blacks socially based in the black church denominations. The broad-based sentiments of American blacks are not rooted in the ideologies of violence, or black nationalism, or black separatism, or in any of the various militant postures of "black liberation" fronts of the Sixties. Black intellectual apologists for the militant fronts were inwardly aware of the ideological distances between the main body of black thought and that of the young ideologues of militant, direct-action protest. The former has always aspired, in the main, to democratic inclusion (not assimilation, as Cox proposed) in the constitutional folds of the American Dream. What separated most blacks from the elite ideologies of militant protest was a gap that black radicals tried unsuccessfully to bridge in competition for the loyalties of King's immense following. Despite all the militant and revolutionary slogans avidly espoused by a Robert F. Williams, a Stokely Carmichael, a Rap Brown, a Malcolm X, and no matter how radical the *zeitgeist* of the Sixties generation who could not abide King's nonviolence, none of them could compete with King for the "soul" of black America.

There were two fundamental reasons for this strange paradox: 1. What the militants wanted was not what the vast majority of blacks wanted, with the utilization of black militant methods. 2. The *Brown* decision and the Montgomery Bus Boycott, and all the militant trends that followed, confronted built-in structural societal limitations at the outset. To one degree or another, the majority of blacks were more aware of the nature of these social restraints and how they functioned than were the liberal-inspired doctrines of racial equality. The aims of the Black Revolution were already delimited within the restrictive scope of civil rights reformism built into the societal framework of American race relations—*before Brown,* before King *and* Montgomery.

Did King understand this? Was his insistence on the strict moral legitimacy of nonviolence a recognition that civil rights gradualism was the preordained path, the only sure road open to black protest? This remains an open question. At any rate, his emphasis on the ethics of nonviolence could evoke no principled opposition from the NAACP or the National Urban League because these two traditional "race better- ment" organizations preferred the peaceful approach of either legal re- dress or social legislation reformism to outlaw racial segregation. Thus, these two old-line organizations had no other recourse but to support King as a matter of reform principle, if not pure moral ethics. But the young generation of the militant Sixties assumed no such methodological loy- alties to King's nonviolence.

King defined his role as bringing to bear upon a secular struggle for social justice the moral weapons of a religious imperative for racial rec- onciliation. Segregation was more than just a matter of the oppression of an "inferior" race by a "superior" race; more than just the continued imposition of an inferior "caste" status on a racial minority for the pragmatic purposes of maintaining the political, economic, cultural, and social supremacy of white people by legal and other means. Segregation was more than merely a violation of constitutional precepts: For King, segregation was immoral, a mortal sin, a violation of divine law. In black leadership terms, this was something new in the annals of social protest. No previous black religious leader had openly espoused such a creed on a national scale. It was as if to imply that Gunnar Myrdal was correct in his analysis of the "American Dilemma" as being, at the core, a moral issue transcending all class interests, group interests, or caste interests. In fact, King asserted: "In the final analysis the problem of race is not a political but a moral issue. Indeed, as the Swedish economist Gunnar Myrdal has pointed out, the problem of race is America's greatest moral problem."[21] Myrdal, however, was not espousing "morality" from a doctrinaire Christian point of view, but from the point of view of what philosophers cite as ethical values judged from sociological and/or psychological criteria. King, in contrast, attempted to wed the ethics of theology with the ethics of utilitarianism. For him, politics was a false veneer that obscured the original sin, the immorality of defying the will of God. This outlook placed King's moral authority above the utilitarianism of the NAACP or the social welfare tradition of the National Urban League:

> Government action is not the whole answer to the present crisis, but it is an important partial answer. Morals cannot be legislated, but behavior can be regulated. The law cannot make an employer love me, but it can keep him from refusing to hire me because of the color of my skin. We must depend on religion and education to alter the errors of the heart and mind; but meanwhile it is an immoral act to compel a man to accept injustice until another man's heart is set straight.[22]

With this evolving conviction still not publicly avowed, King, upon assuming the pastorate in Montgomery, immediately set out to revise the Dexter Avenue Baptist Church program. He was concerned with broadening the auxiliary prospectus of the church, whose activities consisted chiefly of the Sunday school, the Baptist training union, and the mission society, "which carried the message of the church into the community":

> Among the new functions I decided to recommend were a committee to revitalize religious education; a social service committee to channel and invigorate services to the sick and needy; a social and political action committee; a committee to raise and administer scholarship funds for high school graduates; and a cultural committee to give encouragement to promising artists.[23]

King admitted that he proposed these innovations with some trepidation, since they were a "definite departure from the traditional way" of black Baptists. The creation of a "social and political action committee" and a "cultural committee" was, indeed, a progressive step for traditional Baptists of any class composition in Alabama (or New York State) in 1955, and Dexter Baptist was a *middle-class* church. To King's supreme gratification, Dexter Baptist heartily approved of his recommendations.

King never fully elaborated on his concept of the cultural committee, or what specific genres or artistic fields he had in mind when he referred to "promising artists." However, black churches, in pursuit of cultural advancement for promising artists always had an overriding predilection for vocalists. "The Black church is a singing church," wrote one critic and chronicler of the black church who appeared inspired by the persona of King, "a fact well documented by the legions who have risen to fame and fortune in the world of secular music, but who began their careers in the choirs of local black churches. Of equal importance is the fact that the transition from church choir to night club, or to stage, screen, or opera is usually accomplished with a minimum of artistic or emotional adjustment."[24] The entire corps of black church historians agrees on this particular cultural aspect of the church's inner rituals.

Even before he officially became a Baptist preacher, King had already evinced an appreciation for Western music, specifically that of the Italian Donizetti, a musical taste probably not shared broadly in his Baptist congregation. In more ways than just his intellectual grounding in philosophy, King was a unique cultural cut above the traditional black preachers of his religious calling who led congregations that favored singers, especially female singers. There the middle-class black congregations' interest in promising artists usually stopped; their collective tastes or appreciation rarely encompassed the talents of jazz musicians, blues singers, dancers, actors, painters, writers, or entertainers. In more ways than one the black middle class is culturally one-dimensional; it has proven incredibly slow in getting beyond its cultural provincialism in the creative arts. In this respect the black church shares many of the social and cultural values of its origins in white Protestant puritanism. A segment of creative individualists may depart from the canons of church morality and take up the secular arts with a minimum of emotional adjustment, but with little or no encouragement from the churches unless they are singers.

For one thing, in the view of many black church people, many creative and performing arts carry a moral, i.e., "worldly," stigma. "From the most primitive times art and religion have been closely intertwined," wrote the historian cited above in his panegyric to the King saga. But this writer's main intent was to praise King's artistry in the delivery of his sermons: "Though Dr. King received an academic training in the North where he learned the formal use of rhetoric, he also relied largely upon the emotional poetry of the traditional black sermon. 'His oratory carried the emotional stuff, while his analysis carried the moral message.' "[25] The only branch of the arts this author mentioned as being "intertwined" with black religion was singing: "There is an element of religion in every form of black music. The difference between what happens when Mahalia Jackson sings and Aretha Franklin or Billie Holiday or Bessie Smith sings may be a matter of theme and setting but hardly a matter of essence."[26] However, this genre of black music was, as King unconsciously intimated, racially far removed from the cultural roots of his favorite aria in Donizetti's *Lucia di Lammermoor*.

In this regard, King's moral philosophy as well as his cultural appreciation were transcendentally universal. Rooted in the most deeply racial of all black institutions, the church, King's social perceptions and cultural affinities extended beyond its cultural range. To what extent this can be attributed to the influences of his northern educational exposure and his wife, Coretta, can only be surmised. If, in fact, Coretta King's extensive musical training rubbed off on King and broadened his music appreciation, it was an indication of her trained musical qualities, rather than a prior bent in King himself. As an aspiring professional singer, Coretta King was but another of a long line of the black church's favorite artistic progeny—the female singer—going back to Marian Anderson in the 1920s. These singers became the main ambassadors of good will between middle-class blacks and upper-class whites. They were proxy cultural symbols, allegedly indicating that the European music they sang to predominantly white audiences proved the black middle class's own cultural coming-of-age. In point of fact, these accomplished black singers were mainly symbols of personal achievement, rather than reflections of a general interest by the black middle class in furthering the musical fortunes of blacks as a whole. It would have been rare to discover an album of Donizetti's *Lucia di Lammermoor* or a Beethoven symphony or a Bessie Smith blues recording in a black middle-class living room. Hence, King's early plans to establish a cultural committee at Dexter Baptist to encourage promising artists would have made but a small dent in the black middle class's cultural provincialism with regard to the secular arts.

In 1955 the expanding consciousness necessary for embracing the secular arts either as sponsors, devotees, patrons, or entrepreneurs was not a priority in the black middle-class struggle for upwardly mobile existence or on the agendas of its churches (this cultural spirit had died after the 1920s). Even when an outburst of black creative culture occurred in the Sixties, inaugurating an updated version of the renaissance of the

1920s, it was outside the ideological range of the civil rights leadership. The NAACP and the National Urban League, which had sponsored the Harlem Renaissance of the 1920s had to avoid identifying with the cultural renaissance of the Sixties because it was culturally "nationalistic." It would not even have mattered much if the fates had left King alone to pursue his local career as a Montgomery Baptist preacher and cultivate his ideas for encouraging artists. The black middle-class, as it was then constituted (even in the North), was not committed to any serious sponsorship of promising artists or to any involvement in the "politics of culture." More than that, King's rather cryptic reference to "promising artists" might have been inspired by the effect Coretta's compromise of her professional career ambitions had on their marriage. It is not often recalled that soon after King had achieved national media celebrity, Coretta King attempted to launch a professional singing career. At that time, the rather awkward implications of this career foray by the wife of a now prominent black leader was not lost on a number of critical observers.[27]

However, the creation of the political action committee by King was symbolic of the implied social role of the black church, especially within the regional context of the Southern states. This social movement was intrinsically a *southern* one, and his political committee would reflect nothing beyond the priorities that the black middle-class considered were in consonance with its "class interests." In Montgomery these civil rights class interests had already been demonstrated before King arrived. Prior to King, the traditional regional civil rights groups, whether South or North, had always been led by middle-class blacks and their professionals. In Alabama middle-class blacks, in concert with struggling NAACP chapters, had been active on a number of fronts, openly or covertly, testing out stratagems for cracking the stout walls of segregation in both the private and public sectors. In Montgomery middle-class blacks had for years been negotiating with white power in business, politics, and the public arena for fairer treatment of black citizens in all areas of Montgomery life. Thus, when King arrived, "a change in race relations, subterranean, cautious, and only tentatively directed, was under way in Montgomery."[28] After at least one aborted plan to stage a bus boycott, the action of Rosa Parks successfully revived the idea, and King was elected head of the Montgomery Improvement Association to lead the boycott.[29]

Prior to King, the class interests of the civil rights spokesmen in Montgomery had coincided with the goals of the secular NAACP. When King mobilized the boycott, he also mobilized the church along with other sectors of black life. Thus, the NAACP, essentially northern-based, had to take a backseat to the new southern middle-class self-assertion. The NAACP could never have sparked such a protest in any event and, moreover, it had to avoid the expected charge by local whites of northern "meddling" in southern affairs. King later made it clear that his leadership and movement were *not* in competition with the NAACP. Yet the moral authority that King was able to project was, in fact, in competition with the authority the NAACP had always commanded in the civil rights arena. In the process of this regional transfer of civil rights hegemony, the southern black middle class added to its new ascendancy the community prestige of the organized black church. With King as the standard-bearer, black preachers and their powerful church network emerged as new symbols of authority for a new age in the black community. Soon the organized power of the black preacher-as-leader would manifest itself in the Southern Christian Leadership Conference (SCLC), organized in Atlanta in 1957 with King as chairman. In this fashion the Montgomery Bus Boycott, led by King, ushered in a new phase in the seventy-five-year-old civil rights protest struggle, if one reckons it from the demise of Reconstruction. More than that, the varying class interests of Montgomery were unified, if only temporarily, around a specific civil rights issue for the first time. King was to emphasize this point when he wrote about the mobilization of the black community around the boycott:

> The mass meetings also cut across class lines. The vast majority present were working people; yet there was always an appreciable number of professionals in the audience. Physicians, teachers, and lawyers sat or stood beside domestic workers and unskilled laborers. The Ph.D.'s and the no "D's" were bound together in a common venture. The so-called "Big Negroes" who owned cars and had never ridden the buses came to know the maids and the laborers who rode the buses every day. Men and women who had been separated from each other by false standards of class were now singing and praying together in a common struggle for freedom and human dignity.[30]

And so it was—nothing succeeds in unifying a people or a nation like a war, a national catastrophe, or an all-embracing social crisis. The southern civil rights crisis, beginning with Montgomery, brought about a unity of purpose among the classes the likes of which had not been witnessed in the twentieth century. It was a kind of class unity of purpose not possible in the North. Despite the ensuing strains and stresses within the southern movement, brought about mainly by disaffections with King's nonviolence, this overall class unity prevailed throughout the months and years of the many-sided southern struggle for racial parity. In the long run, however, this class unity was to prove conditional. More than that, the heightened role of the black church in the civil rights movement, inspired by King's charisma, did not obscure that the black church is itself a class-ridden aggregation of denominational bodies. King's own Dexter Baptist congregation was not composed of maids, domestic workers, and unskilled laborers. King's talk of Montgomery blacks "separated from each other by false standards of class" applied to the class elements predominant in his own congregation. As one observer pointed out: "Dexter Avenue Church was not large in membership by the standards of King's father's church, but it was definitely the church of the able Negro professional class."[31] Had Dexter Baptist *not* been composed of black professionals with B.A.s, M.A.s, and Ph.D.s, it is doubtful King would have accepted the invitation to its pastorate. He had been offered a teaching post and a deanship in black colleges—professional sinecures which, guided by divine providence, he elected to turn down. King was no ordinary black Baptist preacher, as some black radicals at first were inclined to think.

As class factors *really* operate in the black community, the middle class usually has to be in the forefront of the civil rights struggle or there is no struggle at all. Since the black church has forever been the denominational barometer reflecting the upwardly mobile progress of aspirants to the black middle class, King's placement in Dexter Baptist was in tune with the times. Yet his moral philosophy, translated into a black version of the social gospel tradition, called *all* the black churches out of the cloistered role of soul-saving into a secular struggle for social justice. How has the black church responded during King's reign and after his demise?

Historically, the church is the only indigenous black institution that American blacks have been allowed the untrammeled freedom to control. Since the beginning of the nineteenth century, black churches and their preachers have come in all denominational shapes, sizes, religious intensities, and secular and antisecular theologies. Black churches have been safe havens from the pain and strife of life in the outside world, sponsors of educational institutions, social welfare agencies, missionary headquarters for proselytizing in Africa, depositories of corporate wealth, and initiators of lucrative business enterprises. To the overwhelming majority of blacks through the ages, the church has been all things to all manner of men (and women). Many critics, black and white, have claimed that blacks have been much too religious for their own worldly good. Some of the white critics were counted as "friends of the Negro." The famous defense lawyer, Clarence Darrow, who would later figure prominently in the Scottsboro defense, wrote that he would be the last to interfere with the blacks' "religious orgies," but that he was interested in the "Negro as a 'race' or a people." He could not avoid the conclusion that "their slow and painful struggle for greater opportunities would be made easier if they were less religious":

> The development of any people is greater in proportion to their dependence on reason, and an ability to face facts, however hard the facts may be. Assuming there is a God, what reason has the Negro to praise him? Is God his friend? If so, why has he made the Negroes the hewers of wood and drawers of water through all the long and dreary past?[32]

Since the end of World War II, wry complaints by "free-thinking" secularized blacks that too many preachers are living off the meager resources of the black poor have notably increased. This view is shared, less vocally, by many of the middle-class, educated, ordained black ministers themselves. They frown at the proliferation of black preachers with storefront, hole-in-the-wall churches inside and around the fringes of lower-class communities. This type of self-elected, self-taught preacher was once described as "jackleg," representing a religio-institutional phenomenon that appeared when large numbers of southern blacks migrated to northern and western cities. These migrations disrupted and undermined the social composition of the traditional southern black churches.

At the same time, with the expansion and secularization of the black middle class, both North and South, an all-but-rigid class stratification within and among the black denominations, based on social and economic (and skin color) status, slowly altered the traditional rituals and membership in black churches. In 1963, E. Franklin Frazier observed of the expanding black middle class:

> Their ambiguous position in American society together with their recent rise to middle-class status are reflected in the religious behavior and attitudes of middle-class Negroes. There is first a tendency for middle-class Negroes to sever their affiliations with the Baptist and Methodist churches and join the Presbyterian, Congregational and Episcopal churches. The middle-class Negroes who continue their affiliation with

the Baptist and Methodist churches choose those churches with intelligent ministers and a relatively large middle-class membership.[33]

This shifting class-church affiliation helps explain the character of King's Dexter Baptist, and also that the bulk of King's wide support among black preachers came from Baptist and Methodist congregations, not the more *elite* churches. Most of the extensive network of black preachers affiliated with King's Southern Christian Leadership Conference are Baptists and Methodists, the denominations which historically had the greatest influence in the christianization of the slave population before the Civil War. The problem was, a vast uncharted number of black church members of lower-class character neither belonged nor were attracted to the Dexter Avenue type of Baptist (or Methodist) church. This was despite King's charismatic ability to transcend class lines and weld class unity among southern blacks all through his thirteen-year civil rights crusade. But with the passage of the Civil Rights Act and the Voting Rights Act of 1964–1965, followed by the rise of Black Power in 1966, the binding class-unity factor lost its imperative.

Moral visions of social justice compelled King personally to extend the black struggle into the economic arena of class poverty and into the political arena of moral opposition to the Vietnam War. However, for middle-class blacks per se (plus newly emergent upwardly mobile aspirants) *their* civil rights needs would be served for the time being; their economic status would be enhanced by the new era of growing economic opportunities in American society. After King's death, the SCLC vowed valiantly to carry out and expand the black church role that King had envisioned. This was an exemplary ambition for the SCLC, for it was beyond the scope of its collective social imagination, beyond the range of its *institutional* experience, to understand that as a *social organization* the black church could not give the kind of leadership that had been lacking since the 1920s unless *the black church changed itself*. Martin Luther King left the soul-saving role in the pulpit to step out and involve himself (and the church) in the secular affairs of his black public. However, his moral message represented leadership capital that could sustain him only so far, his martyrdom notwithstanding. The economic, social, political, cultural, and institutional problems of American blacks are beyond the reach of moral preachments—as King was, finally, forced into understanding.

In this sense Oliver Cromwell Cox was justified in rejecting Myrdal's liberal thesis on the moral imperative as "mysticism." However, it was not just the "political ruling class," as Cox asserted, that wanted to produce the social illusion that the race problem is "pre-eminently a moral question" to be solved by moral means. To this category must be added also the liberals. It was overwhelmingly white liberals, *not* the political ruling class, who flocked to the support of Martin Luther King on the question of the moral imperative. No one knows better than the political ruling class that the political, economic, and cultural policies that monitor the internal affairs of American society are not inspired by moral considerations, but are based on the imperatives of power—especially economic power. Placing segregation and race prejudice on the nation's up-front agenda for examination by means of moral suasion had its unquestionable value. However, after that, practical solutions require not moral means, which are unavailable, but a pragmatic reorganization of the institutional bases of race relations by *both blacks and whites*. As the ongoing, organized extension of the individual role of King, the SCLC was faced with the necessity of transforming his lofty moral idealism by qualifying the black church's social role in political, economic, and cultural terms—either that or it would return to its former pulpit soul-saving role without leadership pretensions.

Following King's death, church historians, church educators, and denominational adherents of his moral philosophy dedicated their loyalties to the fallen martyr by outlining a "New Agenda for the Black Church." One advocate of this new agenda wrote in 1969:

> The first priority for the Black Church is to recapture the leadership of the black people. It must reclaim the unqualified trust and commitment traditionally associated with the Black Church and the Black community. It must restore its original identity with the fortunes of Black people.[34]

Between King's death and 1975, some twenty-five books of varying quality on black religion were published by black authors, many of whom echoed the above sentiments on the church's mission of black liberation. Coming on the heels of all the civil rights legislation of the 1960s, it was presumed that these apostles of black liberation via black religion had little faith in the ideologies, the programs, the approaches, or the implied goals of all the secular protest fronts of the Sixties. Alternatively, the goals were acceptable but not the methods employed across the spectrum, from the legalistic NAACP to the militant activism of the Black Panthers. Whatever the case, the leadership of black people had to be "recaptured" for the black church. This recaptured leadership would, of course, redound to the elevation of the most forceful, dynamic, and educated black ministers to be found in the Baptist or Methodist congregations. This leadership ascendancy, of course, was already exemplified by the emergence of the Southern Christian Leadership Conference, sponsored and inspired by the guiding spirit of King himself. By the 1980s, this church-sponsored leadership network displayed a highly prestigious galaxy of black ministers on its board of directors. The SCLC board listed fifty members, of which twenty-seven would be identified as "Reverends" (in black middle-class churches the title "Doctor" is interchangeable with "Reverend"). From 1981 to 1982, these fifty board members represented seventy-nine SCLC chapters or affiliates from nineteen states, including Washington, D.C. On the leadership question, it should be mentioned that although the Nation of Islam was a significant black religious movement since it exhibited the personality of Malcolm X, black Islam was pointedly downplayed as a legitimate aspirant to the recaptured leadership role claimed for the black church. One church-inspired critic claimed that the "Black Muslim Movement is clearly a sect," not a church:

A major goal of the Muslim leadership a decade ago was the general acceptance of the Movement as a legitimate religion—specifically, as a legitimate sect of orthodox Islam. This is no longer considered necessary: the Muslims' self-respect does not hinge on such acceptance. Muhammad has stated that the Muslims *are* legitimate and Islamic, and so far as the Muslims themselves are concerned, this settles the matter. Nor is it an expedient directed at the black community any longer, for the aegis of orthodox Islam means little in America's black ghettos. So long as the Movement keeps its color identity with the rising black peoples of Africa, it could discard all its Islamic attributes—its name, its prayers to Allah, its citations from the Quran, everything "Muslim" without substantial risk to its appeal to the black masses.

In pressing their demand for complete acceptance as a legitimate religion and a Moslem sect, the Muslims had their eye primarily on the white community.[35]

In this article the author stressed the religious and political implications of the Black Muslim sect, but *not* the economic one, which was the real base (rather than the superstructural) glue that held the Nation of Islam together. Leave it to the black historians, trained to think and write by the liberal academic tradition, to remain true to the liberal intellectual policy of superficially obscuring and evading fundamental social facts. The "economic nationalist" factor behind the tight organizational success of the Black Muslims was the manifest rejection of the noneconomic liberalism that permeated the ideology of the official civil rights movement. Thus, a significant number of "leaderless" blacks in the ghettos (and the jails) were led to reject black Christianity *and* the philosophy of the civil rights movement. The communal clash of theologies (Islam versus Christianity) obscured the economic determinism that helped sustain the Black Muslim movement. The emergence of black Jews, another fractional group rejecting black Christianity, was explained when one of the converts to "Black Judaism" wrote that:

> The failure of the Black Church to take care of the total needs of the black masses in the cities influenced the existence of Black Judaism. The Black Church is itself, in some sense, an aspect of the general failure of Christianity in America, for slavery and Christian morality were obviously incompatible, and the segregated White Church precluded the possibility of reasonable religious fulfillment for black Christians, forcing them to establish their own traditions. Blacks were probably influenced also by the "strong communal bond" existing among Jews, and by their high level of economic success. Even Booker T. Washington urged his followers to "imitate the Jew" if they hoped to overcome their racial and economic obstacles.[36]

The reference to "racial and economic obstacles" is significant.

This religious departure of the Nation of Islam within the sociological and religious experiences of the northern black communities was (and is) more significant than Christian spokesmen were about to admit. For the real challenge to the traditional black church and its social role was the basic economic nationalist character of the Nation of Islam rather than its religious character. Moreover, its leader, Elijah Muhammad (*né* Poole), was a "leader" in the truer social meaning of the term than were Christian preachers who commanded the loyalties of a vaster number of Christian followers than Elijah Muhammad had Muslim followers. Black Christian ministers and their literary and historical adherents, who collectively adopted the moral imperative that dominated King's social thought, had to confront the hard fact that the eradication of legal segregation, legalized discrimination, legalized oppression, and so forth, did not, could not eliminate poverty. Economics would exacerbate the ghetto pathologies in inverse degree to the economic and social elevation of the black middle-class professionals and their expanding mini-elites with upwardly mobile aspirations. Stripped of all its adopted Islamic theology, the Nation of

Islam, similar to all nationalist movements among nonwhite nations and minorities the world over, was basically economic in motivation. The Nation of Islam was born at the moment during the 1930s when the catastrophic impact of the Great Depression on blacks was most severe. As an erstwhile member of Garvey's defunct Back to Africa movement, Elijah Muhammad had learned his black economics lessons well. Divested of all its "Back to Africa," "race pride" phraseology, the Garvey movement was fundamentally economic nationalist in motivation, inspired by Marcus Garvey and a coterie of uprooted West Indians from the impoverished Caribbean yearning after a black economic power base. They had visions of such a base lying fallow on the African continent, since the Caribbean was controlled economically by the British Exchequer in London. But the potential economic power base in Africa the Garveyites saw was also mainly controlled by the same British Exchequer. Thus, the only *economic* source of wealth from which to extract the wherewithal necessary to establish an economic power base in Africa would be found *in the United States*—not in the black population of the Caribbean, or in England, or Brazil, or Panama, or in any other black population concentration in Latin America. In the case of both the Garvey movement and the Nation of Islam, remove the group-molded substructure of their economic enterprises; their semicooperative organization; their authoritarian imposition of black versions of the puritan ethic of thrift, industry, sobriety; the apotheosization of business enterprise; the strong personality cult built around the "Leader"; the catechisms of personal morality— and neither nationalistic movement could have been as successful as it was in the beatification of "race pride."

Nothing much in the racial psychology of American blacks prevents black Christian preachers from accomplishing the organizational achievements of a Marcus Garvey or an Elijah Muhammad—if only they had the motivation and the will to do so. The basic reasons black preachers fail as promising candidates to recapture "the leadership of black people" is that they, for the most part, are just as indoctrinated by the American-induced *laissez-faire*, unrestrained individualism, egotistical personal "liberty" drives, competitive self-elevation as blacks of *all* classes in their search to realize black versions of the American Dream.

Martin Luther King, too, had a "dream" that truly inspired his followers to the extent that it could. Unfortunately, economic institutions in the United States do not, and never did, distribute rewards to either groups or individuals on the basis of just deserts measured by any demands of any moral imperative. Moreover, the American nation was founded as a constitutional republic, not as a constitutional theocracy with divine doctrine inscribed in its governing covenants. From 1955 to 1968, King's Christian-inspired moral preachments could play a significant role in supporting the struggle for legal redress, for constitutional legitimacy in furthering social justice. But for many of his followers, King's crusade instilled the hopes of unrealizable expectations, hopes that civil rights justice would be the equivalent of complete liberation of body and soul. Not all his followers thoroughly read King who, as a visionary, did not fail to see the secular restraints of the real world in the quest for black liberation. He pointed out the built-in defects long noted in black social polity. At the end of the Montgomery struggle, King said that "the constructive program ahead must include a vigorous attempt to improve the Negro's personal standards." He said that if the "behavior deviants" within the black community stem from economic deprivation, emotional frustration, and social isolation, these were the "inevitable concomitants of segregation." But what befalls blacks *themselves* when segregation is eliminated? Blacks, said King, "must be honest enough to admit that their standards so often fall short," and that one of the "sure signs of maturity is the ability to rise to the point of self-criticism":

> Our crime rate is far too high. Our level of cleanliness is frequently far too low. Too often those of us who are in the middle class live above our means, spend money on nonessentials and frivolities, and fail to give to serious causes, organizations, and educational institutions that so desperately need funds. We are too often loud and boisterous, and spend far too much on drink. Even the most poverty-stricken among us can purchase a ten-cent bar of soap; even the most uneducated among us can have high morals. Through community agencies and religious institutions Negro leaders must develop a positive program through which Negro youth can become adjusted to urban living and improve their general level of behavior. Since crime often grows out of a sense of futility and despair, Negro parents must be urged to give their children the love, attention, and sense of belonging that a segregated society deprives them of.[37]

King submitted his list of self-criticisms. Later, when his Christian spiritual inheritors talked about the "New Agenda for the Black Church," one said:

> The issue facing the majority of black churchmen and black churches is, Will we or will we not involve ourselves in the struggle for black

liberation? Fortunately, we have but one choice, for if the Black Church
is to survive she must enter the arena of struggle. If she does not do
so, her existence is indeed irrelevant and her demise will be welcomed.
For no institution needs to exist in the midst of black people unless it
is inextricably bound to the liberation struggle of our people. Many
churchmen see this and certainly the growth and development of the
National Committee of Black Churchmen is indicative of this insight.[38]

He then cited the ''class'' of the black community to which the black
church owes its main leadership allegiance:

It is this great host of people that the Black Church has most conspic-
uously neglected and it is among those people that we must find our
credibility. For to be found in this number are the welfare families, the
households that are headed by women, the alcoholic husbands, the
teenage drop-outs and dope addicts, and the sons who are being slaugh-
tered in Vietnam. This is the *powerless majority*—these are the superfluous people. They constitute the church's mission.[39]

These ''superfluous people'' and ''powerless majority'' are the large
body of blacks whose material existence was not even minimally affected
by civil rights legislation. Yet if King recognized, as he plainly said he
did, that ''if first-class citizenship is to become a reality for the Negro,
he must assume the primary responsibility for making it so. [That] integration is not some lavish dish that the federal government or the white
liberal will pass out on a silver platter . . . ,'' then why did he continue,
over and over again, to espouse his insistent moral variation of the NAACP's
integration refrain that *all* answers to *all* problems relating to black citizenship *had* to be solved, indeed *must* be solved through full integration?
Why did King continue to say this?
    By virtue of the immense moral authority vested in Martin Luther
King by accidental political and social circumstances in the 1950s, he
boasted a mandate possessed by no other black spokesman in the twentieth
century. From 1955 through 1965, King, with the impetus of a judicial
decree *(Brown)* creating a favorable ''climate of opinion,'' molded a
leadership philosophy justifiably infused with all the moral indignation
that segregation deserved. But with the advent of the Black Power enthusiasm, King should have changed course. He *should* have turned the
thrust of his moral imperative back toward the black social polity with
this message: Now that the Civil Rights Acts of 1964 and 1965 have
been legislated, let us get our house in order! King had the moral authority

to do exactly that. His first target should have been the fringe network of street-corner churches and their overinflated society of superfluous preachers; he could have chastised them into playing the kind of *institutional* role in black communities that black critics of Christianity (both black and white) insist belongs to them by historical antecedents. Many of these fringe churches are mini-enclaves of parasitic social escapism that ought not to be further tolerated in the black communities. They should be ridiculed and their moonlighting preachers ostracized. But they *are* tolerated—more than that, they are zealously supported by those seeking the opiate of religious escape from worldly responsibility. In the midst of urban poverty, squalor, crime, family disorganization, and other accumulated pathologies, outcast and insolvent blacks support opportunistic, socially irresponsible preachers. There was a time during the 1920s, 1930s, and 1940s when these storefront churches served to ease the pain and shock of northern urbanization—the social isolation, the aches of uprootedness, the culture shock of migratory displacement. But as a continuing religious character of the ghettos, the fringe churches have become regressive havens for fifty-seven varieties of religious escape from reality. Even in these days of civil rights enlightenment, they persist to exist at the individual call of the jacklegs, most of whom would consider leadership for any purpose other than a prayer meeting to collect money a blasphemy against God.

However, King, in this regard, minced words and missed out on the real potential of his calling. At the outset he circumspectly chided some "Negro clergymen who are more concerned about the size of the wheelbase on their automobiles than about the quality of their service to the Negro community," or he softly scolded the failures of "Negro leaders to arouse their people from their apathetic indifference to [the] obligations of citizenship"; he criticized the black middle class, the black elites, the black press, the black fraternities, etc., for the shallow quality of their "social consciousness." But he could not use his moral authority, his unquestioned intellect to explain clearly the social, political, economic, and cultural limitations of racial integration and the future consequences of these limitations. When faced with the challenge of the Black Power revolt against integration, he could only reply:

> There is no theoretical or sociological divorce between liberation and integration. In our society liberation cannot come without integration and integration cannot come without liberation. I speak here of integration in both the ethical and political senses. On the one hand, in-

tegration is true intergroup, interpersonal living. On the other hand, it
is the mutual sharing of power. I cannot see how the Negro will be
totally liberated from the crushing weight of poor education, squalid
housing and economic strangulation until he is integrated, with power,
into every level of American life.[40]

No doubt, the first flush of success in Montgomery heightened King's
conviction that moral suasion potentially held unlimited powers to transform. The "sociology" of segregation and legal discrimination could
ultimately be transfigured into a thoroughly renovated "sociology" of
"liberation and integration"—by moral suasion and the will to protest.
But his conclusion was a graphic example of a history of ideas repeating
itself, however qualified by time and place. Summed up here was the Du
Bois-NAACP debate on the meaning of segregation in 1934. George
Santayana, one of Du Bois's Harvard University mentors, was never
more profound than when he wrote that "those who cannot remember
the past are condemned to repeat it." In this reasoning on integration
King could conclude nothing beyond what the NAACP's leadership had
concluded in 1934, prompting Du Bois's departure. But the NAACP's
stand in 1934 was not a rationally reasoned position based on sociological
and psychological fact or demographic realities; it was the *ad hoc* and
expedient rationalization of an inept leadership. It reflected a dilemma
posed by the imperatives of race and ethnicity—a dilemma that the NAACP
could neither face nor resolve intellectually. King brought the outlines
of the dilemma up to date and, at least, in clearer focus. He admitted
that he couldn't see how poor education, poor housing, and economic
strangulation would be ameliorated without the full integration so dear
to the hearts of the NAACPers. Until there was integration "with power"
into every level of American life, there could be no liberation. But in
the process of thinking the matter through, he could not help adumbrate
other dimensions that qualified the meaning of integration—the "intergroup" dimension and the "mutual sharing of power." What he was
intimating, without saying so, was that individuals should integrate *but
still remain identified with a group in order to share intergroup power.*
The mere fact that a percentage of blacks, large or small, integrate into
certain sectors of the larger society does not mean, ipso facto, a sharing
of any group power. Integration, in the NAACP's definition, has meant
the actual shedding of any special group identification. Individuals cannot
integrate in this fashion and at the same time insist on maintaining a
group identity in order, in King's vision, to gain a mutual sharing of

intergroup power. One might gain an enhanced degree of "interpersonal living," but it will be won at the price of giving up any basis or claim to both the "ethical and political senses" of intergroup power. And in this regard, it remains totally unclear what King meant by integration in both the ethical and political senses.

Apparently King did not comprehend that there *is* a theoretical and sociological divorce between liberation and integration, and the "theoretical" position is *pluralism*. With all his education in philosophy, ethics, political economy at Boston University, plus his more important life experience, King, the trained social thinker, could not understand "theoretically" what thousands of grass-roots blacks understood instinctively (if not methodologically) when they abandoned black Christianity and the civil rights goals of the Sixties for more congenial ethical and political faiths. In this regard, King was no different in his social naïveté regarding integration than were the NAACP spokesmen who, in 1954, thought the *Brown* decision heralded the elimination of all forms of segregation. The essential difference between King's ideal of integration and that of the NAACP was that King's ideal was to be achieved on moral and ethical grounds, while the NAACP persevered on constitutional grounds and legal redress.

It was one thing, however, for the NAACP programmatically to turn full integration into a legal and sociological fetish mainly because its leadership felt no obligation to represent or even defend the perpetuation of any "separate" or "segregated" all-black institution. But King was the preeminent representative of the one and only traditional and "separate" institution that blacks not only controlled but held both sacred and inviolate against the social onslaughts of institutional racism—the black church. True to the institutional legitimacy of the black church, neither King nor any of his brother preachers ever contemplated, intimated, or suggested that the black church should be integrated out of existence in deference to anyone's concept of racial equality. In this regard, King's transcendent moral postures on the universal brotherhood of man, regardless of race, were not inconsistent with his secular position that there can be no black liberation without integration. They were, however, inconsistent with the secular position of the black church as a traditional institution. King knew very well that black preachers would be the last to sanction the dissolution of the church for the ultimate realization of King's goal of liberation through integration. Since King, in expounding his theory of the relationship between liberation and integration, did not specify "integration where, when, why, and how," he also did not have to specify what the role of the black church might be in the integrative process. In other words, King did not realize that he was merely reiterating the dimensions of an old dilemma in a new way. In 1934, Du Bois asked the NAACP leaders whether they would defend or reject the existence of the black church as a separate institution—they could not answer.

The black church, before and after King, remains a black institution. It is not only a social institution for godly worship, it is also a collective repository for various kinds of incorporated wealth, a source of employment for reigning ministers of the gospel and other dignitaries or subordinates in the church hierarchies. In short, the institutionalized black church is an economic, political, social, and moral power base. For several decades into the twentieth century, as E. Franklin Frazier so cogently pointed out, "the Negro church organization became the most important arena for political life among Negroes. It was in the contests carried out within these organizations that Negroes struggled for power and position and the members could exercise some choice in the selection of men to govern them. Thus, the Negro church organizations became the most effective agencies of social control among Negroes in their relatively isolated social world."[41]

But the patterns of social control produced the authoritarian, strongman personality in the raiments of forceful male preachers with almost unlimited powers. Some of these preachers developed into what Frazier described as "petty tyrants" who ruled in black churches and "who have their counterparts in practically all other Negro organizations." As a consequence, said Frazier:

> Negroes have had little education in the democratic processes. Moreover, the Negro church and Negro religion have cast a shadow over the entire intellectual life of Negroes and have been responsible for the so-called backwardness of American Negroes. Sometimes an ignorant preacher backed by the white community has been able to intimidate Negro scholars and subvert the true aim of an educational institution.[42]

However, although backed by broad sections of the white community, especially the middle-of-the-road and left-leaning liberals, King was certainly not an ignorant preacher. King's emergence coincided with the middle-class secularization of the black church, a process during which the church lost much of its former position as the main refuge against the emotional ravages of American racism. Thus, black churches, to maintain their institutional authority, had to "place less emphasis upon

salvation and death and [direct] their activities increasingly to the economic, social and political problems of Negroes in this world. The reorganization of the religious life of Negroes in the urban environment
has been influenced largely by the new class structure of Negro communities, especially in the North, which is the result of the increasing
occupational differentiation of the Negro population."[43] Adding to this
pressing need for reorganization, especially in the North, was that increasing numbers of blacks chose *not* to maintain church affiliations.

As said before, King's movement was not northern but southern;
hence, the *Southern* Christian Leadership Conference became the organized continuation not of the church as a spiritual refuge, but of King's
moral crusade for social justice. However, at this juncture of black social-
class evolution, an obvious question was not even asked: Had not the
secularization and urbanization of the formerly uprooted blacks so dis-
tanced them from traditional moorings; had not the accumulation of ghetto
pathologies, the persistent demographic segregation, the migratory scattering of increasing black populations from coast to coast; had not the
social consequences of all these effects rendered the black situation beyond the ability of even the transformed black church to redress with
King's secularized moral message? The SCLC and King both assumed
that it had not, *but it had*. When King stepped onto the stage of leadership
in 1955, the "Crisis in Negro Leadership" was of some forty years
existence. The product of a black generation that understood very little
of its own civil rights history, King never grasped the full scope of the
indigenous crisis in black leadership philosophies and the full range of
its *real* consequences for the Sixties generation.

Building on King's mobilizing achievements and, of course, legitimized by civil rights legislation, the SCLC performed admirably. The
SCLC's own published miscellany of recorded documents and media
propaganda attests to the reforming zeal of its leaders in many crucial
areas of black life, especially during the 1970s. On the death of King,
the leadership of the SCLC was taken on by Ralph D. Abernathy, one
of King's closest lieutenants from the days of Montgomery. Lacking
personal charisma, Abernathy was a sincere disciple with a journeyman's
zeal that could not even begin to emulate the gifted touch of the departed
prophet. With the passing of King, the crusading impact of his moral
imperative subsided and vanished amid the din and clamor growing out
of the national disasters connected with the Vietnam War. King's decision
to extend his crusade on domestic race-relations problems to the international arena of the immorality of an unjust war split the civil rights

leadership. More than that, his attempt to extend his southern-based movement into the North by way of Chicago in 1966 ran afoul of the urban pathologies of an embittered racial and ethnic caldron. If Memphis was to become King's Calvary, Chicago would be his Armageddon on the road to the cross. Later, another King disciple, the Reverend Jesse L. Jackson, would establish a strong outpost of SCLC in Chicago that bore the stamp of King's gospel of humanitarian confrontation—People United to Save Humanity (PUSH). All in all, the preachers would consolidate their claim to the throne of black leadership, ratified by King, plus the prior claim of the black church to the institutional regency in the black community.

However, this SCLC association of ministers could not transcend anything that King had accomplished; nor could they create programmatically any innovation in the quest for racial equality that had not already been devised by the NAACP, the National Urban League, the Student Nonviolent Coordinating Committee (SNCC), the Congress of Racial Equality (CORE), or King himself. Programmatically SCLC could organize, consolidate the civil rights gains of the Sixties; SCLC could mobilize and alert people for the defense and perpetuation of gains already won. But the realities of the American social structure and the built-in dimensions of its racial and ethnic makeup effectively delimited SCLC to the selfsame protest tactics that had been the hallmark of civil rights movements during the King era. In sum, the SCLC of the post-King Seventies became the ideological inheritor of the NAACP's social logic of racial integration and it could neither alter nor reverse the force of that social logic in civil rights practice. SCLC had to uphold and project King's social philosophy on integration and, like King, it became functionally trapped in a dilemma. If King could not, or would not, consent to the proposition that the black church ought to be integrated out of existence as a product of segregation, neither could the ministers who made up the SCLC leadership. This ongoing and deeply embedded contradiction broadened and perpetuated the dilemmas of black leadership. Consequently, the more civil rights achievements that were won, the deeper the dilemmas of black leadership, not to speak of the mass of black followers and those who were not even followers.

Although many black leaders are profoundly aware of the implications of their dilemma, an unwritten law exists against such a dilemma being admitted in public policy issues. From time to time, however, individual leaders will refer to it obliquely. Andrew Young, a minister and member of the SCLC hierarchy, is a case in point. Four years after

King's demise, Andrew Young, a ranking spokesman on the SCLC board of directors, had a number of second thoughts on black secondary education, which the good preacher-politician addressed under the title "Urban Education: A Challenge of the Seventies."[44] He said:

> There is a crisis in public education. In Atlanta, in New York, small towns like Evanston, Illinois or Palo Alto, California. And most of us can agree on that. But when we start to try to define the crisis we come up with all kinds of conclusions. Some of us use the word [sic] "quality education," others insist that financing is the crisis, and it certainly is because property taxes, the predominant method of financing public education in this country, have already been found unconstitutional in four different state courts; which means that on the financing question, we're going to have to have greater federal funds.[45]

Andrew Young foresaw a reversal of the use of property taxes for school financing and an increasing reliance on federal funding. But he admonished that *"as we get more federal funds, I think we're going to have to see to it that we also don't lose local control. The diversity of our society and the complexity of most of our urban areas demands that we have control as close to the neighborhood as we possibly can."* (Italics added.) This statement on public school education comes from a leading ideologue of the SCLC, eighteen years *after* the *Brown* decision mandated the complete desegregation of public school education in the South, inspired by the NAACP. But in the legal battle for outlawing segregated public schools, did the NAACP emphasize the maintenance of "local control" as "close to the neighborhood" as was racially or ethnically feasible in any given instance? No, the NAACP did not; the NAACP maintained that the neighborhood school was, in fact, nothing but the product of imposed segregation and should be outlawed. Since one could not achieve "quality education" in such an arrangement, court-enforced busing of schoolchildren was the only answer. However, Andrew Young, in his address to the Hungry Club of Atlanta, made a play on what he called "code words": "It's too bad we don't have a train system in our city already, and then the dialogue about education would be on training our children rather than on busing them."[46] But this is precisely what untold numbers of ordinary blacks said about court-ordered busing of children long before 1972—they asked for the improvement of the existing schools in the neighborhoods. "People are crying for neighborhood schools and they're right," Young continued, "but they've not yet realized that there are no more neighborhoods or communities. We live in geographic proximity to each other, but we don't even know the names of people on our block, much less care for the upbringing of their children'':

> To place children in a classroom for six hours a day with no surrounding loving community is simply repression; and repression always leads to revolt. This repressive and authoritative atmosphere is really what's responsible for much of the violence in our schools.[47]

Without specifying who among the black leaders had, prior to 1972, been the most adamant and class self-righteous in pushing the busing issue, Young revealed that it was his personal experience in visiting the Ocean Hill-Brownsville district in Brooklyn, New York, during the public school community-control struggle of 1968–1969 that taught him the importance of emphasizing local control as opposed to busing. The Ocean Hill-Brownsville struggle was over decentralization and the concept of community-based local control over administration of racially or ethnically distinct neighborhood school districts. This conflict between local black community spokesmen and the New York City Board of Education had resulted in the longest school strike by teachers and supervisors in American history. ''The strike paralyzed a school system of more than 1,000,000 children, 60,000 teachers and supervisors, and 900 schools. It also put into sharp focus some of the most troubling questions of urban education,'' to wit:

> What can be done about the present unmet needs of slum children for the kind of schooling they must have to escape the vicious circle of poverty, neglect, and ignorance?
>
> Is decentralization an effective answer? Does it provide genuine educational advantages, or is it merely a method of redistributing political and economic power? Can it be achieved without anarchy? Does it institutionalize racial segregation?
>
> What kind of qualifications, background, and experience should teachers and principals in the ghetto possess? Are black teachers more effective than white teachers in teaching black children? Are seniority, tenure, and other teacher rights obsolete?
>
> And finally, is integrated education a viable concept in cities that are becoming increasingly segregated?

The conflicts that had erupted in each of those districts; the long teacher strike and the chaos that followed; the militant posture taken by self-proclaimed spokesmen for the "community" and their apparent indifference to existing law, court orders and Board of Education directives—all these had caused many New Yorkers (and their legislators) to view the prospect of community control with anxiety and even alarm.[48]

Such questions and issues posed in 1968, and reiterated by Andrew Young in 1972, threw into question, not the purely judicial, but the purely racial and ethnic, i.e., the purely sociological and political ratiocinations implicit in *Brown*. This sweeping mandate ruled out any consideration of the concept of local control of public school administration *anywhere* or at *anytime*. Hence, the leaders of the Ocean Hill-Brownsville protest were in opposition to the *Brown* mandate. During the entire year of 1968, during which the Ocean Hill-Brownsville conflict was in progress, *The Crisis*, official organ of the NAACP, published but one noncommittal statement on Ocean Hill-Brownsville. And later, Andrew Young, as a prominent member of the ruling board of the SCLC, could not *publicly* differ with the NAACP's official position on public school integration. *But, then, neither did Martin Luther King* during his thirteen-year reign as moral spokesman. Moreover, neither did the SCLC, following King's departure. During King's career, he and Andrew Young and the entire leadership of SCLC complained about the slowness, the foot-dragging tactics by which the district courts and the southern white liberal leadership delayed or otherwise obstructed the court-ordered decree on desegregating public school districts. Similar to the NAACP braintrust, King and his SCLC forces continued to echo the same views and pursue the same public school integration issue (of children, no less!) as if it were the sociological, political, and civil rights touchstone, the *sine qua non*, the main public battle front in the overall struggle for racial democracy between or among the parents of children in the adult world. Of course, King, being particularly southern, was preoccupied with southern regional problems. Hence, the rigid public school segregationist policies of the South assumed the character of a number one moral issue among others in King's imperative. This obviously obscured the fact for King that the many instances of *de facto* integration in northern schools had never resulted in any noticeable degree of interracial reconciliation. In writing about the condition of blacks in the North, King often wrote as if all northern blacks actually lived in Harlem-type ghettos. Hence, King, like Andrew Young, could not differ publicly with the NAACP on crucial principles of functional goals. Even though the NAACP program on public schools differed from the policies of the leaders of Ocean Hill-Brownsville, one must *not* impugn the NAACP's policies, neither must one openly support the principles of the leaders of Ocean Hill-Brownsville. Like Young in 1972, one can only equivocate in retrospect on matters of programmatic principles, i.e., local control. The total thrust of the civil rights movement, initiated by the NAACP philosophy, places the idea of local control in apposition to the idea of racial integration in all intraracial and interracial affairs, thus laying the ground for a moral and functional dilemma for the black leadership, for King, for the SCLC, and for the blacks who follow them, and for the blacks who follow no one or nothing. Because his life was cut short, King never had time to attempt to solve this dilemma, caught up to the very end in the social logic of his own moral imperative.

The implication of Young's analysis was that *Brown* had not wrought the simple justice many of its fervid supporters had prophesied. Blacks, said Young (meaning black leaders), were in danger of missing the real crisis, and "getting caught up in the emotion, prejudice, and politics of education . . . leaving our children to suffer needlessly in an irrelevant situation."[49] He saw the "real crisis" in the fact that educational philosophy, public and private, "had not adapted to the urban environment."[50] Being an Atlantan, by way of New Orleans, nothing in Young's urban experience in politics had impressed him more regarding the "real crisis" in public education than the struggle in Ocean Hill-Brownsville. *Even in Atlanta,* said Young, one sees children carrying weapons, breaking windows, attempting arson, not just in public schools, but also in private suburban schools. One sees the complete alienation of children from adults, teachers facing tough and hostile pupils. As a result, "we produced a complete new problem for educators." "Basic skills of reading, and writing and computing are necessary for survival. Without them there can be no possibility of life, liberty and the pursuit of happiness." Blacks were not acquiring these basic skills because of segregation, said the NAACP, led by the "social scientism" of Kenneth Clark and others; eliminate segregation and all will be well. Now, said Young, "somehow, we must structure an education process which is relevant to our urban situation; one which can cope with the change, the challenge of chaos in the total community and establish some order and knowledge in the minds of our children."[51] *But what about integration?* Said Young:

> But an integrated education involves a great deal more than simply integrating pupils. We must see to it that there is a continually integrated

school board, that there be an integrated administration, that integrated school planning and construction takes place. We must make sure that integrated curriculum and textbooks are part of the education system, that we have integrated supervisory and training personnel, integrated faculty, integrated custodial staff, and finally integrated classrooms.[52]

This was not what *Brown* or its implementation either demanded or promoted. The implementation of *Brown* in the South (such as it was) eliminated black teachers, black principals, black administrators, a whole generation of experienced administrative public school personnel made superfluous by integration. The only way such a corps of black administrative personnel could have been developed would have been to retain the nucleus that already existed under the separate school systems by the discrete implementation of the principles of local control; by the elimination of public school segregation by law, while allowing the parental option of voluntary choice of local school enrollment. Such public school policies *ought* to have been implemented at the very outset of school desegregation no matter *what* the *Brown* decision said or did not say. When in 1952 South Carolina aimed to equalize racially separated school districts by allocating funds for upgrading black facilities, the NAACP turned down both the legal and the sociological rationale for this effort. What occurred was a misapplication of a legal judgment that allowed for no objective consideration of alternative social consequences. The *Brown* decision was intrinsically a legal opinion limited to the public administration of school systems. Social segregation in other areas of public life *was something else*. Instead of using *Brown* as a means of readjusting the lines of racial division or racial separateness in defending local black control, a totally irresponsible and romantic black leadership allowed the nebulous issue of integration to eliminate one of the natural foundations of political leverage in the coming struggle for *black political power*. The events leading to the *Brown* judicial decree meant merely that the American Constitution could no longer uphold doctrines of *legally* enforced segregation, *legally* supported racial discrimination, *legally* supported denials of racial equality. The judicial removal of such restrictions only opened the door for the establishment of racial "justice" within the social framework of a voluntary reordering of interracial, or better, intergroup relations. In other words, the separate-but-equal doctrine that *Brown* ruled unconstitutional *should* have been supplanted by the truly democratic doctrine of "*plural but equal*." Such a pluralistic doctrine (already socially implicit in the racial and ethnic composition of the United

States) would have given legitimate credence to Andrew Young's conclusions in estimating the nature of the "real crisis" in black education:

> Now, what do we do to restructure a school system in the light of some
> of these observations? First, I think the task of an urban education
> system would be to involve more adults in the process. This can be
> done by making greater use of para-professionals, people from the
> community who can share in the routine of school life and who are
> there to love and discipline as well as to assist the teacher in indivi-
> dualized instruction. This should free the teacher to become more of a
> planner and trainer, and enable him or her to be more creative in meeting
> the needs—the specific needs—of the children.[53]

From *Brown* in 1954 to the SCLC in Atlanta in 1972, the absence
of this approach to education had contributed to the breakdown of "traditional patterns of community," giving rise to what Young called "the
challenge of chaos in the total community." Andrew Young apparently
borrowed that very suggestive phrase from King's prophetic title of his
last book, *Where Do We Go from Here: Chaos or Community?* The die
cast by the immanent image of the martyred King would continue to
guide the SCLC. However, the intellectual superficiality of King's SCLC
progeny was like unto King as the bubbling patter of a nervous rivulet
feeding the majestic depths of a mountain lake. During the long odyssey
from Montgomery to James Meredith's attempted march from the University of Mississippi to Jackson, which culminated in the call for Black
Power, King could not help but become a changed leader. This did not
alter his views on the ultimate efficacy of nonviolence as the only sure
method of social change. However, King was confronted with problematic
realities of black life and aspirations that seriously challenged *not* his
moral convictions, which were unassailable, but his social philosophy as
the end product of his moral philosophy. Neither Andrew Young nor any
of King's disciples would subsequently face these challenges and debate
them. (On matters of strict leadership principles and policies, black leaders will not seriously debate each other.) Andrew Young's indirect criticism of school integration and busing was *not* aimed at the NAACP
philosophy. For Young, *Brown* was, from the first, acceptable in *principle,* and though educational *practice* had gone awry, this was not the
fault of *Brown*! (Nor of King's acceptance of *Brown*.)

By the time of the James Meredith march in Mississippi, King had
to face the shocking personal affront of being openly booed at gatherings
by increasing numbers of young-generation black militants who rejected

not only his nonviolence but also his political and economic policies whenever such specific policies were spelled out by King himself. When King, at one meeting, asked why certain of his followers refused to sing the verse "Black and white together" from that rousing civil rights anthem "We Shall Overcome," the reply was: "This is a new day, we don't sing those words anymore. In fact, the whole song should be discarded. Not 'We Shall Overcome,' but 'We Shall Overrun.' "[54] King was shocked. He related that "as I listened to all these comments, the words fell on my ears like strange music from a foreign land. My hearing was not attuned to the sound of such bitterness."[55] What King was hearing for the first time was the rising sentiment behind the Black Power slogan— a concept that King categorically rejected. The significant thing about King's rejection of the Black Power idea was that *he understood its meaning so well, but still had to reject it*. Completely gripped by the spell of his own self-righteous moral imperative on racial democracy, King could not perceive that his rejection of Black Power symbolized the end of his effectiveness as a black social philosopher. (His appeal as a black social moralist was to continue until even that sainted role would be eclipsed by a rifle blast from the minions of antimorality oppositionists to the social advance of blacks in *southern* society.)

But the barrier to black social advances during King's career was not only the power of racist opposition, which was formidable enough. The other side of the white-black equation was that blacks themselves were not sufficiently organized to engage seriously in the game of ethnic or racial-group contention for shares in the American pie. Black Power rhetoric was but a belated vocal reflection of black political, economic, and cultural powerlessness—a powerlessness made all the more graphic when civil rights legislation abolished both legal and certain *de facto* restrictions that had held blacks in bondage prior to *Brown*.

The intellectual legacy of this bondage affected the social, political, economic, and cultural ideologies of the contenders for black leadership born during the 1930s and after. In the evolution of their thought, they would act as though they were "new" leaders, not the end products of a "Crisis in Negro Leadership" extending back to the 1920s. Hence, "new" leaders would act out their roles from scratch, just as if the thirty or forty years during which blacks existed in an urbanized state of social makeshift—an unorganized migratory marginality—did not matter and had no essential bearing on contemporary issues. The "new" leadership would be so far removed from the 1920s that it would act as if the New Deal had never happened; as if a fundamentally changed relationship of the black minority to a social welfare role of the federal power had never occurred. Briefly stated, the "new" leadership would speak on behalf of the destiny of a black minority that lacked a history of the *politics of organized self-determination.* This was the real significance behind the rise of the Black Power concept, which King had to reject.

The racial politics of a racist (or, better, an ethnocentrically imbued) capitalistic society such as the United States cannot tolerate for long the brand of moral imperative that King was preaching. The free-enterprise money markets know no morality other than the morality of the power to determine marketable exchange values. In this regard, King elected to misconstrue what the Black Powerites were really alluding to. Put off by their apparent predisposition to cathartic violence, King did not want to understand that the Black Powerites were really hungering after a genuine program that, *nationwide,* spoke seriously to the question of how blacks could achieve various measures of local control over the political, economic, and cultural fortunes of black communities (especially in the North). To this incipient, grass-roots demand, King responded with the NAACP-inspired declaration that unqualified integration is the answer to all questions. He rejected Black Power as some racially inspired, but youthful, exuberance that suggested black separatism when what it really meant was pluralism. Even Malcolm X, after his expulsion from the Nation of Islam, the ultimate expression of black separatism, retreated from the impossible position of separatism. Blacks cannot be separate in the United States, but they *can* be functionally *plural.*

Even King himself, in his arguments against Black Power, admitted the pluralistic nature of American society, but he refused to countenance the most efficacious approach to the American pluralistic reality: "To succeed in a pluralistic society, and an often hostile one . . .," he said, *"the Negro obviously needs organized strength, but that strength will only be effective when it is consolidated through constructive alliances with the majority group."*[56] (Italics added.) But King, as educated as he was, turned the answer on its head. The majority group *does not have to* and *will not*—in fact, *cannot*—effectively ally itself with a minority group (for the latter's benefit) if the minority group itself fails to organize its *own* economic, political, and cultural potential for a showdown across the bargaining table to obtain an equal share of the resources of any society. If King understood that blacks obviously needed "organized strength," then he must have known that blacks were woefully deficient in organized strength. No doubt, setting up the Southern Christian Leadership Conference satisfied King that it might help to fill the organizational vacuum. But though the SCLC represented a valiant effort in defense of civil rights gains *already* achieved, it could not even begin to encompass the full range of organizational forms that had been lacking for forty years. Such forms had not been established because the white liberalistic thinking that had permeated the ideology of civil rights leaders since the founding of the NAACP had discouraged them on the assumption that they weren't needed. *Such was the legacy of noneconomic liberalism:* It led ultimately to a Supreme Court decision outlawing legal public school segregation, but decreeing the total integration of schoolchildren by ruling out optional local administrative community control. This was done in the name of guaranteeing universal, nonsegregated, nondiscriminatory quality education.

If this were not the case, then Andrew Young would not have been moved in 1972 to mount the platform in Atlanta lamenting that the biracial public school system had, detrimental to the educational interests of black children, degenerated into a "real crisis" because Atlanta blacks had failed to achieve local control. Why did they not have local control? Precisely because the movement that inspired the integration of black pupils into the segregated but mainstream educational channels functionally ruled out both the necessity and the (Black Power) legitimacy of local control. Said Young: "Integration as part of an urban education emphasis is quite different from a consolidation of school systems which would put suburbanites in control of urban education. Urban education is most likely to be developed by people who live in and love the city. It's hardly likely that a commuter from Lithonia is going to have much empathy with the life styles of urban children."[57] But it is the *"life styles of urban children"* that predominantly characterize black schoolchildren in Atlanta and elsewhere. Thus, commuters from the suburbs *(be they black or white)* cannot be expected to have much empathy with the life-styles of (black) urban children. Which was precisely the unavoidable outcome of racial integration across the board in education (both lower and higher), housing, political representation and participation, and so on. The civil rights movement demanded unqualified racial integration. King went along with that demand unreservedly; so did Andrew Young and the entire corps of black preachers who later made up the leadership of the SCLC. In the process, they elected to barter away all potential claims that the urban black community had to retain local control over black education as if it were an unnecessary entitlement.

Appearing before the Supreme Court justices in the *School segregation Cases* beginning in December 1953, John W. Davis, a Southern-

bred white lawyer, argued in support of South Carolina's efforts to equalize state funding of the racially separate school districts of Clarendon
County and asked the Court to consider the problem it would confront
"if it ordered the schools desegregated in a heavily Negro district such
as the one in Clarendon County where there were 2,800 black pupils and
300 white ones."[58] In this "clear and present" example, it would have
been beneficial to have accepted South Carolina's *forced* gesture as a
necessary step in the direction of *black political control* over the administration of the already heavily black-populated school districts. Such a
compromise along the way would not have negated the judicial significance of *Brown* five months later because it would have left the legal
door open for *free choice* in the matter of what *kind* of public school
parents could elect to send their children to: *all black, all white, or in
between.* Whatever the choice, the principle of black local control could
have been safeguarded. Both the NAACP lawyers and the bevy of social
scientists mobilized by the NAACP turned thumbs down on such arguments. Hence, the various responses to the predecision arguments, pro
and con, led Chief Justice Warren to write the "unanimous" *Brown*
decision. However, the arguments of John W. Davis, with respect to the
racial situation in Clarendon County, which was the locus of *Briggs* v.
Elliot, one of the five school segregation cases subsumed under *Brown*,
is worth repeating:

Who is going to disturb that situation? If they were to be reassorted or
commingled, who knows how that would best be done?

If it is done on the mathematical basis, with 30 children as a
maximum . . . you would have 27 Negro children and three whites in
one schoolroom. Would that make the children any happier? Would
they learn any more quickly? Would their lives be more serene?

Children of that age are not the most considerate animals in the
world, as we all know. Would the terrible psychological disaster being
wrought, according to some of these witnesses, to the colored child be
removed if he had three white children sitting somewhere in the same
schoolroom?

Would white children be prevented from getting a distorted idea
of racial relations if they sat with 27 Negro children? I have posed that
question because it is the very one that cannot be denied.

You say that is racism. Well, it is not racism. Recognize that for
centuries and more, humanity has been discussing questions of race and
race tension, not racism. . . . [T]wenty-nine states have miscegenation
statutes now in force which they believe are of beneficial protection to

both races. Disraeli said, "No man," said he, "will treat with indifference the principle of race. It is the fact of history."[59]

But *Brown* did disturb that situation on the assertion that any other interpretation of the facts amounted to "racism." John W. Davis opined that an alternative assessment of the school district situation was not necessarily racism. He declared that the intent of the state of South Carolina was to "produce equality for all of its children of whatever race or color" as it had done in equalizing the schools of Clarendon County *without* an upcoming *Brown* decision. However, in his characterization of both the NAACP's position on South Carolina's equalization efforts and those lawyers and social scientists who unreservedly supported the NAACP's position, Davis said:

> I am reminded—and I hope it won't be treated as a reflection on anybody—of Aesop's fable of the dog and the meat: The dog, with a fine piece of meat in his mouth, crossed a bridge and saw [his] shadow in the stream and plunged in for it and lost both substance and shadow.
>   Here is equal education, not promised, not prophesied, but present. Should it be thrown away on some fancied question of racial prestige?[60]

But the NAACP opted for a Court decision on a species of "equal education" that promised to eliminate all racial and social barriers against upgrading black "racial prestige." Despite some very cogent arguments from certain justices who questioned whether *Brown* could "constitutionally" deliver what it promised, the Court rendered a unanimous decision.

As time passed, shifting urban demographics defeated the grand design of *Brown*—and produced more separation of the races than had existed when *Brown* was rendered. In protest against the ineluctable social forces leading toward more separation, the NAACP and King conveniently called it more "segregation," a description that was sociologically time-serving and inaccurate. All around these black leaders was the spectacle of immigrant groups flocking into the cities, creating concentrations of community ethnicity with never a complaint that they were the victims of segregation. Instead, they defended their communities and strenuously exerted the rights of territoriality whenever and wherever possible. From thence, taking advantage of every liberty, every opportunity—political and economic—that was available, they moved up the social, political, and economic ladders and into the American mainstream faster than blacks, and were more readily accepted by American whites for such demonstrations of Americanization.

In any event, the urban sprawl and bottled-up racial and ethnic enclaves created more extended and predominantly black school districts—all lacking Andrew Young's version of local control, and exacerbated by mounting black-on-black crime, unemployment, the menace of drugs, illegitimate births, teen delinquency, family disorganization, and a full catalogue of each and every malaise under the heading of ghetto pathology. All these pathologies were, of course, in consonance with the conventional wisdom of liberal interpretations, attributable to the searing consequences of segregation, which, historically and sociologically, *is* true. But it does not follow, sociologically, that the magic solution for the elimination of these pathologies is racial integration. Supplementing King's moral strictures against the sin of race discrimination was the civil rights notion, a thoroughly simplistic one, about the need for action, a "strategy for change," or, as King said, "a tactical program that will bring the Negro into the mainstream of American life as quickly as possible. So far, this has been offered by the non-violent movement. Without recognizing this we end up with solutions that don't solve, answers that don't answer and explanations that don't explain."[61]

Afro-Americans, who constitute the black disadvantaged with their accumulation of ghetto pathologies, are, by the moral stroke of white repentance for past sins, to be brought into the mainstream of American life—and that will solve everything! For King, every institutionalized result of racial segregation—all-black public schools, all-black housing arrangements, all-black urban communities (i.e., ghettos), in short, any all-black consequence of segregation (except, of course, the all-black church)—had to go in order to demonstrate society's payment of its debt for the historical denial of the "humanity" of all blacks. However, later on, he had to backtrack in consideration of the real nature of the dilemma of the black position in American society: "The dilemma that the Negro confronts is so complex and monumental that its solution will of necessity involve a diversified approach. But Negroes can differ and still unite around common goals." Hence, in this regard, said King:

There are already structured forces in the Negro community that can serve as the basis for building a powerful united front—*the Negro church, the Negro press, the Negro fraternities and sororities, and Negro professional associations. We must admit that these forces have*

*never given their full resources to the cause of Negro liberation. There
are still too many Negro churches that are so absorbed in a future good
"over yonder" that they condition their members to adjust to the present
evils "over here."*[62] (Itallics added.)

It became painfully clear (or at least it should have) that when Gunnar
Myrdal outlined the nature of the "American Dilemma," it was before
Brown, Martin Luther King, the Civil Rights Acts of 1964–1965. But
as the tumultuous black Sixties drew to a close, the burden of the "American Dilemma" was dropped by society at large into the unready hands
of blacks themselves. The *real dilemma is the blacks' own to deal with,*
implied King. And although the blacks' dilemma required a diversified
approach, King had to be vague as to what these approaches should be.
He *had* to be vague, because as the most prominent representative of the
new black leadership continuum, he had arrived on the scene devoid of
organizational precedent outside of the NAACP and the National Urban
League. Thus, King had little or no conception of the various kinds of
organized strength that blacks sorely needed, but which he belatedly
recognized as nonexistent. In 1966–1967, King was discovering that the
blacks' dilemmas were more complex than he had imagined during the
Montgomery Bus Boycott. Negro fraternities and sororities, the press and
professional associations might alter and adapt their racial form and content; formerly all-black colleges and universities might cease to be "all
black" under the impact of civil rights and desegregation; only the all-
black churches multiply and endure. In the very eye of the racial storms
of the Sixties, in the midst of the shifting, uncertain winds of desegregation, of integration, of the upward mobility of the expanding black
middle class, or in the downward drift into the pits of ghetto pathologies,
these churches remain racially unaltered social institutions. Sociologically, they form the bedrock institutional bases, the social fulcrum around
which is grounded the pluralistic relationship of the black minority in the
American nation, divided among the three major religious power
groups—white Anglo-Saxon protestants, white Catholics, and white Jews.
With all the liberalistic agitation and propaganda, pro and con, relative
to the issue of "social integration" that has been bandied about since the
Brown decision, these power groups want social integration only insofar
as access to wealth, professional, political, and cultural prestige are concerned. Psychologically secure in the convivial folds of their racially
separate religious church affiliations, black religionists are no different,

in the main, regardless of what Martin Luther King said about racial integration as a "moral imperative."

Very early in his career King observed that the black needed a program "to improve his own economic lot. . . . He must not wait for the end of segregation that lies at the basis of his own economic deprivation; he must act now to lift himself up by his own bootstraps."[63] But this self-help tactic, one of the demands of pluralism, is not sanctioned in the propaganda arsenal of integration. In this regard, the Nation of Islam graphically demonstrated, with its economic and social rehabilitation efforts within the black communities, both the moral and social bankruptcy of black Christianity in the arena of social responsibility. As limited in community impact as was the Nation of Islam, and as controversial and objectionable to many as were its authoritarian methods, its rigorous discipline, its "hate the white man" ideology, this movement demonstrated what a "church" *can do if it wills it* by the voluntary assumption of social responsibility and without ideological coercion. King was instrumental in rehabilitating the social image of black Christianity by joining his moral imperative with the issue of civil rights. But the King-inspired secularization of black Christianity, despite the SCLC continuum, could not encompass the totality of the programmatic needs of blacks. The problem is that the black church, despite being the only existing institutionalized basis for the pluralistic legitimacy of blacks in a pluralistic society, remains politically narrow-minded, intellectually and socially provincial, culturally one-dimensional, economically self-serving, and parochial. The black church is not intellectually equipped to extend King's *avant-garde* function onto other social fronts.

Since the 1930s, when W.E.B. Du Bois clashed with the NAACP leadership over its integration philosophies, the fundamental conceptual defect in the entire civil rights thrust was the concerted effort to negate both the realities and the leadership imperatives of minority-group plurality. Although in the heat of those internal NAACP executive board controversies, Du Bois and his few supporters were unable completely to spell out the future demands of black-group plurality, Du Bois tried to lay down the programmatic basis for it *within the NAACP*. He already knew in 1934 that no amount of integration, no matter to what degree it would be constitutionally or legally supported, would diminish the sociological essentials of group plurality—especially a nonwhite minority like American blacks. If the American assimilationist melting pot has not, in all these decades, erased the plurality of white-skinned ethnics, what purblind romantic nonsense it is to expect that integration is going to eliminate the social consequences of skin-color barriers to equality in a society whose dominant ethos is saturated with the ideas not only of racial "purity" but racial puritanism.

The conceptual linking of integration with civil rights effectively obscures that by eliminating discrimination in public accommodations, in voting rights, and in employment opportunities, neither "ethnicity" nor "cultural diversity" is thereby divested of any social meaning or function—the cultural pluralism remains operative. As a consequence of civil rights legislation, the dominant group culture is still left free to thwart, or otherwise limit, the social range of integration of the minority group. But on the other hand, the elimination of legally enforced exclusion by reasons of race or ethnicity, does in fact enhance the minority group's freedom and flexibility to develop the internal resources of its own political, economic, and cultural plurality. Only when a minority group develops such resources can it have any effective power in a plural society. In pursuit of such plurality goals, the majority group cannot become a proxy for the minority, but it could assist in mutual functional-plurality interests. The real problem with American society is that it is sociologically multiracial, multiethnic, and culturally pluralistic, but economically, politically, and culturally, *it does not want to act that way except at election times*.

As one result, the black civil rights leadership "theoretically" misconceived the essential function and necessity of civil rights. Because a set of unique racial, social, and legal circumstances justified the prerogative of civil rights leaders to maintain that *full priority* be given to the struggle for the legal enforcement of the rights established by the Fourteenth and Fifteenth Amendments, these leaders misconstrued the end results. As has been pointed out elsewhere, the Civil Rights Acts of 1964–1965 outlawed "the use of race as a basis for making decisions affecting individuals," *but not groups*. It was an ill-conceived conclusion on the part of civil rights leaders to expect that desegregation in the private and public sectors of an institutionalized economy would transform American society into a nation of desegregated hearts and minds. King's Christian ideal of Love does not penetrate here. Thus, the civil rights acts, contrary to expectations, merely lowered the barriers in favor of a more unrestricted evolution of black minority plurality. But lacking beforehand an internally institutionalized infrastructure by which to reorganize all aspects of black community life, the successful passage of civil rights legislation of the Sixties left civil rights leaders, including King, *without a viable leadership program*. Not a single leader of the Sixties understood the meaning and consequences of this programless dilemma better than King himself.

Like many other major and minor black leaders who were his contemporaries, King began an intellectual retreat in the face of what he saw were the immense complexities of the black position in America. The rousing and exuberant pursuit of civil rights of the Fifties and Sixties had been satiated. In the face of the white backlash, civil rights and integration slogans became simplistic and banal, lacking in clearly defined purpose. King began to universalize the black situation in America and link it with the uprising of poor and oppressed peoples in Africa, Asia, and Latin America:

> However deeply American Negroes are caught in the struggle to be at last at home in our homeland of the United States, we cannot ignore the larger world house in which we are also dwellers. Equality with whites will not solve the problems of either whites or Negroes if it means equality in a world society stricken by poverty and in a universe doomed to extinction by war.
>
> In one sense the civil rights movement in the United States is a special American phenomenon which must be understood in the light of American history and dealt with in terms of the American situation. But on another and more important level, what is happening in the United States today is a significant part of a world development.[64]

As politically inspiring as this international symbolizing of the worldwide unity of purpose of the oppressed might have been, it was, insofar as American blacks were concerned, like grasping at straws in the Atlantic tradewinds. Many Third World countries, in requesting foreign-aid funds, were in competition with domestic blacks for the same federal coffers. At the same time, a casualty rate that would ultimately add up to more than 57,000 American soldiers dead was mounting in Vietnam. An as-yet undetermined percentage of those dying were black soldiers from the ghettos of America. King had been led, unwisely, to compromise his established civil rights legitimacy by taking a public stand against the Vietnam War. This was the internationalization of his original moral imperative on domestic rights issues. The catch here was that the privileges of equal citizenship carried with them an equal obligation to fight America's wars, whether these wars were considered just or unjust. After all, it was the NAACP and the civil rights radicals of the late 1940s who were in the forefront of the fight for the integration of blacks in the military. Whether a war is just or unjust depends upon which side of the battle lines the critic of the war is speaking from. In the Vietnam War, American leaders attempted to impose their version of democratic political institutions as a governing principle for that country. Whether or not the American government is justified in attempting to impose democratic political institutions on another country (especially in the Third World) is a question that *ought* to be internally debated. It ought to have been debated by civil rights leaders except that King was the only one who entered the debate in some fashion. However, seeing the issue from the black position in the American system poses very critical questions from an international perspective. The truth was, and is, that King in particular was demanding racial equality within the American democratic political and economic system. It is not only Americans who put forth the nationally egotistical claim that American economic and political democracy is the most advanced and the most powerful; it is also the peoples of the Third World upon whose unwilling backs the American power attempts to impose democratic political institutions who say the same thing: *American capitalistic democracy is the world's best, richest, most liberal, most powerful, and most desirable.* Thus, despite all the physical, moral, military, and other depredations Americans wreak on Third World countries in the name of imposing democratic institutions, the most prized goal of many of these Third World peoples is American citizenship. They will risk almost as much danger to life, limb, and sanity to gain entry into the United States as an American soldier does who is sent to defend them against their own dictators and corrupt political leaders.

On the other hand, the dissatisfied American blacks' favorite complaint about American democracy is its inherent racism. It is American racism that stands in the way of blacks receiving their just economic and social rewards from American democracy. Late in his career, Martin Luther King began to take the position that "American society needed a radical redistribution of wealth and economic power to achieve even a rough form of social justice." He is quoted as saying to the SCLC staff: "We must realize recognize that we can't solve our problem now until there is a radical redistribution of economic and political power."[65] Later on, King's thinking had evolved to the point where he took the position that the "issues of economic class were more crucial and troublesome, and less susceptible to change, than were issues of race."[66] America, he said to one interviewer, "is deeply racist and its democracy is flawed both economically and socially." King added that:

The black revolution is much more than a struggle for the rights of Negroes. It is forcing America to face all its interrelated flaws—racism, poverty, militarism, and materialism. It is exposing evils that are rooted deeply in the whole structure of our society. It reveals systemic rather than superficial flaws and suggests that radical reconstruction of society is the real issue to be faced.[67]

The writer who described this evolution in King's thinking interpreted the process as "his journey from reformer to revolutionary." Probably a more factual explanation was that King's thinking was being influenced by certain Communist party Marxists known to be in close collaboration with him. This collaboration helps explain the intensive FBI harassment and surveillance of King. But his alleged transformation from reformer to so-called revolutionary was both dubious and too simplistic an interpretation. By 1967, King had to face the hard reality that his moral preachments had suffered a diminishing power of appeal. Legislation had blunted the cutting edge of the protest movements, leaving the civil rights legions shorn of any tangible goals. Thus, for the black minority in particular, the objectively hard facts about the nature of American political, economic, and cultural institutions were laid visible and bare. As social practices, discrimination and segregation were like guardian sentinels forestalling and blocking the way to the inner sanctums of institutional power. But outlawing segregation and discrimination did not mean instant black liberation, and King came to the conclusion that racial equality was not achievable in American society as presently organized. Conclusion? "The whole structure of American life must be changed," he said. "We are engaged in the class struggle." Later: "We're dealing in a sense with class issues, we're dealing with the problem of the gulf between the haves and the have nots."[68]

Whether King's final conclusions about the black situation in American society were warranted; whether he was right or wrong is still, in 1986, an open question. But the interior question he posed was: *What is the future of blacks in American society?*—a legitimate question! However, King's "Marxist" conclusions about the need to restructure American society were nothing really new. They have been stated many times over by various black revolutionary thinkers since 1920, the beginning of the "Crisis in Negro Leadership." But these former revolutionary thinkers, beginning with A. Philip Randolph, were faced with the fact that blacks in general did not subscribe to revolutionary doctrines. In King's day few, if any, of his followers were imbued with any so-called revolutionary ideas about restructuring society. Indeed, historical circumstances have placed blacks into the most ironic and contradictory position of any nonwhite minority in the Western Hemisphere, including the American Indians. At least, the Indians have a legal claim to masses of American land, which blacks do not. The only claim blacks have against American institutions is their inherent racism, yet blacks reverently uphold American political and economic values. Blacks may have agreed with King that their civil rights struggle had international connotations and was "a significant part of a world development." In fact, blacks are so much aware of Third World societies "stricken with poverty" that while *they must condemn the discriminatory racism that pervades American society, they are called upon actively to champion the rights of nonwhite immigrants from the Third World to gain entry into the United States as a land of refuge from tyranny and poverty, a land of opportunity, a land of freedom.* Moreover, very few of these Third World immigrants care one whit that American society is racist, and soon begin to look rather dubiously at blacks for complaining about racism with the oft-heard rejoinder: *American blacks do not take advantage of American opportunities.*

For years American blacks accepted a trundle of racial myths about the situation in Haiti and other parts of the Caribbean and Latin America. Propagandized by the notion that there was no racism in Haiti, Brazil, the West Indies, or Latin America, American blacks were made to feel inferior and were literally looked down upon by blacks from those countries who very naturally wanted no part of American racism, especially in the South. However, the level of poverty known to most blacks in those countries was unimaginable to American blacks. Black poverty in America was mild compared with poverty in the Caribbean and Latin America.

It was once the custom of West Indians to flaunt the history of Haiti as the one and only black independent nation in the Western Hemisphere, and its glorious revolution under Toussaint L'Ouverture as the record of blacks who fought for their freedom. The innuendo was that American blacks had never fought for their freedom. But the 1980s saw the unprecedented spectacle of Haitian refugees risking death by drowning in shark-infested seas to gain entry into the United States—the land of freedom, liberty, and opportunity *in the racist southern state of Florida no less!* Here was a historic reversal of the role of independence and national freedom in the international relations between the United States and the Caribbean. Yet, the most vociferous supporters of the rights of black Haitians to the privileges of American citizenship were American blacks! Some of them agreed with Martin Luther King that America is a thoroughly racist and sick society—so racist and corrupt that they even deprecate their own black American citizenship as being worthless. Which raises the question, If their black American citizenship is so empty and unrewarding, why do they go to such extremes to champion the rights of Third World peoples (especially black ones) to emigrate to the United States, the land of freedom, equality, and opportunity? It must be that (black) misery loves company.

All of these shifting and changing nuances on the international scene since the demise of King can be cited to suggest that King had been led, unwisely, to misread the implications of America's role in international relations with the Third World as it related to the black position in American society. While there *were* certain political, economic, and military linkages between blacks in America and oppressed peoples of the Third World, these peoples see America (and the blacks within it) as the most affluent of the "have" nations. Their "revolutions," while breaking with what they see as the shackles of Western imperialism, are fundamentally the means by which they seek to catch up with Western economic affluence, political power and military prestige. Afterward, they seek foreign aid from the West, principally the United States. Whenever possible, these Third World nations wink at the history of American imperialism in their own countries, allowing their surplus and discontented citizens to seize every opportunity to emigrate to the United States. Many arrive and enter into immediate competition with American blacks for the economic and political rewards of citizenship. Black Africans are involved, whenever possible, in the same international emigration-to-America syndrome. In the meanwhile, American blacks continue complaining that racism operates against *their* citizenship ambitions.

The history of America and the world since World War II, and especially since the emergence of Martin Luther King and the civil rights movement, amply demonstrates that out of the international turmoil of social revolutions, wars, atrocities, famine, droughts, communal religious strife, and secular terrorism, the United States, with all its flaws and imperfections, takes on the semblance of the "best of all possible worlds" in a fashion that Voltaire's Pangloss never dreamed. This is especially true, and ironically so, for American blacks, who are just about the only nonwhite minority group in the entire world having no options to pack up and emigrate anywhere (including the African continent). For better or worse, the American black minority is stuck with the American version of political and capitalistic democracy. Their future lies with the rise or fall, the decline or the re-creation of the American economic ability to create social wealth. There will be no social revolutions in the United States because historically the American nation is an evolutionary society. By virtue of its very nature as an evolutionary society, its existence at the apex of world economic, political, and military power has eliminated and precluded the endemic Third World need, and rationale for, social revolution.

For these essential reasons King's civil rights allies were outraged when he left aside the pressing problems of domestic civil rights to assume an internationally moral posture on the American involvement in Vietnam. In addition, the very powerful federal establishment, including President Johnson, up to then "morally" in King's corner, began to turn against the King crusade. The irony was that, in terms of international *realpolitik,* nothing that happened in the Third World, including the Vietnam War, could directly benefit American blacks. Because the United States is at the apex of international world power, the United States cannot avoid being involved in Third World revolutions. However, the American political establishment, from the White House on down, did not (and does not) understand how to use political and military leadership in the best interests of *both* the United States and the nations of the Third World. Educated in the political and economic traditions of an evolutionary world power, Americans do not understand how to deal with Third World revolutions. Embarrassed by King's unwise and impolitic foray into the Vietnam quagmire, the federal establishment repudiated King.

During his last months, King transferred the legacy of an economic program named Operation Breadbasket to the leadership of his lieutenant, the Reverend Jesse L. Jackson, who established the program in Chicago. King's eclectic, mixed-bag ideas for black empowerment ventures had attracted offers from the national business community to invest in black enterprises toward the end of creating jobs and financing black business ventures. Jesse Jackson was launched into national prominence. Operation Breadbasket, practical and useful from the standpoint of fostering minor free-enterprise entrepreneurs, would hardly scratch the economic surface of the black disadvantaged. But no matter: American foreign aid to the Third World was accomplishing the same ends—enriching influential Third World entrepreneurs. Operation Breadbasket, an acceptable palliative, was not really an innovation but a newer version of the original "Buy Black" movement organized mainly in New York City and Chicago during the 1930s Depression. Then, the goal was to force jobs for blacks from white merchants profiteering off black communities. But Jesse Jackson was able to carry his program another step up, into higher finance, and in the Seventies he would achieve what Booker T. Washington had vainly tried to accomplish between 1900 and World War I. Washington, the prototypical philosopher of black capitalism, spent fruitless years trying to induce powerful white industrialists to help finance a corps of black businessmen.

Contrary to Jackson's flamboyant exercise in Operation Breadbasket's "class" economics, King was driven to appeal to "reverse classism" against the establishment by attempting to organize several thousand poor whites, American Indians, Mexican Americans, and a majority of blacks into a "Poor People's Campaign" aimed at Washington, D.C. The goal was to force Congress to act against poverty. In this way, though, King's emphasis on the racial crusade was transformed into an incipient version of the class struggle. This attempt to link the economic plight of poor blacks with that of poor whites and other minorities merely posed the threat of a symbolic demonstration of economic problems that the American establishment would not even begin to confront, short of a disastrous economic slump. It posed the threat of a class war—but it was a confrontation in which the underclasses possessed neither a power nor a political clout that the establishment would respect beyond the momentary annoyance of urban disruption. The degree to which American society, and its political and economic institutions, is essentially an evolutionary society was misunderstood by King—as has been the case with a long line of would-be American revolutionaries since World War I. Faced with the irrefutable fact that American society had neither the capacity nor the will (or even the need) to transform itself into *his* supermoralistic ideal of interracial harmony, King was led to repudiate the end results of the evolution of American society that he confronted in 1967. Thus, he was unable insightfully to assess his *own* considerable contribution to the achievements of his own era. Misreading, with the best of intentions, the international role of the United States, King overromanticized the hopes, ambitions, and the indigenous realities of the Third World. If indeed, as King himself concluded, "the civil rights movement in the United States is a special American phenomenon which must be understood in the light of American history and dealt with in terms of the American situation," then he should have been wise enough to limit his social and moral concerns to the complex issues of the domestic American front. Wars, like the Vietnam War, just or unjust, once begun cannot be stopped at will by anyone's moral preachments; wars are fated to run out their bloody course to the logical end of inherent exhaustion. Martin Luther King, caught up in a moral dilemma between developing international and domestic negatives, was slowly undermined and negated and suffered a worsening mental state of diminishing personal morale.

The martyrdom of Martin Luther King marked the passing of the most influential leader produced by black America in the entire twentieth century. His intellectual scope, even at the young age of thirty-seven, outmatched that of the collective black leadership of his day. His all-embracing intellectual range lacked only the cumulative depth that comes with age and experience. For the black civil rights movement, the irony of King's role was that it was only the black church that could have produced him; the further irony was that the secular civil rights organizations could not have produced a leader with his charisma. Martin Luther King's undoing can be likened to that of a young, potentially great field general who, not lacking in certain military skills or in sufficient mobile forces, does not know when to retreat, when to consolidate, when to back up and regroup, when to give up territory for strategic purposes. Carried away with an intensified, morally self-righteous zeal, King became trapped in the momentum of a social logic of his own making and was destroyed. His overzealous moral idealism in the interests of the "brotherhood of man" led him to dissipate the moral authority he possessed. Better for American society and for the black minority as a whole, had he turned his moral authority *back on the black minority itself* with the secular message: *Get Your Own Minority House in Order. Civil rights laws have done nothing but remove the segregationist barriers, the social dam, which held in check a black backwater of the internalized consequences of racial oppressions. Once the legal barriers are removed, pent-up minority energies are released with few real outlets. Racial integration is not the complete answer for the social disabilities we have historically incurred.*

To be sure, such a turnabout from the social protest direction pre-destined, as it were, by the Montgomery Bus Boycott was asking King voluntarily to accept the leadership of a most difficult enterprise. At the outset, the Afro-American was, by all counts, the most inadequately organized racial minority in the entire nation, having had close to a hundred years of bitter experience of surviving in a hostile society. More than that, the psychological ravages of segregation, discrimination, and racial harassment have left their mark on the collective psychologies *of all classes*. For many, the winning of civil rights legislation was similar to the legal release of a prisoner who has been pardoned, finally, after serving a life sentence for a crime he did not commit. But a long incarceration has left the unlucky prisoner bereft of the means of coping constructively with the social demands of his freedom. King possessed the moral authority to lead the struggle for the release of the prisoners, but shied away from the more difficult task of exerting the same authority to tell them how they might reorganize their lives to cope with the demands of freedom in a plural society. No black leader prior to King had been able to exert such authority—not even Marcus Garvey in the 1920s whose foreign-derived superego led him to misguide and subvert the lasting effectiveness of the very social movement he had successfully organized.

In the most fortuitous fashion, however, and contrary to all the fashionable radical prophecies of the post-World War II era, King, in his own way, proved the pundits of social change wrong in their forecasts about the necessary path for black liberation. When Oliver Cromwell Cox wrote, with his *a priori* Marxist convictions, that black leaders "cannot give Negroes a 'fighting' cause. None can be Moses, . . . even be Mohandas Gandhi—a Lenin will have to be a white man"—King proved him wrong. Among other things, King proved that a "Lenin" could not be a white man leading a liberation movement in America. King's assassination also demonstrated that the ultimate leader of black liberation *must* be a black man (or men). The assassination of King also revealed the extent of the *vulnerability of the black male as a leadership symbol* in the continuing struggle for black equality in the coming period.

PART FIVE

The black Seventies unfolded as an era in which the civil rights legislation of the black Sixties would be put to the crucial test in public policy legitimization. Also, in retrospect, the Seventies would unfold as the transitional decade leading to the fateful 1980s. By 1970 the black population had grown to an official census count of 22,581,000, or 11.1 percent of the total population. This total of twenty-two and a half million was of course an undercount. However, this undercount (which had occurred in every census since Reconstruction) was less significant than the scattering, in black migrations since 1940, of millions across the American continent in many big-city, medium-city, small-town, regional, and sectional demographic formations.

If the older black generation was the progeny of the New Deal, the younger generation, coming of age in the Seventies, would be the "Children of the Age of Civil Rights," harboring unprecedented assumptions about the meaning of freedom, equality, and democracy. Thus, in the wake of all the agitation, confrontation, proliferation of movements, rise, decline, and passage of leaders through the glare of grass-roots fame into obscurity, the innate limitations of civil rights would wax clearer and clearer. The millennium was not to be; the pre-NAACP prophecies of T. Thomas Fortune's 1890 declaration had never been a part of the civil rights legacy. Being present-minded, like most Americans, the Children of the Age of Civil Rights had scant knowledge of where they came from, and only the faintest comprehension of where they were headed. Since the present appeared to be a gradual negation of their expectations, there were feverish and spasmodic attempts at stocktaking—*where do we go from here? And why?* Once the reality sank in, certain perceptive black spokesmen would admit that the civil rights cycle was over—that 1970 could be summed up as a replay of the issues of 1870. Nineteen-seventy, by some unique play of historical forces, set the stage for the reenactment of the *political* issues of Reconstruction. Thus, the Seventies would usher in a new emphasis on black politics. One writer would describe transition later in an article titled "From Civil Rights to Party Politics: The Black Political Transition:"

> The political history of American blacks since the middle Sixties is in large part the history of the new Afro-American political class: the black elected official or party politician. The emergence of this new class is closely linked with the politization of the American Negro's ethnic experiences. Politization facilitates what can be called the vertical integration of an ethnic group's social structure, reducing the normally sharp status and class cleavages within an ethnic group. . . . Politization was one of the few ways to enhance an ethnic group's political efficacy—its capacity for unified action—in the face of limited political resources, societal barriers, and the keen competition of city politics. Because of their relative exclusion from city machines in the years between 1900 and 1960, urban Negroes were deprived of this crucial political experience for more than two generations.[1]

It required the cyclic playing out of the civil rights thrust to the very limits of its constitutional enforceability before many blacks would seriously reconsider the politics of civil rights via political integration versus what this writer cited as the "politics of black ethnicity." The two ideals, most often functionally incompatible, would not be easily accepted as a fact of political life. More than that, the innate contradictions between "integration" and "ethnic unification" would not be easy to reconcile in the social arena of political activism.

At the threshold of the black political Seventies, the black populations, scattered across the width and breadth of the continent, found themselves bound together not by ethnic-group *political* unity, but by an imposed unity of race and color, and conscious (if conscious at all) only of the persuasive influence of one ideology—the dominant one of the civil rights movement. Civil rights leaders had not, *could* not organize or mobilize the necessary kind of political unity, or political consensus, blacks required to hold fast to and further to enlarge upon the gains and the initiatives won during the Sixties:

> As political leaders, . . . the civil rights leaders lacked the authority and influence—the political clout that could sustain and increase federal efforts to meet the massive social-economic needs of blacks. In American politics, this kind of political authority is accorded only to elected politicians. The organization of civil rights leadership outside of party politics—and thus outside the competition for elected office—prevented this leadership from achieving the most legitimate type of American political leadership.[2]

These political science writers in their new analyses, did not make clear here exactly *why* the civil rights leaders neither desired black political leadership nor pursued the kind of policies that would have encouraged the legitimacy of black leadership *inside* the battleground of party politics. Trapped as these leaders were in the social logic of full integration, even the eclipse of the civil rights era of federal good feeling could not induce them to reassess their strategies and adapt to the demands of the politics of black ethnicity. Approximately ten years later, the political consequences of this flawed approach would be evident in the historic bid by Jesse Jackson for the presidential candidacy of the Democratic party.

The advent of the Jesse Jackson campaign, which could not have been foreseen during the Seventies, was not what it *should* have been, i.e., the coming-of-age of the politics of black ethnicity. In the context in which the Jackson campaign occurred, it was only symbolic of what the campaign *could* have been. *The Jackson presidential candidacy campaign should have been the political leadership front for the mobilization of an independent black political party.* Jesse Jackson *should* have revived the failed efforts of the three conventions that had been called to launch an independent black political party in Gary, Indiana, in 1972, Little Rock, Arkansas, in 1974, and Cincinnati, Ohio, in 1976. Eschewing that challenge, the Jackson campaign of 1984 was essentially a political *tour de force* of the preacher-as-leader syndrome that thrived off the motive power generated by Martin L. King, Jr., and carried over into the political arena. It was merely the accident of the quadrennial presidential electoral reenactment that supplied the setting and the stage for the Jacksonian histrionics. But Jesse Jackson entered the presidential fray unsupported by a previously organized political base that the two-party system would even begin to take seriously. Thus, he had no choice but play the theatrical role of a devil's advocate within the folds of the Democratic party, which already had the black vote securely pretabulated in the voting booths. This black pro-Democratic party consensus had been manifest for almost fifty years; what was needed was only the right kind of leadership to wield this consensus into an independent political force. Despite the extensive inner-group network of social, fraternal, and church organizations that blacks have always maintained, blacks continued into the Eighties to be poverty-stricken in the area of political and/or economic and cultural organization. As one astute observer put the matter, historically:

> Among black organizations, only the trade union of sleeping car porters and the Southern Christian Leadership Conference have approached [a] degree of organized and institutional power. And today, with the catalytic force of Martin Luther King, Jr., and A. Philip Randolph no longer on the scene, there is no viable body of institutionalized black power in this country capable of putting significant nonviolent black consensus pressure into action. Indeed, throughout the country there are many organizations of "black educators," "black engineers," "black lawyers," and so forth. These are loose affiliations of black people that display no power traits at all.[3]

What this amounts to is that, outside the religious and social functions of black churches, not one political, social, economic, educational, or cultural institution can truly claim to speak for a black-majority consensus on any issue in terms of "leadership." Thus, even the long-distanced staying power of the NAACP and the National Urban League does not represent a definitive leadership influence for those blacks who remain outside the membership affiliations of the NAACP and the NUL and the churches. Hence, the arrival of the politics of black ethnicity in the Seventies was not the outcome of any conscious effort to build community bases toward the aims of black political power, but of the realization that civil rights legitimacy alone no longer guaranteed the upward scale of black survival.

Moreover, the arrival of the Seventies brought to the fore a rash of other contingencies in the politics of ethnicity. The black civil rights hegemony of the Sixties produced a number of unforeseen and unintended consequences for the black position that critically altered the comparative status of the black minority vis-à-vis other minorities who were already American citizens. Blacks would also see their hard-won gains threatened by the arrival of competitive new ethnic immigration from Asia, Latin America, and the Caribbean. In California it could be observed during the Jesse Jackson campaign that in Watts, Los Angeles, the scene of the bloody racial uprising of 1965, by 1984 "LITTLE PROGRESS IS SEEN IN RIOT-SCARRED WATTS":

> Nearly twenty years after rioting ripped through Watts, living conditions are as bad or worse and the community feels "helplessness, despair and disenchantment. . . ." Conditions are as bad, or worse, in South Central Los Angeles today as they were 19 years ago. . . .[4]

On the same newspaper page where the above was printed, it was reported that "U.S. BACKS WHITES' BIAS SUITS: The Justice Department today intervened in a civil suit in support of two white firefighters in Birmingham, Ala., who contend that they have been victimized by reverse discrimination." The city administration of Birmingham was being accused of *violating the Civil Rights Act of 1964* by promoting two blacks to lieutenant and captain "in preference to demonstrably better qualified white firefighters and fire lieutenants." Here again was reflected the constitutional controversy surrounding the interpretation of the embattled Fourteenth Amendment's application to not "civil" but "economic" rights.

However, during a worsening national economic recession—with mounting unemployment among the native-born American working classes and bitter competition for the right to jobs and economic security involving blacks and whites—the federal authority permitted what amounted to an unrestricted immigration of indigent escapees from the poverty-stricken Third World. Self-appointed social welfare agencies went so far as to boast, in one prominent example of American liberalistic profligacy, that "CAMBODIAN FAMILY FINDS A HOME IN GREENWICH [Connecticut]." A seven-member Asian family was brought to the United States and given a four-bedroom house in an affluent suburban neighborhood rent-free for one year, during which time the family was promised all possible help in learning English, finding suitable work, and adapting to American culture. Thus goes American largesse to indigent foreigners in the midst of an economic employment crisis affecting the general well-being of the native-born. Not a single democratic society in the world would permit such a degree of internal economic insolvency to be exacerbated further by the free entry of indigent outsiders, while it condemns its unlucky insiders for what American society now calls extravagant demands for the rights and privileges of economic favoritism. Today, both the liberals turned neoconservatives and the traditional conservatives of the Reagan administration term the demands of native-born minorities (meaning, of course, blacks) for economic redress not only morally and ethnically excessive, but also *unconstitutional*.

As has been the case from time immemorial, these "new immigrants" will be sponsored into the social, political, and economic position of being used *against* blacks in the same fashion that all the *old* immigrants from Europe were used. Thus, it was not unexpected that during the Seventies the descendants of those old European immigrants opened up with a chorus of profound complaints. Michael Novak's "unmeltable ethnics" rose up in concerted indignation. The black civil rights thrust produced the loudest public reaction ever heard from the white ethnics in this century, while inspiring a new wave of ethnic self-assertion. For decades the vast American mosaic, the nation of nations, the quiescent communal ingredients of the melting pot of Horace Kallen's pluralist vision had lain dormant; in response to the impact of the blacks it began to simmer and then fretfully to bubble up. White ethnics issued a series of demands for special dispensations *from the federal power,* demands for recognition and for what they saw as long-deferred rewards from the total society.

Added to these white ethnic ingredients was the new self-assertion of the Mexican Americans of the Southwest. The upward surge of Mexican Americans lent a new quality to the racial encounters of the Sixties and Seventies because historically this group had kept company neither with Anglos nor other white ethnics. Gradually the Mexican-American element would be qualified to mean Chicano or Latino, definitions that would ultimately embrace all Hispanics.

Thus would the social history of American minorities from the *Brown* decision of 1954 into the Seventies and Eighties redefine the indigenous plurality of American society, a development inspired by *one* minority —the outcast blacks. And within the context of this evolving qualification in interracial and interethnic positions, the status of American Indians (the so-called Native Americans) would remain unchanged and problematic to any concept of domestic plurality. However, the presence of American Indians, the new self-assertions of Mexican Americans, plus the catalytic role of American blacks set these three minorities apart in the *racial sense* as the most outcast and excluded among all social groups designated as minorities.

More than that, unlike white ethnics, blacks and Indians are historically inseparable from the original establishment of the American nation
by the founding ethnic group, the White Anglo-Saxon Protestants. Despite
the negation of citizenship status to blacks and Indians by the English-
heritage exponents of the "White Nation" ideal, Article 1 of the Constitution (Section 2, Part 3) *had* to read: "Representatives and direct taxes
shall be apportioned among the several States which may be included
within this Union, according to their respective numbers, which shall be
determined by adding to the whole number of free persons, including
those bound to service for a term of years, and excluding Indians not
taxed, three-fifths of all other persons. . . ." Since this article said nothing about Indians who *were* taxable, or *would be* taxable, or those blacks
who *were* or *would be* "free persons," the implication was that full
citizenship for blacks and Indians, although deftly avoided, could not
forever be deferred, short of extermination or expulsion.

Black and/or Indian citizenship was a normative constitutional issue
at the outset. Not so with the Mexican Americans, who did not figure at
all in the original constitutional arrangements of the social and political
relationships between the races in the thirteen colonies. Unlike American
blacks, whom certain Mexican Americans (i.e., the Chicanos) disdain as
Black Anglos, Mexican Americans are in reality "Brown Spaniards."
Whatever ethnic designation (Mexican American, Chicano, Latino, or
Hispanic), this minority, ethnically speaking, is the outcome of the fif-
teenth-, sixteenth-, and seventeenth-century struggle between England
and Spain to establish Spanish-speaking and English-speaking empires
in the New World. The existence of the United States today is a consequence of the English victory over Spain in establishing a political and
military hegemony over the geographic spoils of the New World. As a
fait accompli of the four-hundred-year expansionist struggle between European nations, the United States, in the interests of national sovereignty,
reserves the historical right to determine the legal and constitutional conditions for granting citizenship within its established borders, *especially
with regard to its official language.* Just as long as American citizenship
(*sui generis* or by naturalization) is maintained or granted within the strict
confines of legally established, constitutional principles, no *ex post facto*
considerations involving the ethics and morality of "territorial conquest"
prerogatives can hold much water. Thus, Chicanos, for example, have a
right to American citizenship on the grounds of either their historical
presence in Texas or California or by subsequent naturalization. However,

the territorial prerogatives the Chicanos claim as supplementary supports for American citizenship are without accurate historical or legal foundations.

Ethnically speaking, Chicanos, similar to most Hispanics, are a mixed-blood social caste or class with Spanish and Indian antecedents. The original inhabitants, the aborigines of Mexico and Texas and California, were various pure-blooded Indian tribes or nations. In Mexico today, and all over Latin America, Indians are second- and third-class citizens—political, social, cultural, and economic out-groups. Moreover, Latin American blacks, the racial progeny of the African slave trade in Latin America, are without political power and, for all intents, are *next to invisible* as far as the internal domestic policies of Latin American nations are concerned. American blacks, in their *pluralistic* relationships with Chicanos, should take these important historical facts into account.

On the other hand, because they are a nonwhite ethnic minority in the United States, Mexican Americans, for the most part, are, like American blacks, not *immigrants* as this classification was applied to the European antecedents of present-day white ethnics. However, the progeny of European immigrants, being of the white race, achieved more economic, political, and social privilege by their *voluntary* emigration to the United States than either blacks, Indians, or Chicanos, who historically are more *native* to the United States than white ethnics. Yet, prodded by the black struggles of the Sixties for civil rights and minority-group parity, the white ethnics found cause to voice bitter grievances over their treatment as American citizens—citizens who have never suffered a single violation of their *constitutional* rights or privileges as members of an ethnic group. Their right to vote has never been violated. Their right to work for a living has never been restricted. Their right to acquire and own property has never been violated. Their right as naturalized citizens to equal protection in every political, economic, cultural, and social sphere of advancement has never been hindered or restricted by adverse state action. Which is to say that whatever citizenship restrictions have been levied against European white ethnics have been the result, not of legal or extralegal penalties imposed or upheld by the state, but of the operative folklore of class and minority-group prejudices that conflicted, competed, clashed, or compromised or cooperated in the ultimate self-interest of social advancement in pursuit of the American Dream. The Irish and the Poles, the WASPs and the Jews, the Italians and the Greeks, the Finns and the Slavs, etc., met and conflicted, argued and competed, but compromised and intermarried and cast the trappings of their specific ethnicity behind them. It was because of these evident facts in the social history of white ethnics that one critic could write off their tendencies to claim any legitimate pluralistic demands for special dispensation from the total society on grounds of ethnic disadvantage. Speaking to the "rise of the unmeltable ethnics" of the Seventies as delineated by Michael Novak, this critic of what he described as the "ethnic myth," wrote:

> Pluralist principles, however, have been on the ascendancy precisely at a time when ethnic differences have been on the wane, and though the United States may now proclaim itself a "nation of nations," never before has it been closer to welding a national identity and culture out of a melange of ethnic groups that populated its soil. Instead of cele-brating the triumph of pluralism therefore, it might be more appropriate to ask why Kallen's dream of a "democracy of nationalities" has been unattainable.[5]

The critic pointed out that the trouble with American pluralism was that "it was built upon systematic inequalities that constituted an unten-able basis for long-term ethnic preservation. This was the pitfall—the fatal flaw—that robbed ethnic pluralism of its cultural innocence."[6] Moreover:

> It is fashionable and convenient to blame "the WASPS" for the de-struction of ethnic subcultures, but more subtle and complex forces were at work. Ethnic groups were not just passive victims to cultural repression, but played an active role in their own demise—not out of any collective self-hatred, but because circumstances forced them to make choices that undermined the basis for cultural survival. To be sure, these choices were difficult ones, and they were accompanied by a painful sense of cultural loss.[7]

Thus, he continued, "not only have ethnic groups sacrificed much of their own ethnicity in a quest for economic mobility, but they have also been instrumental in subverting the ethnicity of groups above them in the class hierarchy. Because Jews escaped poverty more rapidly than others, they were often in the vanguard of an attack on WASP exclusivity in residential areas, in schools and colleges, and in resorts and social clubs. Needless to say, WASPS stubbornly resisted the intrusions of outsiders and sought to preserve the ethnic character of their neighbor-hoods and institutions. However, antidiscriminatory legislation, com-bined with a long series of court decisions, has narrowly restricted the

basis for lawful discrimination."[8] On this point, the critic found it unnecessary to emphasize the irony that the "long series of court decisions"
that had restricted the basis of lawful discrimination was *not* initiated by
any such thing as a "white ethnic" or a "Jewish" civil rights protest
movement, but by a prolonged black civil rights struggle against "lawful
discrimination." But concomitant with the prolonged history of this predominantly black-inspired civil rights effort, "the cultures of ethnic groups
have been radically transformed after several generations of accommodation and change, and the lines of ethnic distinctions are more blurred
than ever. Yet the ethnic pluralists insist that ethnic groups are holding
their own, and they scoff at the very idea of the melting pot."[9] In the
meantime, the theorists of ethnic pluralism, such as Michael Novak, while
making their principled case for ethnic-group particularism in the face of
their glaring *whiteness,* wax indignant about the civil rights particularism
of the blacks. They act out their assumed ethnic claims for citizenship
recognition with bland disregard for the accumulated privileges they have
enjoyed in the United States purely on the racial grounds *that they are
white:*

> The literature of the ethnic pluralists devotes remarkably little space to
> the problem of inequality, though their vision of a pluralist society
> implicitly assumes a basic equality among constituent groups. Otherwise
> pluralism might degenerate into a domination of some ethnic groups by
> others, as is typical of plural societies throughout the world. . . .[10]

Consequently, the white ethnic pluralists, *"rarely have confronted
the issue of how blacks would fit into the pluralist schema. . . ."* The
theorists of ethnic pluralism have all been white and European, thus,
*"the pluralist thesis from the outset was encapsulated in white ethno-
centrism."*[11] (Italics added.)

A classic example of white ethnocentrism took place within the
Democratic party ranks in Chicago, Illinois, during and after the mayoralty campaign of Harold Washington. Chicago represents one of the
most ethnically partitioned cities in the United States and one of the most
antiblack. The mayoralty campaign of Harold Washington highlighted
the fact that the politics of black ethnicity of the Seventies, while coming
late in this century, was better late than never. The campaign recognized
not only that the civil rights cycle of the Sixties had run its course, but
also that the white world, which for so long had been held responsible
for black deprivation, was peopled by ethnics who did not consider them-

selves morally responsible for the racist sins against blacks in the American past. More than that, the exponents of this assertiveness, as demonstrated in the political battle zones of Chicago, were ethnic politicians who were already strongly enough entrenched to make certain that their political superiority over the blacks be permanently maintained. As the critic of the "ethnic myth" pointed out:

> Indeed throughout American history, ethnic groups have espoused [ethnicity] doctrine in order to protect their class interests, but have been all too willing to trample over ethnic boundaries—their own as well as others—in pursuit of economic and social advantage.[12]

During the Seventies, the most vocal representatives of the white ethnic resurgence were Slavs and Italians, who were among those with whom blacks had encountered the sharpest racial animosities in the cities and the suburbs. The militant black Sixties in the quest for racial democracy brought into the open their counter-grievances:

> Voices of the white ethnic working class rose in anger at being ignored by government and the press, anger at being ridiculed by intellectuals, anger at being exploited by right wing reactionaries like George Wallace. . . .[13]

This theme was sounded in a series of ethnic conferences during the Seventies attended by "priests, politicians, and community workers." It signaled what was then called the beginning of a major social movement among an estimated forty million people of European descent in scores of older industrial cities in the Northeast and Midwest. The emphasis on "European descent" was significant. It implied that the ancestors of some other white people in the United States might have originated on some continent other than Europe. If only Europe supplied the ancestors of the white ethnics, from where did the other whites derive? The none-too-subtle implication behind this claim to European antecedents was the cognizance of not being WASPs—one of the long-standing citizenship-status problems of the white ethnics. But these forty million ethnics of European descent actually outnumber the blacks if their population count is nearly accurate. More than that, white ethnics are more socially and economically solvent than blacks—they possess a more disciplined, tighter, and more controlled male-dominated family structure than the blacks. They defend their hegemony over their ethnic communities. Exhibiting strong tendencies toward territoriality, white ethnics readily turn their community bases into political power bases. The existence of these populous ethnic enclaves in the industrial cities of the Northeast and Midwest would render the NAACP's racial integration prognoses utterly comic if it were not for the seriousness of this demographic miscomprehension by civil rights leaders. Next to the staunchly segregationist white Anglo-Saxons of the southern states, the most pronounced anti-integrationists were to be found among northern white ethnics. While indeed white ethnics are white Americans, a major theme sounded throughout the ethnic conferences was resentment against being "stereotyped" white Americans:

> The ethnic American is sick of being stereotyped as a racist and dullard by phony white liberals, pseudo-black militants and patronizing bureaucrats. . . .[14]

Measuring themselves against the standards and norms of WASP group behavior, status, and culture, the white ethnics, as late as the Seventies, found it difficult to take a "joke." Social inferiority complexes ran surprisingly deep. At least it was not the blacks who denigrated the white ethnics with the charge of being "dullards," even in jest, but ethnic animus was not directed at the "phony white liberals" and "patronizing bureaucrats" so much as at the activities of the "pseudo-black militants." In the course of the ethnic conference discussions, the "phony white liberals" and the "patronizing bureaucrats" were further identified, rather cryptically, as the "elites." But who these elites were either as a group or a class was never stated. What they meant was the WASPs, who once held the monopoly of the elites. But the elites, since World War II, have been increasingly infused with a variety of Catholic ethnics—Irish, Italian, Polish, and so forth. The Jews in America have fused the Judeo-Christian tradition into its ultimate consummation with full membership in the elites. Since 1952 we have had a president of German-American ancestry, a president of Catholic Irish-American ancestry, a vice-president of Greek-American ancestry, a secretary of state of German-Jewish American antecedents, a national security adviser of Polish-American background, and a leading presidential candidate of Norwegian-American ancestry with a female vice-presidential running mate of Italian-American background. People do not laugh derisively at ethnic jokes anymore— they only amuse themselves with the memory of what ethnic jokes (e.g., the dumb Pole) *used* to mean. Out of the entire lexicon of racial and ethnic stereotypes—Polacks, Hunkies, Wops, Dagos, Kikes, Hebes, Hymies, Chinks, etc., only "niggers," "spades," and "spics" remain epithets of derogation. Today there is no real basis for the white ethnics' continual complaint about being stereotyped. "Racist" they *are*, but only to the varying degrees of antiblack attitudes they have absorbed as a consequence of their Americanization. But since it was not bureaucratic or white liberal patronization or stereotyping that finally prodded the white ethnics to air their suppressed grievances, they are obliged to admit that the charge of racism by the "pseudo-black militants" is a fact, not a stereotype. But added to their list of grievances was the complaint about being victims of "class prejudice." The most vocal of the ethnic spokesmen was a woman of Slavic heritage who made the charge:

He [the white ethnic] pays the bill for every major government program and gets nothing or little in the way of return. Tricked by the political rhetoric of the illusionary funding for black-oriented social programs, he turns his anger to race when he himself is a victim of class prejudice.[15]

Another spokesman, an Italian American, charged that "nobody has done anything for the ethnics since Social Security. Yet they are being blamed for white racism." The Slavic-American woman added:

He [the white ethnic] has worked hard all his life to become a "good American," he and his sons have fought on every battlefield—then he is made fun of because he flies the flag. . . . The ethnic American is overtaxed and underserved at every level of government. He does not have fancy lawyers or expensive lobbyists getting him tax breaks on his income. Being a home owner, he shoulders the rising property taxes—the major revenue source for the municipalities in which he lives. Yet he enjoys very little from these unfair and burdensome levies. . . .

The ethnic American feels unappreciated for the contribution he makes to society. He resents the way the workingclass is looked down upon. In many ways he is treated like the machine he operates or the pencil he pushes. He is tired of being treated like an object of production. The public and private institutions have made him frustrated by their lack of response to his needs. At present he feels powerless in his daily dealings with and efforts to change them.

Unfortunately, because of old prejudices and new fears anger is generated against other minority groups rather than those who have power. What is needed is an alliance of white and black, white collar,

blue collar and no collar based on mutual need, interdependence, and
respect, an alliance to develop for new kinds of community organization
and political participation.[16]

Thus did blacks make the transition from the age of civil rights to
the decade of the "politics of black ethnicity" amid a newly inspired
white ethnic resurgence contesting the apparent gains made by blacks.
More than that, an increasing influx of "new immigrants" would bring
another class of ethnic competitors for the benefits of the social programs,
government-sponsored legislation against discrimination on the "basis of
race, color or national origin" with regard to employment, educational
programs, public services, and affirmative action. Although the fruits of
all these liberalistically inspired social benefits would be broadly distrib-
uted among groups that played no role in initiating civil rights legislation,
the conservative backlash is directed against blacks *and blacks only*. In
its political contest against the Reagan offensive to cut back government
spending on social programs, the Democratic party was faced with the
necessity of *disavowing the political aspirations of its black constituency*.

In urban politics, the new politics of black ethnicity would have to
contend with a Democratic party that was also the party of the political
conservatism of white ethnics, as was displayed in the dirty politics of
Harold Washington's mayoralty campaign in Chicago in 1983. During
the ethnic conference cited above, the Italian-American spokesman said:

> It's not that we are against the black man getting his, but it's time we
> got ours too. . . . If the real needs of these people—for housing, re-
> habilitation for their elderly—are not responded to by government, then
> there is going to be a sharp move to the right—even beyond [George]
> Wallace.

He added, however, that "the enemy is not the black man. It's the power
structure that plays off one group against the other." The Slavic-American
woman asserted:

> America is not a melting pot. It is a sizzling cauldron for the ethnic
> American who feels that he has been politically courted and legally
> extorted by both government and private enterprise.

As for the blacks, the Slavic American, who lived in Baltimore,
admitted that white ethnic homeowners in her area did not attempt any

protests against the threat of highway construction through their residential sections until the blacks did, and noted that the issue brought the blacks and white ethnics together in an alliance: "But now we're together. We don't hold hands and sing 'We Shall Overcome.' We don't say we're interacting socially according to an affirmative model. And we're still at the point where we have to meet on neutral turf." Speaking of a younger-generation ethnic, an Italian-American organizer of Cleveland, Ohio, said:

> All he knows is he's in a confused community. He sees his dad's $9,000 job in jeopardy. His mother can't go downtown on a bus without being afraid of having her purse snatched. He can't go to a swimming pool without it meaning a fight with black kids. He can't afford to go to college. If you don't think that kid is angry you've got to be crazy. . . . And it's not that he's antiblack. The black kids don't know this. They don't know where the white ethnic is coming from in attitude. He wants what he thinks they're getting—so they call him a racist.

If this Italian American considered that the ethnic youth were products of a "confused community," he probably could not have imagined the state of confusion rampant among the black youth of the Seventies. Their rites of passage from adolescence to adulthood would be distorted and marred by the absence of a positive education for the demands of uncertain futures; they would be designated by the economics, the sociology, and the "culture of poverty" as the chief candidates for the ranks of the unemployed. At least, white ethnic youth had the "head start" of a strong male-controlled, tightly knit family structure that monitored their passage into adulthood. This would not be the case for vast numbers of black youth, especially in the northern urban ghettos. For the black youth of the Seventies, the black male leadership symbols of the Sixties—King, Malcolm X, Carmichael, Cleaver, Seale, Newton, Baraka, and others—would be canceled out either by death or by the demotion of militant fads in the conformity of eclipsed ideologies. As the children of the Children of the New Deal they would find incomprehensible the urban world of the fading New Deal inheritance of their parents.

Thus, had *all* the forty million ethnics been coming from the vantage of the Italians and the Slavs, blacks would have been in deeper trouble than they were with the coming of Reagan Republicanism. But the black predicament at the lower-class level was bad enough. Significantly, little was heard from the Irish-American ethnics on this imagined black threat to hard-won minority status. Reaching back more than one hundred years into the racial history of the United States, one of the most fervent antiblack immigrant groups had been the Irish. But the election of an Irish-Catholic to the presidency in 1960 must have been, at least, the symbol to Irish-Americans that the melting pot had politically assimilated the Irish to the extent that a Kennedy and a Bouvier could match pedigrees in the Oval Office; that an O'Neill and an Agnew could commune and conflict with a Nixon to the tune of a Sirica and a Jaworski; that a Carter and a Brzezinski could aspire to high plaudits in political history only to leave the last dance to a Mondale and a Ferraro. In one degree or another, the same might be said for practically all the forty million white ethnics plus those former ethnics whose ethnicity had, by sociological osmosis, been steamed out in the melting pot, i.e., the Germans, French, Swiss, Scandinavians, Greek, Dutch, Spanish, Welsh, Jews, Russians, Hungarians, and the variety of Slavs. There is not a single area in the professions and cultural arts, in politics, or the corporate business world where the descendants of the European immigrants of yesterday have not been represented. Even the corporate world of organized crime, dominated by Irish, Italian, and Jewish representatives has been glamorized into a folk legend with heroes who could outwit the constraints and prohibitions of law and order in pursuit of the riches promised by the American Dream. All of these successes and concessions were granted because European immigrant descendants were of the white race. In the world of corporate crime, while the white gangster hero is glamorized along with prosecutory slaps on the wrist, the blacks are condemned to the obloquy of derogation for the sins of petty crimes committed in pursuit of sheer economic survival. The relativity involved in estimating what are wealth and poverty; what are privilege and penury; what is success or failure; progress or stagnation; retrogression or class and/or racial repression was lost on the white ethnics, startled out of conformist accommodationism by the so-called pseudo-black militants. The one thing Americans worship and applaud (above religion) is the religion of economic success; it is only *black* success that arouses the enmity of the seekers of the American Dream.

This was so evidently the case that at the conference of white ethnics, the Italian American cited above argued for the creation of:

> A study group to develop a social agenda for white urban ethnic groups. This is to include community organization and economic development similar to that done in black communities in the mid-nineteen sixties.[17]

More than that, the Italian American argued that the budding ethnic movement was then "wonderfully parallel to where the blacks were a few years ago." All of which revealed that white ethnics, like many blacks and their black leaders, had misread the meaning of the black Sixties. Blacks *would* come a long way socially, educationally, and economically in search of racial-group parity. But this advance would prove highly deceptive when measured against the level of black expectations. It would prove two strides forward in making up for backward steps previously made. It would be like the fast pace of progress being made on a treadmill. If it were true that the blacks did not understand where the white ethnics were coming from, the reverse was also true—the white ethnics were, for the most part, unmindful of where the blacks had been in relation to the status the white ethnics had already achieved in terms of American citizenship.

The ambition of the white ethnics during the Seventies to catch up with and surpass the blacks was a both ludicrous and ironic case of the perceptive disparities of social illusions versus social realities. The prevalent idea of black progress (that blacks were getting too much) was mostly illusory. The civil rights crusade had eliminated the legal, extra legal, and constitutional barriers against black equality; had wiped discriminatory and segregationist laws off the books; and morally, at least, had condemned extralegal or institutional racial practices within the body politic. Civil rights legislation *had* pried open the doors of opportunity for employment, for education in particular. But only a favored percentage of the black population would reap the educational, economic, and social rewards. While this percentage would be upgraded in educational and professional training, achieve a new high in employment in previously restricted fields of career advancement, at least half the black population would be pushed farther down the economic scale into a permanent slough of poverty, unemployment, and welfare. Not since the early decades of the twentieth century, or since the 1930s, have any white ethnic immigrant descendants experienced the economic or political deprivation of the disadvantaged class of native-born American blacks. What the white ethnics perceived during the Seventies was the unprecedented growth and advancement of a new black middle class, accompanied by a similarly unprecedented growth, stabilization, and horizontal extension of a permanent black underclass whose chances for escaping the poverty and unemployment traps were practically nil. More than that, the creation of this permanent black underclass would give the lie to the claims of *both* the advocates of government-sponsored full-employment programs and the conservative champions of unfettered free enterprise as the proper or economically pragmatic answers to the growing pauperization afflicting not only the blacks but various other *white* class components in American society.

Class stratification among the blacks would be hastened and intensified by the civil rights gains of the Sixties, encouraging a number of illusions not only among white ethnics regarding blacks, but also among growing numbers of blacks themselves. One black social scientist even went so far as to found a new school of thought among blacks, white liberals, and (black and white) conservatives predicated on the notion of "The Declining Significance of Race."[18] All of those new, flourishing opportunities for professional advancement by upwardly mobile blacks in both private and public sectors only demonstrated, it was implied, that racism was becoming less and less a real barrier against blacks in the competitive marketplace. Following this new vogue came a spate of so-called ethnic studies relating to the market economy and the place of ethnics and blacks in the workings of that economy. Prominent among these commentators on the Seventies' outcome of the black fortunes of the Sixties were a few black neoconservatives. Their central argument is, to quote one black economist, Walter E. Williams:

> What is reducible to racism, bigotry and callousness on the behalf of whites is most often featured as the cause of the current condition of many blacks. The assumption is made that since blacks do not differ biologically from whites in ways that should affect socio-economic status, the different status of blacks in the society reflects racism and mistreatment by whites. Therefore, the fight to promote equality and opportunity is portrayed as a struggle between the forces of good and the forces of evil. To the extent that the problems of blacks are cast this way, more-effective policies are ignored and people seeking to help blacks set out to find evil people and punish them. . . .

However:

> Finding and punishing evil people cannot explain the economic progress of minorities in the United States or anyplace else. For example, Jews in the U.S. and elsewhere did not have to wait for the end of anti-Semitism in order to prosper as a group. Japanese-Americans did not have to wait to become liked in order to be the second highest group in the U.S. in most measures of well-being. West Indian blacks did not

have to wait for racism to end to earn a median income in the U.S. that is just slightly below that for the nation as a whole. People discriminated against elsewhere frequently exhibit similar patterns. . . .

. . . Clearly, the experience of Orientals, Jews and West Indians calls into question the hypothesis that racial bigotry can be a complete explanation of the difficulties that blacks face in America. *The point is that if racial discrimination is not the most important cause, then economic and political resources need to be reallocated to address the more important causes of the disadvantages faced by many blacks.*[19] (Italics added.)

Here was expressed a "new" (but not so new) historical twist in the evolution of the economics of black leadership philosophies. In the new age of the politics of black ethnicity, black conservative economists appear with the message that the politics of black ethnicity is crippled at birth because the civil rights movement of the Sixties did not (in fact, could not) solve the basic problem of black *economic* disadvantages. The implication was that *without a viable economic base of social organization in American society, there cannot be a viable politics of black ethnicity.* Although the advocates of these conflicting positions never got together around some kind of black consensus, the salient issues were more than clear. In a backlash, whites (including white ethnics) claimed that blacks were "getting too much"; the black civil rights leadership contingents were protesting that civil rights legislation had not delivered all that was legally due (or at least promised) to blacks in the way of full employment; but the new-vogue black conservative economists countered with the argument that civil rights legislation was doomed before it was even voted upon because black economic disadvantages were not really due to racial discrimination. Unlike other "deprived" ethnic groups such as black West Indians, nonwhite Japanese, and non-WASP American Jews who suffered discrimination but did not need antidiscrimination laws to succeed economically, the problem with black Americans is that they were unable to pull themselves upward by their own economic bootstraps. All of which was a replay of the racial economics of Booker T. Washington in an age of the new Republicanism, and Washington, in his day, was a true-blue black Republican. For Booker T. Washington, the surest road to racial equality for blacks was through black economic enterprise, *not* civil rights legislation *as a programmatic priority.* In 1912 in his annual address to the National Negro Business League, Booker T. Washington asked his audience:

If the white man can secure wealth and happiness by owning and operating a coal mine, brick yard, or lime kiln, why cannot more Negroes
do the same thing? If other races can attain prosperity by securing riches
on a large scale from our seas, lakes and rivers . . . thousands of Negroes
can do the same thing. Activity in all these directions finds no races or
color line.[20]

In the 1970s and 1980s, Thomas Sowell and Walter E. Williams,
among others, qualify the ethnic parameters of race and economics by
shifting the group comparisons to include American blacks, West Indian
blacks, Japanese Americans, and American Jews. The three latter groups
"made it" economically despite racial discrimination; that black Americans did not implies deficiencies in the group "culture" of black Americans or, perhaps, in the "family" or the "social organization" or the
"psychology" of black Americans that are perhaps traceable to their
black slavery heritage. Most of the arguments raised here by the black
neoconservatives and others deserve serious debate. Moreover, since the
black (and white liberal) civil rights advocates cannot face the reality that
the crusade has run its effective course, the crucial question of the present
and future economic status of blacks becomes central. Civil rights parity
has been achieved, more or less, but not *economic* parity. However, the
conservative arguments used to explain away racism or racial discrimination as the most important cause of black economic disadvantages,
while *statistically* plausible in the 1980s, are historically and sociologically of dubious validity. The use of median-income indices for economic
comparisons between ethnic groups does not explain the background or
the outcome of other social factors surrounding the evolution of ethnic-
group behavior. An examination of such factors—historical, geographical,
sociological, psychological, cultural,—effectively qualifies or undercuts
what median-income comparisons are meant to prove.

Approximately 226,504,825 people live in the United States, according to the last census. The black population is estimated at 26,488,218.
The Jewish population was estimated at 5,290,000 in 1980. In 1970 the
Japanese population was estimated at 588,324, of which 217,175 lived
in Hawaii. The West Indian population in 1970 was estimated at a mere
315,000. Although the highest concentration of American Jews is on the
eastern seaboard, Jews are widely scattered across the United States.
However, neither the Japanese nor the West Indians established viable
economic communities in the southern states, which still hold at least
half the American black population.

The geographical locus of the most intense racial discrimination and most rigid racial segregation existed, historically, in the southern states. However, it is not necessary to cite the intricate legal and extralegal structures of laws and ordinances, the complex webs of social customs, occupational or business licensing, labor practices of employers, banking, real estate, and corporate practices that monitored race relations in the southern states to understand the social, political, and economic consequences of racial discrimination. It is merely enough to repeat the blatant assertion by the leading literary southern racist, Thomas Dixon, Jr., that if blacks were not checked they would become *such an economic competitor of the white man that they would have to be massacred.* In the pervasive sway of this racist ideology all over the southern states, it required an inordinate degree of pragmatic and level-headed fortitude for Booker T. Washington to deemphasize civil rights agitation in favor of economic development, property ownership, and black economic self-sufficiency. Washington argued that black ownership of property, productive farms, industrial-skills education, and black business development were more important than agitation for a passel of empty civil rights bills. But he was assailed for this "conservative" philosophy by the white liberals and the black civil libertarians with their advocacy of noneconomic liberalism. However, in the black Seventies the newborn black neoconservatives go several decades up on Washington by questioning the efficacy or the philosophical legitimacy of the civil rights interpretation of racial discrimination *after the historical fact* of the *Brown* era.

The black (and white) neoconservatives ask: If racial discrimination was truly the root cause of black economic disabilities, why, "in the wake of legal litigation, antidiscriminatory laws and affirmative action . . . why do these differentials remain [in the 1980s]." The differential referred to here "is the fact that black median income is roughly 60 percent of white median income."[21] This black economist finds this persistent differential a "mystery." If some 371,149 Japanese Americans, or 315,000 West Indians, or 5,290,000 Jews each can boast a higher median income than the American white population groups, it only proves that racial discrimination cannot be the sole cause of American black economic disabilities. In other words, it is a mystery why 26,226,000 American blacks have not achieved, at least, median-income parity with American white groups.

One neoconservative economist, in arguing that factors other than just racial discrimination account for black economic difficulties, cites such plausible but unquantifiable factors as age, education, experience, class background, family structure. However, from a macroeconomic perspective, the conservatives also cite governmental intervention into the domestic economy, which imposes severe restraints on "voluntary exchange" and results in "the diminution of free markets in the United States." The most prevalent economic disability among blacks is their high rate of unemployment or underemployment (and, by inference, the persistence of the welfare bureaucracy). In other words, the answer to unemployment is not government-sponsored programs to ameliorate poverty (or to fight racial discrimination), but a full-cycle return to the voluntary free-market milieu of the free-enterprise system. Barring such a revisitation of the unrestricted free-enterprise economy of the pre-New Deal era, of Harding, Coolidge, and Hoover, blacks will be unable to escape the toils of economic despond. In sum, it is a case of "the state against blacks." In support of "the state against blacks" argument, this neoconservative black economist cited about twenty-four Supreme Court cases dating back to the 1870s:

> Black handicaps resulting from centuries of slavery, followed by years of gross denial of constitutional rights, have been reinforced by government laws. The government laws that have proven most devastating, for many blacks, are those that govern economic activity. The laws are not discriminatory in the sense that they are aimed specifically at blacks. But they are discriminatory in the sense that they deny full opportunity for the most disadvantaged Americans, among whom blacks are disproportionately represented.[22]

The substance of these arguments is that judicial decisions in constitutional law since the 1870s have tended to violate a citizen's right to work, which was not a part of the American value system in the past. The founding Americans, plus the waves of immigrants, sought not only religious and political freedom but also *economic freedom:*

> They thought that a man should not have to get permission from a king, a mercantile association or a guild in order to pursue a particular trade. They thought that the right to work was part and parcel of the natural rights of man. What modern Americans have done is resurrect the mercantile system of monopolies and other state privileges that the Founding Fathers sought to escape.[23]

In other words, American constitutional jurisprudence has progressively undermined and subverted the pristine American philosophy of free enterprise. Cited was Munn v. Illinois, 94 U.S. 113 (1877), "one of the most far-reaching decisions of the nineteenth century Supreme Court. It instituted state economic regulation of private businesses." Specifically, *Munn* v. *Illinois* upheld an Illinois law that fixed minimum rates for grain storage. A dissenting opinion by Justice Fields declared:

> If this be sound law, if there can be no protection either in the principles upon which our republican government is founded, or in the prohibition of the Constitution against such an invasion of private rights, all property and all businesses in the State are held at the mercy of a majority of its legislature.[24]

Justice Fields's contention was that any state law that supports economic regulation violates the due process clause of the Fourteenth Amendment. From that point on, the Supreme Court showed a reluctance to uphold, on the grounds of unconstitutionality, a number of state laws that regulated economic activity. The Court made what it deemed an appropriate distinction between "businesses affected with public interest" (e.g., railroads, water, electricity, gas) and other categories of "private businesses." What the black neoconservative economist saw was significant in regard to racial discrimination in economic activity, was that the Supreme Court did not begin to alter its earlier views on what is and what is not a "business affected with public interest" until 1934. In that year the Supreme Court's decision in *Nebbia* v. *New York* upheld the New York State law that fixed the minimum price of milk at the retail level.[25] With regard to the controversial issue of state action or judicial intervention into the meaning of racial discrimination in the context of economic activity, the inference here was that during the last forty-five years (prior to Reagan), government intervention in the economy *was a New Deal social, economic, legislative, judicial, and constitutional venture*. It was a profound turning point in American social and political history that would ultimately lead to federal intervention into the arena of racial discrimination in *both* private and public economic interests. Whether or not the economic activity was of private or public interest, blacks especially would find themselves disadvantaged because of generally discriminatory practices based on race. In extending the New Deal heritage, government programs would be instituted to eliminate racial discrimination. But the neoconservatives of the Seventies and Eighties would declare the government programs ineffectual, ill-advised, inappropriate, and of questionable constitutionality. Granted that blacks, after all the civil rights legislation of the Sixties, would continue to be heavily represented in the ranks of the economically disadvantaged, it is not demonstrable that this situation is the sole result of racial discrimination—so say the neoconservatives.

Thus, in the ironic aftermath of the Sixties, blacks wound up at the lowest median-income range (compared with whites) in economic comparisons, but at the same time *white* ethnics were rebuking them for the undeserved privilege of "getting too much." However, it was not so much that blacks were "getting theirs," as it was now incumbent on white ethnics to "get theirs too." Even though it was increasingly evident by the Seventies that blacks in the aggregate weren't progressing very far, white ethnics felt the need to "catch up with the blacks"! In the meantime, black civil rights leaders and their vocal constituencies would continue to press for more supports and more guarantees for the civil rights of black economic redress and government-sponsored parity because of continued racial discrimination in economic activities. Enter the (black) neoconservatives with the belated argument that the persistent economic disabilities of blacks were not due solely to racial discrimination. Black economic disadvantages resulted from a history of government interference into the economy so as to hamper the functioning of a free-enterprise open-market economy *that blacks could not fit into because of certain innate group, social, or cultural inadequacies that had little to do with racial discrimination.* Did not the black West Indians have economic parity with whites? Did not the Japanese Americans make it in economic parity? Did not the Jews also make it despite anti-Semitism? Despite racial, ethnic, or religious bigotry in America, these ethnic groups found economic success—what *is* wrong with the blacks?

In assessing the controversies surrounding the effects of racial discrimination, the neoconservatives are prone to ignore serious discussions of the history of purely civil rights court decisions, or legislation passed in favor of court decisions that affect macroeconomic regulation by the states. They infer that economic regulation by the states hampers the free play of free-enterprise, free-market, relations to such a degree as to be detrimental to blacks' ability to better their depressed economic situation. Since it is patently clear that the civil rights legislation of the Sixties did not eliminate the economic scourge of black poverty, something critical remains to be said about either the need, the intent, in fact, the historical justification for civil rights legislation. But as economists specializing in the *economics* of civil rights, the neoconservatives reveal they are especially poor historians when it comes to the *economic history of blacks.*

The comparative *median-income* arguments are exceptionally shallow and explain very little about the purely economic history of blacks in the United States. For one thing, one cannot even begin to discuss the ramifications of black economic status in the twentieth century without a serious assessment of the philosophy of *noneconomic liberalism* that dominated the civil rights movement from the outset. Thomas Sowell, for example, writes his conservative economic critiques on the outcome of civil rights practices just as if black spokesmen on black economic problems had not voiced such critiques as far back as the age of Booker T. Washington. Of course, since the earlier spokesmen were not the educated products of Harvard, Columbia, Cornell, Temple, and the Hoover Institute, their arguments were not as learned and would not have been published in books even if they had been. But one salient fact of the vaunted American economic mystique that these early-twentieth-century black spokesmen did recognize very clearly was that one of the chief corollaries of the American free-enterprise system was the *freedom to discriminate using purely racial criteria as a means of defending the privilege of White Anglo-Saxon Protestants to set competitive ground rules for what race or ethnic group shall have the freedom to profit from free-market economic relations.* The sectional, racial, political, and economic origins of the so-called civil rights Supreme Court decision in *Moore* v. *Dempsey* (1923) thus make it a landmark case. And it is not accidental that neither the liberal-oriented civil rights historians nor the neoconservative economic historians review the profound implications of this case in either civil rights or economic free-market terms.

Thomas Sowell, the black, and also "fair-haired," protagonist of the neoconservative vogue that sprang up in the wake of the civil rights debacle of the Seventies, writes a number of highly intelligent and provocative books on the economics of "ethnicity" versus the civil rights renditions of equal opportunity, affirmative action, etc., but ends up calling the *Brown* decision: "A momentous day in the history of the United States, and perhaps the world."[26] As an avowed economic historian of some perspicacity, Sowell had already demonstrated that he was at a loss seriously to interpret the *Brown* decision, and was also negligent as an economic historian in dealing perceptively and informatively with *black economic history.* If the *Brown* decision of 1954 was a landmark Supreme Court rendition of the Fourteenth Amendment with reference to race relations (and it was), then so was the *Moore* v. *Dempsey* ruling of 1923 a landmark decision if for no other reasons than the NAACP leadership, Louis Marshall of the American Jewish Committee, and Su-

preme Court Justice Oliver Wendell Holmes, Jr., said it was. But *Moore*
v. *Dempsey* actually implied much more than either the civil rights historians
or the neoconservative economic historians find it necessary to admit.

The black economic factors behind the civil rights outcome of *Moore*
v. *Dempsey* graphically showed that southern white Protestants were
organized to use racial discrimination as the most potent means for the
supereconomic exploitation of southern blacks in the private agricultural
sector of the southern economy; *they were also prepared to use the
organized police and judicial apparatus of the state to prevent by force
all efforts by blacks themselves to organize a self-help, self-engendered
black cooperative economic organization for their own improvement within
the context of the free-enterprise, free-market economy which, with or
without the interference of the state, dominated the southern economy.*
Both the civil rights and black economic implications of *Moore* v. *Dempsey* have been argued earlier in this study, and enough stated to refute
arguments by the neoconservatives of the 1970s and 1980s that racial
discrimination was not (and is not) a dominant factor in the persistence
of black economic disadvantages. However, the implications of the economic factor behind *Moore* v. *Dempsey* are even relevant to a more
thorough analysis of why the median-income comparisons of Japanese
Americans, Jewish Americans, West Indian Americans, and Afro-Americans made by neoconservative black economists are not only superficial
but *ahistorical*. Japanese Americans did not concentrate in the southern
states; nor did West Indian Americans. American Jews did settle in the
South in considerable numbers. However, Jews established themselves
there as industrialists and merchants catering to both whites and blacks
via the open market. Leo Frank's pencil factory was only one important
instance of a southern Jewish enterprise using *both* black and white labor.
Jewish merchants also served black and white customers, but hired only
black menial labor in keeping with southern racial etiquette. In this regional context, even to pose the question, *Could an individual black
entrepreneur or entrepreneurial group organize a business enterprise
that served both black and white customers, and hired both black and
white labor, be accepted on its economic merits in the free-enterprise
atmosphere of the southern states?*, would be asinine and rooted in an
abysmal ignorance of the racial climate of the South. The answer would
be an emphatic *No*! Why? *Institutionalized racial discrimination* was only
a degree removed from the South African system of apartheid because,
contrary to popular liberal comparative social-science interpretations, there
were as many racially mixed residential communities in the South as in

the North. Racial discrimination was one thing in the American South, something else in South Africa, or in California or New York City. Which raises the following questions: Could Japanese Americans have managed their high levels of economic success if they had settled in the South instead of California, Oregon, or Washington? Could black West Indian Americans have achieved their higher median-income levels if they had settled in Georgia, Alabama, Florida, or Mississippi instead of New York City and the eastern seaboard? In both cases the answer is again emphatically *No*! The politics and economics of race and ethnicity in the southern states were under the rigid racial control of White Anglo-Saxon Protestants.

In Mississippi during the 1920s, a Supreme Court decision in *Gong Lum* v. *Rice*, 275 U.S. 78, allowed the state of Mississippi legally to classify an "Oriental girl with Negroes for purposes of assigning her to school."[27] Which meant that in the eyes of the ruling white caste system in the South, Asians of any variety were classed as merely another category of "nigger." In this rarely talked-about lawsuit, Chinese citizens in Mississippi objected to sending their children to segregated black public schools in compliance with rules on race relations enunciated by the Mississippi state constitution written in 1890.[28] Thus, a *Yick Wo* v. *Hopkins* civil rights case would not have arisen in Mississippi as it did in California. And Why? Because Mississippi was *not* California. Observers of Chinese-American life-styles in Mississippi report that, unlike California or New York City, "there is no Chinatown in the Mississippi Delta."[29] Although Mississippi attempted to force Chinese children to attend black schools, Chinese parents circumvented that rule. During the 1920s in Mississippi, *the Chinese established their own purely Chinese-American public school institutions in which they enlisted Chinese-American teachers from out of state to make certain that their children would be inculcated with the educational values that Chinese-American adults preferred them to have.*[30] They also fashioned a Chinese Baptist Church by which "baptism was the single most important prerequisite to economic and social acceptance in backwoods America's version of the Protestant ethic. A Chinese Christian identity—implanted by means of a separate church—helped to lift the hated epithet colored from the Chinese and elevated them above the Negroes."[31] In this accommodation between immigrant Chinese and Mississippi Delta whites, the Chinese Americans did not indulge in the public school–racial integration lament of the black civil rights leadership involved in *Brown* some thirty-five years later.

In the descending scale of social status based on race differences,

Japanese Americans on the West Coast were *also* elevated above the blacks in the eyes of whites. Despite anti-Japanese alien land laws, racial discrimination against Asians was of a different quality than that against blacks and stemmed from different cultural, racial, political, and economic motivations.

Unlike the southern, midwestern, and eastern states, California from the beginning of its statehood, was a virtual open territory for in-migration. The second largest state, it represented 158,693 square miles; in 1850 its population was only 92,597; in 1900 the population was only 1,485,053. Between 1900 and 1910 almost three times as many people lived in New York City as in the whole state of California. Unlike the South, where most blacks lived, California was an immense stretch of virgin land with a vast agricultural potential. Thus, the drive for land ownership between the whites and the Japanese was *not* a competition for a scarce commodity, but a strategy aimed at delimiting Japanese ownership of land mainly because the Japanese had proven highly successful in cultivating the land they had *already obtained*. In 1900 there were only 10,151 Japanese in California, 5,617 in Washington, 2,501 in Oregon. The combined Japanese population in the entire United States in 1900 was 24,326. The total black population was estimated at roughly nine to ten million. If, say, ten thousand blacks had migrated from Mississippi or Arkansas to California in 1900, it is extremely doubtful that they would have had the same access to land as the Japanese immigrants. In California by 1921, despite anti-Japanese racial discrimination, Japanese farmers were raising and marketing 12.3 percent of the state's total farm products. This was achieved during the same period of the Phillips County, Arkansas, race war that grew out of an organized attempt by black farmers to market their crops in the free market. Thus, racial discrimination against the Japanese was one thing; against the blacks, something else.

The two qualities of racial discrimination cannot be compared in terms of purely economic results in the free-market system. Ten thousand American blacks migrating to California for a stake in the booming agricultural market would have been considered an invasion to be checked with the same brutality witnessed in Arkansas. If as of 1970 the so-called median income of 588,324 Japanese-Americans, 217,175 of whom live in Hawaii, is higher than the median income of twenty-six million blacks, it only means that racial discrimination works in mysterious ways in its economic inequalities. Economic liberalism would not be at all hard put to allow 371,149 Japanese Americans an equitable share of the median-income benefits of the United States' vast wealth. For some twenty-six million blacks such a liberalistic dispensation of economic rewards implies a degree of racial or economic equality that liberalism, as such, never intended. It implies a degree of economic equality that not only would be prohibitive because of the sheer numbers of American blacks, but also because the very *real* legacy of slavery—black labor exploitation and a racial discrimination that permeated race relations under free-market capitalism—can be remedied only through a piecemeal parceling out of charity, philanthropy, enlightened labor practices, antidiscrimination legislation, and/or affirmative action–sponsored employment. Even when liberalism is pushed to allowing blacks (or some of them) to compete freely in the free market for jobs and positions in the businesses, corporations, industries, and institutions of either private or public sectors of the economy, it still remains economic liberalism tinged with charity.

A graphic example of the economic liberalism of charity is the charity American Jews extended to blacks. From, say, World War II to 1970, the Jewish population was estimated to have been four million to over five million. In 1900 the Jewish population was just over one million, or 1.4 percent of the total population. In 1980 this percentage had increased to but 2.7. Long before the new-vogue black neoconservative economists appeared on the scene, it was well known among economists that American Jews as an ethnic group had the highest *median* income of any white group in the United States. As far back as the age of Booker T. Washington, wealthy Jewish capitalist-industrialists were extending financial charity to blacks. To maintain that American Jews became one of the wealthiest ethnic groups in America despite racial discrimination related to anti-Semitism is a gross misinterpretation of the historical, sociological, and economic roles of racial discrimination and anti-Semitism in American life. Jews themselves would not admit to such a distorted assumption. Jewish writers are able to boast that Jews played a prominent role in "laying the economic foundations" of American society because each wave of immigrants brought not only impoverished Jews but also those with extensive backgrounds in European mercantilism, banking, trade, and commerce. Thus, in any assessment of the role of racial discrimination in the economic life of the United States, how can one make the preposterous comparison of the median income of Jews with the median income of twenty-six million blacks? The neoconservative economists, in attempts to explain the failures of equal opportunity and affirmative action to eliminate black economic disparities, use this kind of logic: "Jews in the U.S. and elsewhere did not have to wait for the end of anti-Semitism in order to prosper as a group," so what, then, is the problem with blacks? (Their answer: *the problem is in themselves!*) Thomas Sowell, one of the most voguish exponents of this school of thought, had to admit:

> It would be hard to find a minority with a more different background from black people than Jews, who had centuries of urban experience behind them when they first set foot on American soil. A more reasonable comparison might be made with groups from a peasant folk-culture background, without an intellectual tradition, and a social pattern in which they were not only in the bottom income class but also in which there was a "caste" position from which no one expected them to rise.[32]

Sowell, the economist, might have been more explicit by pointing out that the Jews' urban experience in Europe was part and parcel of their experience in free-market trade, commerce, and banking. The lowly blacks could not have been expected to gain such commercial training in Africa or in the southern states, when they themselves were, for the most part, nothing but *property and a commodity*. And in this regard, it would be morally extraneous to this racial, ethnic, and economic argument to bring up the pejorative fact that in the pre-Revolutionary class of the slave-trading elites there was a scattering of Jewish merchants. Or, in pursuit of the historical and sociological reasons behind the blacks' failures to perform up to median-income par in competition with Jews in a capitalist culture, one could also cite the assessments of Karl Marx, of all people. One of the leading nineteenth-century anti-Semites was Karl Marx, himself the offspring of a rabbinical family. Marx's father adopted Christianity in 1816 in order to practice law in Prussia: "Like many converts Marx found it necessary all his life to justify the mass conversion of his family by attacks against his blood brothers."[33] Karl Marx was a convinced enemy of the capitalist system in all its forms. He also implied (without substantive foundation) that "capitalist culture-banking," "the bill of exchange," money, etc., were synonymous with Judaism. In explanation, and also expiation, of Marx's anti-Semitism, one commentator hastened to explain that "in the middle of the nineteenth century anti-Semitism was mainly a religious and social not a racial issue, and among converts such as Karl Marx are to be found vitriolic enemies of Judaism."[34] This explanation of what anti-Semitism is, or was, also applies to the United States. Anti-Semitism in the United States was not a racial but a social and religious issue. Thus, racial discrimination had nothing to do with American Jewish economic successes, or failures, here. Such failures were of little economic consequence. While anti-Semitism was *not* a racial discrimination issue in the United States, "anti-Negroism" *was* and *is*. The anti-Semitism of Georgia whites did not stop Leo Frank from operating a successful pencil-making company in Atlanta because it brought a measure of labor prosperity to that region. Leo Frank was lynched because his alleged crime got confused, inadvertently, with the race question, and somebody was forced to pay.

But more to the point, if Karl Marx was an anti-Semite he was also a racist, *but* a benign racist in the sense that he was a benign anti-Semite, similar to Henry Ford, or like the KKK, which railed against Jews (and Catholics) but did not go around randomly lynching Catholics and Jews or Japanese or Chinese (only blacks!). The organic connection between European capitalism and African slavery (i.e., that slavery was an adjunct of Western capitalism) was very clear to Karl Marx. But Marx did not fully understand *American* slavery, and its subsequent racial and economic consequences, mainly because Marx never visited the United States. His views on blacks and their relationship to the white labor classes were oversimplistic. He was not able to foresee that the abolition of slavery, which he called for as a prerequisite for the military victory by the North over the South, would not lead to a full emancipation of either black or white labor. He could not have foreseen that the abolition of black slavery would merely lead to the establishment of another quality of subjugation of black labor to the profit demands of capitalist farming and capitalist industry. If Marx *thought* he understood the political, economic, and racial consequences of American slavery in connection with the Civil War and emancipation, it is yet unknown to what extent he understood the consequences of black slavery in the Caribbean and Latin America as correlates to Western Hemispheric capitalism. Out of the crucible of black slavery and capitalistic agriculture in the Caribbean, a class, color, labor, and capitalistic configuration evolved that was quite unlike the outcome of capitalism and slavery in the United States.

Which brings this analysis to a consideration of how immigrant black West Indians in the United States as a special ethnic group have impacted on the economic, political, and cultural status of native-born black Americans. "West Indian blacks did not have to wait for racism to end to earn a median income in the U.S. that is just slightly below that for the nation as a whole," say neoconservative critics of civil rights dispensations. In other words, if about 315,000 black West Indians living in the United States as of the 1970s could achieve a median income just slightly below that for the nation as a whole, then what is wrong with twenty-six million American blacks that *they* cannot accomplish the same economic parity? If West Indians, or Jews, or Japanese Americans can work an economic miracle as ethnic groups *without* government programs or affirmative action or civil rights legislation or urban uprisings, then all the 1960s civil rights legislative supports were of doubtful legitimacy since in the Eighties blacks are still struggling to narrow the median-income gap between blacks and whites, and falling progressively behind. Even acceding to the neoconservatives' contention that perhaps there *is* something "wrong" with American blacks, merely citing median-income comparisons explains next to nothing about the racial and ethnic situation in America. Out of a total of twenty-six million American blacks one could quite easily *select* 315,000 who enjoy a rather high median income compared with poor whites in Appalachia—but what would *that* prove? No one knows, for example, the approximate number of whites who share the profits from organized crime—gambling, drug peddling, prostitution, theft, extortion, labor racketeering, etc.—but let us agree to an estimate of 350,000 (there are probably considerably more). It would not require any special knowledge of free enterprise to grasp that the median income of 350,000 operatives in organized crime would be higher than that of 350,000 high school dropouts, clerks, or seasonal farm workers. What, then, does this median-income figure for black West Indians in the United States prove? Organized crime is a form of free enterprise requiring considerable skill, resourcefulness, a high degree of organization, discipline, and ingeniousness. But it would be extremely impolitic to attempt to round up 350,000 organized-crime operatives to discover their median-income levels. It would not prove that "crime does not pay," and would offend the sensibilities of certain ethnic groups well known to be numerically highly visible in organized crime. The median-income level of organized-crime operatives as a distinct population group would prove little about the national median-income levels for other groups or classes except that the United States is an extremely rich country with vast disparities in the distribution of the national wealth. Beyond that, what, then, does the high median income for black West Indians really say about the median income of black Americans generally?

As in population ratios of Japanese Americans and American Jews, there is less of "them" and more of the "others." No one knows for sure how many West Indians there used to be (or are now) in the United States. As one West Indian commentator, Reed Ueda, has noted: "No exact figures are available for the size of the black West Indian population in the United States in the early 20th Century. The U.S. Census and the Bureau of Immigration distinguishes British West Indian immigrants from Puerto Ricans and Cubans but not from the French, Dutch and Spanish West Indians.''[35] But like the Japanese Americans, West Indian Americans were to a great degree the results of *selective* migration. When the sociologists and economists cite the economic or educational successes of West Indians, one of the initial factors is *selective* migration: "British West Indians of mulatto background entered the United States in the early 20th Century with considerable skills, training and education. They were in their prime years of productive activity. The statistics seem to confirm impressionistic reports from that period ascribing to British West Indians notable advantages in training and schooling, especially in comparison to southern Negroes migrating to northern cities from a rural environment that had offered them few educational and employment opportunities.''[36] Another factor influencing West Indian economic status was that the largest waves of West Indian immigrants, like the Japanese, had the good fortune to gain entry into what was "open territory." That open territory (marketwise) was Harlem, New York City, and, to a lesser extent, Brooklyn.

The arguments the neoconservatives put forth regarding the median-income differentials between American blacks and West Indian blacks are always based on what each group achieved, or did not achieve, in *one* regional area—the eastern seaboard (comprising New York State, Massachusetts, and New Jersey). More specifically, the median-income comparisons are not only reduced to one city, New York, but also to one municipal subdivision of that city—Manhattan; more than that, the comparative assessment boils down to merely one black community within that municipal subdivision—Harlem. As the West Indian writer cited above has noted under the rubric of "Accommodation and Assimilation, 1900 to 1940":

In the 1920's British West Indians were most numerous in New York City. They probably formed 10 to 15 percent of the city's black population, and they were perceived by American-born blacks as a foreign social element. British West Indians had a distinctive English accent, worshipped as Anglicans (less frequently as Methodists or Baptists) and often expressed allegiance to the British crown. In the island home lands British West Indians had taken for granted their membership in a majority population of blacks and mulattoes; in the United States they were viewed as strangers by native-born blacks and whites, and furthermore they became members of a distinct racial minority group. In the British West Indies, mulattoes were considered superior to blacks; in the United States, mulattoes and blacks were usually considered to belong essentially to the same group. British West Indians struggled to adjust to the discriminatory treatment and prejudice directed toward Negroes in general, *which they often found much worse in the United States than in the West Indies.* Many highly skilled and educated immigrants were forced to take *jobs beneath their level of training or experience; they patiently waited for the opportunity to leave jobs as elevator operators or cooks* and to resume their previous occupations as *teachers, lawyers, and craftsmen.*[37] (Italics added.)

This was written by a contemporary scholar of West Indian affairs who, similar to new-vogue neoconservative economists, reads present-day professional upward-mobility values some sixty-five years back into the social and economic history of the black community. As such, it results in a contemporary obfuscation of what is fact or myth involving black urban and black economic history. First, these black ethnic economic conclusions are posed as if Harlem, New York City, represents the race and class and ethnic profile of black communities in the entire United States. Not considered here are the black populations in Chicago, Detroit, Cleveland, Washington, Atlanta, New Orleans, Kansas City, Boston, Los Angeles, Durham (North Carolina), Birmingham (Alabama), Jackson (Mississippi), or Little Rock (Arkansas). West Indian blacks did not compose "10 to 15 percent" of the black populations of these cities. In fact, West Indian migration into these cities was either nonexistent or else so infinitesimal as to be of little consequence as an ethnic factor in black social, political, or economic life. New York City's black Harlem *was* an important urban concentration. In fact, it was so important that James Weldon Johnson described it as "more than a community; it is a large-scale laboratory experiment in the race problem, and from it a good many facts have been found."[38] Yet black Harlem was *not* representative of the total black urban population of the United States in 1920, especially in terms of median income.

In 1900 *there was no black Harlem* as such. In 1902 only 650 black families lived in Harlem, the descendants of the original Harlem blacks from nineteenth-century settlements. Harlem was a predominantly genteel white community composed mainly of WASPs, Jews, Germans, Irish, and immigrants from England. At that time, Harlem (the original Dutch name, Haarlem) was considered a prime Manhattan residential area, the very first upper-middle-class suburb of New York. The less-than-accurate census techniques of those days listed the general area of white Harlem as being composed of 103,570 families; the black population in *all* of New York City was given as 60,606 in 1900. However, *between the national census of 1900 and that of 1930, Harlem was transformed from an upper-middle-class elite white community into the largest single all-black urban concentration not only in the United States, but also in Latin America, the Caribbean, and the African continent.* In 1930 the black population of New York City was estimated at 327,706 (the bulk living in Harlem); in Chicago, 233,903; Philadelphia, 217,593; Detroit, 120,066; Cleveland, 71,899. The rate of increase for these urban populations from 1920 to 1930 were as follows: New York City, 115 percent; Chicago, 114 percent; Philadelphia, 64 percent; Detroit, 194 percent; Cleveland, 109 percent.[39] This phenomenal growth was the result of one of the greatest internal mass migrations of any racial or ethnic group in the United States—the movement of southern rural and small-town blacks out of the South into northern and midwestern cities. Since the end of the Civil War there had been "a steady but small movement of Negroes northward. It averaged 41,378 persons for each decade between 1870 and 1890."[40] Among them was a small number of British West Indians. Those who came to New York City settled into largely segregated black enclaves in various sections of Manhattan. "There were more foreign born Negroes in New York City than in any other city in America," approximately 5000 in 1900.[41] By 1914 the National Urban League estimated that some 49,555 blacks had clustered into some 1,100 houses within a twenty-three block area of Harlem. By 1920 two thirds of Manhattan's black population lived in Harlem, which became "the Mecca of the colored people of New York City."[42]

In addition to being a mecca, Harlem also became known as the "Cultural Capital of the Black World" in the United States. However, it became more than that, economically speaking. Harlem gradually became open territory for an increasing number of black migrants from both the South *and* the West Indies. By offering an expanding supply of much desired housing and real estate for blacks, Harlem was transformed into a self-contained market open to black economic entrepreneurship. Similar to the way the open territory of California agricultural development accommodated in-migration of the Japanese from 1900 on, Harlem afforded an open market for blacks escaping from agricultural poverty in search of prosperity in the industrial, commercial, professional, and service occupations.

How did all this occur? What was the phenomenal combination of forces that created black Harlem? In economic and racial and ethnic terms, the question becomes more important when it is realized that in 1930, there were more than twice the number of blacks in one city, New York, than there were Japanese Americans (whose population was estimated at 138,834) in the entire United States.[43] Seen against the historical, sociological, ethnic, and racial antecedents to median-income levels, comparisons become ludicrous. This is especially the case since racial discrimination, which *is* an operative factor, is also *relative* in its social uses. Discrimination against Jews is not the same thing as racial discrimination against blacks, *and never was*. Racial discrimination against the Chinese and Japanese is not the same thing as racial discrimination against blacks, *and never was*. For example, despite the white racist animus that infused the American military engagement with the Japanese during World War II, Japanese Americans, by virtue of the industrial significance of Japan, have attained today the same "racial" status as "Honorary White Men" that the Japanese have held in South Africa for many years.

Viewing the comparative median income as it relates to race, ethnicity, immigration, civil rights, and racial discrimination, the neoconservatives have raised their disclaimers to the liberal consensus on civil rights on purely economic, i.e., median-income, grounds. Japanese Americans, Jews, and West Indians did not need civil rights legislation to achieve a high income level in the United States. These ethnic groups (and others) gained economic affluence within the free-market system, unhampered by government regulations and equal-opportunity programs. But as a corollary to these contemporary arguments, the West Indian-American scholars point out how difficult it was psychologically for black West Indians to "adjust to the discriminatory treatment and prejudice directed toward Negroes in general." Black West Indians were saying the same thing in the Seventies. West Indian scholars, for example, are noted for voluntarily entering the United States, where they are granted the kind of lucrative salaries, honorariums, prizes, educational fellowships, and positions that would never be granted blacks in England, France, or elsewhere, while steadfastly protesting American racism, which treats *them* like other blacks. The irony is that all the educational and professional rewards accruing to foreign-born blacks in the Seventies are the direct results of the benefits goaded out of the system by *the American black civil rights movement*.

West Indian scholars and the neoconservatives both cite the extraordinary economic success of West Indians in New York City, and only in Harlem, as proof that the general complaints of American blacks about racial discrimination are hollow—*there is something culturally deficient about American blacks*. Reed Ueda writes:

> Many striving [West Indians] discovered that they could improve their status through small business enterprises. The West Indians seized opportunities in urban areas to open retail stores and purchase real estate, and rapidly gained a reputation for drive, ambition, thrift and cleverness. George S. Schuyler, an American black journalist, expressed admiration for their "enterprise in business, their pushfulness." A contemporary student of British West Indian social life in the 1920's and 1930's observed that the West Indians were "legendary in Harlem for their frugalness and thrift."[44]

In terms of ethnicity, race, and foreign origins, this partially explains an aspect of the social history of black West Indians (in Harlem). Since the neoconservative economists compare the entrepreneurial successes of West Indians in Harlem with the entrepreneurial successes (or lack of them) of American blacks all over the United States, it is notable that West Indian American writers do not cite black Chicago, black Detroit, black Washington, D.C., or black Atlanta. For example, during the 1920's and 1930's, Chicago had the second largest black population, as a consequence of the great migrations, but the presence of black West Indians is not noted in that city.

What is not cited in the history of West Indians in New York City are all the facts about the evolution of black Harlem from a predominantly all-white, upper-middle-class suburb in the 1890s into the open territory of an expanding black economic and real estate market that had never before existed for American blacks in the entire economic history of the United States. Thus, if it could be recorded that West Indian immigrants discovered they could improve their economic status through business enterprise by applying "drive, ambition, thrift and cleverness" in "urban areas," they would have discovered an expanding market of the kind that was nonexistent in the West Indies. However, this widening market was not initially opened up by West Indians, but by the "drive, ambition, thrift and cleverness" of Afro-Americans. The Afro-American Realty Company was organized in 1904—when Harlem was still a predominantly all-white, upper-middle-class Manhattan suburb—by one Philip A. Payton, Jr., who was a protégé of Booker T. Washington's National Negro Business League, *established in 1900*. At that time, "the existence of a loosely rooted Negro population ready to settle in Harlem was primarily the result of ever-increasing Negro migration into the city." Migrating blacks from the South faced a grave housing shortage, which seriously complicated the problem for those New York blacks who had already secured a precarious residential base in racially segregated Manhattan. In addition, the general commercial expansion of midtown Manhattan was dislocating the black population. Many all-black apartment blocks in Manhattan's midtown were destroyed, for example, to make way for the construction of the famous old Pennsylvania Railroad Station. Pushed about, willy-nilly, by housing segregation, commercial expansion, bitter and bloody racial conflicts with the Irish and Italians, the police, and administrative authorities, native-born American blacks had been buffeted about in New York City, pushed into and squeezed out of a succession of miniature ghettos ever since the end of the Civil War.[45] Thus, when an enterprising group of Booker T. Washington protégés created the Afro-American Realty Company in 1904, this corporation's main objective was to capitalize on the serious housing shortage by maneuvering to open up all-white residential areas to black occupancy. The situation "offered unusual money-making opportunities to Philip A. Payton, Jr. Payton was keenly aware of the housing needs of the growing black population. As a result, Manhattan blacks flocked to Harlem and filled houses as fast as they were opened to them."[46] From 1900, Payton and his associates operated in the growing field of Harlem real estate management for blacks until the Afro-American Realty Company went out of business in 1908.

The black invasion of all-white Harlem began with the purchase by the Afro-American Realty Company of one or two apartment houses on 134th Street, just west of Lenox Avenue, around 1903. Later, black congregations bought apartment houses a few blocks away. "St. Philip's Episcopal Church, one of the oldest and richest coloured congregations in New York, bought a row of thirteen apartments on One Hundred and Thirty-Fifth street between Lenox and Seventh Avenues."[47] At first, the local whites used every available means, including establishing the Hudson Realty Company, to buy back the black-owned properties and evict the black tenants. Thus, the black-versus-white struggle for control of Harlem began. For a tense period, blacks moved in and held out against the organized white pressures to oust them. However, more blacks succeeded in moving into buildings adjacent to the first black nucleus. "Then, in the eyes of the whites, the whole movement took on the aspect of an 'invasion'—an invasion of both their economic and their social rights. They felt that Negroes as neighbors not only lowered the value of their property, but also lowered their social status. Seeing they could not stop the movement, they began to flee. They took fright, they became panic-stricken, they ran amuck. . . . The presence of a single colored family in a block, regardless of the fact that they might be well-bred people . . . was a signal for precipitate flight. The stampeded whites actually deserted house after house and block after block. . . . And this was the property situation in Harlem at the outbreak of the World War in Europe."[48] Thus was born black Harlem; thus originated the new black, economic market of the northern states established by the pioneering efforts of *native-born American blacks*. As one of the first chroniclers of these racial and ethnic events wrote in 1930:

> The move to Harlem, in the beginning and for a long time, was fathered and engineered by Philip A. Payton, a colored man in the real estate business. But this was more than a matter of mere business with Mr. Payton; the matter of better and still better housing for colored people in New York became the dominating idea of his life, and he worked on it as long as he lived. When the Negro New Yorkers evaluate their benefactors in their own race, they must find that not many have done more than Phil Payton; for much of what had made Harlem the intellectual and artistic capital of the Negro world is in good part due to this fundamental advantage: Harlem has provided New York Negroes with better, cleaner, more modern, more airy, more sunny houses than they ever lived in before. And this is due to the efforts made first by Mr. Payton.[49]

One of the great ironies in the entire liberal-historical interpretation of the outcome of the Washington–Du Bois civil rights conflict was that Payton and his associates were mainly prominent members of Booker T. Washington's anti-NAACP camp, and also officials in Washington's National Negro Business League. The ideological split between these two camps, of course, predates the founding of the NAACP. Although the Afro-American Realty Company folded in 1908, the ideological and philosophical divisions between these two camps carried over and became institutionalized as dissident factors in the NAACP's civil rights continuum from 1910. However, by 1908 the Afro-American Realty Company had at least succeeded in demonstrating in social practice Washington's emphasis and insistence that black *economic* enterprise should take precedence over civil rights agitation. The Afro-American Realty Company thus played a pioneering *economic* role in solving the severe housing problem that *all* blacks (native or foreign-born) faced in New York City in 1900. The fundamental *economic* importance of this achievement did not bear its greatest fruit until after the beginning of World War I in

1914, when mass migrations of southern blacks (and from the West Indies) were drawn to New York City for "better jobs" in response to the industrial impact of the war.

At that point, another civil rights irony occurred which has been overlooked by many civil rights historians of ethnicity and immigration. As pointed out earlier, as of 1914, anti-immigration forces in Congress attempted to pass legislation to bar entry to the United States *by all peoples of "African descent" from Africa, the Caribbean, and Latin America.* Among the lobbyists that fought successfully to defeat this legislation was the NAACP. *In fact, the NAACP's defeat of this antiblack immigration legislation was the most successful civil rights lobby the association had achieved since its founding in 1910.*[50] Consequently, the door was opened for the influx of black West Indians who desired to emigrate to the land of opportunity. From 1910 to 1920 the population of black Harlem increased from approximately 49,555 to approximately 73,000. Since in 1920 the National Urban League estimated that about two thirds of the blacks in New York City actually lived in Harlem, these statistics are only estimates.[51] By 1930 of an estimated 327,706 blacks, 54,754 "foreign Negroes" lived in New York, 39,833 of them living in Manhattan (or Harlem).[52] By the 1930 census, the progressively growing municipal boundaries of this black urban market had been established. Southern and West Indian black migrants had arrived simultaneously into the open territory of an expanding economic market. Unlike in Chicago, for example, migrating blacks captured Harlem's open territory without a physical struggle. It was a case of white population retreat and abandonment. In Chicago housing occupancy by migratory blacks was achieved only by physical and often bloody confrontations with mostly ethnic whites, who resisted black housing encroachments, neighborhood by neighborhood, street by street, block by block.

The in-migration of southern blacks to Chicago, Detroit, Cleveland, St. Louis, Kansas City, urban centers far removed from the northeastern United States, did not involve West Indian or foreign-born black ethnics. Thus, it was only in New York City, and especially in Harlem, that British West Indians as an ethnic group, could lay claim to an economic market extensive enough for them to succeed in the entrepreneurial business field, the professions, and the arts. Essentially, the population-mass factor that comprised the exchange basis of this economic market was Afro-American. It was a fact that about "25 percent of Harlem's population in the twenties was foreign-born."[53] However, only about "10 to 15 percent of the city's black population" was British West Indian, considered to have been the most prosperous group. The entrepreneurial and professional successes of this ethnic Caribbean group could not have been achieved without the labor, exchange, and clientele of a predominantly American black population. Thus, for example, Boston's 3,287 West Indians (in 1930) could not claim the extraordinary achievements of the West Indians in New York City. Nor did foreign-born blacks figure in the economic or political successes of blacks in Chicago, the blacks' "second city" of the 1920s. From an entrepreneurial point of view, the Marcus Garvey movement of the 1920s was a phenomenal and short-lived success—1919 to 1925. But the Garvey movement, organized mainly by West Indian blacks, could not have been achieved without the economic base created by the mass migrations of southern blacks into New York City. Ultimately, neither black Harlem, nor black Chicago, nor black Detroit, Cleveland, or Philadelphia, became what they are known for today because of the black migrants' prior conscious intent to establish these communities. It was the international impact of World War I, and the resulting need for industrial labor, voluminous, tractable, cheap, that spawned the rate of growth of these black cities.

In view of arguments by the neoconservatives of the Seventies about the relevance of racial discrimination and civil rights legislation in the Sixties, what was the state of civil rights between 1900 and 1930? Moreover, how is the black economic situation to be assessed overall during that period? Patently, the general economic position of blacks cannot be explained by reference to the localized economic performance of one ethnic group (West Indians) in one urban location, New York City. What is not adequately understood in all this civil rights history is the significance of twin philosophical legacies that characterized the period—the civil rights philosophy of the NAACP (organized in 1909–1910), and its factional antecedents, versus the economic philosophy of Booker T. Washington, reflected in the National Negro Business League of 1900. That the Afro-American Realty Company was a functional extension of Booker T. Washington's philosophy extolling economic enterprise in preference to civil rights agitation is lost on the latter-day neoconservative economists. In their negative response to the failed efforts of civil rights legislation to remedy black poverty, they remain historically oblivious that the legacy of the civil rights movement was noneconomic liberalism dominating the NAACP tradition. The NAACP avowed no interest in black self-generated economic efforts. Moreover, the southern blacks' migration was so overwhelming in its northern civil rights challenges (such as race riots as in Chicago, 1919) that the NAACP had few options but to pursue its adopted noneconomic legalism. In addition, *still* ongoing were civil rights challenges in the South, as exemplified by *Moore* v. *Dempsey* in Arkansas and other cases.

Both the neoconservatives and contemporary West Indian writers *correctly* approach black progress and achievement in economic terms. Without *economic* progress there is no progress. If all the civil rights advances have not brought a full measure of economic progress, then there is something questionable about civil rights activities. The West Indians (at least the British West Indians) espouse the idea that their ethnic group has achieved a high median-income level *without* the reinforcements of civil rights legislation. Sowell writes that "discrimination clearly cannot account for the incomes of minorities who earn more than the national average, since these groups have neither the size nor the control necessary to discriminate against the general population."[54] The writer Reed Ueda, mentioned above, notes:

> Studies in the 1930's disclosed that West Indians owned a disproportionate number of small stores in Harlem and Columbus Hill. Another contemporary observed that they frequently formed small private companies consisting of a half-dozen investors who would pool several thousand dollars to purchase apartment buildings that they later rented out at a good profit. They also organized corporations to buy and manage larger "elevator" apartment buildings. The Antillian Realty Company and another realty investment firmed by a combine of British West Indians and native-born blacks each had holdings totaling $750,000 in this period.[55]

This scope of business activity, from the point of view of free-enterprise efforts, was exemplary. However, as one observer has noted, in the 1920s *"less than 20 percent of Harlem's businesses were owned by Negroes."*[56] This meant that the grand new black economic market of Harlem remained a profitable, exploitative appendage to the capital of white absentee ownership. Which further meant that a high median income for any black group in Harlem was won at the high cost of intense interracial and intraracial entrepreneurial competition. (There was no room for the elevation of everybody's median income.) But in the racial struggle for economic self-advancement, especially in business enterprise, Sowell implies that American blacks (as differentiated from West Indians) made their poor showing because "entrepreneurship varies greatly from group to group. It is commonplace among Jews, Armenians, Chinese or Japanese, somewhat less common among the Irish, *and rare among blacks.*"[57]

(Italics added.) However, the record shows that in black Chicago, where the West Indian population was practically nil, the number of black-owned businesses, between 1915 and 1937, increased from 727 to 2,464; during this time the black population increased from 83,316 to 237,105. One observer noted:

> The Great Migration created the "Negro Market." Both white and Negro merchants, as well as the Negro consumer, became increasingly conscious of the purchasing power of several hundred thousand people solidly massed in one compact community. The rapid growth of the Negro community between 1915 and 1929 was accompanied by expansion in all types of Negro-owned businesses, *not the least lucrative of which was speculation in real estate.*[58](Italics added.)

(Shades of Harlem's Afro-American Realty Company!) This shows the statistical fallacy of using West Indian median-income levels to prove what such economic statistics are meant to prove—that entrepreneurship is rare among blacks. In terms of pure business activity, the situation in Harlem only proves that as an ethnic minority within a larger minority, black West Indians were furnished an extensive, self-contained black market. Obviously, such an open entrepreneurial black market did not exist in the West Indies, especially in Jamaica, the largest West Indian island. Writer Reed Ueda described West Indian immigrants as exemplary for their "frugalness and thrift," and their "genius for business." In the professions in black New York, it was said that "as high as one-third of the Negro professional population—particularly physicians, dentists, and lawyers—is foreign-born."[59] However, undelineated here were the economic, political, and educational conditions in the Caribbean in the 1920s and 1930s. In other words, to what extent was the black economic market in the West Indies open to black "frugalness and thrift" or "genius for business"? Thirty years after the high crest of West Indian migration to New York City and the eastern seaboard, Amy Jacques Garvey, the wife of Marcus Garvey, a native of Jamaica, described the situation in the island during the 1920s and 1930s:

> The birth-rate increased with unemployment, as idleness encourages child production. Despite infant mortality the population pressure, not finding an outlet abroad, would at some time, let steam. The grocery trade—wholesale and retail—were in the hands of the Chinese, whose ancestors came to the Island as indentured labourers. Now their offspring were the Traders. The Syrians and Lebanese practically monopolized

the clothing and shoe trades. Thus money that had to be spent to buy the barest necessities of life went into the hands of alien traders.[60]

"Alien traders"! Jamaica was then a British colony with blacks, whites, mulattos, East Indians, Syrians, Jews, and Chinese—a multi-colored, multiethnic population. According to varying census estimates, this population fluctuated around two million, the whites being a gross minority. Had the question been posed, Since black Jamaicans represented the overwhelming majority of the island population, why did not a black business class dominate the trade and commerce of its black economic market?, the answer would have been because of colonialism. One of the attributes of colonialism is racial discrimination. But since in the Caribbean blacks constitute a vast majority of the island populations, West Indians generally did not admit that racial discrimination existed in the West Indies (at least, not in the sense that it exists in the United States). Yet, though blacks in Jamaica had an economic market geographically larger than several black Harlems, the black economy was dominated by "alien traders." Thus, the unemployment, the idleness, excessive child production, infant mortality. *Black poverty*, however, was *not* the result of racial discrimination, but was due to money for the barest necessities of life going "into the hands of alien traders." Very similar racial and economic conditions were to be found all over the United States wherever blacks lived. However, American blacks' complaints that exploitation and racial discrimination are the causes of their economic poverty (or low median income) are refuted by both black conservative economists and West Indian scholars, the latter implying that racial discrimination *ought not to be an issue*. West Indians imply that the problem with American blacks is that they "lack confidence and initiative." Because of rationalizations like these West Indians would complain bitterly about racial discrimination in the United States, *but they never identified with the black civil rights movement, which was fighting the racial discrimination they resented.*

These West Indian ethnic arguments, rationalizations, and ambiguities about racial discrimination, either at home or abroad, are offered as explanations for their economic successes in the United States without having to admit the real reasons for their inability to exercise economic control over the island black economic markets. Thomas Sowell, who writes extensively on the comparative study of race, ethnicity, and economics in international and historical contexts, says that compared with

American blacks, West Indian blacks possess greater self-reliance. He explains this historically:

> The greater self-reliance of the blacks in the West Indies deriving from the economic necessities of the plantation, combined with the greater prospects of permanent escape and survival off the plantation, made resistance and rebellion more feasible, since there was not the near certainty of being crushed that there was in the United States.[61]

There *was* a slave-plantation system in the West Indies, just as there was in the United States. However:

> The West Indian setting permitted and fostered more self-reliance, more economic experience, and more defiance of whites. . . .[62]

Since the overwhelming proportion of blacks in the population made Jim Crow laws unfeasible, no such laws existed for West Indian blacks. Thus:

> There could be a very few jobs reserved for whites only, but *only* a very few (since there were very few whites), leaving a whole spectrum of work, skills, and status for blacks. None of this implies that the British were any less racist than the Americans. Certainly the British in the West Indies were noticeably *more* racist than Latin rulers were in other Caribbean islands. . . . What differed were the *economic conditions under which this racism existed and the limitations which this placed on the forms it would take.*[63] (Italics added.)

This observation is acceptable so far as it goes, historically. Economically, however, and given the employment and skills opportunities Sowell describes, it does not explain why one hundred years after the gradual termination of slavery in the West Indies, the economic functions of trading, wholesale and retail, fell into the hands of "alien traders"— the Chinese, Syrians, and Lebanese. Moreover, Sowell's generalizations do not correspond with what West Indians who did not migrate estimated as the racial character of the Caribbean economy. West Indian blacks were up against "The Plantocracy—the Land Barons, the white Shipping and Fruit Companies (who made millions yearly out of the Islands . . .) newspapers, whose policy was to make the Island safe for Big Business at any cost, they being the stock-holders."[64] Consequently, wrote Amy Jacques Garvey:

> The subtle economic thralldom of Colonial Powers in the Caribbean fools many West Indians who say, "All I want is money to do business, or good paying steady work. . . . I can buy a good house anywhere I want to live, I can send my children to good schools as long as I can pay for them. . . . I can live like a real man and be respected. . . . All I want is money." But to get it for the masses, was the almost impossible task. To make this possible at once, would necessitate revolutionary measures.[65]

Obviously, it was from the class of ambitious Jamaicans whose dreams of money making could not be realized under the "thralldom of Colonial Powers" and "alien traders," that Harlem got its influx of black West Indians. It was these, Reed Ueda writes, who were the "highly skilled and educated immigrants [who] were forced to take jobs beneath their level of training or experience, who patiently waited for the opportunity to leave jobs as elevator operators or cooks and to resume their previous occupations as teachers, lawyers and craftsmen."[66]

Like the black neoconservatives, Reed Ueda misinterprets economic realities of the 1920s and 1930s. Reading contemporary upwardly mobile expectations into the 1920s, he does not understand that for anyone black (West Indian or American) being a cook or an elevator operator *was a good job*. Neither the American South nor the Caribbean was noted for a proliferation of high-rise elevator-equipped apartments or office buildings that required the specific job classification of elevator operator. Therefore, an elevator operator, although a "menial," meant black male ex-peasants or college graduates from Alabama or Jamaica could earn a higher wage than they were formerly accustomed to, and it also meant upgrading the ascending categories of manual job skills. A migratory worker out of Jacksonville, Florida, A. Philip Randolph was an elevator operator before he became editor of the famous *Messenger* magazine during World War I. He also led an organization of hotel workers into a union. A cook's job was highly prized by both blacks and whites in New York City during the 1920s; it is still highly prized in the 1980s. In the social history of the West Indies there is no indication that the cuisinier's art had sufficient commercial-enterprise refinements to make the job a lucrative attraction.

As for lawyers, teachers, and craftsmen, American black colleges like Howard, Atlanta, Lincoln, Fisk, and Tuskegee had been turning out scores of graduates in these professional and skilled classifications, the great majority of whom could not find work except as elevator operators, cooks, chauffeurs, or manual laborers. As for lawyers, Reed Ueda does not mention how West Indian lawyers got their training in the 1920s and earlier. For one thing, in the West Indies they were not called lawyers, but "solicitors" or "barristers." For another, they were not trained in the West Indies, but in England, if they were British. When West Indian lawyers came to New York, they could not practice law without passing a bar examination, which meant more schooling in order to qualify. There is no record of how many West Indian lawyers got their certification from Howard University's law school. Paul Robeson received his law degree from Columbia in the 1920s, but was saved from a black lawyer's penurious practice by the stage and concert hall. At the same time, black lawyers out of Little Rock, Arkansas, attempting to defend the black victims of the Phillips County, Arkansas, race riot were being chased out of the county with threats of death. Ueda does not compare the opportunities for the practice of law in New York City with those in the West Indies. Moreover, the University of the West Indies was not established until 1962; Ueda does not point out that American black education (with all its limitations) was far in advance of that for blacks anywhere in the world at that time, including the West Indies or Africa. As for jobs for black schoolteachers (Americans or West Indians), Ueda writes as if they were as plentiful in New York City as they were for cooks or elevator operators, *which they were not.* It had taken a lengthy legal battle with the New York City school board to secure a permanent appointment for a black schoolteacher in a predominantly white school in 1895.[67] Before black Harlem was established, the shifting black population in New York City had severely limited opportunities for black schoolteachers making the profession risky and insecure. Even as late as the 1930s, when black Harlem had taken over all the original public school sites, public school teachers remained overwhelmingly white.[68] Still, in regard to West Indian immigrants who resumed their previous occupations as teachers, Ueda makes no reference to the primary and secondary public school situation in the West Indies and what the actual teaching opportunities were for black teachers.[69]

Sowell, who characteristically downgrades the academic qualities of black college education, cites proof of the black West Indians' eager pursuit of professional education: "Black immigrants in the United States have succeeded economically, educationally, and in other ways much more than native Americans."[70] Another West Indian writer, Aubrey W. Bonnett, asserts that it is "the West Indians' emphasis on education that propels them to do well in this country [U.S.] where universalistic criteria are stressed and meritocracy via education is the name of the game."[71] In both cases, the inference is that black American education, via black colleges, for example, was not equal to West Indians' expectations of what ought to be the measure of "meritocracy" in blacks' educational process in the "universal" sense. Sowell is justified in low-rating the educational accomplishments of many black colleges as he does.[72] Bonnett, however, cites David Lowenthal, the London author of *West Indian Societies*. Lowenthal did write about the educational, economic, and political successes of West Indians in the United States, but, like the neoconservatives Thomas Sowell and Walter E. Williams, he could only cite West Indian success as it related to one American city—New York. Lowenthal did, however, cite the West Indian attitude *toward black education in the West Indies:*

> Europe continues to attract those who are ambitious, energetic, and impatient with, or fearful of, local conditions. Elite and middle-class West Indians regularly travel abroad for business or pleasure. To many, a first-class education still means a European education. The University of the West Indies, too elite to cater for most local needs, is not elite enough to suit some; more than half of all Commonwealth Caribbean college students attend British and North American institutions. For French West Indians, university and professional training still more frequently entails Paris.[73]

In other words, if the more sought-after educational advantages of West Indians meant attending the universities of Paris or London, a more lucrative black economic market in which to promote their ambitions for group or personal advancement in business, the professions, and politics was not in London or Paris, but Harlem and Brooklyn, New York. On the question of initiative or self-confidence, it has to be repeated that this extensive and expanding black economic market was *not started by West Indians*, but by the pioneering business initiatives of American blacks in the wake of the great migration from the South.

Unlike in California, no amount of anti-Japanese legislation or racial ideology could really hinder the Japanese from capitalizing on the wealth lying dormant in the "agricultural potential of California's soil, the diversity of its natural wealth, the beauty of its landscape, and its mild climate. . . ." In California these attractions had been advertised long before "modern chambers of commerce were organised."

> Beyond the boosterism found in letters of hide and tallow traders, whalers, and gold seekers lay other qualities, intangible yet real. These gave California a romance and a glamour that exerted a magnetic influence even in distant countries. Visitors in the early days came under the same spell that, through the years, has turned tourists into permanent residents.[74]

The West Coast open-territory paradise of California was not open to any American native-born blacks who might have desired to abandon Mississippi and Georgia because of lack of opportunities in agriculture. What provided release from the economic oppression that Thomas Sowell and Walter E. Williams claim did not really exist in any meaningful way was the northern cities—especially New York, where British West Indian escapees from lack of opportunities or "alien traders" arrived in unprecedented numbers. The peculiar aftermath of black slavery in the New World rendered both American and Caribbean blacks a migratory people. Reed Ueda for example, begins his study of the migratory history of British West Indians by observing that "over a half-million black immigrants have moved from the British West Indies to the United States since 1820."[75] Why did they migrate? He says that "they were attracted to the United States by its growing industrial economy and its opportunities for social mobility."[76] But "social mobility" how? Since the end of Reconstruction in the southern states, American blacks began to migrate northward also in pursuit of social mobility. However, the black neoconservative assessment of this migration claims that this pursuit of social mobility turned out to be a failure, especially in economic advancement or median income. Here again, a more extended comparison is in order taking into account all the factors—economic, educational, cultural, historical, geographical, and international—that sum up this vast migration. The motivations and responses by Afro-Americans and West Indians to the migratory push and pull do not yield simplistic conclusions.

As late as 1972, David Lowenthal was able to say:

> Today most Caribbean territories are striving toward universal education and equal opportunity. But the persistence of colonial patterns of rewards and prestige, together with shortages of funds and personnel, keeps school systems elitist and unsuited to local needs.[77]

As late as 1964 in Barbados, "only 4.5 percent of those over 15 had secondary-school certificates. Elsewhere, far fewer are schooled; just one in six Windward Island children were in secondary school in 1964, *one in ten in Jamaica. . . .*"[78] (Italics added.) All over the West Indies, Lowenthal writes, secondary-school children are predominantly elite and middle class; the smaller the proportion of students to the population, the more elite they are. Managerial and professional families, mostly white, light-colored, Portuguese and Chinese, constitute half the secondary enrollment in such places as Guyana and Surinam. "For the West Indian majority, formal education is brief and perfunctory. Primary schooling is mostly free and in theory compulsory. . . . In Jamaica fewer than two-thirds of those on the rolls ordinarily turn up."[79]

It was this educational, economic, and political "thralldom" that motivated black West Indians to escape. Their migration was, of course, more intensely self-motivated than the northward migration of American blacks, who needed more externally generated inducements to pack up and move. However, West Indian writers tend to play down the absence of upwardly mobile opportunities for black West Indians as a prime reason for their migratory propensities. Bonnett describes the West Indies as "migration-oriented societies." However, "the West Indian migration to Europe was not as substantial as that to North America, numbering fewer than one million." By the Seventies, this writer was able to estimate that there were:

At least 300,000 West Indians in Britain, an estimated 300,000 in France and about 200,000 in the Netherlands. Despite their small numbers these immigrants bear the brunt of resentment from their European hosts. A mere generation ago the British, French and Dutch all took pride in the absence of racial conflict and felt more or less at home with Caribbean visitors. Today Britain, France and the Netherlands exhibit profound patterns of discrimination, residential segregation and turmoil. *Nowhere is the situation worse than in Britain where the West Indian youth find their unemployment the highest, a consequence of prejudice and inferior educational opportunities.*[80] (Italics added.)

This quotation is taken from a footnote to the study entitled "Institutional Adaptation of West Indian Immigrants to America," written in 1981. Herein is reported the irony that, in the Seventies, some 300,000 West Indians of immigrant stock in Britain were voicing the same complaints about racial discrimination and segregation that American blacks were struggling against during the high crest of West Indian immigration to the United States in the period, 1920–1930. What happened, then, between World War I and post-World War II, to all the innate, "cultural" abilities of black West Indians to succeed in "business enterprises," in the professions, in the skilled occupations, in trade? West Indian immigrants in Britain did not, as their antecedents did in New York City, resume previous occupations of "teachers, lawyers, and craftsmen." They did not achieve the high median-income levels so highly regarded by the neoconservative critics of black American economic performance in comparison with other ethnic groups.

As a matter of fact, one can look at West Indian economic performance just across the border, in Canada. Canada, similar to the British West Indies, is part of the British Commonwealth. As used to be said of British West Indians in Harlem, "West Indians had a distinctive English accent, worshipped as Anglicans . . . and often expressed allegiance to the British Crown."[81] For these reasons, to many Jamaicans Canada was more attractive than New York City. Canada at least *was* British and would prove much more amenable to black West Indian ambitions than the United States because Canada did not exhibit the intense degree of racial discrimination for which the United States was noted. At least Canada would not treat West Indians as if they were indistinguishable from American blacks in Georgia, New York City, or Arkansas. The facts were that West Indians had been migrating to Canada throughout the nineteenth and twentieth centuries. "The first significant migration of non-white West Indians was during the 1910's when many came to Canada to work in steel mills and coal mines in Nova Scotia, as sleeping car porters and as domestic servants."[82] But this early West Indian immigration was halted as a result of Canadian immigration policy. Canadian officials "were directed to put every impediment in the way of black immigration on the basis of a climactic [sic] theory of race."[83] But in the 1950s, Canadian policy shifted slightly and immigration from the Caribbean was renewed "on the assumption that black immigration would be acceptable if certain conditions were right." The changed Canadian assumptions were premised on the need for West Indian domestic service (i.e., women). However:

> Most domestics were black and lower class and in many instances faced severe social and emotional isolation in Canada. On the whole Canada's immigration policy was and still continues to be restrictive and racist.[84]

Consequently, the restrictive nature of Canadian immigration legislation has been under attack from West Indian lawyers citing how "racism has affected immigrants from Third World countries." This West Indian agitation over the civil rights of black immigrants was in progress as late as the Sixties and Seventies in Canada and Britain. Thus, West Indians in Britain and Canada did not match the accomplishments of West Indians in New York City. In terms of pure economic achievement and opportunities, West Indian migration into those countries was encouraged by a shortage of unskilled and service labor such as existed in the United States during World War I. Jobs for West Indians, like sleeping car porters, domestics, steel mill and coal mine workers, were the kinds of jobs American blacks had filled ever since post-Reconstruction. Neither in Canada nor Britain did the vaunted West Indian "contempt for manual labor" hold up as in New York City. If in New York City, West Indians could eventually eschew manual or low-status unskilled labor to resume "previous occupations as teachers, lawyers and craftsmen" it was because, inadvertently, such immigrants were afforded the open territory of an expanding black economic market. Obviously, then, for those statistical thousands of West Indians who migrated to Canada, Britain, the Netherlands, and France, no such convenient black market was in the offing. Sowell, in spite of his negative assessments of black American economic performance in the economy, had to tender a qualifying rejoinder to his own simplistic statistical generalizations about group median-income averages:

West Indians in the United States have continued to hold sizable advantages over American Negroes in incomes and occupations. As of 1969, West Indians' incomes were 28 percent higher than the incomes of other blacks in New York City, and 52 percent higher nationally. *Second generation West Indians have higher incomes than whites.*[85] (Italics added.)

Note again the specific reference to New York City, not Chicago, Detroit, Philadelphia or Atlanta! Although this claim for a 52 percent West Indian median-income national average is specious enough, it is even more statistically specious to claim that second-generation West Indians have a higher national income than whites. How can one neoconservative economist make such an assessment when another liberal sociologist can offer the median-income argument that, given the current condition of race relations in contemporary American economics, narrowing the income gap between *blacks and whites* is not in the immediate offing: "In the example of family income, if the growth rates of 1959–1982 persist without interruption, the median incomes of black and white families in the United States will be equal in about three centuries."[86] Sowell, however, expanded on his median-income American black–West Indian statistical theme:

> West Indians, as such, are too small a group to have any political power, so West Indian individuals, in public office hold their positions as "representatives" *of the black population as a whole*. . . . Moreover, the many West Indians in civil rights movements must attribute black poverty and unemployment almost solely to white racism, although the West Indians' experience itself seriously undermines the proposition that color is a fatal handicap in the American economy.[87]

But if "color" is *not* a fatal consideration in parceling out economic rewards under capitalistic free-enterprise *American* conditions, then the white-black economic income gap that affects *blacks*, but *not* West Indian blacks, has to be explained by a congruence of other factors. Since West Indian immigrants in Canada, Britain, France, and the Netherlands did not even begin to match the economic, professional, and entrepreneurial achievements of West Indians in the United States, Sowell was forced to conclude that:

> Even those West Indians in the private sector of the economy may be dependent on the large black population for their prosperity. Many are business men, doctors, lawyers, publishers, and others whose customers or clienteles are American Negroes. West Indian immigrants in England are not nearly as successful there, *perhaps because of the absence of a large non-West Indian black population to provide them with a constituency*.[88] (Italics added.)

Instead of "constituency," Sowell really should have said the "open territory" of an expanding black economic market; also, it was not a question of "perhaps"—it was a clear fact of a unique black urban experience that could not have been duplicated anywhere else in the Western world. Black West Indians possessed a much larger constituency in the Caribbean but could not exploit it. West Indian immigrants in Canada, England, France, and the Netherlands found no constituency on which to build an economic structure. *Thus, in England and, to a less-publicized degree, in Canada, West Indians found themselves faced,*

during the post-World War II period, with the necessity of organizing a
civil rights movement actually patterned after the methodology and ide-
ology of the black civil rights movement of the 1960s, even to the extent
of adopting the Black Power slogans.[89]

Sowell, and other new-vogue neoconservative critics of the functional legitimacy of the civil rights movement in eliminating black poverty
in the United States, would logically have to answer the question, Since
the civil rights movement of the Sixties and Seventies failed to eliminate
the black poverty of the white-black median-income gap, then what would
be the significance of the civil rights movement of black West Indians
in Britain and Canada? If racism (racial discrimination) can no longer be
charged as the main reason for the inability of blacks to achieve median-
income equity in a free-enterprise economy in the United States, then
what is the legitimacy of civil rights movements among West Indian
blacks in Canada and England? If, as the West Indian Bonnett reports,
"nowhere is the situation worse than in Britain where the West Indian
youth find their unemployment the highest, a consequence of prejudice
and inferior educational opportunities," then, according to Sowell and
Williams, such a situation cannot be attributed solely to racism or racial
discrimination. Either the national economic systems of Britain and the
United States must be radically different in their treatment of nonwhite
minorities, or there is something characteristically deficient in the social,
economic, and cultural makeup of the 300,000 or more West Indians in
Britain. About blacks in the United States, Sowell writes:

> The example of the West Indians suggests that it is not slavery alone,
> or even brutal treatment during slavery, that serves as a crippling hand-
> icap for generations after emancipation, but rather the occupationally
> and psychologically constricting world in which the American Negro
> developed in the United States. Their example also suggests that the
> current disabilities of black Americans are not due only to current
> discrimination but also to past deprivation and disorganization that con-
> tinue to take their toll.[90]

In other words, the "toll" of past mistreatment and social disorganization unavoidably places American blacks in general beyond the
economic range and capability of civil rights movements, government
programs, affirmative action, etc., either to ameliorate or seriously affect
them. *Does this imply that the historical and legal and sociological origins*
of the American civil rights movement were, perhaps, ill-considered, ill-

advised, illegitimate, misdirected, misled, or perhaps even unconstitu-tional, or what? The question becomes not only difficult, but also prob-lematic because Sowell, and the neoconservative school, in downplaying the effectiveness of civil rights programs to ameliorate economic dis-abilities, overlook that the black civil rights movement was grounded in the ideals of *noneconomic liberalism*. This Joel B. Spingarn's philosophy was willingly adopted by the NAACP leadership. W.E.B. Du Bois, circumstantially a prisoner of this noneconomic liberalism, could not break with it until 1934, with rather disastrous and denigrating personal results. However, thirty-four years prior to this break, black leadership had been divided over the priority to organize principally for civil lib-ertarian economic goals. Put simply—What was more important: *the struggle for civil rights justice* or *the struggle to develop the arts of how to earn a living in a free-enterprise economy?* This core issue of the Washington–Du Bois leadership controversy broke out precisely when Booker T. Washington's protégés were establishing the Afro-American Realty Company and laying the *economic* basis for the growth of the world's largest black urban community, Harlem, which was also the largest black urban economic market in the United States. But true to the intellectual influence of the philosophy of noneconomic liberalism, liberal-consensus historians have (along with the radical left) misinter-preted and obfuscated the root implications of the Washington–Du Bois leadership split. On this question, neoconservative economic historians are not much better. Sowell, for example, while exceedingly thorough in making ethnic-group economic comparisons that are enlightening as generalizations, ignores specifics that relate to his generalizations. In assessing Booker T. Washington, Sowell writes: "While . . . Washing-ton's approach was primarily adapted to situation of the black masses, W.E.B. Du Bois emerged in the early twentieth century as a spokesman for what he called 'the talented tenth'. . . . Du Bois's educational em-phasis was on liberal arts, rather than on the vocationalism of Washington, and his political emphasis was an unrelenting pressure for full civil rights as soon as possible. He was one of the founders of the National Asso-ciation for the Advancement of Colored People. . . . These were differ-ences of emphasis rather than principle. . . . Despite a divided leadership much was accomplished by both camps. There was more than enough work for both to do."[91]

But this was true only as a long-standing historical generalization concerning the evolution of black civil rights, economic, and educational movements. Du Bois himself did not characterize Washington so simplistically. Washington, said Du Bois, "*. . . is striving nobly to make Negro artisans business men and property-owners; but it is utterly impossible, under modern competitive methods, for workingmen and property owners to defend their rights and exist without the right of suffrage.*"[92] (Italics added.) *Suffrage?* Here, specifically, Du Bois was alluding to the *South*, where blacks had been effectively disfranchised, the inference being the absence of *political rights* in the South. In the NAACP programmatic context, it meant the absence of *civil rights*. Yet the NAACP was not created in the South but in the North—New York City—from which locale it was feasible to espouse the doctrine of noneconomic liberalism without declaring it as such. Thus, even before the NAACP was actually established, Du Bois, in splitting with Washington in those seminal years of black leadership conflict, was forced to espouse the civil rights priorities of noneconomic liberalism in order to attack Washington effectively. Seventy-five years later, the new-vogue black neoconservative economists would declare that absence of civil rights safeguards against racial discrimination is not acceptable as an excuse for the failure by American blacks to gain median-income parity with American whites. Walter E. Williams says the Japanese Americans, Jewish Americans, and West Indian Americans did not allow racial discrimination and the absence of civil rights legislation prevent their ascent to a high economic status. Sowell asserts that the West Indians' economic achievements disprove the notion that color or racial discrimination present any real, insuperable barriers against the color black in economic life. What is shown, says Sowell, is that there is something flawed in the social organization factors in black life, something "culturally" deficient that results from the peculiar American slavery experience, that continues to affect black family organization or perhaps black psychology. *But what exactly does all this mean?*

In Sowell's assessment of the leadership quarrels between Washington and Du Bois, his purely *economic* interpretation is flawed. As a neoconservative economic historian concerned with the history of ethnic economic behavior and business development, it is curious that he makes no reference to Booker T. Washington's important National Negro Business League (NNBL) established in 1900. *How important was this league?* In the 1980s the NNBL is still in existence with a few branches in certain cities. Sowell makes no historical references to Washington's book, *The Negro in Business*, published in 1907, nor to Du Bois's study on the same theme in his famous "Atlanta University Social Studies" of 1899. Washington's 379-page study of the role of American blacks in business

enterprises contains a comprehensive survey of black business achievement in the North, South, Southwest, and Midwest. Washington explained that in preparing the study, he "sought rather to refer to such
examples as would show the variety of business enterprise in which
colored people are engaged rather than the total amount of business being
done by Negroes. Furthermore, I have in every case been influenced in
making my choice less by the actual material success gained, measured
in dollars and cents, than by the enterprise and energy and moral ear-
nestness displayed. I have done this because I believe that the success
won by hard work, rather than by lucky chance, is the only success that
is of any importance to the race as a whole."[93]

But Sowell, economic historian and critic of civil rights outcomes,
explores only Washington's educational philosophies, *not* his economic
philosophies, which is, of course, intellectually inconsistent. This is especially the case since Booker T. Washington was an ideological foe of
civil rights programming at its inception—that is, seventy years *before*
Sowell's discovery that civil rights legislation alone could not and would
not solve the black economic disadvantages of a low median income. In
other words, it was not so much that Washington was against civil rights
as he was *instinctively* opposed to the ideals of noneconomic liberalism
that dominated the civil rights traditions, the historical influence of which
Sowell, the economist, does not comprehend. Hence, despite favoring
the virtues of the free-market system to deal more generously with the
problems of black poverty, Sowell ignores the leadership ideals of Booker
T. Washington, who among all black leaders was the truest believer in
the free-enterprise virtues of American capitalism! In this regard, Roger
W. Babson, one of the prominent white economists of national stature,
was a statistician who "guided stock market investors for half a century
with periodic assessments of trends." Babson, who died in 1967 at the
age of ninety-two, established the Babson Institute in Wellesley, Massachusetts, "for the training of young men for business and finance,"
and predicted the October 1929 economic crash two months before it
happened. Babson is also remembered as having claimed that one of the
great inspirations of his life was Booker T. Washington, who, he said,
was an economic man "much handicapped" by the inability of his race
to bootstrap itself upward in the American economy.[94] Sowell poses the
same economic problem, but for the purposes of decrying the failure of
government programs to proxy for blacks in the free market. Because
the black West Indian ethnic group did not need the help of government
programs, this group has become an economic, professional, or entre-

preneurial barometer by which the successes (or lack of them) of black economic progress in the entire nation are measured.

Given the marginal and often precarious position of at least half the black population, these conservative arguments emerge as crucial for the Eighties, if for no other reason than that their history deserves more than a superficial review. Both the liberal social critics and those of the Left have decried all the real or pretended black economic programs as either romantic or futile solutions to the blacks' problems.[95] The most thorough of these critics was E. Franklin Frazier, who decried the "myth of black business" and called it "Negro Business—A Social Myth," no matter what local or national claims were made about the scope of black business enterprises. Generally, Sowell's conclusions agree with Frazier's, but *after* the fact, in that Sowell incorrectly asserts that black entrepreneurial efforts were rare among (American) blacks, but *not* West Indian blacks (in New York City). Capital investment, represented by black business, said Frazier, was "insignificant from the standpoint of the American economy and [that] it provided an exceedingly small amount of employment and income for black workers."[96] Frazier proceeded to explain how false ideas arose concerning the importance of black business enterprise, how it became a myth, and how the myth had been propagated among blacks. Although the campaign on behalf of building black business arose in the 1890s, Frazier pointed out that the idea became institutionalized in Booker T. Washington's National Negro Business League of 1900. Frazier traced the development of the league's educational and inspirational program from its first meeting in Boston to its fiftieth anniversary meeting in 1950. He traced the fortunes of numerous black merchants' associations throughout the nation's black communities. During that time the number of black colleges giving business education courses grew from six in 1900 to more than twenty in 1940.[97] However, during the same period numerous attempts by blacks to establish industrial undertakings resulted in failure. Many such ventures had been supported by northern white capitalist philanthropy. Nevertheless, said Frazier, "northern philanthropy has been sympathetic to the efforts" of blacks to create business enterprises. This has been shown especially in their financial support of the study of black business:

A quarter of a century ago, the Spelman Fund, established through Rockefeller contributions to social research made an initial grant of $15,000, which was supplemented by $5000, for the study of Negro business. The chief results of this study, which comprised less than fifty pages, were to show that almost all Negroes' businesses were small retail businesses and undertaking establishments serving Negroes, that they were conducted by their owners, and that they were in Negro neighborhoods.[98]

Frazier charged that these studies did not point out the fundamental causes of the failure of blacks to carry on successful business enterprises either on a small or large scale: *"They did not deal with the simple but fundamental sociological fact that the Negro lacks a business tradition or the experience of people who, over generations, have engaged in buying and selling."*[99] So much for the "myth of black business." Sowell would agree, but with a different emphasis. He would assert that, historically, even small-scale entrepreneurial enterprise was rare among blacks. Frazier concluded that it was not a question of the scarcity of black entrepreneurial ambitions, but that business efforts failed because of a universal lack of business knowhow and expertise! This requires from Sowell a more thorough economic analysis for his conclusions about the superiority of West Indian professional and entrepreneurial successes in New York City. If, as Frazier concluded, the scope and economic impact of black business enterprise is a myth, then to what extent is the West Indian ethnic-group economic success factual or mythical? Black West Indians arriving in the United States possessed no more essential training in buying and selling than American blacks inasmuch as the black Caribbean economy was dominated by absentee colonial landlords based in London (or Paris or the Netherlands) or by Chinese, Syrians, Lebanese, and Jewish "alien traders." Thus, ambitious black West Indian *would-be* entrepreneurs, or professionals, or lawyers or teachers, or doctors had little or no control over "their" economic market. That was the why and the wherefore of black West Indian migratory societies. Interestingly enough, Frazier did not mention the significance of the West Indian ethnic group's economic and professional success in his discussion of the "myth of black business." However, the West Indian writer Bonnett has reassessed Sowell's and Williams's thesis on the economic significance of West Indians in New York City. His 1981 study on the "Institutional Adaptation of West Indian Immigrants to America" is subtitled "An Analysis of Rotating Credit Associations."[100] The overall substance of this study is that West Indian accommodation to the northern urban American milieu (i.e., New York City), in terms of economic survival and upwardly mobile economic success, and also ethnic-group stability in terms of social organization (i.e., family), was based on two salient factors:

1. The social and economic role of West Indian class divisions transferred to the United States.
2. The social role of economic cooperative enterprise that often cut across class lines in West Indian immigrant groups, especially in New York City.

Bonnett claims that his study of West Indian "mutual aid societies" updates history, "since it is probably the first serious study of self-help institutions among Black immigrants to have been done since the turn of the century. Thus, in this regard, it brings a present perspective to what is an ongoing and still useful and much needed association for people still labouring under the very real social and economic handicaps. Also, its currency today is quite obvious at a time when this country is still in an economic recession and the availability of sources of funds to Blacks through regular financial channels is severely limited or entirely cut off."[101] Moreover, Bonnett showed how these West Indian credit associations served as "structural shields" to enable the immigrants to "cope with the complexities of urban life." In other words, *in contrast to the generality of black Americans, West Indian immigrants founded their main social organization on the principle of the "rotating credit association," their traditional version of what was known in America as the "economic cooperative." These credit associations are described as urbanized adaptations of forms of economic cooperation indigenous to Caribbean and West Indian societies in Latin America. In the indigenous terminology of traditional West Indian societies, this form of association was known as the susu,* or *esusu,* sometimes translated to mean "partners" (in credit), or *sou-sou.* The origins of the rotating credit system are placed in Africa and Asia, and variations of the *susu* were transplanted to the West Indies. Bonnett contends "that the Chinese, Japanese and black immigrants to the USA have been much more successful in their commercial enterprises because of a suprafamilial social structure and in particular the use of rotating credit associations."[102] The use of these rotating credit associations served to assist *"in small scale capital formation."* In this way, immigrants to the United States from southern China and Japan employed the traditional rotating credit association as their principal device for capitalizing small businesses. The cooperative nature of rotating credit associations, then, was a means of amassing capital:

> By far the most extensive use of these [rotating credit] associations in the United States is among black West Indian immigrants. Although Americans tended to lump all black immigrants together into a uniform image, it is important to realize that these immigrants represented a diverse group from dozens of different islands in the Caribbean each with a strong attachment to their respective homelands.[103]

Thus, the rotating credit associations were "functional and instrumental institutions serving socio-economic functions in the immigrant community." Bonnett cited a cultural trait connected with the social practices of the rotating credit association "which promoted self-confidence and initiative rather than regimented dependence fostered among black Americans."[104] Another corollary attributed to the value system of West Indians was, as cited before, one in which "universalistic criteria are stressed and meritocracy via education is the name of the game." Such conclusions represent in certain ways an extrapolation of the Sowell conservative economics thesis—racial discrimination per se does not account for the persistent economic disadvantages of at least half the black American population; there are other *cultural* flaws in their styles of social organization (one of which is the family structure). Black West Indians achieved a high median income despite racial discrimination and, therefore, did not need the reinforcements of civil rights legislation because they had not been psychologically immobilized in terms of "self-confidence" and "initiative" by the "regimented dependence" fostered among black Americans. Moreover, since civil rights legislation, government programs, and affirmative action have failed to alleviate the consequences of black Americans' economic disabilities, these disabilities must be alleviated by the economic self-help initiative of blacks themselves. Which, of course, signalizes the swan song for civil rights dispensations. Hence, the latest Sowell *dernier cri* becomes *Civil Rights: Rhetoric or Reality?* (1984).

Viewed retrospectively from the political, economic, cultural, and educational civil rights questions that comprise the social history of these arguments, Thomas Sowell's thesis has validity but only as a *generalization*. Had all the contending forces (racial, ethnic, economic, political, civil rights,) remained equal from 1900 to 1980, Thomas Sowell would have inherited the mantle as the new Sage of Tuskegee, for his "economics" but not as a result of his demonstrable elite education. Booker T. Washington preached black economics—i.e., black economic initiative, self-reliance, self-help, entrepreneurial ability—as the surest way to racial equality. By contrast, Sowell is a modern-day product of the kind of elite education that Washington was not enamored of. Moreover, Sowell owes his lofty academic prestige, in part, to the influence of the civil rights movement in breaking down racial discrimination in higher education. The Du Bois generation of black academics was never so honored. But this does not deny Sowell the intellectual prerogative of questioning whether or not civil rights are, in fact, rhetoric or reality. The actual outcome of the civil rights movement of the Sixties and Seventies demands that certain questions be answered, and certain obdurate facts be faced. Where have American blacks come from? Where have they arrived? Where are they going? In arguing where blacks have come from, Sowell either misses a number of signposts or doesn't acknowledge them.

American blacks represent the single largest nonwhite (ethnic) minority in the United States. Consequently, sheer numbers would rule out the kind of functional ethnic cohesion in economic organization that Sowell and Williams allude to in their comparative assessments of American blacks, West Indians, Japanese, and Jews. In economic terms, the comparisons are so preposterous as to cast well-deserved doubts on the ability of demographic statistics and macroeconomic analyses to form a compatible marriage. Black migrations out of the southern states since World War I have deposited some twenty-six to thirty million blacks in a variety of urban settlements, differentiated by local, state, sectional, and regional configurations. Japanese, West Indian, and Jewish ethnographic concentrations are associated with distinct localities—California and New York City. The Japanese are judged principally on their economic achievements in California, Jews and West Indians by their ethnic accomplishments in New York City, in terms of median income. Sowell cites capitalistic, free-market free enterprise as the testing ground for who makes it or who doesn't. Liberalistic idealism (fortified by left-wing radical idealism) has consistently indoctrinated the black leadership that because of ingrained practices of racial discrimination, it is the economic system or the state that must reorient its racial practices to accommodate black economic grievances. Hence, civil rights programs. But when civil rights programs fail to deliver economic parity, then the onus for black economic deprivation is shifted back to the blacks themselves. Historically, liberalistic idealism was never of a mind either to aid or encourage black American self-generated, self-help economic enterprise of any kind. The "regimented dependence fostered among black Americans" cited by Bonnett was a heritage fostered by liberal idealism that downgraded and discouraged indigenous black self-help economic enterprise. In one sense, the liberals had a point in throwing their moral and financial support behind black civil libertarians rather than behind Booker T. Washington. A nonwhite minority as large as the blacks had little chance to win economic parity with whites in the competitive free-market name of the game. More than that, dissident black critics themselves would decry the outcroppings of the Booker T. Washington school of economic thought as predicated on the hopes of patently unrealizable black economic goals. Thus, the "myth of black business" as pronounced by E. Franklin Frazier in the 1950s and later by one of the black intellectual prodigies of the Sixties and Seventies, Robert L. Allen, in his study *Black Awakening in Capitalist America*. Allen did not see "black capitalism, Negro organization men, foundation grants, business-managed welfare or token political victories as aiding Black Liberation, but as producing an atmosphere conducive to even more comprehensive exploitation."[105] Robert Allen's thesis was an extension of the Frazier thesis that viewed the impact of black business enterprise as social myth. Interestingly enough, Thomas Sowell did not see fit to comment on Robert Allen's study despite its genesis in the civil rights contention of the Sixties that Sowell decries. In the final analysis of the outcome of black civil rights progress as "myth" or "fact," "rhetoric" or "reality," there are myths and there are other myths to be either sown or blown.

If E. Franklin Frazier could decry all the boasts of American black business enterprise as social myth, the West Indian scholar Aubrey W. Bonnett could also qualify the exaggerated claims of West Indian ethnic successes in black business enterprise in free-market New York City. It was necessary for Bonnett to analyze this peculiar ethnic business activity with a more strict accounting of the larger black economic market in which it occurred. In this regard, Bonnett writes that for "whatever the reason, the tendency has been to focus on the relative economic success, the educational attainment, the growing ethnic pride of these [West Indian] immigrants."[106] Under the heading of "The Black West Indian Immigrant—The Myth and the Reality," the author qualifies the realities behind the ethnic hubris. With regard to black Americans, both the neo-

liberal and the neoconservative schools of economic thought reverse the
analysis by focusing on the relative economic failures. But regarding the
West Indians, Bonnett continues:

> This overly optimistic slant, the local gossip and home folklore abound-
> ing with the success stories of those who have made it, have added a
> halo complex to their immigrant experience. Few of the failures are
> taken notice of, and if so, with severe criticism rather than compassion
> for those involved. The culture of poverty to which these immigrants
> are exposed and their daily battle to survive is hardly stressed.[107]

Sowell's (and Williams's) economic assessments of the "culture of
poverty" regarding Afro-Americans brook severe free enterprise–inspired
criticism and little compassionate understanding of Afro-American economic successes *or* failures. What exactly *were* the root social-organi-
zation causes of Afro-American or West Indian economic successes or
failures? A key to the answer is given by Bonnett. In his analysis of the
West Indian immigrant use of rotating credit associations as a mechanism
for small-scale capital formation, he says:

> We contend that for the most part the self-reliant West Indian blacks
> were invariably from the already successful mulatto class and were not
> indicative of the black population from which the majority of poor
> working class migrants to the United States came. It was these blacks
> who used rotating credit associations in their islands to help cope with
> their situation of poverty, and, faced with urban poverty and other types
> of deprivation, it was to these very associations that these poor immi-
> grants turned. We shall concern ourselves with the instrumental function
> of these associations in an urban milieu.[108]

In other words, in the evolution of New York City (especially Harlem) as an expanding black urban economic market, not-so-apparent or
admitted class factors were operative within both the black American and
the West Indian immigrant populations. Beyond New York City, in other
major northern black urban communities, class factors within the evolving
black communities were operative (without the West Indian immigrant
ingredient). How these class factors operated in the economic, political,
cultural, educational, religious, and social evolution of these numerous
black urban communities is what differentiated those cities. *They were
not all alike in every economic, political, and cultural detail. Yet black
civil rights and political leaders even today continue to espouse "lead-*

*ership" pretensions just as if all these variegated black communities are
alike simply because they are all black!*

In the context of the accumulated northern black urbanization process
beginning in World War I, Harlem stands out as unique in more ways
than simply reflecting the outcome of West Indian median-income levels.
As James Weldon Johnson pointed out in 1930, Harlem, unlike any other
black community, became "more than a community," it became a *"large-
scale laboratory experiment in the race problem."* (Italics added.) Such
an assessment could not apply to Chicago, Detroit, Philadelphia, Washington, D.C., or Cleveland. It was no accident that the headquarters of
the NAACP and the National Urban League were in New York City,
with their main satellite branches in Harlem. It was no accident that the
world's largest aggregation of black history and cultural materials is not
in Chicago or Washington, D.C., but in Harlem, in the Schomburg
Library Collection. The Garvey movement could *not* have been launched
from, say, Kingston, Jamaica, because, for one thing, Jamaican black
entrepreneurial hopefuls were moving out in order to put, as Bonnett
indicates, their rotating credit associations to more effective use. They
put it to use in New York City, especially in Harlem. However, evidence
reveals that the Afro-American black middle class was in default in its
social obligations to seize the time to utilize its collective economic
resources cooperatively in Harlem, *even in its own economic and political
interests*. In New York City the established but penurious black middle
classes deeply resented the in-migration of the southern-bred blacks even
before black Harlem was created. Toward their own black workers and
peasants in Jamaica, the West Indian middle classes were just as intol-
erant, if not more so. Hence, the four-way class, color, and caste Afro-
American–West-Indian splits, divisions, factions, fusions, fights, fits and,
interethnic fustian. But because the West Indian black community was
considerably smaller, *it was also considerably better organized*, especially along the economic lines of the rotating credit associations. The
Harlem Afro-Americans, who were much more numerous, were, conversely, woefully lacking in any comparable economic cooperative organization. This lack led inexorably to an absence of *political organization*
among Afro-Americans.

If, as Bonnett suggests, the "already successful mulatto" West Indian middle class was more economically adroit in Harlem than the Afro-
American middle class, what, then, was wrong or perhaps inept about
Afro-American middle class economic enterprises? Bonnett argues that
the West Indian middle class at least set an organizational example for

its impoverished half brothers, the migrants to the United States, by
forming viable partnerships as a variation on the rotating credit method
of economic organization. What, then, was missing in the *social consciousness* of the Afro-American middle class (at all levels)? A number
of social and ideological characteristics were incompatible with its natural
class function of "leadership." Frazier generalized on these negative
characteristics:

> For example, a group isolated to the extent of the Negro in America
> could have developed cooperative enterprises. There has been no attempt
> in schools or otherwise to teach or encourage this type of economic
> organization. The ideal of the rich man has been held up to him. More
> than one Negro business has been wrecked because of this predatory
> view of economic activity.[109]

In fundamental terms of *black urban economics*, middle-class leadership has set few positive examples in social organization or influenced
working-class black Americans toward improving the organizational qualities of their lives. Such as assessment, of course, does not take into
account the role of the black church in influencing black social life.
Sowell, and others, have cited the striking differences between Afro-
American and West Indian family structures. Black family structure is a
key factor in maintaining cooperative economic organizations such as
rotating credit associations. And it is a matter of record substantiated by
more than mere "local gossip" or "home folklore" that the West Indian
family structure, unlike the Afro-American's, was patriarchal in the extreme. On the level of small-scale capital formation, family structure
becomes a key element for failure or success. David Lowenthal, whom
Bonnett cites regarding the economic successes of the rotating credit
associations, also presents a vivid portrayal of the patriarchal nature of
West Indian societies and West Indian families:

> Upbringing is felt to require physical chastisement; parents regularly
> resort to the rod. Outsiders may interpret frequent beatings as symptoms
> of parental insecurity, but West Indians consider them normal and ap-
> propriate. Flogging is considered essential not only for effective pun-
> ishment but for education; teachers vie with parents as disciplinarians.
> Beatings are no evidence of cruelty, opines a local authority: "People
> of nearly all classes in Jamaica . . . who are very violent with children
> at any other given moment are often at other times very loving and

warmhearted.'' West Indians also approve a show of authority from man to wife: ''They don't love you 'less they beat you,' '' as the saying goes. In New York, West Indian husbands a generation ago gained a reputation for savage cruelty; Harlemites wondered why their women put up with it. Black Americans continue to view West Indian families as ''slaves to the man of the house''; West Indians say that ''American Negroes do not discipline their children.''[110]

Another corollary to this assertion is that if Afro-American men do not (and cannot) control or discipline their children, *it means they cannot control their families and, ultimately, cannot control or discipline their women* (to the extent that West Indian men dominate their women). This fact is not refutable even as a generalization. Afro-American men of all classes may mistreat women, attempt to dominate them, may even succeed in dominating or ''disciplining'' them to a degree. However, generally speaking, *Afro-American men have never been able successfully to dominate and control Afro-American women because they never possessed either the social, economic, or political power to do so in American society*. This is one of the consequences of the slavery heritage that Sowell and others have suggested but have never fully admitted in slave-family studies. In addition to the ''myth of black business,'' Frazier highlighted the bases for the myths surrounding the so-called stability of black family life, and the tenor of male-female relationships within that context. In dissecting the elements of male-female relations in black middle-class life, Frazier pointed out:

There is much frustration among the black bourgeoisie despite their privileged position within the [separate black] world. . . . They cannot insulate themselves against the more subtle forms of racial discrimination. These discriminations cause frustrations in Negro men because they are not allowed to play the ''masculine role'' as defined by American culture. They cannot assert themselves or exercise power as white men do. . . . In the South, the middle-class Negro is not only prevented from playing a masculine role, but generally he must let Negro women assume leadership in any show of militancy. This reacts upon his status in the home where the tradition of female dominance, *which is widely established among Negroes, has tended to assign a subordinate role to the male. . . .*[111] (Italics added.)

In one degree or another, this male-female relationship is a conjugal factor present in *all* classes of the black American population as of the

1980s. Contrary to all the gender mythologies emanating from the feminist movement about the subordinate role of black women in a racist society, the main brunt of the physical, psychological, economic, emotional, and status denigration stemming from racial discrimination *is borne by the black male.* Moreover, in black group sociology, the problem of the "endangered black family"[112] undercuts all analyses, forecasts, and social programming regarding the future of black leadership in politics, economics, culture, and education from now until the year 2000. In West Indian family organizations, in the Caribbean or Harlem, rotating credit associations were successful to the degree that patriarchy could enforce or assure the economic cooperative effort necessary for the accumulation of small-scale capital formation. In Afro-American social life or social organization, no such economic cooperative organization could be either induced or enforced mainly because of the progressive breakdown of communal family life resulting from the mass migrations of southern blacks into northern cities during and after World War I. Added to the inherent contingency of the in-migration of southern blacks into New York City, Chicago, Detroit, Philadelphia, Cleveland, and other cities, it is safe to conclude that the indigenous and established northern-based black middle-classes of that era were not about to assume much economic, political, cultural, or social responsibility for the welfare of what they considered unwelcome additions from Georgia, Alabama, Mississippi, Arkansas, Louisiana, Oklahoma, etc. Thus, the in-migration drama of southern Afro-Americans and West Indians in Harlem had ramifications for the fate of "black cities" all over the United States. James Weldon Johnson wrote in 1925: "I believe that the Negro's advantages and opportunities are greater in Harlem than in any other place in the country, and that Harlem will become the intellectual, the cultural and the financial center for Negroes in the United States, and will exert a vital influence upon all Negro peoples."[113] *The financial center!*

James Weldon Johnson wrote his estimate of Harlem as a "financial center" in 1925, five years before the 1929 crash left the nation (and its black communities) in economic disarray. Thus, it is more than just random economic or ethnic sampling that conservative black economists in the 1980s select the economic performance of blacks (and black ethnics) in *one* community, Harlem, as the median-income gauge for American blacks all over the nation! Though in the 1920s blacks and the rest of the nation were riding the crest of an industrial and commercial boom, conservative economists in the 1980s discuss the rise or decline of ethnic median-income ratios *just as if the 1930s Depression decade never hap-*

pened. The New Deal ushered the federal power into the national economy with its retinue of alphabetized agencies—NRA, AAA, TVA, FERA, PWA, WPA, CCC,—aimed at rescuing the economy from culpable mismanagement by free enterprise and the free-market system. The need for the social engineering of the New Deal programs was *not* the fault of blacks' failures to maintain a high median-income level under the free-enterprise system, it was the innate failures of the free-market system itself to accommodate to black economic aspirations. Which, of course, raises the legitimate questions—How did American blacks make out? How did they fare in Harlem when presented with the almost unrestricted opportunity to make their entrepreneurial mark on what was described as the financial center of black America?

When an economic historian like Sowell compares West Indians' and American blacks' median income, he does not talk about Harlem in the same terms as Johnson did, i.e., Harlem as a black "financial capital" or, better, as a newly created black economic market. Despite Johnson's glowing assessments of Harlem as the possible financial center of black America, he had some lingering doubts about its future when he asked the vital question, Can the blacks hold Harlem, having gained population control over one of the most "beautiful and healthful sections of the city"?:

> [Harlem] is not a slum or a fringe. . . . There is nothing like it in any other city in the country, for there is no preparation for it; no change in the character of the houses and streets; no change indeed, in the appearance of the people except their color. . . . The Negroes of Harlem, for the greater part, worked and saved their money. . . . [Churches] set an example by purchasing [property]. . . . Buying property became a fever. . . . Often companies of a half dozen men combined to buy a house—these combinations were and still are generally made up of West Indians—and would produce five or ten thousand dollars to put through a deal. . . .[114]

The next forty or fifty years would demonstrate that Harlem blacks did not hold onto Harlem through economic control. And one of the key reasons they did not gain majority control of the totality of Harlem real estate was the insufficient corporate methods used, or *the absence of any corporate approach at all*. The West Indian writer Bonnett records that "West Indians would also *combine* to buy a house. Of the several corporations organized for this purpose, the Antillean Realty Company had holdings in excess of $750,000."[115] The word "combine" is a key to the failure of black American corporate endeavors. Frazier has pointed out that one of the negative "class traits" of the black middle class is an inability to *cooperate* toward any positive economic or political objective. Although Bonnett misquoted the facts and figures contained in his sources, he amply revealed that American black and West Indian entrepreneurs represented two divergent styles of black economic enterprise. Johnson wrote that when black real estate buying began to make itself felt in Harlem, corporations were organized for this purpose:

> Two of these, the Antillean Realty Company, composed of West Indian Negroes, and the Sphinx Securities Company, composed of American and West Indian Negroes, represent holdings amounting to approximately $750,000. Individual Negroes and companies in the South have invested in Harlem real estate. About two years ago a Negro institution in Savannah, Ga., bought a parcel for $115,000 which it sold a month or so ago at a profit of $110,000.[116]

Johnson noted also that the height of this black corporate accumulation of real estate in Harlem was 1920–1929, the period immediately following World War I, when the second major wave of West Indian immigration caused by the war had reached its peak. However, this accentuated wave of black corporate real estate accumulation took place *thirteen years after the collapse of the pioneer Afro-American Realty Company in 1908*. A thorough assessment as to why this truly pioneer black business enterprise collapsed has never been made. However, one study that offered a sketchy review of the financial operations of this company attributed its failures to "internal dissension," "fraudulent stock" promotion, "overextension of the company's holdings," and general opposition on the part of stockholders to the leadership of the company's board of directors. "The Realty Company promised the world and delivered little. It had hopefully been incorporated for fifty years, but folded after four. During its short and hectic existence it was wracked with internal dissension." However:

> The Afro-American Realty Company played a significant part in opening homes for Negroes in Harlem. Philip A. Payton, Jr., owned and managed apartment houses and brownstones in sections never previously rented to Negro tenants. His holdings were scattered throughout Harlem from One Hundred and Nineteenth to One Hundred and Forty-seventh Streets. When the company folded, white realtors and mortgagors took

over its property but the Negro tenants remained. The new owners
continued to advertise the Negro company's former houses in the colored
press. The speculations of Philip A. Payton, Jr., led to the downfall of
the Afro-American Realty Company, but they also helped lay the foundations of the largest Negro ghetto in the world.[117]

No mean accomplishment! The historian who wrote this, forty years
after the Harlem events of the 1920s depicted by Johnson, was describing
the "making of a ghetto," but Harlem was not then a ghetto but a choice
residential quarter. Although racially segregated, it was an ideal black
community that became a ghetto because of overcrowding and gross
physical neglect. However, the West Indians or other Caribbean immigrants never loudly complained that Harlem was a ghetto or that it was
the consequence of racial segregation; neither did the working-class blacks.
This baleful complaint came from representatives of the American black
middle class, their professionals, and their leadership spokesmen as represented in the ruling echelons of the NAACP.

In the 1980s it can truly be said that the blacks have lost Harlem,
as Johnson feared in 1925. *But why?* Because of the irresponsibility, the
organizational incompetence, the ideological disaffections, in sum, the
failure of the black middle class to give leadership. These defaults in
black economic (also political) organization represent the hallmarks of
the failures of the black middle class and its professionals. In varying
black urban contexts across the nation, these middle-class leadership
defaults are duplicated. Chicago, of course, was an exception in that it
set a superior example of political organization, but Harlem failed abys-
mally to realize Johnson's hopes as the *financial center* of black America.
One cannot, of course, discount the terrible economic impact of the 1930s
on the economic fortunes of black Harlem (as both Sowell and Williams
are prone to do in their economic analyses). However, the steady economic and political decline of Harlem as the Cultural Capital of the Black
World was not offset by the economic activities of West Indian or Afro-
American black business entrepreneurs. The economic, political, physical, and sociological decline of black Harlem reached its nadir in the
Sixties. By the Seventies, Harlem confronted its most denigrating negation of community pride rooted in the seventy-year-old traditions connected with its birth as the most important black urban community in the
entire world. *By the Seventies, Korean small-business entrepreneurs were
moving into Harlem and taking over every available commercial access
to profiteering off Harlem as a black economic market. Also during the*

Seventies, even newly arrived Africans from poverty-stricken nations were openly ridiculing New York blacks—American blacks—for crying the civil rights blues while having failed organizationally to make the most of the opportunities that had been offered by the free-market capitalist system.

Today, the black neoconservative economics school of Thomas Sowell can place the blame for the malaise of *all* blacks *on them* in their competitive race with the ethnics for economic, professional, and even educational rewards in the free-market system. For Sowell *blacks were not entrepreneurial enough.* At the other extreme, E. Franklin Frazier ridiculed all black pretensions to black business as "over-rated exaggerations" and an unadulterated "social myth," insofar as it was assumed that black business enterprise could solve, for blacks, the problem of racial discrimination. Thus, American blacks in the 1980s are caught between two widely divergent schools of economic thought on just how the largest nonwhite minority is to achieve what the liberal consensus terms median-income parity with the grand majority white population. The Sowell school argues that government programs will not, cannot do the job, thus exit civil rights as the cure for economic ills. Frazier's position implied that only through the continuing integration of blacks into the various employment categories of the corporate private sector, the governmental public service sector, and, perhaps, the democratically administered trade-union sector would blacks have the remotest chance to overcome the effects of racial discrimination in economic life.

One theory that is definitely out of consideration is the solution for black economic disadvantages long trumpeted by the radical left, *socialism.* Aside from the average black being so saturated with the values of economic individualism that socialistic ideas are as foreign as unemployment benefits are to an African tribesman in Tanzania, the Reaganite political revolution of 1980 was partially inspired by the notion that civil rights-sponsored government programs were perilously akin to federally administered socialism.

All of which leads to the third critical black economic assumption. The comparisons between West Indian American and Afro-American organizational behavior, the median-income ratios argued by Sowell, Williams, and Bonnett point to one conclusion: Unlike the West Indians, Japanese, and Jews, American blacks failed to adopt and master the ethnic-group techniques of *economic cooperative organization.* What Bonnett described as the origins of West Indian rotating credit associations had counterparts that the Japanese, Chinese, and Jews brought to the

United States as a part of their immigrant cultural baggage.[118] This, of course, takes the issue of economic cooperative organization among Afro-Americans back to the 1920s, back to the legal, economic, and racial events surrounding the Phillips County, Arkansas, race riot that culminated in the civil rights victory of *Moore* v. *Dempsey* of 1923. There, it was shown that racism, racial discrimination plus the southern imperatives of the free-market system, successfully thwarted black attempts to organize the Progressive Farmers and Household Union of America, an economic cooperative. Phillips County reflected the racial and economic tenor that prevailed in all the southern states. Even in the less racially restricted northern states, neither the NAACP nor the National Urban League (nor the black church) was able or willing to extend much, if any, leadership guidance in this important field of black economic cooperative survival.[119] Frazier described black American business and entrepreneurship as unschooled, predatory, and exploitative. Hence, the "social myth" of black business: *But what is left?*

In the foreseeable future (let us say until the year 2000) black Americans, with or without civil rights reinforcements, must strive to survive economically within the "rules of the game" of free-enterprise, free-market American capitalism. The dominant white American economics ideology will neither foster nor sanction any other form of national economic organization (whether the political ideology is Democratic, Republican, or "Liberal"). Another feature of the nagging debate on black economics and racial discrimination is that Sowell, Williams, and even Frazier play down the factor of the sheer numbers, the millions that make up the black population (compared with the West Indians, Japanese, and Jews). Although Bonnett can argue in the 1980s for a reevaluation of economic self-help institutions among black immigrants because it "brings a present perspective to what is an ongoing and still useful and much needed association for people still lingering under the very real social and economic handicaps," it might also be argued that *for blacks it might be much too late*. For the overwhelming majority of blacks, integration since the *Brown* decision has meant very little either socially or economically. However, enough upwardly mobile economic integration has taken place since the Fifties to create a very substantial and enlarged middle class. As Frazier pointed out:

> The employment of Negroes in the field of marketing or distribution by large American corporations is a phase of the integration of the Negro into American life.[120]

This was, however, the process of class integration, and Frazier wrote the above in 1957. By the 1980s the impact of political Reaganomics would begin to threaten even the economic gains of the new black middle class. For the black lower classes, economic survival becomes problematic, tentative, and unpredictable as the national economy attempts to shift its corporate gears, its private and public economic sectors, back toward the pre-New Deal era of an unrestricted free-market economy. In the process the purely "group" economic aspect of black survival is in extreme jeopardy resulting from exacerbated class divisions engendered by economic integration. Because of this widened economic class division, the Seventies thrust toward organizational expressions of the "politics of black ethnicity" was compromised at the outset by ideological divisions in black politics. The politics of ethnicity is more exactly the "politics of plurality." The demise of the civil rights era, beginning with 1980, points to political organization as the only alternative. Political organization also permits a renewed opportunity to make up for long-standing *organizational* deficiencies that have hampered black progress in economic, cultural, educational, and other social fields.

The entire seventy-year social process following the mass migration and northern urbanization of blacks since World War I created the "Crisis in Negro Leadership." It has also been a social process during which blacks, in the aggregate, have failed to master the art of *cooperation,* or cooperative methods of social organization. This overall failure is attributable to the nature and composition of *black leadership.*

PART SIX

If the black Seventies witnessed the shift from the politics of civil rights to the politics of black ethnicity, the advent of the Reagan administration in 1980 revealed that the black political leadership had failed to make the most of the potential that had accumulated up to the end of the Carter regime. During the Seventies the creation of an independent black political party became more than obligatory. The political leadership, however, accomplished nothing more than three half-hearted attempts by way of three political conventions. These conventions were staged in Gary, Indiana, 1972; Little Rock, Arkansas, 1974; Cincinnati, Ohio, 1976. Organized under the sponsorship of the National Black Political Convention, which developed out of the National Black Political Assembly, these conventions were advertised as vehicles for launching a *national independent black political party*. Had this party indeed been launched, it would have laid a political groundwork that would, in turn, have given Jesse Jackson's presidential candidacy bid of 1984 much more impact than it did. However, an independent black political party was not established in the Seventies.

From the point of view of black politics per se, this failure to carry out the threat to organize a black independent party is significant. Before 1972 two attempts had been made to establish such an independent black party, once in 1960 and again in 1964, when the Freedom Now Party nearly made the grade but collapsed. During the 1960 Kennedy-Nixon campaign, *the Afro-American Party was launched and actually got on the ballot in a few states,* but it disappeared after the Kennedy victory. The real story behind the launching of the Afro-American Party, the reasons it was launched, and why it disappeared from contention has never been told.[1]

The idea of creating a black political party was not new, even in 1960. By the time of the Gary, Indiana, convention of 1972, the idea was fifty-six years old, having been first clearly expressed in 1916 by W.E.B. Du Bois. The intervening years made it clear to black leaders, especially in the North, that a "Crisis in Negro Leadership" had developed:

> There is for the future one and only one effective political move for [black] voters. We have long foreseen it, but we have sought to avoid it. . . . But self-defense knows no nice hesitations. The American Negro must either vote as a unit or continue to be politically emasculated as at present. . . . The situation is this: At present the Democratic Party can maintain its ascendancy only with the help of the Solid South. The Solid South is built on the hate and fear of Negroes; . . . The Republican Party is the party of wealth and big business and, as such, is the natural enemy of the humble working people who compose the mass of Negroes. Between these two great parties, as parties, there is little to choose. On the other hand, parties are represented by individual candidates. [Blacks] can have a choice and they can vote for or against them. Their only effective method in the future is to organize in every congressional district as a Negro [Black] Party to endorse those candidates . . . whose promises or past performances give greatest hope for remedying the wrongs done the [Blacks]. If no candidate fills this bill they should nominate a candidate of their own and give that candidate their solid vote. This policy effectively and consistently carried out throughout the United States, North and South, by [black] voters who refuse the bribe of petty office and money, would make the [black] vote one of the most powerful and effective of the group votes in the United States.
>
> This is the program which we must follow. We may hesitate and argue about it, but if we are a sensible, reasonable people we will come to it and the quicker the better.[2]

Black political spokesmen and political scientists who in the Seventies were hailing the arrival of the politics of black ethnicity, were ahistorical enough not to have made reference to the above remarks by one of their most highly praised Elder Statesmen! If Du Bois's description of the relationship of blacks to both the Democratic and the Republican parties in 1916 carries a familiar 1970–1980 political flavor, it only means that for blacks, the more things (political) change, the more they remain the same. However, the issue of the black political party was raised in 1916 at a time when black loyalties were going through a highly ambiguous reevaluation. Traditional loyalties to the Republican party, the party of Lincoln, were being questioned by an increasing number of black voters. But not until Roosevelt's second-term reelection in 1936 did blacks switch loyalties en masse to the Democratic party. This black–Democratic party alliance would endure until the 1980s.

The core issue that represented the binding glue for the black–Democratic party alliance was civil rights. More than that, for forty-eight years the Democrats remained the chief proponents of the federally sponsored programs legislated for bettering the economic, social, educational, and other conditions of the underprivileged classes and special interests like labor. This legislative tradition in support of government programs led eventually to Democratic party sponsorship of civil rights programs. In the transition from civil rights to party politics, however, an aspect of the black civil rights–Democratic party alliance that was rendered passé and obsolete was "clientage politics":

Clientage politics and the civil rights movement were essentially two parts of the same political process—a process of black dependency on white friends. They differed in that clientage politics was usually limited to an individual (a clergyman, a doctor, a lawyer, an educator) whereas civil rights politics assumed a more institutional form, through an organization with a permanent staff, a budget, a political manifesto, and an ideological elan. Of course, this classification is not perfect. Some Negro clientage politicians also functioned within organizations, especially within middle class Negro professional and civic associations. And at the same time Negro clientage politicians sought, in their own way, the goals of civil rights organizations—namely, the reduction of explicit restraints imposed by whites on black access to the institutions of American society.[3]

However, the civil rights institutional formations, such as the NAACP and the National Urban League, differed from being purely clientage leadership in that they were "general purpose organizations serving the needs and concerns of Negroes in education, housing, public accommodations, employment, medicine and health. Unlike Negro clientage politicians, the civil rights bureaucracy dealt directly and explicitly with white racist constraints on Negro needs in these fields."[4]

Yet "the achievements of the civil rights movement and its leadership in the 1960's—still the preeminent political leadership among Negroes in that decade—had unintended consequences. The movement's success in stimulating a massive presence of the federal government in the affairs of Negroes—especially the affairs of that 40 percent of the Negroes who were poor and lower class—created a situation in which the Negro's appetite was whetted for further changes."[5] But *what* changes? *"Where do we Go from here?,"* as Martin Luther King, Jr., put it. The change *had* to be *political* both in form and content, *there was nothing else*. Unfortunately, the changes that were so avidly sought were taking place in the broader white society *outside of* and *beyond* black society. It was not generally understood that a *prior* set of changes of an *organizational* character had to occur *within* the black group itself. Despite the handwriting on the walls of the capital that the era of civil rights ascendancy was ending, the black civil rights leadership still could not shift gears and divest itself of its sixty-year-old heritage. This leadership, which had been accurately described as the leadership of clientage politics, did not measure up to the demands of a political leadership. Nevertheless, the emergence of the politics of black ethnicity did inspire a new turn in black political orientation. "As political leaders, however, civil rights leaders lacked the authority and influence—the political clout—that could sustain and increase federal efforts to meet the massive social-economic needs of blacks. In American politics, this kind of political authority is accorded only to elected politicians. The organization of civil rights leadership outside party politics—and thus outside the competition for elected office—prevented this leadership from achieving the most legitimate type of American political leadership." An important result is that:

> The political history of American blacks since the middle 1960's is in large part the history of the new Afro-American political class; the black elected official or party politician. The emergence of this new class is closely linked with the politization of the American Negro's ethnic experiences. Politization facilitates what can be called the vertical integration of an ethnic group's social structure, reducing the normally sharp status and class cleavages within an ethnic group.[6]

By the mid-Seventies, this "vertical integration" resulted in the creation of some three thousand black elected politicians, most of whom lived outside the South. These politicians were found in 41 of the 50 states. They included 15 congressmen; over 170 state legislators; over 50 mayors in cities such as Cleveland, Newark, Gary, Raleigh, Atlanta, and Los Angeles; nearly 600 city officials; and nearly 500 school board officials. At that time, they made up almost 1 percent of all elected officials nationally. This elected vanguard of the new "Afro-American political class," as it was called, would enhance the new era of the politics of black ethnicity. *This political development would, for all general-purposes, render the social roles of the NAACP and the National Urban League obsolete.* In fact, in the middle of the Seventies, the NAACP experienced its first serious internal organizational crisis since the Du Bois debate of 1934. In the same way that Martin Luther King could not come to terms with the political and economic implications of Black Power, the NAACP and the NUL could not make the transition from either civil rights or clientage politics to the imperatives of the politics of ethnicity. During the sixty years of northern urbanization, black political development had been neglected:

> The worst aspect of this neglect was that, for the first five years of this century, the black elites and the black middle-class were deprived of the power inducements provided by city political machines. Whereas city machines helped the elites among the Irish, Poles, Jews, Italians and other white ethnic groups to establish an effective political organization of their communities by transforming their voters into cannon-fodder for city machines, the black bourgeoisie was not induced to exert its leadership skills and institutions to politicize the Negro lower strata in order to bring black votes to the service of city machines.[7]

But, historically, the politization and economic organization of the black lower strata were two sides of the same civil rights coin, or two parts of the same, generic failures of the black elite leadership. The NAACP, which could not, or would not, attempt the economic cooperative organization of blacks in the 1930s, proved incapable of organizing blacks politically in the 1970s. Even the political resurgence of the white ethnics in the Seventies could not move the NAACP to reexamine its traditional policies. The association, still fixated on the ideals of non-economic liberalism that sanctioned its birth in 1910, failed to confront the fact that the very successes of its long civil rights crusade during the 1960s had rendered its programmatic existence almost obsolete and canceled out its organizational *raison d'être*. Having been, since the New Deal, clients of the Democratic party, neither the NAACP nor the NUL could face the *political* fact that the party of Roosevelt had by 1968 fulfilled its civil rights mission on behalf of blacks to the fullest constitutional and statutory limits of the Fourteenth Amendment. From that point on, the civil rights agenda would increasingly become the "Lost Priority." "What happened to the civil rights movement in America?" one articulate white liberal spokesman asked in all sincerity in 1970.[8] Among his several answers to this American minority-group contingency was that:

> The basic trouble was never "the system" as many blacks and white radicals contended. It was the prevailing attitudes of the people in a democracy. One of the negative attitudes of the late 1960's was the absence of a sense of history and identity and continuity. . . .[9]

Americans generally (both black and white) had very little sense of history—the true history of the black struggle for parity beginning with the collapse of Reconstruction. But the accumulated consequences of these black failures to achieve racial parity left an almost indelible mark on blacks themselves:

> Paradoxically the Negro is struck with his whiteness, not his blackness. It is a cultural and historical fact which cannot be denied or ignored— it can only be dealt with on a basis which will allow Negro society to get "moving again" culturally and emotionally Understanding and helping to alter this destructive whiteness within the Negro—by external social action, a change of public attitude and the kinds of relations which may alter this destructive white image—is basic to any approach to better race relations. Society needs to provide a more compassionate image of the world for the Negro to internalize and to help directly in the process of altering that image on the inside.[10]

Which was, of course, precisely what the Supreme Court *Brown* decision of 1954 failed to do, thereby setting the civil rights movement on a studied course that led inevitably to its programmatic impasse by 1970. The Supreme Court could not understand, in contemplating its *Brown* decision, that its historical role *should* have been to frame its judicial decisions in such a way as to pave the road for the black minority to function more effectively in a racially, ethnically, politically, and culturally plural society. Racial integration in the public school systems would not alter one whit the essentially plural nature of American society, nor result in any greater degree of melting-pot fusion of races, ethnic groups, or cultures in the United States of 1980 than in 1930. The political, economic, cultural, and even educational implications of the American plural imperatives were beyond the juridical purview of the nine justices who voted unanimously in favor of the *Brown* decision. *One* consequence of this, and there were several, was that by the Seventies the NAACP was incapable of reorienting its program to conform to the politics of black ethnicity. The Black Power and "black consciousness" movements of the Sixties were actually *minority* viewpoints within the majority civil rights sentiments inspired by the NAACP.

As gestures toward meeting the organizational demands of the new political age of the Seventies, the three black conventions held in Gary, Little Rock, and Cincinnati became the most significant indicators just how far the new Afro-American political class would go toward fulfilling the potentials of the politics of black ethnicity. Crucially, *they would not establish an independent black political party*. As a matter of "political" fact, these black conventions were formal inspirational responses to the Voting Rights Act of 1965, which led to voter-registration drives in the southern states. This stepped-up enfranchisement of southern black voters had a spill-over effect in not only enhancing southern black electoral participation, but also increasing northern black political activity to the extent of phenomenally increasing black elected officials (BEOs) in the North and West. Hence, a most extraordinary increase occurred in the number of BEOs that had not been seen in the United States since the heyday of Reconstruction. Having nothing else left of a dwindling "civil rights" persuasion on its agenda, the NAACP joined in with belated support to up the body count in registering black voters in the South. The association could risk this most "political" adventure without the least threat of the charge that the NAACP was at last disavowing the politically nonpartisan image it had striven for so many decades to maintain. But in terms of resurgent black enfranchisement:

> Higher levels of registration and voting, made possible by the Act of 1965, have been responsible for the sizable increases in the number of black elected officials: in the period from 1969 to 1974, there has been an increase in the total number of black elected officials from 1,185 to 2,991, an increase of 152 percent. Most of this increase, again, is reflected in the gains made in the South.[11]

However, the rising number of black elected officials hastened the formation of new black political organizations:

Several organizations have developed in consonance with the rise of the black elected official; *they embody the continuing collective search for institutions that will provide a basis for the exercise of effective black power. As such, they are the heirs to the movements of the 1960's.*[12] (Italics added.)

These new black political institutions included the National Black Caucus of Local Elected Officials, which operated within the framework of the National League of Cities. Next most important was the Congressional Black Caucus (CBC), formed in January 1969, when there were seven black members in the House of Representatives. By 1974 there were sixteen blacks in the House and one black senator (the first since Reconstruction).

When the CBC was born in 1969, it enthusiastically championed its role as the only legitimate organized national political spokesman for the black community, and it developed this role quickly, forcefully and visibly.[13]

However, the Congressional Black Caucus found itself unable to maximize its assumed role as an "organized national political spokesman." Without a doubt, such a political role on a national scale was an obligatory development growing out of the Sixties, but a purely political leadership is insufficient unless backed up by other institutional forms of social organization. Inasmuch as blacks were functionally poor in the necessary institutional forms, other than those of civil rights, black political leverage during the Seventies would be limited to the pragmatic necessities of electoral politics. The arrival of the black political Seventies found blacks nationwide lacking in the economic, social, and cultural institutions necessary to supplement the limited degree of electoral leverage won during the Seventies. Because of this failing, the Congressional Black Caucus was forced to limit its role to a purely legislative one. And this legislative role was influenced by the CBC's being trapped within the political agenda of the Democratic party.

Having pushed civil rights legislation to its outer social limits, the Democratic party had nothing else to offer blacks but good will and some moral support in memory of Martin Luther King. During the Seventies, the most basic pressing issue facing at least half the black population was economic, or to state it constitutionally, the translation of "civil rights" to "economic rights." Civil rights legislation had implied that the equal protection clause of the Fourteenth Amendment could be stretched to guarantee equal economic opportunity enforceable by federal power. To maintain its New Deal heritage as the political champion of black progress, the Democratic party had no choice but to support the economic goal of "full employment." So full-employment legislation became the main platform issue relative to the cause of blacks. Thus, the Congressional Black Caucus could do substantially little other than to champion full-employment legislation, but only such as conformed to the already established economic priorities of the Democratic party. This kind of legislative work, admirably performed by the CBC, involved tax reforms, saving the Office of Economic Opportunity (OEO), and revenue-sharing. The foreign policy issue, that was declared of special interest to blacks was, of course, the United States' policy toward Africa, which begs further clarification and debate, but is not subject to analysis here. In sum, the Congressional Black Caucus's main contribution was the Humphrey-Hawkins Full Employment and Balanced Growth Act. There the political leverage of the Congressional Black Caucus stopped. The Humphrey-Hawkins bill eventually passed, but its passage did not, could not, stem the rising levels of black unemployment. One critic implied in 1974 that because the Congressional Black Caucus lacked the resources to continue to develop its legislation aspirations, "it, indeed, inferred a lack of policy and a clear direction,"[14] which, of course, was true in a most profound and prophetic sense. Similar to all the transient spokesmen and ideologues of the Sixties and the Seventies, the Congressional Black Caucus would also inherit the ongoing consequences of the 1920s "Crisis in Negro Leadership."

Following the creation of the Congressional Black Caucus in 1969, the impact of the new class of black elected officials, inspired by the burgeoning movement of black political ethnicity, had produced not only the National Black Political Assembly, but by 1972 had launched the National Black Political Convention movement. This movement staged its first black political convention at Gary, Indiana, in 1972, "amidst the high aspirations of 8000 national delegates that was to be the birth of a new political force in America."

The convention produced a national black political agenda, a document that reflected the militant and substantive issues of the convention, as the basis on which black and white politicians would bargain for black votes. This process, however, was not followed because part of the convention leadership bolted prematurely in the direction of George

McGovern during the 1972 presidential campaign, leaving the agenda
an almost meaningless instrument of political strategy.[15]

The basic reason for this convention's failure was that the black
political convention movement promised to produce an *independent black
political party* (something that no single nonwhite minority in the United
States could even contemplate doing!), which was the only logical reason
for calling a black political convention. Such a bold, independent step
meant breaking with the Democratic party, however, which black elected
officials had little intention of doing. For this reason, the black political
conventions of 1972, 1974, and 1976 were poorly attended by the new
black elected officials.

The eight thousand delegates at Gary arrived expecting, no doubt,
that an independent party would be launched, but it was not to be. Why?
The reasons were numerous, and also compelling: 1. An independent
black political party would have smacked of separatism, which functionally was an unsound political position to pursue. However, an independent
black political party *should* have been perceived as a *plural* imperative,
rather than a separatist proposition. 2. Nothing resembling a majority
consensus existed that an independent black political party was either
necessary, or advisable, or even possible. 3. At these black political
conventions there was abject fear of the political consequences of breaking
cleanly away from the Democratic party. 4. There was also an instinctive
recognition that the difficulties confronting the potential organizers of
such a venture were near-insurmountable. 5. *Lastly, some of the participants had to be influenced by the long-standing dictum upheld by the
American two-party system that the "Third Party" idea was an* a priori
impossibility.

What was transpiring during the Seventies indicated that *the only
force capable of dismantling the structure of the two-party system was
the black political constituency.* But in the Seventies, the long-standing
"Crisis in Negro Leadership" was still vividly evident. To have launched
an independent black (Third) political party would require the kind of
daring, insight, skill, and imagination that the new black elected officials
did not possess. A *theoretical* Third Party in the United States would
have had to be a movement of several independent parts, a *coalition* of
independent components anchored around an organized base. The total
political history of the United States, comprising the politics of race,
ethnicity, region, (geography, class, and demography) indicated in the
Seventies that the Third Party had to be built around a solid base—*of*

the largest nonwhite minority in the United States. Not until 1984 would this seminal idea appear on the political horizon, and then only in embryonic form. Jesse Jackson's Rainbow Coalition was merely a germinal conceptualization of a Third Party political movement. However, trapped within the confines of the Democratic party like his predecessors of the Sixties, Jackson had no choice but to subordinate his Rainbow Coalition to the electoral destinies of the Democratic party. Thus, the Rainbow Coalition was not a bona fide political movement but an unrealized political idea to be squandered in the presidential futilities of an already lost Democratic party cause.

However, Jesse Jackson had no option but to seize the opportunity to parade the mere symbolism of the possibility of a black president of the United States for the real and intrinsic political substance lying fallow beneath the popular imagery of the Jackson campaign sensationalized by the media (and, of course, championed by blacks themselves in the pre-election spectacle of grasping at political straws). Given the programmatic deadlock of the American two-party system, the presidency is an office whose leadership capabilities are severely restricted. The American executive is trapped and immobilized between the contending issues of the politics and economics of liberalism and conservatism. The national economy founders in the administrative embrace of functional disarray, while blind economic forces drift further and further from political control. In such a situation, the presidency becomes the office of a chief caretaker whose politics become a "holding action" of programmatic expediency. It therefore no longer matters very much who is president—a Democrat or a Republican; a libertarian or an anarchist; a black or a white; a male or a female; a liberal or a conservative; a middle-aged neoconservative or a liberal septuagenarian. For a Jesse Jackson to have contended for the presidential candidacy (the race factor aside) was but a footnote to the political drama of two-party systemic insolvency. The Democratic party had nothing to offer blacks but the empty promise to defend the civil rights gains already won from being whittled away. Jesse Jackson, in turn, had nothing to offer the Democrats to save the party of Roosevelt and Truman from being the party of past accomplishments and good intentions. The Democratic party leadership, considering the black vote already bought and paid for, did not feel obligated even to make the purely symbolic gesture of offering Jackson the equally symbolic office of the vice-presidency.

The meteoric rise and passage of Jackson's political charisma, however, was like the finale of a political drama whose main plot had an irresolute dénouement. In the rough-and-tumble world of presidential politics, Jesse Jackson was a contender without a track record, an aspirant lacking a genuine political base, devoid of a politically equipped army. If between 1972 and 1984 the new political class, the black elected officials, had supported the black independent political party movement, and had created even the mere structural format for such a party, Jesse Jackson's Rainbow Coalition would at least have had the core of a prepared black political base. *It has now become a manifest political truism (not accepted by political science, of course) that a truly viable Third Party movement in the United States has to be structured around a black political base.* A number of historical antecedents and contemporary exigencies give political legitimacy to this point of view. Important here are the two pre-Seventies attempts at black Third Party organization, the Afro-American Party of 1960 and the Freedom Now Party of 1964, both of which failed. More important, however, not only has the flag of the independent black political party been waved several times during the twentieth century, but the "balance of power" potential of the black population has been a well-gnawed bone of political contention since Reconstruction. Black disfranchisement in the South, as well as tight machine control of the black vote in the North, have been rooted in the morbid fears of organized black political independence in whatever degree of expression.

However, it would not be true to political history to assert that either the Republicans or the Democrats have *not,* in some phase of their history, been supportive of black interests or sources of considerable political patronage. To Frederick Douglass in the late nineteenth century, the "Republican Party is the Ship, all else is the open sea." It cannot be claimed that the Democratic party has not served the economic, political, social, educational, and cultural interests of blacks to the limits of its programmatic capabilities, within the contexts of the Roosevelt, Truman, Kennedy, Johnson, and Carter regimes. However, the Democratic party's programmatic potential to champion the social causes of blacks reached its constitutional and legislative zenith during the 1960s. By the arrival and departure of the Carter administration, the Democratic party's ability to extend or transcend its achievements on behalf of purely black causes began to falter, and clear signs of a rift between blacks (that is, black leaders) and the Democrats began to appear. Caught in a vortex of contending domestic and foreign policy issues, the "civil rights" of the Sixties were internationalized by Carter into a "human rights" crusade. Political morality in foreign policy became an issue of international concern for the United States following the moral debacle of the Vietnam War. This moral dilemma trapped Martin Luther King. President Carter, the last Democratic party hope for the black cause of the Seventies, was also a victim of the same moral dilemma in political terms. By 1979 an open break between Carter and the black leadership loomed in response to the president's new budget proposals, which promised to undercut, if not negate, any executive support for what black leaders viewed as the urgencies connected with the Humphrey-Hawkins full-employment bill. The Congressional Black Caucus declared an all-out fight against Carter's proposed budget cuts affecting the poor (that is, specifically blacks). One prominent CBC member declared, "We are trying to help Carter save the presidency from self-destruction." A well-known black journalist described the Carter–Democratic party situation in 1979: ". . . The [congressional] black caucus and black leadership throughout the land are faced with an immense contradiction. And they know it."

. . . They must publicly oppose Carter even with the prospect of a very low black voter turnout for the 1980 elections. The trend is not good. Less than 35 percent of black registered voters went to the polls in 1978. Despite the fact that blacks gave Carter 93 percent of their ballots in 1976, black registration and election day activity were disappointing.[16]

In other words, the waning months of the Carter administration represented the last stand of the Democratic party as the political vehicle for black advances. Said one important black congressman: "There must be an alternative to Carter without going Republican."[17] But the question was, Where to after a break with Carter? And the answer was: *Politically, blacks had nowhere to go!* Trapped in the perennial two-party tug-of-war, blacks were back in the political predicament of 1916 out of which grew the "Crisis in Negro Leadership" of 1920. But America and the blacks of 1920 was not the America and the blacks of 1980. Volumes of evolutionary social, political, and economic history would transpire over the ensuing six decades. Blacks of the 1920s possessed a social consciousness uninfluenced by the New Deal program of the welfare state, reinforced by the philosophy of a political party whose guiding principle of government was that the federal power had the obligation to guarantee the economic, social, and political well-being of the underprivileged. The high point of this federal commitment to such a brand of social engineering arrived during the Sixties and carried over into the

Seventies—the decade of the new black politics, the politics of black ethnicity.

But the new era of black politics, ironically, arrived at the beginning of the end of the age of civil rights ascendancy. The Democratic party's effective civil rights advocacy was ending, although the NAACP and the National Urban League could not accept this factor in the future course of federal social policy. If the higher echelons of black leadership could not face this reality, lower-echelon black political spokesmen sensed the significance of the shift during the Nixon administration. This recognition was evident when observers described the black political reaction as the shift "from civil rights to party politics: the black political transition." Out of necessity, the new era of the politics of black ethnicity had a potential for black political mobilization as the only means to safeguard the limited civil rights legislation of the Sixties. However, this new era of political mobilization occurred within the tactical strategies related to black loyalties to the Democratic party. This meant that black political mobilization did not translate into independent black politics but blacks gained an enhanced voice in shaping Democratic party policies. This strategy was based on what the Seventies revealed as a political illusion. The Democratic party coalition grounded in the New Deal heritage—the continuum of labor, social welfare, the Great Society, and civil rights— became progressively a coalition in political disarray. After forty years, Roosevelt's New Deal was running out of vitality and losing its national power to persuade. In fact, the Democratic party was running out of goals that had not already been won.

Thus, the growing Democratic party debacle was leaving the black civil rights leadership stranded on the shoals of a civil rights program the achievements of which had, by the Seventies, become programmatically redundant. This leadership, composed prominently of lawyers, could not deal perceptively with the inherent limitations of the Fourteenth Amendment; nor could it alter its sights enough to take advantage of the implicit options of the Fifteenth Amendment by way of the Voting Rights Act of 1965. Although throughout the Seventies the NAACP concentrated on supporting voter-registration drives among blacks in the North, South, and West, it did so because it had little else of real consequence to push.

In 1972, however, the NAACP exerted its influence to dash cold water on the implied political aims of the National Black Political Convention movement. Here was a case in which traditional civil rights leadership could not read the clear writing on the crumbling walls of the Great Society of the Sixties, nor the political consequences for blacks that would follow the Nixon administration's Republicanism of the Seventies. The NAACP boasts even today that politically it is a nonpartisan organization. But in March 1972, the NAACP stated that the draft preamble of the National Political Agenda to be adopted by the National Black Political Convention was at odds with the NAACP's basic principles. Whether or not the conveners of the National Black Political Convention actually *sought* the approval of the NAACP beforehand is not known. However, when the convention stated in part, "We begin here and now in Gary. We begin with an independent political movement, an independent Black Political Agenda," the NAACP objected by way of memorandum to the conveners. The association objected on the grounds that the National Black Political Convention spelled out "its separatist and nationalist intent by specific calls for black control of all the economic, social and political agencies, undertakings and institutions presently to be found in the black communities and neighborhoods. At almost no point does the Agenda also demand an equitable share of control in institutions and agencies now controlled by whites." In emphatically opposing the agenda of the National Black Political Convention, the NAACP declared:

Our action is taken primarily because of a difference in ideology as to how to win equality for the Negro minority in the United States.[18]

And that was, and is, the crux of the black leadership crisis today and yesterday. The famous Du Bois–NAACP split of 1934 was being reiterated on another level of debate, under political, economic, and social conditions that Du Bois could have imagined but did not experience. In retrospect, from 1934 to 1965, the NAACP can be excused and even championed for its insistence on the primacy of its ideology. At that moment in history, its sixty-two-year-old struggle against segregation and racial discrimination had been waged on purely constitutional grounds. But after the national judiciary and the legislature had removed all legal and semilegal supports for segregation and discrimination in the Sixties, the NAACP's program became increasingly irrelevant in the Seventies. The NAACP was being pushed by the combined dynamics of social reform to become a programmatic anachronism.

Thus, it was no accident in the NAACP's long struggle for the legitimacy of its constitutional reforms in race relations that an internecine power struggle erupted within its top echelons in 1983, the third year of the Reagan administration. The attempt by the NAACP's national chairman, duly elected, to oust the national executive director, duly elected, was symptomatic of the NAACP's arrival at the first stage of its functional obsolescence as the main traditional civil rights organization. It was the first major outbreak of internal strife since the Du Bois–NAACP controversy of 1934. At that time, only the New Deal saved the organization and legitimized its program for the next fifty years. With the arrival of the Reagan administration came the first concerted political assault on the federally sponsored social welfare–social reform administrative infrastructure established by the New Deal and defended by successive Democratic party regimes. Despite being increasingly beset by problems of dwindling membership, inadequate staff, decreased funding, and internal disorganization, the NAACP leadership could not read the message clearly written on the walls of the federal establishment in Washington, D.C. While announcing frantic shifts in strategy in the search for new directions in civil rights programming, the NAACP leadership could not understand the historic, political, and also constitutional significance of Reaganism. Reaganism personified the political vanguard not only against the federal role in defense of civil rights enforcements but also against federal sponsorship of economic-support supplements in civil rights advocacy. Thus, the futile NAACP attack on Reagan and Reaganism was like condemning political agnosticism for being devoid of the Christian morality of a Martin Luther King. At that moment, none other than Kenneth B. Clark, one of the main architects of the sociological arguments in support of the 1954 *Brown* decision, declared that unless the NAACP returned to the policies, principles, and clarity of leadership that had made it effective in the past, it could have no value in the present and future struggle for racial justice. Kenneth B. Clark said that the NAACP, as an organization, was "verging on irrelevance."[19]

Coming from a spokesman such as Kenneth B. Clark, these were fateful assertions. The NAACP could *not* return to *past* policies and principles to regain clarity of leadership in the present and future, since it was precisely its past policies and principles that hopelessly trapped it in its contemporary programmatic crisis. In 1954, Clark and the NAACP leadership had concluded that the social dynamism initiated by the desegregation of public school systems would ultimately transform and reform American society's race relations in social life, politics, and economics. As pointed out at the outset of this study, *how Clark and the NAACP leaders of 1954 could have been so naïve was a demonstrative commentary on the profound truth of Du Bois's vision in 1934.* Clark's assertion in 1983 that the NAACP was "verging on irrelevance" was but a reiteration of the Du Bois critique of the NAACP in 1934. During the Seventies the NAACP could have redeemed its flagging prestige and legitimacy by casting aside ideological differences, which had become totally irrelevant, and encouraging the National Black Political Convention movement to pursue the organizational possibilities of the independent black political thrust. As the oldest and most prestigious social-reform organization functioning on behalf of the black cause, the NAACP *maintained the prerogative to discourage and delegitimize black ideological departures not consistent with its leadership ideologies*. It helped dampen and discourage the National Black Political Convention because many of the leading black elected officials maintain sentimental and ideological attachments to the principles of the NAACP by force of its civil rights traditions. Despite its belated enthusiasm for black voter registration campaigns, the NAACP could still maintain its traditional political nonpartisanship. Its vaunted stance of allegiance to neither of the two mainstream political parties was by inference a nonallegiance even to the idea of an independent black political movement.

However, the Seventies was the decade of the black political coming-of-age. Civil rights evolved into another sphere—it went from constitutional rights into political rights, which were outside the range of purely constitutional guarantees. At this point, the NAACP's integrationism, the propaganda equivalent of the measure of civil rights, had reached effective saturation level, as E. Franklin Frazier's sociological analyses had foreshadowed in the Fifties. When social policies reached the limits of federal enforcement, the NAACP's ideal of full integration became an end in itself, impossible of achievement in a racially and culturally plural society. This is what Republican President Nixon alluded to in 1970 when he asserted that "civil rights is a field in which government can pass laws but can do little to combat or control human prejudices."

The dreary imperatives of economically determined public policy took over; black economic survival had to be weighed in the scales of the free market versus federal intervention on behalf of the underprivileged in the richest country in the world. In this context, the moral legitimacy of civil rights would be weighed against the free-market economy, and the black cause would come up on the short end of both federal economies and competitive profits. Throughout the Seventies, the National Urban League would report an annual widening gap between the median incomes of blacks and whites. The Census Bureau reported in 1970 that in 1969, "the median income for [blacks] was $6,000, compared with $9,800 for Whites." Throughout the Seventies this gap would widen. But in 1970 National Urban League leaders would oppose the

NAACP leadership attacks that the Nixon administration was consciously antiblack. Whither civil rights?[20] This National Urban League defense of the Republican party's civil rights record was more than political; it was a not so subtle shift in leadership opinion over the legitimacy of the traditional civil rights philosophy. Not only was the NAACP doomed to experience an *internal* organizational and leadership crisis in the Seventies, the National Urban League position also represented a break in the sixty-year ideological unity between these two organizations. By the Eighties, this ideological split would widen even more.

Neither the National Urban League nor the NAACP was programmatically prepared for the Seventies, let alone the Eighties. Even if they had been, the spread of black urbanized and regional populations across the United States, North and South and West, was beyond the functional capabilities of these two old-line organizations. The new era of the politics of black ethnicity had arrived, but blacks were politically subservient to the regional politics and economics of the eastern seaboard states, the southern states bloc, the midwestern bloc, the Southwest region anchored in Texas, and in the Far West, the Pacific Coast states with their black populations practically lost in a melange of Asians and Latinos, all prevailing and countervailing for minority handouts from the golden pot of the American Dream. In this newly emergent national political context, blacks had only electoral and legislative reinforcements vested in their black elected officials and the National Black Caucus. And despite a steady increase in such officials on state and local levels, the stark truth was amply spelled by a number of astute black observers: At the same time in the entire society, because of total reliance on economic development to solve all social problems there has been a total failure to build any institutions or procedures which might develop the population politically—in social responsibility and in the political skills and procedures needed to cope with social problems.

American politics, like all politics, is rooted in the aims, interests, and designs of extremely powerful economic enterprises. Thus, while the civil rights victories were legitimate and necessary, they did not address themselves to the central problem of black people in the aggregate—economic powerlessness. This powerlessness was to become most glaring only after the consummation of all the favorable social legislation. But heightened awareness of intrinsic black powerlessness was the other side of the coin of a heightened black consciousness. Broad sections of the black populations—coast to coast, North to South—reflected a search for group autonomy in economic life and in political expression. In the cultural spheres, this racial-group identification was reflected in literature and various creative arts—music, theater, dance, and even in the most debated and controversial of all—the film. Even today, the record of black exposure in the most visual and socially visible art form, the film, has not been adequately assessed.

In 1970 a national committee of black churchmen, forty-one church and community leaders, issued what it called the "Black Declaration of Independence." These spokesmen came from large urban centers, north, south, east, and west. They labeled themselves "Concerned Black Citizens of the United States of America in Black Churches, Schools, Homes, Community Organizations, and Institutions Assembled." The declaration enumerated a long list of grievances against white society and the federal power for the "exploitation and injustice" heaped upon black people, for the "unrelenting Economic Depression" created in the black communities. The declaration accused the federal power of allowing *"election districts to be so gerrymandered"* as to deprive the black electorate of its just representation in the legislatures. It accused the United States of allowing the *"dissolution of school districts controlled by Blacks."*[21] This litany of grievances reiterated the substance of black protests against discrimination, racial bigotry, racial exclusion, etc., that had been voiced during all the decades prior to the civil rights legislation of the Sixties. Coming during the Seventies as the declaration did was a graphic revelation that broad sections of the black population placed little trust in the promises of the civil rights legislation of the Sixties. These community and church spokesmen were *not* representatives of Martin Luther King's Southern Christian Leadership Conference (SCLC), nor were they affiliates or associates of either the NAACP or the National Urban League. The temper of the declaration also indicated that these spokesmen did not represent any of the ideological carry-overs from the separatist or militantly nationalistic Black Powerites of the Sixties. This Black Declaration of Independence revealed a *profound black leadership vacuum that would appear and would grow in converse ratio to the deepening crisis within the NAACP and the decline in the relevancy of its program. Thus, between the upper-level dominance of the NAACP and the National Urban League and the lower levels of black community-based leadership contenders, there was an absence of leadership. Moreover, the social horizon held no indication of an organized movement out of which a new style of leadership might emerge on a national scale.* The civil rights successes of the Sixties had, for all functional purposes, left the NAACP even more obsolete than the National Urban League, which, in certain respects, had the option of shifting its social welfare orientation to speak to the economic contingencies of the Seventies. But the National Urban League alone could not fill the leadership vacuum because, historically, its heritage was of the same traditional mold as that of the NAACP.

It is debatable to what extent the historical root cause behind the long-standing black leadership deficiencies is understood even in the Eighties. An accumulation of discernible evidence indicates *that the true nature and origins of the problem are not understood at all.* But the consequences are more than apparent, and the varied black publics and factions responded to this central leadership issue from different angles. The white liberals, conservatives, and radicals responded in kind. The civil rights movement had shaken American society to the extent of nearly undermining the stanchions of its stability. No other nonwhite (or even white) minority group could have achieved such a reordering of the nation's domestic priorities as did the blacks—neither the American Indians nor the Hispanics; nor the white ethnics, Protestant, Catholic, or Jewish. And nor could women have initiated a social movement in the United States with the impact of the black movement. Yet, in the final accounting of the civil rights drama, all these minority groups, and women, have profited by way of an enhanced social, political, and economic status as a direct result of the catalytic potentials of the black minority.

Another ironic consequence of the civil rights crusade that went unchallenged, and further canceled out the prerogatives of black leadership, was the white liberal propaganda of the Seventies that relegated blacks to being just another "immigrant group." All white ethnic immigrant groups had classic histories of having to fight their way up the social, economic, and political ladder; after all the civil rights struggle, contention, and bloodshed, American blacks were simply late arrivals at the gates of democratic ethnic parity. Ideologically trapped in their naïve faith in the Fourteenth Amendment's ability to guarantee the social and economic millennium for blacks, the black leadership did not even possess the authority to declare that *American blacks were not to be classified as an immigrant group, and would not allow themselves to be classified as such; that American black history involved a specific relationship to the constitutional history of the United States not shared by other ethnic immigrants.*

At the same time, blacks, in general, were buried deeper in civil rights anonymity when the federal power broadened the concept of a "minority" to *"minorities and women."* To be more precise, the class category of women was placed in the selfsame category as blacks, not only as being oppressed but as suffering from the identical quality of segregation, disfranchisement, exclusion, discrimination as blacks! Constitutional violations of the rights of women to equal citizenship were equated with constitutional violations of the rights of blacks. Women (white) were not segregated or denied access to quality education; nor were there violations against their voting franchise (at least not since 1920). And even before the Nineteenth Amendment was passed, white women in the forefront of the struggle for "votes for women" were not intimidated by either the police or lynch mobs in pursuit of their rights. The original intent of the black civil rights movement was a moral and constitutional protest against *racial* indignities. In fact, the entire social history of lynch law in the southern, southwestern, and western states had as one of its main extralegal rationalizations the protection of "white womanhood" against the threat of depredation by blacks (read, black men). The original intent of the black civil rights movement up to 1964–1965 was a constitutional and moral protest against the oppression and indignities based on race, not sex. The Voting Rights Acts of 1964–1965 outlawed disfranchisement based on race not sex. Yet liberalism would rationalize civil rights legislation on the premise that sex oppression was similar to racial oppression and that sex and race discrimination were two sides of the same coin. More than that, the black minority and its leaders had to accept this Seventies interpretation of civil rights doctrine. This was the price blacks had to pay for being in the catalytic vanguard of a civil rights reformation that bore the bulk of the physical, emotional, moral, and psychological travail in defense of the cause.

When the countervailing politics of white conservatism began to exert pressures during the Nixon administration, federal agencies began to relax enforcements in minority hiring on the premise that such enforcements opened the door to charges of "reverse discrimination." At that moment, the classification "minorities and women" obscured the fact that at least half the minority populations were female. Thus, tabulating women who were *not* of minority groups resulted in a censual count that was a vast majority compared with the total minority populations. But it was to become evident in the anticivil rights or affirmative action backlash that the term "minority" was a code word for blacks (and blacks only). Even though resistance to the civil rights of women took its most extreme expression in opposition to the ERA, the issue of women's rights (i.e., sex discrimination) actually pushed civil rights issues related to race into the background.

However, the developing anticivil rights or anti-affirmative action backlash was predominantly a conservative white male consensus. Tangentially, the white male consensus was also construed to reflect an antifemale (i.e., anti-ERA) sentiment. But since the strategic centers of economic and political power in America are controlled by white males, so-called Women's Power does not denote the same threatening intensity as political or economic Black Power. By the 1980s the Republican pro-Reagan white male consensus was fueled by the conviction that enough, if not "too much," had been done by the federal power for "minorities," meaning, *for blacks*. By including the gender factor in the competitive struggle among minorities for the rewards of affirmative action, the black minority was relegated closer and closer to last place in the pecking order. But insofar as the gender factor was concerned, *the black male emerged as most vulnerable* to the conservative, neoconservative, *and* liberal backlash fueled by the Reagan ascendancy. Even the most vocal liberal opinion had to admit by 1980, during the last days of the Carter–Democratic party ascendancy, that in the final analysis, *"Black Men Are Last"*:

> Corporate affirmative-action programs have been far more productive for white women than for black men. Black women—labeled "twofers" by some personnel managers because they are counted twice on Government compliance reports, once as a woman and once as minorities —are being employed and advanced less rapidly than white women but faster than black men.
>
> The National Urban League recently reported that the nation's work force grew by nearly 5.2 million employees between 1974 and 1977. Of these, 3.5 million entered private industry. Fifty-three percent of all new employees entering private industry were white women, 26 percent were white men, 5 percent were black women, 12 percent were of Hispanic background and 4 percent were Asian. At this same time, as many black male employees left private industry as entered, so there was no net increase in their number.[22]

These were the results of the civil rights spoils system by the 1980s. And when it is recognized that this sociological, political, and legislative rendering of the meaning of constitutional American democracy was precipitated by blacks, *and blacks only*, then the causes and implications of the conservative antiblack "nullification" process become graphically apparent. If blacks as a minority become last, then black males ultimately become more "last" than others. What does this say for the black minority as a whole? One thing is clear: The process of equalizing political and economic right. according to gender means *undermining the political and economic rights of nonwhite minority groups as minority groups.* The issue of women's rights is a *class issue.* For blacks, in particular, the irony is that this unavoidable civil rights summation has been legitimized by the white liberal consensus on the legal and sociological meanings of civil rights. More ironical is that it is *conservative* opinion on the constitutional implications of civil rights that has more often debated this crucial question of sex versus race. In an article titled "Sexual Distinction vs. Racial Discrimination," one conservative critic argued:

> Little by little, a new legislative history is being created for the Equal Rights Amendment, and in the process some troubling thoughts are taking shape.
> If ratified, the amendment manifestly would work some change in our law. The question is: What change?
> For the record, we are talking about this proposed amendment to the Constitution: "Equality of rights under the law shall not be denied or abridged by the United States or by any state on account of sex."

Quoting another prominent critic on the constitutional implications of this amendment, this conservative wrote:

> My own view, . . . is that there is something terribly wrong with a Constitution that puts the sexual exclusion of a Catholic seminary or a traditional women's college on the same plane with the racist bigotry of a white supremacist "segregation academy." I will not here attempt to argue the moral differences between race discrimination and sexual exclusion. I will simply record my strong impression that Americans now share this sense that sexual differentiation should not be regarded with the same intolerance as race discrimination.[23]

The problem was that all the mounting media evidence showed that the liberal public consensus on civil rights had come to believe that sexual differentiation was to be regarded with the same intolerance as race discrimination. It was one means of relegating race discrimination to the back burner as a public policy issue. This public policy shift in emphasis away from blacks by means of the gender question coincided with the gradual relegation of the black minority to the historical status of an immigrant group! In short—*enough of black minority civil rights!* Also —*enough of black men!* And what were the true sociological-gender facts of both racial and sexual discrimination:

Irritated at having to attain any Government-imposed hiring goals many managers are more comfortable advancing white women than black men. . . .

Many of these white male managers are contemptuous of black men, whose advancement in business and the professions they ascribe to "reverse discrimination." . .

Needless to say, this white male attitude permeates the political, business, academic, professional, cultural, and social worlds:

It is difficult to find black men qualified for managerial positions since only 6 percent of the graduates of four-year colleges are black and the proportion of black students in graduate schools has been declining.

Women, on the other hand, now constitute 43 percent of the work force and receive nearly half the degrees being awarded by universities and colleges.

The result? "White male managers devote more attention and effort to recruiting and training women and far less to advancing black men."[24] However, contrary to all claims that prior to the Civil Rights Act of 1964, racial and sexual discrimination had been two sides of the same coin, it had to be admitted in 1980 that *"white women have also been in the corporate world far longer than black men."*[25] But prior to the Supreme Court decision of 1954, any knowledgeable black person (male or female) already knew about the status of white women in the economic, political, cultural, educational, business, and social worlds. Gender discrimination was *not* to be compared to racial discrimination, inasmuch as the white female, no matter what degree of political, economic, and social equality she held (or did not hold), was able to participate in racial discrimination *against* blacks. But it would be the white male who would establish and maintain the rules of race and gender discrimination and/ or exclusion. And in the final analysis, in sorting out the race, gender, and minority privileges and prerogatives, *black men would be last.*

However, the black leadership, forever tied into and subordinated to the white liberal consensus on the race, gender, and minority equation, remained strapped, immobilized, and subordinate to the point where it could not confront the fact that gender was one of a number of factors undermining the social viability of the black minority issue as a whole. As early as 1970, it was obvious that with the newly arrived gender issue in civil rights, the black male was in serious trouble. The assassination of Martin Luther King was more than an attack on the civil rights move ment oy right-wing extremism; it was, more pointedly, an attack on the most visible and vulnerable symbol of black male leadership. Here, King's intimate social philosophy became a secondary consideration—*the black male had to be tamed and constrained*. At the same time, the articulate black female was growing more and more querulous over the changing role and status of the black male. One black women's opinions soon became, during the Seventies, a rising crescendo of black-gender contention:

> What is the hang-up of the American black man? Who is the greatest deterrent to his progress—the white man? Why is his every step upward marked by a trail of blood, sweat and tears? Why is it that in the year of our Lord 1972 we find him slipping back into the era of Reconstruction?
>
> I think it is high time for the black man in America to take a good, hard look at himself and analyze the factors that have slowed his progress. It is time that he sat down and found out what has stopped him from ticking. The day has come when the black man must face himself and his own shortcomings.[26]

Not only was the black minority group as a whole set up for the white backlash of the Seventies, the black male was coming under increasing fire. White corporate managers (those in the professions, government, business, the arts, academia, etc.) characterized black men as: "Arrogant, impatient, unwilling to conform to [business] standards and lacking in basic [job] skills." Black women, in the meantime, were marshaling a compendium of critical opinions on the black male, summed up in charges such as: *"They don't know what to do about the situation now that the high hopes of the Sixties have been proven a delusion."* Another black female opinion muttered *sub rosa,* was *"our worst enemy is the black male!"* Generalizations as to what degree black male–female diffidence extended throughout the entire black population during the Seventies cannot be assumed to be definitive. But in one degree or another, silent or vocal, a question permeated the atmosphere of the faltering civil rights hopes: *"What is wrong with this black male?"* But in the real world at large, the black male's performance was judged on the basis of his *leadership* role, *because of his efforts at leadership* or *because of an absence of leadership authority.* In the professions, in politics, in government, in academia, in the arts, the black male's performance could be gauged by the judgment coming from the corporate world:

The few black managers who did succeed found themselves in the lonely position of being the only black at the job level they had attained. Loneliness, a feeling of being endlessly judged not as a manager but as a black man, and having no confidence that they would be advanced to their fullest potential all combined to damage their spirits and careers. Many white managers, impatient with black subordinates, withdrew what little support they had been providing. The failure rate of black men accelerated.[27]

The women's movement, which rode into legislative and political contention in the wake of the black civil rights movement, brought into view the heretofore unacknowledged existence of the gender gap within the black minority itself. However, like white feminism, black feminism had *always* been present, even if in muted forms. Actually, black female–black male dissensions were vocalized during the late 1940s. However, the black male–female diffidence of the post-World War II period had none of the manifestations of the "male-female split" of the 1970s and 1980s. Such a development was as unforeseen as the emergence of the white ethnic and other minority bones of contention. In addition to and contrary to all vaunted claims for the concomitant growth in solidarity of the black minority as a consequence of the civil rights crusade, the veneer of "black unity" was deceptive. Thus, the black female opinions cited above summed up the Seventies situation as follows:

We are divided. "A house divided within itself cannot stand," we often read Black America's house is in shambles! Yes, we get together and go to church. We get together briefly in a protest march. On Saturday nights, we get together to drink, dance, and have a ball. But, for serious, constructive meeting of the minds, for a planning session and for carrying out those plans, we are not interested. We'd much rather sit and air our gripes over a beer with a friend than get together and remedy situations. Each unit wants to operate within its own little sphere. Each wants to project its own image. There can be no response to one cry, Black America.[28]

However, who in the house of Black America is to blame for this immobilizing division? *It is the black male,* according to this black-gender-gap complaint. Put into historical and sociological and political terminology, the blame is placed on black male leaders as their minority function is understood in black communities across the wide geographical expanses of the United States. In other words, the "Crisis in Negro

Leadership" graphically evident since the 1920s was not really overcome and rectified in the 1960s and 1970s. This is despite the fact that black women (like white women) would gain, as a result of the civil rights movement, unprecedented preferential advantages in education, professional employment, and political office.

The outcome of this minority-group-cum-gender issue coincided with a Seventies situation in which blacks (in the median aggregate) wound up in a worse *economic* position as a minority group than *before* all the Sixties civil rights legislation. Groupwise, the equal-opportunity legislation catapulted at least one third of the black minority into the middle-class economic range, while the remainder experienced a descending level of economic impoverishment.

However, at the lower levels of the economic-class spectrum, black minority-group disunity had its most disastrous sociological consequences. Black family insolvency, already a problem of endemic proportions long before the Sixties, became exacerbated in the Seventies to become an urban blight in the Eighties. Black lower-class poverty, black-on-black crime, degenerating educational facilities, incremental family pathologies, mounting teenage-pregnancy rates, paternal absenteeism— all these negative factors would multiply to the degree that black urban communities would be faced with impending social disintegration. Aside from the basic factor of economic insolvency, which was always present, northern urbanization since the world wars intensified black family insolvency, rooted in the uncertain *economic* functions of the black male as "provider" and "man" of the household. Historically, *black males as a class were never granted the full economic option to play out the role of man of the household to the fullest extent of its evolutionary and functional capabilities,* prior to the advent of the female equality movement. Thus, by the 1980s the controversial Moynihan Report of 1965, which described the black family emergency as a *"case for national action,"* would come back to haunt civil rights leaders, most of whom had rejected the report as unwarranted in 1965.

The ending of the civil rights cycle, 1954–1980, would render all original *black* issues a "Lost Priority." But black minority-group issues would remain unresolved, even though partially remedied through the "vertical integration" of a new black middle class. The vast majority of urbanized blacks, for whom the civil rights of integration and upward *economic* mobility were meaningless, still remain separate and unequal. Now that the civil rights cycle has ended, their future lies in the economics and politics of the "equality of plurality," or "plural but equal," as a racially democratic alternative to the separate-but-equal doctrine. However, this next stage in the possible evolution of the status of the black minority can be achieved only through the development of a *new style of black leadership*—a leadership that can measure up to the organizational demands of the politics of black ethnicity.

P ART SEVEN
Conclusions

A summation of the twenty-six years since the 1954 *Brown* decision would have to call 1980 a watershed year for blacks. Only twenty years remained in the twentieth century, and only ٬en years were left to fulfill the Afro-American League's T. Thomas Fortune's prophecy that the civil rights struggle would occupy a century. Indeed, the ninety years that elapsed between Fortune's declaration and the end of the Carter administration in 1980 had not been an exercise in black leadership child's play. On the contrary, it had been an evolutionary saga of black leadership factionalism, contention, and rivalry; opposition and alliances; classism and its social prerogatives; nationalism and separatism versus integrationism and assimilationism; left versus right; black conservatism versus the white liberal left wing and conservative paternalism; Pan-Africanist (and later) Third World internationalism and Afro-American minority-group particularism. But since the harsh banes of racism and racial segregation were the common foes of all these factions, class alignments, and ideological divisions, internal disunity slowed down black progress on all fronts—political, economic, cultural, social, and educational. If the black struggle was not an exercise in child's play, it did trivialize crucial issues caused by a factional disunity that rendered black leadership an exercise in the futility of *political* subordination. This process culminated in the anomaly of more blacks being better off economically, and more being worse off, than their predecessors had been from 1900 to 1960.

Although on the average blacks are better off in the Eighties than their forebears, the tasks they face from now through the year 2000 will be more difficult—calling for more organizational skill, political ingenuity and imagination, intellectual endurance, hard work, and application of thought than before. Historically, the main spokesmen to represent anything approaching a *national* consensus appeal in the twentieth century have been Booker T. Washington, W.E.B. Du Bois, Marcus Garvey, A. Philip Randolph, Martin Luther King, and, recently, Jesse Jackson. T. Thomas Fortune was eclipsed early on by the political and racial consequences of being a "stillborn" leader during the dubious racial decade of *Plessy* v. *Ferguson*. Du Bois, Randolph, Garvey, and their contemporaries faced the "Crisis of Negro Leadership" first evident in the post-World War I period. Thus, King and his protégé Jesse Jackson would personify, both as participants and as advocates, black progress in all social advancements, underwritten in the main by the civil rights engendered by the black–white liberal–Democratic party alliance.

Jesse Jackson's emergence following King suggested the possibility of things to come in the Seventies *and* the Eighties. An assessment of Jesse Jackson as a leadership symbol can dispense with the hero worship that rightly belongs to King. King himself was unprecedented and unexpected among the black leaders produced by the Fifties and Sixties. Jackson has brought back into focus the economic factor that was downplayed and reduced to a nonfactor in black civil rights affairs. This was the philosophy of *noneconomic liberalism*. Tactically, noneconomic liberalism had been one means of expunging from the programmatic movement the procapitalist, free-market ideals of the Booker T. Washington school in favor of constitutional legalism. Unsettled racial conditions in both North and South up to the New Deal obviated any serious debate how blacks would fit into the capitalist, free-market economy except as a cheap labor pool. The New Deal further discouraged economic debates by instituting the federal budgetary innovations of the welfare state. Under the economics of the welfare state, all talk of "black capitalism" became visionary, or at least irrelevant to black economic survival.

It took Jesse Jackson to reintroduce the notion of a black capitalist *clientage* class sponsored by white corporations as an extension of civil rights clientage into economics. More precisely, Jesse Jackson's People United to Save Humanity (PUSH) aimed to revitalize the latent energies of economically deprived black communities. As a description of PUSH operations noted: "Jackson began to direct the flow of white corporate profits earned in the ghetto into black banks as a means of strengthening the black communities' meager economic foundations."[1] PUSH was an extension of Martin Luther King's Operation Breadbasket. In King's conception, Operation Breadbasket was aimed at securing more jobs for blacks at the nonentrepreneurial level.[2] Jackson transcended the scope of King's plan by inducing large corporations to invest directly in black communities at the entrepreneurial level. In this way Jesse Jackson realized the black economic dream of Booker T. Washington after some seventy years.[3] But in the process, Jackson developed the style and momentum for a qualitatively new brand of black leadership. Although PUSH's economic accomplishments would not even begin to dent the surface of growing ghetto poverty at the class level, Jackson's leadership could *politicize* the issue of black economics. During the transition from civil rights politics to the politics of black ethnicity, Jackson's leadership would emphasize the necessity of combining black political organization *with* black economic organization. However, his burgeoning leadership potential would be contained within the range of the fortunes and misfortunes of the Democratic party. Or, more precisely, within the black–white liberal–Democratic party coalition.

Neither the NAACP nor the National Urban League was bold enough, or sufficiently unrestricted by sanctions of *noneconomic liberalism*, to confront the seats of economic power in the manner of Jesse Jackson. The traditional civil rights leadership was in a programmatic bind. Once the ambiguity of the Fourteenth Amendment's equal protection clause became even more indistinct in the process of universalizing both civil and economic rights, the traditional civil rights leadership had nothing substantial to fall back on but the legislative stratagem of a Humphrey-Hawkins full-employment bill. Only a vast federal outlay could have given this full-employment bill any pretense of wiping out unemployment (whether of blacks, whites, or other minorities). Moreover, the corporate leaders from whom Jesse Jackson wangled financial backing for his black business clients were politically unsympathetic to federal funding of full employment programs. Corporate leaders are predominantly advocates of conservative fiscal policies. Thus, the only hope for passing the Humphrey-Hawkins bill lay with the Democratic party, and the entire civil rights leadership and black elected officials were, and had to remain, party loyalists. Hence, the Carter presidency became the last chance for any favorable congressional action on Humphrey-Hawkins. With record-high unemployment levels in the black communities, civil rights leaders, as champions of black progress, had to press for black rights that had become much more economic than civil. Then Carter, who owed his election to the "balance of power" of the black vote, began to hedge his support for the Humphrey-Hawkins bill:

> It started off as legislation that would have made the Government the employer of last resort for the unemployed. The question now is whether the Humphrey-Hawkins full-employment bill, after all the compromises, ended up as a political symbol of last resort for President Carter, Congressional liberals and the Congressional Black Caucus.[4]

But along the line, the sponsors of the bill had to give ground on the definition of full employment. Both Carter and the sponsors agreed that the primary emphasis should be on creating jobs in the private sector. But in its last stages, what the bill left "unresolved [was] how much money the Government is to spend on programs directed to people and places with chronically high unemployment—teen-agers, blacks, decaying inner cities, regions, states."[5] Ultimately, directly due to the swing of public sentiment to the right, the Humphrey-Hawkins bill became one of the domestic issues that helped defeat Carter; it also brought to a close the long reign of the Democratic party as the sponsor of liberal legislation in the stopgap or long-range economic interests of the underprivileged.

Although the category of the economically underprivileged included a larger proportion of the population than blacks, legislative controversies involving government spending centered around the plight of the blacks, not other minorities. The blacks would become the vanguards of social protest, first for themselves and then for other minorities. Blacks would also become the most prominent scapegoats for most of the conservative backlash from critics of liberal public policy. Ultimately, the combined factors that went into this burgeoning backlash from the right pushed Jesse Jackson to take the unprecedented step of running for the presidency in 1984.

With the decline of the Democrats in 1980, black leadership as a whole had nowhere to turn politically. Having been lofted by a considerable black consensus as the leader of the Seventies, Jackson had nowhere to go but up as a means of sustaining at least the symbolic justification for his leadership appeal. As King's immediate successor, more by self-propelled design rather than by consensus, Jackson mobilized his own supporters. When the politics of welfare state economics dwindled under the assault of Reaganomics, leaving Jackson's civil rights colleagues stranded, Jackson pursued his only option, the *leadership summitry* in the open field of electoral politics. However, in bidding for the highest political office in the land, Jackson had to be launched like a helicopter from a rooftop rather than as a turbojet from an airfield. The analogy here refers to the jet-propelled presidential electioneering that was the prerogative of a Walter Mondale, a John Glenn, and a Gary Hart. Which is to say that Jackson's presidential bid was launched without the backup of a well-cultivated and prepared political base. Jesse Jackson's *non-existent political base was the figment of the black independent political party structure that was not formed during the black political conventions at Gary, 1972; Little Rock, 1974; or Cincinnati, 1976*. Because no black independent political party was formed from 1972 to 1980, Jackson's maverick impact on the political culture would be limited. He had no option other than to restrict his potential within the constraining folds of the Democratic party, which had been holding the black vote in ransom since 1936.

The subsequent Reagan Republican sweep demonstrated the dismal fact that the Democratic party's attachments to (and strategical need for) the black vote had evolved into an electoral liability. The Democratic party's identification with blacks was by no means a moral indictment, but a *political* indictment from the point of view of those of the electorate who labeled blacks as the most palpable scapegoats for a hot issue, too much government spending on social programs. Hence, running for the presidency as a black (unheard of racially and politically apocalyptic), Jackson had to criticize the front-runner, Mondale, for failing to address issues important to blacks, while at the same time promising to support the Democratic party ticket on demand.

In doing so, Jackson posed problems for blacks that would not have been solved even if the 1984 election had been won by Mondale or ended in a tie. In playing the politics of "loyal opposition" with the Democrats, Jackson sought to cajole them into a platform emphasis on black interests, while bidding for personal inclusion in the high echelons of Democratic party leadership. Which meant that neither Jesse Jackson nor the civil rights leaders had seriously faced the implications of Carter's defeat in 1980. What more could the Democrats do for blacks that had not already been done or tried? Thus, for Jackson and the civil rights leadership to justify both their demands on the Democratic party and their loyalties to party principles, they had to bring a set of *new ideas* to the party.

The political victories of Reaganism were due to the Democratic party's having run out of ideas. Both the national economy and the social foundations of the entire American society were beset by severe functional strains and stresses. During the Sixties, the civil rights movement itself had disrupted the foundations of society and removed the placid camouflage, revealing festering elements below the surface—an un-American degree of poverty, the organized roots of crime and corruption, widespread family disorganization (especially that of blacks), the terminal stages of urban decay, the advanced stages of interethnic enmities and competition, the degradation of national agriculture (a crucial black issue), and a bloated military budget that resulted directly from a foreign policy that not only gave a low priority to domestic problems but was also a long-run detriment to national interests. The list of domestic exigencies was endless. The decade of the Seventies, while crucial for black interests, was also a decade of a growing national emergency that called for a drastic reordering of domestic priorities. However, with the 1984 presidential campaign, it became increasingly clear that, despite all the good liberal–Democratic party intentions, the Democrats had neither a program with a potential for such a drastic reordering of domestic priorities, nor an electoral mandate for the program even if the party were politically solvent. The growing insolvency of black civil rights leadership only fortified its dependent belief that the Democratic party was still politically solvent enough to project a black issues-oriented program. Jesse Jackson, the unprecedented political maverick, thought the same thing.

Jesse Jackson, in his bid for the presidential nomination, could not break cleanly with the tradition that kept the black vote tied to the fortunes of the Democratic party. Although he had a clear option of turning his voter-registration campaign into a double-barreled political venture by organizing voters into an independent party, he skirted that challenge by projecting the idea of the Rainbow Coalition.

This Rainbow Coalition was, in part, Jackson's admission that the coalition that comprised the bedrock of the Democratic party was either inadequate and unrepresentative or else politically insufficient to propel the party toward victory in 1984. At the same time that he called for a Rainbow Coalition, Jackson did not, or could not, espouse a political program in opposition to or different from that of the Democratic party. The Rainbow Coalition was an interesting political idea because it promised a brand-new party alignment. An important, even crucial, segment of this coalition would, of course, be the black voting bloc. In Jackson's view the only possible avenue for expressing the black voting bloc's independence from the two main parties would be within the Rainbow Coalition. On the one hand, the name itself, Rainbow Coalition, would spell out the group's pluralism. On the other hand, Jackson's idea implied that the existing Democratic party coalition in support of Walter Mondale had lost its political powers of persuasion. Ultimately, the results of the 1984 election indicated that the Democratic party—the party of FDR, Truman, Kennedy, Johnson, and Carter—had reached the end of the line as the liberal–left-wing axis of the traditional two-party system. And since the conservative–right-wing fulcrum of electoral politics, the Republican party, offered no future for realizing the aspirations of the black majority consensus, what loomed as the political hope for the black minority?

The only option left was to organize an independent black party. The ultimate aim of this black party would not be solely for the expedient purposes of electoral politics. Realistically, it has to be faced that black elected officials (BEOs) "fear they can't do much to help their people." In an interview sponsored by *The Wall Street Journal* in 1980, one prominent black state representative admitted, "I have a sensitivity towards poor people [and] Blacks are No. 1." But when pressed to cite specific ways he helped black people, he pointed to his authorship of a bill that made Martin Luther King's birthday a legal holiday in his state. "Many of the 4,600 black elected officials in the U.S. share [this] feeling of helplessness." The interview continued: "Perhaps more than others, they understood the size and complexity of the problems facing black Americans." "Problems don't go away when you elect a black," said another BEO. *"Even the most powerful black leaders can't change very much."*[6] (Italics added.)

Here, the official was alluding to the powerful black leaders on the civil rights front. It is not simply that the continuing vacuity of these leaders' civil rights and welfare programs represent the diminished end products of their futility; it is that the *sheer size and complexity of black America today* reduces all pretenses and pretexts of black leadership, an exercise in verbal-protest symbolism that harks back to the heydays of past achievements when civil rights redress was the order of the day on the national agenda. But for BEOs as the new black political class, electoral politics has ended as a legislative and parliamentary dead-end trap. This is because black elected officials are both latecomers to mainstream politics and functional captives of the liberal–Democratic party alliance. "By the time blacks move into important posts," said a black member of Congress, "they've got too much work ahead of them to get it done."[7] Left unsaid by this black representative was that by 1980, there was little political leverage left in the liberal-Democratic alliance

to accomplish whatever political work lay ahead. The most obvious obligatory work that loomed was more concentrated political organization
by blacks, but *not only* for the elevation of more officials to political
office. The organization of blacks into an independent political party
would belatedly help make up for the abysmal lack of organizational
achievements by blacks over the last sixty years in all areas—political,
economic, cultural, educational, etc. The black woman's complaint cited
earlier was far from being an idle exercise in complaint-mongering about
the "black man's dilemma." Translated into its broader social meaning,
it is a dilemma of the entire black minority group, a dilemma of black
leadership.

With the end of the cycle of civil rights advocacy, only one basic
option remained for the black leadership. This was internal organization
and consolidation of the minority group within a multiracial, multicultural
society. This imperative meant that the traditional black civil rights leadership had reached a societal void lacking a road upon which to lead its
constituency. The situation called for a new black leadership consensus
that was capable of *redefining* the plausible place of the black minority
within the societal complex in which blacks, as a *group,* found themselves
by 1980. Such a redefinition of the legitimate place of the black minority
within the system had to take into full account the meaning of *plurality.*
It meant the systematic *reorganization* of many areas of black life into,
first a *political bloc,* then cultural blocs, and then into whatever internal
economic organizations are possible within a capitalistic, free-market
system. In this context an independent black political party becomes the
initial step toward a total reorganization of black life over the remainder
of the twentieth century. Without such a *total* political, economic, cultural, educational, and *institutional* reorganization of black life, the American black minority will *not* be able to survive into *whatever* system
American society becomes by the year 2000 and after.

However, this attempt at a total reorganization of black life means
that organizing the black political consensus becomes the *first priority.*
In this process the traditional civil rights leadership (mainly the NAACP)
*must arbitrarily be bypassed inasmuch as this leadership, which exists
on the basis of a vested interest, will not voluntarily step down.* The
official, institutionalized civil rights leadership will not (cannot) voluntarily vote itself out of existence. The official, institutionalized civil rights
leadership cannot face the reality that it is passé. It is *not* passé simply
because of the coming to power of the conservative, Reaganite, right-
wing Republican party hegemony. It is passé because under the auspices

of the Democratic party, civil rights legislation over the years has gleaned maximum power from the Fourteenth Amendment to the Constitution to redress the historical civil rights wrongs heaped on the heads of the blacks. Thus, black aspirations are trapped within the ambiguities of the constitutional meaning of the equal protection clause. Continued agitation and leadership confrontations on this issue at the national level of public policy are not only fruitless but counterproductive. The traditional civil rights leadership that aims at perpetuating this mode of agitation is *detrimental* to future development in the political, economic, educational, and cultural dimensions of the black cause. More than that, *the traditional civil rights leadership will oppose any attempt on the part of an alternate leadership to organize blacks into an independent political bloc.* As pointed out earlier, this was demonstrated in 1972 when the NAACP damned the objectives of the first black political convention at Gary, Indiana, by refusing to support the independent political party plank.[8] The traditional civil rights leadership remains the most highly influential body of black opinion. This leadership has the support of white liberal opinion across the board, whether Big Labor, Big Government, Big Welfare State, Big Liberalism, or Big Public Policy of the type that has philanthropized blacks into being, as a group, a semidependency, half liberated, half victimized by disabilities and problems that are beyond the capabilities of present public policy to either redress or solve. Organizationally and politically, blacks require a brand-new set of public policy priorities. Although most blacks are loyal to the Democratic party, the Democrats are no longer capable of accommodating black social priorities, present or future. The decline of the Democratic party's viability represents a turning point in the traditional two-party system's monopoly over national electoral politics.

By implication, Jesse Jackson challenged the sacred hegemony of the two-party system when he proposed the Rainbow Coalition. Jackson, however, could not venture far enough into the uncertainties of party politics fully to define the ramifications of such a coalition. That is to say, Jackson, like civil rights leaders and the great majority of black elected officials, did not really savor the risk of breaking cleanly with the Democratic party. Just about one hundred years ago, Frederick Douglass thought in terms of "political integration" by declaring that the Republican party was the ship, and all else was the open sea. By 1984 blacks had been long programmed to believe that the only ship of state for political survival was the Democratic party, even though the ship had sprung menacing leaks. In this political debacle, the Republican party cannot represent the party of rescue today. What is needed is a brand-new alignment. As political and electoral matters evolved in the 1980s, the black electoral consensus emerged as the only potential base on which a Third, or alternate, party could be built to compensate for the faltering Democratic organization. The problem was that neither the Democratic party leadership nor the black leadership would have *dared* even to contemplate such a sacreligious political assertion. Black leadership shares with the white electorate much of the same mythology about the two-party system. Black leaders (civil and political) must see civil rights as a *constitutional* mandate. They also share much of the same unspoken, subliminal beliefs that there is something sacred about the two-party system that is also *constitutional*.

Jackson's concept of the Rainbow Coalition was an embryonic political idea that reflected the essentially pluralistic makeup of American society. While this essential pluralism exists outside the theoretical framework of constitutional ideals, it is a social, economic, and cultural condition that cuts across all ethnic, racial, cultural, sex, and geographical lines. This obstinate fact would in the Seventies help eclipse and circumvent most of the social policy expectations of the black civil rights movement. It would activate the responses that would ultimately cut the political supports upon which the Democratic party had rested since the New Deal. In the process the impact of pluralism would thrust into competitive contention a catalogue of submerged or otherwise suppressed minorities. The question posed by Jesse Jackson's Rainbow Coalition was: Which of these variegated minorities would, in their supposed self-interest, enter into a definitive political coalition with the blacks? *This was a crucial question in the 1984 election.*

Jesse Jackson's Rainbow Coalition envisioned a minority-group alliance based on the mutual interests of blacks, other minorities, and women. But not unexpectedly, none of the vocal leaders of the other minorities answered the call. The refusal of both Hispanics and women,—the latter represented by the National Organization of Women (NOW)—to align themselves publicly with the Rainbow Coalition indicated that Jackson had misread the political signals of minorities and women for 1984. Women (as represented by NOW) and minorities are not as solidly committed to the Democratic party as are blacks, which throws in considerable doubt the assumption that minorities and women share mutual interests with blacks. There is no telling how many Democratic party dissidents among the minorities and women either supported Gary Hart over Walter Mondale or bolted to the Republicans. For Democrats like Hart, the black civil rights cause was the main bone of contention over the question of the Democratic party's advocacy of "special interests." Thus, Jackson was forced into paying campaign lip service to the media's portrayal of the Democratic party's special-interest civil rights contenders as composed of minorities and women.

Women represent more than one half the national population, but Jackson, caught in the net of the liberal consensus on minorities and civil rights, could not openly declare that they do not constitute a minority. Thus, similar to the entire liberal–Democratic party consensus, he could not openly speculate what this misapplication of the gender population ratios would mean for blacks. If the total population is measured on a percentage scale of 100, women would make up 51 percent. In view of the conservative white shift to Reaganism, it cannot be determined what percentage of women is in favor of the extension of civil rights supports for minorities—especially blacks—and particularly *in the arena of economic rights,* the *real* battleground where substantive civil rights issues are at stake.

An eventual ratification of the Equal Rights Amendment (ERA) would *constitutionally* submerge the *nonwhite minority group,* effectively burying it as a political and/or legal issue. The black minority group, in particular, would be left constitutionally stranded in the legal mire of the ambiguities of the Fourteenth Amendment's equal protection clause. The ERA is meant to transcend the equal protection clause as being an insufficient safeguard against sex discrimination practiced against a *class.* As one consequence, the ratification of the ERA would justify the argument that another constitutional amendment be placed on the political agenda: *an equal rights amendment to the Constitution that would bar economic, political, and cultural discrimination against a minority group based on race.* The idea of such an amendment would not only reassert the *original* substance of the Fourteenth Amendment, but reopen to debate the social policy implications of the equal protection clause's ambiguities. Such an amendment *could* become one of several planks for an independent black political party. It could also become *one* point of organizational departure for realizing the potential of the Rainbow Coalition. The ERA, aside from its social policy gender implications, raises more fundamental questions about the Constitution. The American Constitution is *not* the most advanced document in the world today. Moreover, it thrives off its past accomplishments in extending its democratic ideals and egalitarian principles. As written, the Constitution cannot mandate any further privileges or egalitarian promises to American blacks than it has already allowed. Thus, as the largest and most important nonwhite minority, blacks can no longer deceive themselves into believing that the Constitution can offer any additional unrealized benefits *without being amended*. Whether the American Constitution will ever undergo an overhauling, which in the opinion of some is long overdue, is a matter for speculation. However, barring any amendment process, the only hope left for the political, economic, and cultural survival of blacks into the next century is self-organization.

As American society, representing a national entity of just over two hundred years, approaches the year 2000, the social and economic conditions of American blacks as a group reflect disturbing indications that they might become, racially and ethnically, *an endangered species*. Black social, economic, political, and cultural survival is *not* guaranteed. Even the American nation *in toto,* as *constitutionally* premised, is not guaranteed to survive without some drastic reordering of its domestic priorities. As for the blacks, the only guarantee of group survival lies in reorganizing along political, economic, cultural, and institutional lines.

The end of the civil rights cycle, beginning with *Brown,* left blacks in the Eighties holding the heavy bag of an immense economic problem. This economic problem weighed down the black upward mobility toward the economic parity that the civil rights movement promised but could not deliver. Hence, the fundamental issue facing the black minority for the remainder of the twentieth century is not the fruitless contention with the unresolvable, ambiguous, open-ended legalisms of equal protection, but the reality of the closed, privileged arena of economic competition for the rewards of social status through economic parity. It is true that blacks have made the kinds of advances that would have seemed impossible in the 1890s. To compare the position of blacks in the 1980s with that of the 1890s, the pre-NAACP era, would be even more difficult than to compare the state of race relations of the 1980s with that of the 1920s. Compared with the pre-New Deal era, blacks have made unprecedented advances in politics, culture, economics, and, especially, education. On the all-important economic front, blacks have made a remarkable *relative* advance against the ravages of poverty in a rich society, the wealthiest the world has ever seen, that irresponsibly tolerates and abets that poverty. The century-old struggle against poverty has been harder, as said before, for native-born blacks than for European immigrants, and it has exerted a tremendous assault on the stability of the black psyche. Blacks' struggle for education has been disoriented and misdirected because the struggle took place in an unprecedentedly rich society whose intellectual tradition has neither understood nor sanctioned the true educational needs of non-white minorities. One of the profound consequences of this ongoing "miseducation" of the blacks has been the cultivation and encouragement of the kind of black "value system" that is generally detrimental to coping successfully with the exigencies imposed by a paternalistically racist, economically predatory, and culturally irresponsible society.

The reality of the black economic situation today is the extended but aggravated situation that W.E.B. Du Bois described in 1934 when he prophesied the unavoidable consequences of the NAACP's civil rights philosophy: "This [NAACP] program of organized opposition to the action and attitude of the dominant white group includes ceaseless agitation and insistent demand for equality: the equal right to work, civic and political equality, and social equality. It involves the use of force of every sort: moral suasion, propaganda and where possible, even physical resistance." But "there are, however, manifest difficulties with such a program. *First of all it is not a program that envisages any direct action of Negroes themselves for the uplift of their socially depressed masses: in the very conception of the program, such work is to be attended to by the nation and Negroes are to be the subjects of uplift forces and agencies to the extent of their numbers and need.* Now for obvious reasons of ignorance and poverty, and the natural envy and bickering of any disadvantaged group, this unity is difficult to achieve. In fact the efforts to achieve it . . . during Reconstruction, and in the formation of the early Equal Rights League and the Afro-American Council, were only partially successful."[9] (Italics added.)

Note the reference to the Afro-American Council (formerly called the "League"). This outcome, which was of course unavoidable in view of the ideological origins of the civil rights program, left the NAACP (and the National Urban League) stranded at the waning of the last civil rights cycle. What Du Bois described in 1934 as the black "socially depressed masses" are the magnified black millions of the Eighties existing below the poverty line—the black unemployed, the fatherless families, the high school dropouts, the petty criminals, the urban homeless, the unskilled, the welfare survivors whom the nation and its uplift forces and agencies cannot rescue. Civil rights organizations are immobilized with no other recourse or rationale for their continued existence but to berate the political establishment for its failure to eliminate unemployment and poverty. There is not the slightest indication that these protests will ever cease to fall on the closed ears of the neoliberal and/or neoconservative conscience of the nation and its uplift forces and agencies.

With the coming of the Eighties, the ameliorative powers of the liberal consensus to assuage the economic disabilities of the black masses were politically spent. As the largest nonwhite minority, blacks as a group bear the brunt of the well-entrenched coercive economic power wielded by politically powerful groups that function at the summits of white society. Thus, white society in general benefits in varying degrees from the "trickle-down" dissemination of economic privileges that are indispensable for the operation of the free-market economic system. In the United States, as in all societies, "coercive power is a mighty economic force," as one unconventional and reconstructed white liberal, Theodore Cross, put it:

> There appear to be few records in history of any tribe or nation where the largest share of economic goods and valued positions has not been claimed by those individuals and groups that were economically and politically strong and that had the most secure hold on society's instruments of coercion.[10]

The writer further advises that blacks "must shape their policies and build their lives not on myths and slogans published by the powerful, but on truth and experience about themselves and about how the world around them actually distributes its economic rewards and penalties."[11] One of the distressing corollaries of the civil rights movement was the creation of empty slogans and the propagation of myths: the myth about the ultimate meaning of racial integration, the myth about the redemptive powers of moral suasion, the myths surrounding the legalities of equal protection regarding race and economics in a free-market economy. A proliferation and apotheosization of myths by the official black leadership followed the Supreme Court decision of 1954 to the effect that the millennium in complete racial democracy would be realized in just one more decade. However, the reverse occurred. *By 1980 blacks had collapsed and were deteriorating politically* as a result of having been goaded and lured by a set of false assumptions, plus having been driven to march forward under the banners of conflicting and mutually negating priorities. By skirting around the self-evident necessity of organizing politically, civil rights and political leaders would also evade the responsibility to counsel *collective enterprises* among blacks, to inspire *collective determination*, to engage in *cooperative economic* efforts on *both corporate-business* and *commodity-distribution levels*. Theodore Cross continued:

In the tradition of many other ethnic outsiders who have achieved rank equal to the majority, blacks must also become competent in all the accepted forms of economic and political power that a democracy holds open to its citizens and protects for their benefit and advancement.[12]

However, in the face of this persuasive American economic reality, both white-inspired noneconomic liberals and radical left-wing socialist advisers beguiled blacks into believing they had neither a legitimate nor a functional stake in the power-sharing prerogatives of the capitalistic free-market system. Thus, from the black vantage point:

It would be a seriously inhibiting mistake . . . to treat America simply as an ideologically flawed society that somehow needs a new set of human values and incentives. Rather, the United States should be seen by them for what it is, a liberal but traditional society which, like almost all societies before it, is responsive to the self-seeking needs and wishes of those groups and individuals who, through competence or position, have the ability to persuade others to share or part with valued positions and resources. The struggle by blacks to take an equal place in the economy must not be seen as an effort to overturn or humanize capitalism but rather an effort to move onto its playing fields, become part of its powerful institutions, and to share all the prerequisites and prerogatives of those who run and regulate it.[13]

Civil rights justice, for all intents and purposes of the United States Constitution, has been won; there are no more frontiers to conquer; no horizons in view that are not mirages that vanish over the hill of the next Court decision on the meaning of equal protection. The bottom line for the next black political manifesto is *economic justice,* without which there will be no future black survival. *The truth is, however, there exists in black America no such organized black leadership consensus that is either willing or able either to replace, oppose, or simply ignore and bypass the organized remains of the old, institutionalized civil rights and social welfare leadership:*

Once more, blacks in America must turn to the politics of ethnic solidarity and self-help. As a group, black people must determine in caucus or convention what goals and tactics are going to serve their interests for the balance of the century. They must find and certify a trailblazing leader who will lay down a proper set of marching orders and make the black agenda effective by connecting it with the public interest and the American sense of fair play. Awakening to the pleasures of elective politics, blacks must multiply their political and economic strength by making political and economic alliances with other groups that share common burdens and aspirations.[14]

On the crucial question of the role of contemporary black leadership, the above sentiments are those of a major commentator on the present black political and economic situation. They advocate a new black leadership that would emerge out of a consensus expressed through a "caucus" or a "convention." Even though the format (caucus, or convention) is understated, the substance of the procedure is correct. But what is really needed is a new black leadership organization of *national* dimensions. More than that, this organization requires another concept of black leadership. The age of the *single* Big Leader Spokesman has passed, since no single black leader today is capable of reflecting the many-sided complexities of the political, economic, cultural, educational, and institutional needs of American blacks. What is required, in fact *demanded*, for black survival is a form of *national council of collective leadership—a new concept of leadership*. The nearest approximation to a single trailblazing leader was Martin Luther King, Jr., whose martyrdom was the tragic consequence of being driven by idealism to invoke a "new set of human values" in a society whose moral reflexes are not attuned to social change. Following King came Jesse Jackson, bearing the outlines of black leadership ideals involving both economic and political activism. But even though he was a black leader with a pronounced degree of charisma and national appeal, Jesse Jackson squandered too much of his potential by opportunistically following the imaginary bait of electoral politics at the presidential summit, while neglecting the more crucial and fundamental and *obligatory* task of political organization at the bottom, *the independent black political party*. Jesse Jackson's presidential bid was, in black political terms, politically premature. While Jackson's concept of the Rainbow Coalition was commendable, in his haste for the laurels of political notoriety, he forgot that the sought-after prize of real black political power lies at the "end of the rainbow," not at the beginning. Only the blacks are in a position to form the organizational base for a "third force" departure from the Democratic party's monopolistic hold on the left-wing position of the two-party system. Yet it would be tactically incorrect to premise a black push for an independent political party on the basis of a coalition at the outset. Black political mobilization of any kind that does not aim to transcend mere electoral conventioneering, that does not outline strategies for economic elevation, is, for blacks, dead-end politics. The ultimate goal of any group politics in a pluralistic society has to be self-interest, especially if the self-interest is economic. In this regard, Walter E. Williams, one of the more modish black conservative critics of civil rights who declare that the blacks' poor economic condition cannot be wholly attributed to "racial discrimination," offers this advice:

> If the evidence bears out the argument that there are laws that eliminate economic opportunities, then political resources should be expended in the direction of modifying those laws. The government, at various levels, can exert its authority to ensure that all people have unrestricted access to legitimate markets.[15]

The immediate question is *what* political resources are in fact available to be expended? And how would such political resources be mobilized? True to their twentieth-century origins, such conservative arguments do get to the heart of the black economic situation. These arguments originated with Booker T. Washington in his clash with the civil libertarians led by Du Bois, and with an NAACP imbued with Joel A. Spingarn's noneconomic liberalism. Although Du Bois would abandon noneconomic liberalism in the 1930s, the essentials of these arguments remained embedded in the ongoing ideological evolution of the black protest movements. Today one of the most extreme extensions of these arguments is reflected in the views of the black conservative Republican Clarence Pendleton, and civil rights debates that divided Washington and W.E.B. Du Bois still cast shadows over the black 1980s.

Now that the civil rights cycle has truly waned, a black conservative Pendleton, Thomas Sowell, or Walter E. Williams can challenge the legitimacy of the liberal consensus that "the past gross denial of basic rights of and gross discrimination against blacks in the U.S." is the reason for the continued discrimination in the economic sphere. In the black conservative view, "racial bigotry and discrimination is neither a complete nor a satisfactory explanation for the *current* condition of many blacks in America."[16] The catch here is that the black conservatives claim the option of delegitimizing the *social* results of civil rights legislation because of black *economic* disabilities. However, black conservatives themselves are the prime beneficiaries of precisely those maximum social, educational, and professional advances resulting from civil rights legislation. Thus, at this late date, *both* the conservative and the liberal consensus regarding the present black *economic* situation have become rhetorical, open-ended, and nonconclusive because their views reflect the racial politics of the post-civil rights era, i.e., the *end* of the civil rights cycle. Clarence Pendleton, in his zeal, got caught in the administrative net of ambiguous definitions over what minority rights are civil or economic (or, perhaps, *both*). When Pendleton went out on a "constitutional" limb to declare federally sponsored appropriations on behalf of minority business enterprises (MBEs) were not only unjustifiable, costly, riddled with corruption, nonproductive "shams," but also conducive to "reverse discrimination" against deserving *white* competitive bidders, he was attacked by other more liberal members of the Civil Rights Commission. More than that, Pendleton was *not* publicly upheld in his conservative views in this the matter by the Reagan administration! The key to unraveling this anomalous political debacle over civil rights interpretations is that the program of "minority set-asides" for disadvantaged entrepreneurs among "blacks, Hispanics, Aleuts, Orientals, Indians or other minorities" was *not* a legislative product of a Democratic party administration. The program was created through an executive order by President Richard Nixon, a Republican, in 1969! This political party history helps explain the curious phenomenon of black Republicanism in the 1980s. It is a *class* phenomenon that reflects *class* interests that are much less "civil" than they are "economic" and are *similar to those of Booker T. Washington*. Thus, it was ironic that among the main critics of Clarence Pendleton's actions against the legitimacy of the Nixon-inspired program for the MBEs were *black Republicans!*[17]

Black conservatism does express the view that some of the causes underlying the restrictions that limit black economic opportunities are certain "laws," that is, *legal* restrictions. However, the modification of such laws, if such is possible, can be achieved only through *black political organization*. The problem is that this new-style political leadership must emerge from the black middle class or, at least, from the political elites of the black middle class. It is evident that the economic consequences of the civil rights cycle produced the new, contemporary black middle class or the repository of new versions of what Du Bois described as the black Talented Tenth. Du Bois saw the Talented Tenth as the source of quality intellectual, political, educational, and cultural leadership that blacks would require in the struggle for racial, social, and economic parity with other groups in American society. But by 1940 W.E.B Du Bois had to give up his idealistic notion about the black Talented Tenth. It became demonstrable that the class origins and affinities of the black elites were *nonnationalistic*. "The upper-class Negro has almost never been nationalistic," wrote Du Bois:

> He has never planned or thought of a Negro state, or a Negro church or a Negro school. This solution has always been a thought up-surging from the mass, because of pressure which they could not withstand and which compelled a racial institution or chaos. Continually such institutions were founded and developed, but this took place against the advice and best thought of the intelligentsia.[18]

The same social and ideological conditions still prevail in the post-civil rights era of the Eighties, especially with regard to the creation of *political* institutions. Black political leadership for any goals, economic or otherwise, must emanate from the black middle-class. However, the economic gains that accrued from the benefits of the civil rights cycle, limited as they were, became the bases of affluence for the contemporary black middle class. This new class, over the last twenty-five years, has been the beneficiary of a quantity and quality of higher education, professional and technical training, employment, upward social mobility, corporate ingress, governmental patronage, cultural and artistic expression, and entrepreneurial opportunity that New Deal middle-class elites couldn't even hope to dream of. But measured against Du Bois's assessment of the "upper-class Negro" of the 1930s, their contemporary progeny are even *less nationalistic* than their predecessors. At least, the "black bourgeoisie" whom E. Franklin Frazier berated thirty years ago was guiltily and painfully conscious of its social powerlessness and its inabilities and shortcomings as a class, and aware of the social responsibilities it either refused or was unable to assume. By contrast, and stated in socioeconomic educational, intellectual, political, and cultural terms, the new black middle class, and its elites, is an *empty class* that has flowered into social prominence *without a clearly defined social mission* in the United States. With a scattering of exceptions here and there, the new black middle class, and its elites, is an unprecedented product of specific civil rights conditioning that renders it not intrinsically incapable, but mindless of its own potential or else reticent to mobilize it through any organizational channel that is plainly open to it.

One critical gauge in assisting the general societal deficiencies of this new class is the puny results of its intellectual, scholarly, and creative output compared with the achievements of its predecessors from 1900 to the 1960s. Despite all the preferential benefits bestowed upon it via extended educational opportunities, this new class has revealed only a flickering glimmer of intellectual or creative or scholarly potential reminiscent of the achievements of Du Bois, Woodson, Rayford Logan, Alain Locke, Booker T. Washington, Abram Hill, Sterling Spero, E. Franklin Frazier, Sterling Brown, Mary MccLeod Bethune, Jessie Fauset, Allison Davis, Lorenzo Green, Langston Hughes, Ralph Ellison, and other notables of the Twenties, Thirties, and Forties. This is not said in condemnation of the new class, but is a general assessment that, as a class, *it does not aspire to achieve*. Lacking even a clear consensus of a social mission, except more of the same vague and evanescent idea of "civil rights," the new middle-class is *empty*, it is an indulgent "Me" generation, a class that has ingrowing psychic troubles over portents of an uncertain future.

Because of its unprecedented and unexpected social and economic evolution, this class and its various spokesmen and spokeswomen cannot admit in a political and/or economic fashion that, for all intents, it has written off the contemporary condition of the black underclass as a lost cause. (Apropos of Du Bois's critique of 1934, only the state and the uplift forces and agencies of the nation can help save the black underclass.) Flushed with the civil rights optimism of the liberal consensus, the emergent new class both denied and evaded the self-evident existence and the growth of a permanent underclass with its ominous signs of black family disintegration as outlined in the controversial Moynihan Report of 1965, *The Negro Family—A Case for National Action*. Related to this issue of the black family, the successes of the civil rights cycle ushered in new features in the evolution of minority issues such as *gender politics*. In addition to the proliferation of other minorities, the politics of gender traps the black minority into political immobilization. The introduction of *gender politics* into the post-civil rights era seriously compromises, retards, and threatens the black minority's ability to maximize its organizational potential, especially *political organization*. At the crucial class level where upward economic mobility has created the maximum affluence, a "silent war" between the sexes has become a serious internal liability for black leadership fortunes. A prominent example of this silent war between the sexes over the definitions and imperatives of black leadership is displayed in the controversies over the leadership role of Coretta Scott King, who, in the words of one black male critic, is "out of place in such a post" as Martin Luther King's successor. Another male critic declared: "She anointed herself; no one ever gave her a crown

Black people aren't prepared at this stage in history to anoint anyone with Martin Luther King's crown." These black male critics of Coretta Scott King's role assert that the "grieving widow" does not merit being anointed as the successor to the real essence of Martin Luther King's goals, which is of course debatable. However, Mrs. King's telling reply to her critics was that neither she nor other "civil rights leaders have found a way" to achieve Martin Luther King's civil rights goals.[19] Hence, of all the nonwhite minority groups, the black minority finds itself at the end of the civil rights cycle as the one most compromised. Because it is and remains the largest minority, economic, political, family, educational, and other problems are magnified by its size—when its size should, in fact, become its innate advantage.

The end of the civil rights cycle has left the black minority without a leadership consensus or even a leadership forum that can claim to speak on behalf of the entire black minority inclusive of class, gender, ideological, and factional divisions. It has even been argued on occasion that such an all-inclusive black leadership consensus is neither required nor justified. This raises the crucial question, In what organizational, political, or economic manner should the future destiny of American blacks be determined or guided? Despite the fifty-year history of New Deal political traditions, the United States remains the world's most powerfully organized capitalist society—*and will remain so*. And despite the conservative right's determined political thrust to obliterate the entire corpus of the New Deal legislative record, such a goal *cannot* be fully achieved. Whether the conservative political results of the Eighties are good or bad in terms of the implied social *ethics* of national policy is beside the central point. From the particularist point of view of the American black minority, one salient historical fact has to be kept in mind. No matter how competing political, economic, educational, and minority establishments care to interpret the meaning of traditions, history, and constitutional legality, the United States still has a rendezvous with both the past and the future of its destiny as a nation. In the future context, the blacks must struggle to save themselves because allies are not promised. In organizing to save themselves, any political allegiance blacks would consider extending to other minorities would have to be purely conditional. Despite the false promises of the most recent civil rights cycle of the Sixties and Seventies, American blacks still represent the most crucial minority group, the most strategically positioned to impact on the institutional structures of the total society. What is lacking is the quality of black leadership capable of harnessing black potential.

N OTES

PART I
(INTRODUCTION)

1–6 John Hope Franklin, *From Slavery to Freedom*, 3rd ed. (New York: Alfred A. Knopf, 1967), pp. 407–408; Emma Lou Thornbrough, "The National Afro-American League, 1887–1908," *Journal of Southern History*, Vol. XXVII, November 1961, pp. 494–512; also *T. Thomas Fortune–Militant Journalist* (University of Chicago Press, 1972), pp. 105–116, 119–122, 178–180 passim; Seth M. Scheiner, *Negro Mecca—A History of the Negro in New York* (New York University Press, 1965), pp. 181–182, 186–188, 192–200; August Meier, *Negro Thought in America, 1880–1915* (Ann Arbor: University of Michigan Press, 1963), pp. 35, 60, 70–71, 80–81, 94, 111, 115, 128–130, 172–174, 176, 180–181, 186, 198, 222, 250, 274; *Harper's Weekly*, October 1887, p. 703; James Weldon Johnson, *Black Manhattan* (New York: Atheneum Press, 1930, 1968) pp. 129–130. Elliot M. Rudwick, "The Niagara Movement," *Journal of Negro History*, Vol. XLII, July 1957, pp. 177–200 is an example of a flawed liberal historiography on civil rights that erroneously cites the Niagara Movement as the first pre-NAACP civil rights movement. This interpretive error was corrected by Thornbrough (q.v. 1961). For a more realistic interpretation of the meaning of the Niagara Movement (1905), see Kelly Miller,

Radicals and Conservatives, (New York: Schocken Books, 1908), pp. 25–41. See also Louis R. Harlan, *Booker T. Washington—The Making of a Black Leader, 1856–1901,* Vol. I (New York: Oxford University Press, 1972), pp. 193, 254, 263–267, 270, 296–298; and August Meier, Elliot M. Rudwick, and Francis L. Broderick, eds., *Negro Protest Thought in the Twentieth Century* (Indianapolis, Ind.: Bobbs-Merrill Company, 1965), pp. 145–191 passim.

7–16 Daniel W. Crofts, "The Black Response to the Blair Education Bill" *Journal of Southern History,* Vol. XXXVII, February 1971, pp. 42–65. See also Senator Henry W. Blair, "Aid to Common Schools," speech relating to S. 151, 47th Cong., June 13, 1882.

17–24 The liberal *Nation*'s arguments against the Blair bill were published February 11 and 18; March 4 and 11, 1886. The extensive arguments, pro and con, on the Blair Education Bill were reported in *The New York Times* during 1884 on February 1, March 17, 22, 25, 28, and 29, and April 4, 6, and 8. The most definitive discussion of the national response to the Blair bill is contained in Gordon Canfield Lee, *The Struggle for Federal Aid—A History of the Attempts to Obtain Federal Aid for the Common Schools, 1870–1890* (New York: Columbia University, Teachers College, 1949), pp. 88–170. See also Edgar W. Knight, *Public Education in the South* (Boston: Ginn & Company, 1922) passim; here the author slights the Blair bill as a carryover of southern racial sensitivities in the conflict between "race" priorities and democratic educational philosophies. Conversely, an unabashedly pro-black interest in southern common-school educational philosophy is found in Lewis H. Blair (no relation to Henry W. Blair), *A Southern Prophecy—The Elevation of the South Dependent upon the Elevation of the Negro,* ed. C. Vann Woodward (Boston: Little, Brown, 1964) passim.

24–28 C. Vann Woodward, *The Strange Career of Jim-Crow,* rev. ed. (New York: Oxford University Press, 1966), pp. 145–191.

PART TWO

1 Thurgood Marshall (later appointed Supreme Court Justice), as quoted in *The New York Times,* May 18, 1954, p. 16.

2 In 1940 the NAACP leadership drafted a memorandum to President Roosevelt, the secretary of the navy, and the assistant secretary of war, outlining several provisions for the *"integration of the Negro into military aspects of the national defense program."* This was the first time the NAACP specified the idea of "integration" within the context

of a general policy pronouncement on civil rights. Following World War II, the term "racial integration" was further popularized as the preeminent synonym for all civil rights issues. See *Crisis,* Vol. XLVII, November 1940, pp. 350–351, 357.

3 Extracted from the originally published text of *Brown* v. *Board of Education, Topeka, Kansas* (347 U.S. 483, 1954), *The New York Times,* May 18, 1954, p. 18.

4 Walter White, *How Far the Promised Land?* (New York: Viking Press, 1955), p. 228.

5 *Slaughterhouse Cases* (16 Wall. 36, L ED 394 [1873]).

6 Ibid., p. 398.

7 Arnold M. Rose, *Libel and Academic Freedom—A Lawsuit Against Political Extremists* (Minneapolis: University of Minnesota Press, 1968), p. 6.

8 The original versions of E. Franklin Frazier's *Black Bourgeoisie* (New York: Free Press, 1957) were published under the title "La Bourgeoisie Noire," *Modern Quarterly,* Vol. V, 1928–1930, pp. 78–84.

9–23 E. Franklin Frazier, *The Negro in the United States,* rev. ed., (New York: Macmillan Company, 1957), pp. 687–706 passim.

24 Ibid., p. 702.

25 See W.E.B. Du Bois on "Segregation" extended discussion, *Crisis,* Vol. XLL, January–June 1934.

26 E. Franklin Frazier, *Black Bourgeoisie* (New York: Free Press-Macmillan, 1957), p. 104.

27 Frazier, *The Negro In the United States,* p. 695.

28 Ibid.

29 See John Higham, *Strangers in the Land Patterns of American Nativism 1860–1925* (New York: Atheneum, 1963).

30 See Lerone Bennett, Jr., *Before the Mayflower, A History of the Negro in America 1619–1964* (Baltimore: Penguin, 1966).

31 Slaughterhouse Cases.

32–33 Michael Novak, *The Rise of the Unmeltable Ethnics—Politics and Culture in the Seventies* (New York: Macmillan, 1971), pp. 7–8.

34–35 Frazier, p. 698.

36–39 Armando B. Rendon, *Chicano Manifesto* (New York: Macmillan, 1971), pp. 4–5, 71, 120–121.

40 Frazier, *The Negro In the United States,* rev. ed., p. 697.

41–42 Rendon, cited, pp. 107–108, 281.

43 J. Harvie Wilkerson, *From Brown to Bakke* (New York: Oxford University Press, 1979), p. 249.

44 During the Sixties, sociologist James S. Coleman was the principal researcher in directing an exhaustive study on "Equality of Educational Opportunity," published in 1966 by the U.S. Department of Health,

Education, and Welfare. The study was made in response to Section 402 of the Civil Rights Act of 1964. The survey covered: "Six racial and ethnic groups: Negroes, American Indians, Oriental Americans, Puerto Ricans . . . Mexican-Americans, and whites . . ." and the effects of public school segregation on these groups. Segregation was, of course, predetermined to be detrimental as per *Brown*. But in response to another such study in 1983, sponsored by the National Institute of Education, James S. Coleman declared: "The assumption that integration would improve achievement of lower class black children has now been shown to be fiction."

PART THREE

1–5 Edmund Cahn, "Jurisprudence," *New York University Law Review*, January 1955), pp. 151–169 passim. See also Raymond Wolters, *The Burden of Brown: Thirty Years of School Desegregation* (Knoxville: University of Tennessee Press, 1984).

  6 See W.E.B. Du Bois, "Of Mr. Washington and Others," *The Souls of Black Folk* (Chicago: A. C. McClurg & Company, 1907), pp. 41–59. Du Bois's critique of Washington delineated for the first time in capsule form the political, economic, and educational essentials of the dilemmas and conflicts that became endemic and institutionalized in black leadership thought from 1900 to the 1980s.

7–9 B. Joyce Ross, *J. E. Spingarn and the Rise of the NAACP* (New York: Atheneum Press, 1972), pp. 13, 14, 15. Throughout this study, the author reiterates the ongoing influence of noneconomic liberalism on NAACP leadership philosophy—pp. 18–19, 24, 28, 51, 53, 65, 107, 160, 166, 172, 217. Ross states, "When those like Du Bois and [Abram] Harris, who had grown impatient, demanded an accounting of the concrete fruits of noneconomic liberalism after a twenty-year trial [Spingarn], through little fault of his own, had no wholly satisfactory reply. Lack of public response had made a once daring program appear conservative and ineffective. Although Du Bois and Harris passed from the immediate scene after 1934, the speeches delivered at [NAACP] annual conferences during succeeding years . . . grew more militant in their denunciation of noneconomic liberalism," p. 244.

 10 Du Bois, *Souls of Black Folk*, p. 43.

 11 Ibid.

 12 Edmund Cronon, *Black Moses—The Story of Marcus Garvey and the Universal Negro Improvement Association* (Madison: University of

Wisconsin Press, 1955). See also Tony Martin, *Race First: . . Marcus Garvey and the Universal Negro Improvement Association* (Westport, Conn.: Greenwood Press, 1976); Theodore G. Vincent, *Black Power and the Garvey Movement* (Berkeley, Calif.: Ramparts Press, 1971).

13 T. Lynn Smith, "The Redistribution of the Negro Population of the United States, 1910–1960," *Journal of Negro History,* Vol. LI, July 1966, pp. 155–173.

14 W.E.B. Du Bois, "Segregation," *Crisis,* Vol. XXXXI, February 1934, pp. 52–53.

15 Ibid.

16 Charles F. Kellogg, *NAACP—A History of the National Association for the Advancement of Colored People—1909–1920,* Vol. I (Baltimore: Johns Hopkins Press, 1967), pp. 155–182.

17 *Crisis,* "Immigration Bill," Vol. IX, February 1915, p. 190; March 1915, pp. 246–247; April 1915, pp. 290–291.

18 Cronon, p. 195.

19 *Crisis,* "Immigration Bill."

20 Du Bois, "Segregation."

21–26 Ibid.

27 Claude McKay, *Harlem—Negro Metropolis* (New York: E. P. Dutton, 1940), p. 124. Note that this was the opinion of a West Indian writer.

28 Du Bois, 'Segregation."

29 Ibid.

30 Du Bois, *Souls of Black Folk,* pp. 51–52.

31 Ibid.

32 This was the Niagara Movement launched in 1905 by Du Bois in opposition to the dominance of Booker T. Washington and his considerable following. See note 7, part one—introduction, ref., Elliot M. Rudwick.

33 W.E.B. Du Bois, *Dusk of Dawn—Autobiography* (New York: Harcourt Brace & Company, 1940), pp. 193, 199.

34 Ibid.

35 Booker T. Washington, *The Negro in Business* (Boston and Chicago: Hertel, Jenkins & Company, 1907, reissued by Afro-American Press, Chicago, Illinois, 1969), pp. 1–20, 344–379.

36–38 Bernard K. Johnpoll and Mark R. Yerburgh, eds., *A Documentary History—The League for Industrial Democracy,* Vol. I (Westport, Conn.: Greenwood Press, 1980), pp. 96–125; Leonard C. Kercher et al., *Consumers' Cooperatives in the North Central States* (Minneapolis: University of Minnesota Press, 1941), pp. 116–136; Howard Haines Turner, *Case Studies of Consumers' Cooperatives* (New York Columbia University Press, 1941), pp. 33–34, 310. See also Du Boıs on economic cooperation, "The Immediate Program of the Negro, ' *Crisis,* Vol. IX, April 1915, pp. 310–312.

39 Walter White, *Crisis,* Vol. XXXXI, March 1934, p. 81.

40 See, e.g., Raymond Wolters, *Negroes and the Great Depression* (Westport, Conn.: Greenwood Press 1970), pp. 230–294. See also Herbert Aptheker, ed., *The Correspondence of W.E.B. Du Bois; Volume II, Selections 1934–1944,* (Amherst: University of Massachusetts Press, 1976), especially the letters of George W. Streator.

41 W.E.B. Du Bois, *Crisis,* Vol. XXXXI, August 1934, p. 245.

42 Ibid., March 1934, pp. 81–82; June 1934, p. 173; August 1934, pp. 240, 243, 244.

43 John P. Davis, "A Black Inventory of the New Deal," *Crisis,* Vol. XXXXII, May 1935, pp. 141, 154.

44 Ibid.

45–53 Jack Greenberg, *Race Relations and American Law* (New York: Columbia University Press, 1959), pp. 31–78 passim.

54 Du Bois, *Dusk of Dawn,* pp. 266, 295, 268–326 passim.

55 Ibid.

56–59 Greenberg, pp. 35, 46–61.

60 Relevant here is the outlining of the liberal legal and constitutional point of view that omits *Moore* v. *Dempsey* (261 U.S. 86, 1923) from the "elementary structure of *Strauder-Buchanan-Nixon-Yick Wo* to the edifice of the *School Segregation Cases,*" despite the fact that *Moore* v. *Dempsey* involved the equal protection proviso of the Fourteenth Amendment to a more dramatic and fundamental degree than *Yick Wo* v. *Hopkins.* See Greenberg, p. 34; p. 233, n. 91.

61 Greenberg, p. 33.

62 Stanford M. Lyman, ed., *The Asian in North America* (Santa Barbara, Calif.: Clio Books, 1977), p. 291.

63–68 *Crisis,* Vol. XXV, March 1923, pp. 220–221; April 1923, pp. 259–261. See also Vol. XIX, December 1919, pp. 56–62.

69–71 *New Republic,* Vol. XXXIV, March 14, 1923, pp. 55–57; March 21, 1923, pp. 84–85; April 11, 1923, p. 150.

72 *Crisis,* Vol. XXV, March, April 1923, pp. 220–221; pp. 259–261.

73 Ibid.

74 *New Republic,* April 25, 1923, pp. 228–229.

75 *Crisis,* Vol. XXV, March 1923, pp. 228–229.

76 Ibid., March, April 1923.

77 Ibid.

78 Ibid.

79 *Survey,* Vol. XL111, January 31, 1920, p. 506.

80 "The Object of Workers' Education," *New Republic,* April 25, 1923, pp. 229–230.

81 Ibid.

82 Joseph G. Rayback, *A History of American Labor* (New York: Macmillan Company, 1959), p. 296.

83 Although articles and editorial opinion published in *The Crisis* relating to the Arkansas race riot of 1919 mention this "Open Letter" to the governor of Arkansas, a search of *The Nation*'s indexes for 1919–1923 does not reveal this specific entry.

84 Quoted in Harry Golden, *A Little Girl Is Dead* (Cleveland: World Publishing Company, 1965), p. 249.

85 Louis Marshall, *Champion of Liberty—Selected Papers and Addresses*, Vol. I, ed. Charles Reznikoff (Philadelphia: The Jewish Publication Society of America, 1957), p. 316.

86 Ibid., p. 426.

87 Hasia R. Diner, *In the Almost Promised Land—American Jews and the Blacks, 1915–1935* (Westport, Conn.: Greenwood Press, 1977), p. 3.

88 Marshall, Vol. I, p. 342.

89 Marshall, Vol. II, p. 704.

90 Although B. Joyce Ross, the biographer of Joel E. Spingarn (see note 7) mentions *Moore* v. *Dempsey* as significant in the evolution of the NAACP's civil liberties program (p. 108), neither the case of *Frank* v. *Mangum*, nor Louis Marshall, nor the American Jewish Committee, nor the relationship between Louis Marshall and W.E.B. Du Bois or Joel E. Spingarn are even suggested.

91 *The New Standard Jewish Encyclopedia* (London: W. H. Allen, 1975), pp. 91–92.

92 Ibid.

93 See Kellogg, *NAACP*, pp. 159–165 passim. Only two black intellectual scholars who were contemporaries of Du Bois merit a comparison with Du Bois's achievements—Carter G. Woodson and E. Franklin Frazier, historian and sociologist, respectively.

94 Golden, p. 8.

95 George Cohen, *Jews in the Making of America* (Boston: Stratford Company, 1924), pp. 250–258; J. J. Smertenko, "What America Has Done for the Jews," *Nation*, Vol. 116, April 11, 1923, pp. 409–411.

96 Du Bois, *Dusk of Dawn*, p. 290.

97 *Messenger*, Vol. II, April, May 1920, pp. 13–16.

98 "The Negro Speaks for Himself," *Survey*, Vol. LII, April 15, 1924, p. 71. See also Kelly Miller, "A Negro Sanhedrin" (privately published pamphlet on file at the Schomburg Library Collection, New York, 1924).

99 *Encyclopaedia Britannica*, Vol. 19, 1973, p. 1009.

100 See Miller, "A Negro Sanhedrin."

101 *Messenger*, Vol. VI, April 1924, p. 106.

102 Ibid.

103 Diner, pp. 75 111, 113

104 Ibid.

105 *Nation,* Vol. 116, June 13, 1923, pp. 689–691.

106 Marshall, Vol. I, p. 271.

107 Ibid.

108 Marshall, Vol. II, pp. 859–860.

109 Ibid.

110 Marshall, Vol. I, pp. 397–398.

111 Marshall, Vol. II, pp. 1145–1147.

112 Ibid.

113 Marshall, Vol. I, pp. 425–426.

114 Diner, p. 154.

115 *Crisis,* Vol. XXXVI, March 1929, p. 100.

116 See Nancy J. Weiss, *The National Urban League—1910–1940* (New York: Oxford University Press, 1974), especially pp. 298–309.

117–120 Diner, pp. 114–115, 154.

121 To date, three substantive studies of the Harlem Renaissance have been essayed by three black writer-historians—Nathan I. Huggins, *Harlem Renaissance* (New York: Oxford University Press, 1971); Jervis Anderson, *This Was Harlem* (New York: Farrar Straus Giroux, 1982); David L. Lewis, *When Harlem Was in Vogue* (New York: Alfred A. Knopf, 1981). The David L. Lewis study touches pointedly, but superficially, on "Jews and Afro-Americans," pp. 100–103, 148, 159.

122 Diner, p. 127.

123 Marshall, Vol. II, p. 1147.

124 Diner, p. 132.

125 Robert L. Zangrando, "The NAACP and a Federal Anti-Lynching Bill, 1934–1940," *Journal of Negro History,* Vol. L, April 1965, pp. 106–117.

126–133 Marshall, Vol. I, pp. 423–424.

134 *Crisis,* Vol. I November 1910, p. 11.

135 George E. Cunningham, "The Italian, a Hindrance to White Solidarity in Louisiana, 1890–1898," *Journal of Negro History,* Vol. 50, January 1965, pp. 22–36.

136 Ibid.

137–139 Marshall, Vol. II, pp. 1156, 1154.

140–142 Marshall, Vol. I, pp. 389, 390, 141.

143 Kellogg, p. 10.

144 Marshall, Vol. I, pp. 434–435.

145 Ibid.

146 Cunningham.

147 Ibid.

148 "Arkansas—A Native Proletariat," *Nation,* Vol. CXVI, May 2, 1923, pp. 515–517.

149 Ibid.

150–159 Marshall, Vol. I, pp. 445–446, 466–468, 470. Compared with the volume of cheap or free land won by European immigrants, the black acquisition of land as a result of the Homestead Act of 1862 was less than minuscule. See, e.g., William K. Wyant, *Westward in Eden* (Berkeley: University of California Press, 1982), pp. 25–30, 60–61. See also Charles C. Geisler, ed., *Land Reform, American Style* (Totowa, N. J.: Rowman and Allanheld, 1984), pp. 12, 172–187.

160–162 Albert Bushnell Hart, *The Southern South* (New York: D. Appleton & Company, 1912), pp. 178, 180.

163–164 *A Documentary History—The League for Industrial Democracy*, Vol. I, pp. 36–38, p. 118, Vol. II, p. 1684.

165–166 Du Bois, *Dusk of Dawn*, pp. 266, 295–296.

167 See George S. Schuyler, NAACP Convention remarks, *Crisis*, Vol. XXXIX, No. 7, July 1932, pp. 218–219.

168 See Dan T. Carter, *Scottsboro—A Tragedy of the American South* (Baton Rouge: Louisiana State University Press, 1969).

169 See Langston Hughes, *I Wonder as I Wander—An Autobiographical Journey* (New York: Holt, Rinehart, 1956); George S. Schuyler, *Black and Conservative: Autobiography* (New Rochelle, N.Y.: Arlington House, 1966).

170 *Crisis*, Vol. CXLII, May 1935, p. 141.

171–172 *Crisis*, Vol. XXXVI, August 1929, pp. 261–264, 280. See also *Survey of Negro Colleges and Universities* (Washington, D.C.: United States Department of Interior, Bureau of Education Bulletin No. 7, 1928).

173 *Historical Statistics of the United States—Colonial Times to 1970*, Part I (Washington D.C.: United States Department of Commerce, Bureau of the Census, 1975), pp. 386–387.

174 *Crisis*, August 1929. See also *Negro Land Grant Colleges* (Washington, D.C.: United States Department of Interior, Bureau of Education, Bulletin No. 9, 1930).

175–178 Greenberg, pp. 36–37.

179 *Crisis*, Vol. XLIII, February 1936, pp. 52, 59.

180 *Crisis*, Vol. XLI, August 1934, pp. 239–241.

181 Du Bois, *Dusk of Dawn*, p. 70.

182 *Crisis*, "Which College-White or Negro," Vol. XLI, September 1934, pp. 264–265.

183 Du Bois, *Journal of Negro Education*, Vol. IV, No. 3, 1935, pp. 328–335.

184 Carter G. Woodson, *The Mis-Education of the Negro* (Washington, D.C.: The Associated Publishers, 1933), p. 1.

185–188 Du Bois, *Journal of Negro Education*.

189 "The Courts and Racial Integration in Education," *Journal of Negro Education*, Vol. XXI, No. 3, 1952, p. 242.

190 Du Bois, *Journal of Negro Education.*
191–193 Woodson, pp. 87, 85, 88, 90.
   194 James Q. Wilson, *Negro Politics—The Search for Leadership* (Glenco, Ill.: Free Press, 1960), p. 308.

PART FOUR

   1 W.E.B. DuBois, *Dusk of Dawn—Autobiography,* (New York: Harcourt, Brace & World, 1940) pp. 198–199.
   2 See James MacGregor Burns, *Leadership* (New York: Harper & Row, 1978), p. 36. This prizewinning study is the most definitive analysis ever written on the definition of "leadership."
3–7 Oliver Cromwell Cox, *Caste, Class and Race—A Study in Social Dynamics* (New York: Doubleday & Company, 1948, reissued by Monthly Review Press, New York, 1959, 1970), pp. 508–538 passim; pp. 572–583 passim.
   8 Richard Kluger, *Simple Justice—The History of Brown v. Board of Education and Black America's Struggle for Democracy* (New York: Random House, 1977), pp. 3–26, 395.
   9 Ibid.
  10 See Bernard Sternsher, ed., *The Negro in Depression and War— Prelude to Revolution, 1930–1945* (Chicago: Quadrangle Books, 1969) passim.
  11 See, e.g., Marquis Childs, *Eisenhower—Captive Hero* (New York: Harcourt Brace, 1958), pp. 245–247.
12–13 August Meier and Elliott Rudwick, eds., *Black Protest in the Sixties* (Chicago: Quadrangle Books, 1970), p. 20, Introduction.
  14 Martin Luther King, *Stride Toward Freedom—The Montgomery Story* (New York: Harper, 1958) p. 15.
  15 E. Franklin Frazier, *The Negro Church in America* (New York: Schocken Books, 1964), pp. 72–73.
16–19 King, *Stride Toward Freedom,* pp. 17, 21, 28, 69.
  20 Martin Luther King was described as personifying a revival of the social gospel movement born in the post-Civil War era, linking American Protestantism with the essentials of social reform ideologies and social reform movements. See, e.g., Ronald G. White and C. Howard Hopkins, eds , *The Social Gospel—Religion and Reform in Changing America,* (Philadelphia: Temple University Press, 1976), pp. 244, 273–279, 292.
21–23 King, *Stride Toward Freedom,* pp. 205, 198, 25–26.
24–26 C. Eric Lincoln, ed., *The Black Experience in Religion* (New York: Doubleday-Anchor, 1974), pp. 97, 76–98.

27 See Henry F. Leifermann, "Profession: Concert Singer, Freedom Movement Lecturer," *The New York Times,* November 26, 1972, Section VI, pp. 42–70.

28 David L. Lewis, *King: A Critical Biography* (New York: Praeger, 1970), p. 48.

29–30 King, *Stride Toward Freedom,* pp. 41, 89.

31 Kenneth Slack, *Martin Luther King* (London: S.C.M. Press, 1970), p. 45.

32 Clarence Darrow, symposium on "The Religion of the American Negro," *Crisis,* Vol. XL, June 1931, p. 190.

33 Frazier, p. 79.

34–36 C. D. Coleman, "Agenda for the Black Church," *Religious Education,* November-December 1969, cited in Lincoln, pp. 188, 236, 253.

37 King, *Stride Toward Freedom,* p. 223.

38 Lincoln, pp. 161, 164.

39 Ibid.

40 Martin Luther King, *Where Do We Go from Here—Chaos or Community?* (Boston: Beacon Press, 1968), pp. 61–62.

41–43 Frazier, pp. 83–84, 86.

44–47 *Drum Major,* official publication of the Southern Christian Leadership Conference, Summer 1972, pp. 13–19 passim.

48 Naomi Levine with Richard Cohen, *Ocean Hill-Brownsville—A Case History of Schools in Crisis* (New York: Popular Library, 1969) passim.

49–53 Andrew Young, in *Drum Major.*

54–56 King, *Where Do We Go from Here?,* pp. 25–26.

57 Andrew Young.

58–60 Kluger, pp. 671–673.

61–64 King, *Where Do We Go from Here?,* pp. 50, 59, 61, 124, 168–169.

65–68 David J. Garrow, *The FBI and Martin Luther King, Jr.* (New York: Penguin Books, 1981), pp. 204–219 passim.

PART FIVE

, Martin Kilson, "From Civil Rights to Party Politics—The Black Political Transition," *Current History,* Vol. 67, November 1974, pp. 192–199.

2 Ibid.

3 Theodore Cross, *The Black Power Imperative—Racial Inequality and the Politics of NonViole* .   New York: Faulkner Books, 1984), p. 29.

4 *The New York Times,* January 15, 1985.

5–12 Stephen Steinberg, *The Ethnic Myth—Race, Ethnicity, Class in America* (Boston: Beacon Press, 1981), pp. 254, 255, 256, 257.

13–17 *The New York Times*, June 17, 1970. See also Barbara Mikulski, on "Ethnic American," op-ed page, *The New York Times*, September 29, 1970.

18 See William Julius Wilson, *The Declining Significance of Race* (University of Chicago Press, 1978). Although the analytic content of this study belies its misleading title, the book deserves serious study for its insights into class stratification within the black group. The book does not prove that race has really declined as a factor in the economic status of blacks in the post-civil rights era.

19 Walter E. Williams, *The State Against Blacks* (New York: McGraw-Hill, 1982), pp. xv–xvi.

20 Quoted by E. Franklin Frazier in *Black Bourgeoisie* (New York: Free Press, 1957), pp. 159–160.

21–25 Williams, pp. 125, 127, 130.

26 Thomas Sowell, *Civil Rights: Rhetoric or Reality?* (New York: William Morrow & Company, 1984), p. 13.

27–28 Jack Greenberg, *Race Relations and American Law* (New York: Columbia University Press, 1959), p. 32.

29–31 Robert Seto Quan, *Lotus Among the Magnolias* (Jackson: University Press of Mississippi, 1982), pp. x, xii, 45–46, 49–50, 123–125, 139–140.

32 Thomas Sowell, *Race and Economics* (New York, London: Longman, 1975), p. 54.

33–34 Karl Marx, *A World Without Jews*, trans. Dagobert D. Runes (New York: Philosophical Library, 1959), pp. vi–vii.

35–37 Reed Ueda, "West Indians" in *Harvard Encyclopedia of American Ethnic Groups* (Cambridge, Mass: Harvard University Press, 1980), pp. 1020–1027. In this survey, the author cites three thousand blacks from the Bahamas who were imported to work on farms in Florida and on government construction projects in Charleston, South Carolina, in 1919. These were temporary workers; the author does not state where those Bahamians remained when they converted their status to "permanent residency."

38 James Weldon Johnson, *Black Manhattan* (New York: Alfred A. Knopf, 1930), p. 231.

39 See T. Lynn Smith, "The Redistribution of the Negro Population of the United States, 1910–1960," *Journal of Negro History*, Vol. LI, July 1966.

40–42 Gilbert Osofsky, *Harlem: The Making of a Ghetto, Negro New York 1890–1930* (New York: Harper & Row, 1973), pp. 18, 3, 123.

43 Harry H. Kitano, Appendix, Table 13. "Distribution of the Japanese-American Population in the Continental United States, 1880–1960,' *Japanese-Americans—The Evolution of a Subculture* (Englewood Cliffs, N. J.: Prentice-Hall, 1969), pp. 162–163. See also Hilary Conroy and T. Scott Miyakama, *East Across the Pacific—Historical and Sociological Studies of Japanese Immigration ana Assimilation* (Santa Barbara, Calif.: American Bibliographic Center, Clio Press, 1972).

44 Ueda.

45–46 Osofsky, pp. 92–93.

47–49 Johnson, pp. 147–149.

50 See *Crisis,* February, March, April 1915, Part Three, n. 17 in text.

51–53 Osofsky, pp. 151–152, 131.

54 Thomas Sowell, *Markets and Minorities* (New York: Basic Books 1981), p. 9.

55 Ueda.

56 Osofsky, p. 137.

57 Sowell, p. 62.

58 See St. Clair Drake, "Negro Business—Myth or Fact," *Black Metropolism—A Study of Negro Life in a Northern City* (New York: Harcourt, Brace, 1945), pp. 430–469.

59 Ueda.

60 Amy Jacques Garvey, *Garvey and Garveyism* (Jamaica, W.I.: United Printers Ltd., 1961), pp. 194–195.

61–63 Sowell, *Race and Economics,* pp. 99–100, 101–102.

64–65 Garvey, pp. 12–13.

66 Ueda.

67–69 Osofsky, pp. 10–11, 36, 64, 83, 120, 147–148.

70 Sowell, *Race and Economics,* pp. 32–33.

71 Aubrey W. Bonnett, *The Institutional Adaptation of West Indian Immigrants to America—An Analysis of Rotating Credit Associations* (Washington, D.C.: University Press of America, 1981), p. 6.

72 See Sowell, *Black Education—Myths and Tragedies* (New York: David McKay Company, 1972), pp. 251–263 passim.

73 David Lowenthal, *West Indian Societies* (New York, London: Oxford University Press, 1972), p. 213.

74 Andrew F. Rolle, *California—A History* (New York, 1978). Quoted in *Encyclopedia Americana,* Vol. 5, p. 196.

75–76 Ueda.

77–79 Lowenthal, pp. 118, 121.

80 Bonnett, p. 2.

81 Ueda.

82–84 Bonnett, pp. 2–3.

85 Sowell, *Ethnic America* (New York: Basic Books, 1981), p. 220.

86 Reynolds Farley, *Blacks and Whites—Narrowing the Gap?* (Cambridge, Mass., London: Harvard University Press, 1984), p.15.

87–88 Sowell, *Ethnic America*, p. 220.

89 Lowenthal, pp. 288, 318, 322.

90 Sowell, *Race and Economics*, p. 102.

91 Sowell, *Ethnic America*, pp. 207–208.

92 Du Bois, *Souls of Black Folk,* (Chicago: A. C. McClurg & Company, 1907), p. 52.

93 Booker T. Washington, *The Negro in Business,* 1907. (Reissued by the African Publication Society, London, 1970), pp. 3–4.

94 See Roger W. Babson, obituary, *The New York Times,* March 6, 1967.

95 See, e.g., Robert L. Allen, *Black Awakening in Capitalist America* (New York: Doubleday-Anchor, 1970), pp. 246–253; Earl Ofari, "The Myth of Black Capitalism," *Monthly Review Press,* 1970 passim.

96–99 Frazier, *Black Bourgeoisie,* pp. 153, 162, 165.

100–104 Bonnett, pp. xiii, 6, 17, 53.

105 Allen, quotation from book cover.

106–108 Bonnett, pp. 6–7.

109 Frazier, "La Bourgeoisie Noire," *Modern Quarterly,* Vol. V, 1928–1930.

110 Lowenthal, p. 107.

111 Frazier, *Black Bourgeoisie,* p. 109.

112 For an extended analysis of this issue, see Nathan and Julia Hare, *The Endangered Black Family—Coping with the Unisexualization and the Coming Extinction of the Black Race* (San Francisco: Black Male/Female Relationships Book Publishers, 1984) passim.

113 James Weldon Johnson, "The Making of Harlem" *Survey Graphic,* Vol. LIII, No. 11, March 1925, pp. 639, 635.

114 Ibid.

115 Bonnett, p. 55.

116 Johnson, p. 638.

117 Osofsky, pp. 103–104.

118 Bonnett, p. 20.

119 Frazier, *Black Bourgeoisie,* p. 172.

120 Ibid.

PART SIX

1 During the Kennedy Democratic party campaign of 1960, Reverend Clennon King of Albany, Georgia, launched the independent Afro-American Party following King's call for "all colored people to find

a solution to racial problems" (*The New York Times*, October 30, 1960). The Afro-American Party got on the ballot of five states—Alabama, Connecticut, Illinois, Iowa, and Massachusetts (*The New York Times*, December 16, 1960). Clennon King was the "other King" of the Fifties who gained fleeting notoriety for his biting criticisms of the NAACP's program. For an insight into this Clennon King-NAACP controversy, see *Crisis* editorial, "The Witling of Alcorn," May 1957 pp. 290–291.

2 W.E.B. Du Bois, "The Negro Party," *Crisis*, Vol. XII, October 1916, pp. 268–269.

3–7 Martin Kilson, "From Civil Rights to Party Politics—The Black Political Transition," *Current History*, Vol. 67, November 1974, pp. 194–196, 197–199.

8–10 John Herbers, *The Lost Priority: What Happened to the Civil Rights Movement in America?* (New York: Funk & Wagnalls, 1970), p. 212.

11–15 Ronald Walters, "The Black Politician," *Current History*, Vol. 67, November 1974, pp. 200–205, 233.

16 Vernon Jarrett, "Black Caucus: Where to After Break With Carter?," *Chicago Tribune*, reprinted in *Detroit Free Press*, February 7, 1979.

17 Ibid.

18 "The NAACP and the Black Political Convention," *Crisis*, Vol. 79, August-September 1972, pp. 229–230. See also Bayard Rustin, "Coming of Age Politically," *Crisis*, Vol. 79, November 1972, pp. 296–298.

19 Kenneth B. Clark, "The NAACP: Verging on Irrelevance," op-ed page, *The New York Times*, July 14, 1983.

20 *The New York Times*, June 30, 1970.

21 *The New York Times*, July 3, 1970.

22 Robert W. Goldfarb, "Black Men Are Last," op-ed page, *The New York Times*, March 14, 1980.

23 James J. Kilpatrick, "Sexual Distinction vs. Racial Discrimination," Universal Press Syndicate, reprinted in *Detroit Free Press*, October 10, 1983.

24 Goldfarb.

25 Ibid.

26 Hazel James, "Black Man's Dilemma," Letters to the Editor, *Crisis*, Vol. 79, October 1972, pp. 279–280.

27 Goldfarb.

28 Hazel James.

CONCLUSIONS

1–3 Barbara A. Reynolds, *Jesse Jackson—The Man, the Movement, the Myth* (Chicago: Nelson-Hall, 1975), pp. 23, 9, 100.

4 Edward Cowan, "The Humphrey-Hawkins Bill," *The New York Times*, November 19, 1977.

5 Ibid.

6 David J. Blum, "Minority Report—Black Politicians Fear They Can't Do Much to Help Their People," *The Wall Street Journal*, October 29, 1980.

7 Ibid.

8 See *Crisis*, Vol. LXXIX, August-September 1972, pp. 229–230.

9 W.E.B. Du Bois, *Dusk of Dawn—Autobiography* (New York: Harcourt Brace & Company, 1940), pp. 192–193.

10–14 Theodore Cross, *The Black Power Imperative—Racial Inequality and the Politics of Nonviolence* (New York: Faulkner Books, 1984), pp. 837, 838, 840.

15 Walter E. Williams, *The State Against Blacks* (New York: McGraw-Hill, 1982), pp. xvi–xvii.

16 Ibid.

17 James J. Kilpatrick, "Minority Set-Asides—Set Them Aside," *Detroit Free Press*, April 22, 1985.

18 Du Bois, p. 305.

19 John Herbers, "Coretta King Struggles with Weighty Legacy," *The New York Times*, January 18, 1986.

Index